THE FATHERS
OF THE CHURCH

VOLUME 91

THE FATHERS
OF THE CHURCH

EDITORIAL BOARD

Thomas P. Halton
The Catholic University of America
Editorial Director

Elizabeth Clark
Duke University

Kathleen McVey
Princeton Theological Seminary

Robert B. Eno, S.S.
The Catholic University of America

Robert D. Sider
Dickinson College

Frank A. C. Mantello
The Catholic University of America

Michael Slusser
Duquesne University

Cynthia Kahn White
The University of Arizona

Robin Darling Young
The Catholic University of America

David J. McGonagle
Director
The Catholic University of America Press

FORMER EDITORIAL DIRECTORS

Ludwig Schopp, Roy J. Deferrari, Bernard M. Peebles,
Hermigild Dressler, O.F.M.

Edward Strickland
Staff Editor

ST. EPHREM THE SYRIAN

SELECTED PROSE WORKS
COMMENTARY ON GENESIS
COMMENTARY ON EXODUS
HOMILY ON OUR LORD
LETTER TO PUBLIUS

Translated by
EDWARD G. MATHEWS, JR.
The University of Scranton
Scranton, Pennsylvania

and

JOSEPH P. AMAR
The University of Notre Dame
Notre Dame, Indiana

Edited by
KATHLEEN McVEY
Princeton Theological Seminary
Princeton, New Jersey

THE CATHOLIC UNIVERSITY OF AMERICA PRESS
Washington, D.C.

The preparation of this volume was made possible in part by a grant from the National Endowment for the Humanities, an independent federal agency.

Copyright © 1994
The Catholic University of America Press
All rights reserved
Printed in the United States of America
First paperback edition 2004

The paper used in this publication meets the minimum requirements of the American National Standards for Information Science–Permanence of Paper for Printed Library materials,
ANSI Z39.48-1984
∞

LIBRARY OF CONGRESS CATALOGING-IN-PUBLICATION DATA
Ephraem, Syrus, Saint, 303–373.
  [Selections. English. 1994]
  Selected prose works / St. Ephrem the Syrian ; translated by Edward G. Mathews, Jr. and Joseph P. Amar ; edited by Kathleen McVey.
     p. cm. — (The Fathers of the church ; v. 91)
  Includes bibliographical references and indexes.
  Contents: Commentary on Genesis — Commentary on Exodus — The homily on our Lord — Letter to Publius.
     ISBN 0-8132-0091-1 (cl.) 0-8132-1421-1 (pbk.) ISBN-13: 978-0-8132-1421-4
  1. Bible. O.T. Genesis—Commentaries—Early works to 1800. 2. Bible. O.T. Exodus—Commentaries—Early works to 1800. 3. Jesus Christ—Sermons—Early works to 1800. 4. Spiritual life—Christianity—Early works to 1800. I. Mathews, Edward G., 1954– . II. Amar, Joseph P., 1946– . III. McVey, Kathleen E., 1944– . IV. Title. V. Series.
BR60.F3E64213 1994
[BR632.E5]
270 s—dc20
[270.2]   94-7480

CONTENTS

Foreword	vii
Preface	ix
Abbreviations	xiii
Select Bibliography	xv

General Introduction	3
Commentary on Genesis	
Introduction	59
Commentary on Genesis	67
Commentary on Exodus	
Introduction	217
Commentary on Exodus	221
The Homily on Our Lord	
Introduction	269
The Homily on Our Lord	273
Letter to Publius	
Introduction	335
Letter to Publius	338
Indices	
General Index	359
Index of Holy Scripture	388

FOREWORD

The Editors presented volume 1 of FOTC, *The Apostolic Fathers* (New York, 1947) as the first of a projected series of seventy-two and promised: "In general, these Fathers will prove to be a reproach to all narrowness and exclusivism. . . . If ever we forget the part that Christian poetry has played in the propagation of Christian truth, we have only to recall the hymns and lyric lines of Ambrose, Ephraem, Pope Damasus, Prudentius and Boethius." Already we have gone beyond the projected seventy-two volumes and, while we have had two volumes devoted to the poetry of Prudentius [FOTC 43 (1962) and 52 (1965) trans. Sr. M. Clement Eagen], this is our first venture outside the Greek and Latin Fathers, and it is particularly appropriate that it be devoted to the "Harp of the Spirit," Ephrem.

Like Ambrose, Ephrem composed homilies and commentaries as well as hymns, and we are fortunate to have on our Editorial Board, Professor Kathleen McVey, whose recent volume, *Ephrem the Syrian Hymns,* Classics of Western Spirituality (New York, 1989) will have whetted the appetites of English-speaking readers for more Ephrem, and who acted as editor of the present volume of *Selected Prose Works.* We hope that this in turn will encourage the appearance of other volumes devoted to Fathers whose first language was neither Greek nor Latin.

THOMAS HALTON
Editorial Director

PREFACE

This volume contains a selection of the prose works of Ephrem the Syrian: the *Commentary on Genesis,* the *Commentary on Exodus,* the *Homily on Our Lord,* and the *Letter to Publius.* These four works comprise approximately two-thirds of Ephrem's genuine Syriac prose works known to have survived. Among the others, the *Commentary on the Diatessaron* will appear in a forthcoming volume in this series, and the *Prose Refutations* have already been rendered into English (see bibliography). While Ephrem is justly renowned for his poetic works, the works translated here also manifest Ephrem's genius as spiritual writer, theologian, and teacher. Study of Ephrem has gained tremendous impetus in the last two or three decades, particularly in Europe, but of late in the United States as well. Recent translations of Ephrem's works published here bear clear witness to this. We are proud to have made this small contribution to that ongoing effort and hope that others will soon follow.

With respect to the translations contained in this volume, the division of our labor has been one of nearly total independence. Dr. Amar translated and annotated the *Commentary on Exodus* and the *Homily on Our Lord,* while Mathews was responsible for the *Commentary on Genesis* and the *Letter to Publius.* The introduction, intended to provide a fundamental guide to the world of Syriac Christianity as well as to Ephrem, was researched and written by Mathews, although the final version benefitted much from comments and suggestions by Dr. Amar. Mathews also compiled the bibliography, the purpose of which extends beyond the four works translated here; it is intended to provide for the reader the available editions of Ephrem's works, a generous selection of studies on Ephrem available in English, along with the major studies in European languages. Secondary works pertaining to the *Commentary on the Diatessaron* will be included in that volume.

While we each followed our own paths in our translations, we have both attempted to follow our predecessors to the best of our ability in steering that dangerous course between the Scylla of literalness and the Charybdis of paraphrase. Syriac differs much from English and we confess to no systematic technique of translation. While we have endeavored, following current scholarly practice, to keep the translations as literal as English syntax will allow, some contexts demanded a more periphrastic rendering for the sake of best conveying to the reader the sense of that passage. In other passages Ephrem's exegesis demanded an even more literal translation than might otherwise have been required. In those places, however, where we have erred in steering too far one way or the other we can only ask the reader's indulgence.

In the two commentaries, neither of us made any real attempt to force the Syriac biblical text of Ephrem to conform to any existing English Bible translation. This was all the more necessary as Ephrem's text preserves readings that differ not only from the Peshitta, the *textus receptus* of the Syrian churches, but also from the Hebrew and Greek versions from which our English Bible translations are made. Our translations follow in the main the divisions to the text as found in those edited texts from which our translations were made.

In the notes we have tried to limit ourselves to explaining Ephrem only by reference to his other works. We have made every attempt to note at least the most important references and parallels, though no doubt specialists will find others that we missed. We have made no systematic effort to draw parallels to Greek and Latin sources, nor to later Syriac works. In those cases where it was necessary to draw attention to Jewish sources or parallels, we thought it best simply to refer to the collection of Jewish legends collected by Louis Ginzberg. This collection has the twofold advantage of being generally available while also exempting us from encumbering the notes and burdening the reader with detailed arguments about the dating of Rabbinic and Midrashic sources.

Although no doubt numerous errors and omissions remain, we would like to give special thanks to several people who have helped to lessen their number. Dr. Evan Lawn, Mr. Eugene McGarry, and Dr. Susan Mathews took much of their own valuable time and kindly read through much or all of the manuscript. They each made helpful suggestions and saved us from many errors that had escaped us. To these and to many others who were kind enough to offer encouragement and/or to look at portions of the work, our most gracious thanks.

The editorial board of Fathers of the Church also deserve our most heartfelt thanks. Dr. Kathleen McVey read through the entire manuscript with great care and attention, thus saving us from numerous omissions, and made many useful corrections and valuable suggestions. The entire editing process was handled with patience, kindness, and utmost professional care and skill by Mr. Edward Strickland. Fr. Thomas P. Halton's kindness in accepting our invitation to write the Foreword to this volume is greatly appreciated. Most sincere thanks must also go to the National Endowment for the Humanities, without whose financial support this project would not yet be complete. But our deepest thanks must go to our families whose encouragement, whose support and whose willingness to bear the brunt of other responsibilities gave us the freedom necessary to complete this volume. It is to all of them that we humbly and thankfully offer whatever is of merit in this book.

ABBREVIATIONS

AB	*Analecta Bollandiana.*
ACW	*Ancient Christian Writers.*
ANRW	*Aufstieg und Niedergang der Römischen Welt.*
ASTI	*Annual of the Swedish Theological Institute.*
BJRL	*Bulletin of the John Rylands Library.*
BLE	*Bulletin de littérature ecclésiastique.*
CBQ	*Catholic Biblical Quarterly.*
CBU	*Contributions of the Baltic University.*
CH	*Church History.*
CSCO	*Corpus Scriptorum Christianorum Orientalium.*
CSS	*Cistercian Studies Series.*
CWS	*Classics of Western Spirituality.*
DHGE	*Dictionnaire d'histoire et de géographie ecclésiastiques.*
DS	*Dictionnaire de Spiritualité.*
EA	*Études augustiniennes.*
ECQ	*Eastern Churches Quarterly.*
ECR	*Eastern Churches Review.*
ETL	*Ephemerides Theologicae Lovanienses.*
GCS	*Die griechischen Christlichen Schriftsteller.*
HA	*Handes Amsorya.*
JA	*Journal Asiatique.*
JAC	*Jahrbuch für Antike und Christentum.*
JBL	*Journal of Biblical Literature.*
JJS	*Journal of Jewish Studies.*
JRAS	*Journal of the Royal Asiatic Society.*
JRS	*Journal of Roman Studies.*
JSS	*Journal of Semitic Studies.*
JTS	*Journal of Theological Studies.*
LCL	*Loeb Classical Library.*
LM	*Le Muséon.*
LNPF	*Library of Nicene and Post-Nicene Fathers.*
MGWJ	*Monatsschrift für Geschichte und Wissenschaft des Judentums.*
NT	*Novum Testamentum.*

ABBREVIATIONS

NTS	New Testament Studies.
OC	Oriens Christianus.
OCA	Orientalia Christiana Analecta.
OCP	Orientalia Christiana Periodica.
OKS	Ostkirchliche Studien.
Or	Orientalia.
OS	L'Orient Syrien.
PBR	Patristic and Byzantine Review.
PdO	Parole de l'Orient.
PETSE	Papers of the Estonian Theological Society in Exile.
PG	Patrologia Graeca.
PO	Patrologia Orientalis.
PS	Patrologia Syriaca.
PWK	Pauly-Wissowa-Kröll.
RA	Revue Augustinienne.
RAC	Reallexicon für Antike und Christentum.
RB	Revue Biblique.
REA	Revue des études arméniennes.
RHE	Revue d'Histoire Ecclésiastique.
ROC	Revue de l'Orient Chrétien.
RSR	Recherches de Sciences religieuses.
RTL	Revue Théologique de Louvain.
SA	Studia Anselmiana.
SC	Sources Chrétiennes.
SP	Studia Patristica.
SVTQ	St. Vladimir's Theological Quarterly.
TS	Texts and Studies.
TU	Texte und Untersuchungen.
VC	Vigiliae Christianae.
ZKG	Zeitschrift für Kirchengeschichte.

Other Works

HASO II   A. Vööbus, History of Asceticism in the Syrian Orient. Vol. 2. CSCO 197. Louvain, 1960.

SELECT BIBLIOGRAPHY

Ephrem's Works

Assemani, J. S., ed. *Sancti Patris Nostri Ephraem Syri Opera Omnia quae exstant graece, syriace, latine, in sex tomos distributa.* Rome, 1732–43.
Beck, E., ed. *Des Heiligen Ephraem des Syrers Carmina Nisibena.* CSCO 218–19, 240–41. Louvain, 1961,1963.
_____, ed. *Des Heiligen Ephraem des Syrers Hymnen auf Abraham Kidunaya und Julianos Saba.* CSCO 322–23. Louvain, 1972.
_____, ed. *Des Heiligen Ephraem des Syrers Hymnen contra Haereses.* CSCO 169–70. Louvain, 1957.
_____, ed. *Des Heiligen Ephraem des Syrers Hymnen de Ecclesia.* CSCO 198–99. Louvain, 1960.
_____, ed. *Des Heiligen Ephraem des Syrers Hymnen de Fide.* CSCO 154–55. Louvain, 1955.
_____, ed. *Des Heiligen Ephraem des Syrers Hymnen de Ieiunio.* CSCO 246–47. Louvain, 1964.
_____, ed. *Des Heiligen Ephraem des Syrers Hymnen de Nativitate (Epiphania).* CSCO 186–87. Louvain, 1959.
_____, ed. *Des Heiligen Ephraem des Syrers Hymnen de Paradiso und Contra Julianum.* CSCO 174–75. Louvain, 1957.
_____, ed. *Des Heiligen Ephraem des Syrers Hymnen de Virginitate.* CSCO 223–24. Louvain, 1962.
_____, ed. *Des Heiligen Ephraem des Syrers Paschahymnen.* CSCO 247–48. Louvain, 1964.
_____, ed. *Des Heiligen Ephraem des Syrers Sermo de Domino Nostro.* CSCO 270–71. Louvain, 1966.
_____, ed. *Des Heiligen Ephraem des Syrers Sermones de Fide.* CSCO 212–13. Louvain, 1961.
_____, ed. *Des Heiligen Ephraem des Syrers Sermones.* Vol. 1. CSCO 305–6. Louvain, 1969.
_____, ed. *Des Heiligen Ephraem des Syrers Sermones.* Vol. 2. CSCO 311–12. Louvain, 1970.
_____, ed. *Des Heiligen Ephraem des Syrers Sermones.* Vol. 3. CSCO 320–21. Louvain, 1972.
_____, ed. *Des Heiligen Ephraem des Syrers Sermones.* Vol. 4. CSCO 334–35. Louvain, 1973.

———, ed. *Ephraem Syrus. Sermones in Hebdomadam Sanctam*. *CSCO* 412–13. Louvain, 1979.
———, ed. *Nachträge zu Ephraem Syrus*. *CSCO* 363–64. Louvain, 1975.
Bevan, E. A. and F. C. Burkitt. S. *Ephraim's Prose Refutations of Mani, Marcion and Bardaisan*. Vol. 2. London, 1921.
Bickell, G., ed. *Sancti Ephraemi Syri Carmina Nisibena additis prolegomenis et supplemento lexicorum syriacorum primus edidit, vertit, explicavit*. Leipzig, 1866.
Bojkovsky, G. *Paraenesis. Die altbulgarische Übersetzung von Werken Ephraims des Syrers*. Monumenta Linguae Slavicae Dialecti Veteris, nos. 20, 22, 24. Freiburg, 1984–87.
Brock, S. P. "Ephrem's Letter to Publius." *LM* 89 (1976): 261–305.
Ephraem Latinus. *Patrologia Latina, Supplementum*. Vol. 4. Paris, 1967. 604–48.
Lamy, T. J., ed. *Sancti Ephraemi Syri Hymni et Sermones*. 4 vols. Machelen-lez-Deinze, 1882–1902.
Leloir, L., ed. *Saint Ephrem Commentaire de l'évangile concordant*. Chester Beatty Monographs, no. 8. Dublin, 1963.
———, ed. *Saint Ephrem Commentaire de l'évangile concordant texte syriaque (Manuscript Chester Beatty 709) Folios Additionnels*. Chester Beatty Monographs, no. 8. Louvain, 1990.
———, ed. *Saint Ephrem. Commentaire de l'évangile concordant, version arménienne*. *CSCO* 137, 145. Louvain, 1953, 1954.
———, ed. "S. Ephrem: le texte de son commentaire du Sermon de la Montagne." In *Mémorial Dom Jean Gribomont (1920–1986)*, ed. Y. de Andia et al. Studia Ephemeridis "Augustinianum," no. 27. Rome, 1988.
Maries, L. and C. Mercier, eds. *Hymnes de S. Ephrem conservées en version arménienne*. *PO* 30. Paris, 1961.
Mitchell, C. W. S. *Ephraim's Prose Refutations of Mani, Marcion and Bardaisan*. Vol. 1. London, 1912.
Overbeck, J. J. S. *Ephraemi Syri, Rabulae Episcopi Edesseni, Balaei aliorumque Opera Selecta*. Oxford, 1865.
Rahmani, I. E. *Ephrem Hymni de Virginitate*. 2 vols. Scharfeh, 1907.
Renoux, C., ed. *Ephrem de Nisibe Mêmrê sur Nicomedie*. *PO* 37. Paris, 1975.
Srboyn Ep'remi Matenagrut'iwnk'. 4 vols. Venice, 1836. [In Armenian].
Ter Petrossian, L. and B. Outtier. *Textes arméniens relatifs à S. Ephrem*. *CSCO* 473, 474. Louvain, 1985.
Tonneau, R. M., ed. *Sancti Ephraem Syri in Genesim et in Exodum commentarii*. *CSCO* 152–53. Louvain, 1955.

SELECT BIBLIOGRAPHY xvii

Zingerle, P., ed. *Ephraemi Syri sermones duo ex codd. syr. Rom.* Brescia, 1868.

Selected Secondary Sources

Amar, J. P. "Byzantine Ascetic Monachism and Greek Bias in the *Vita* Tradition of Ephrem the Syrian." *OCP* 58 (1992): 123–56.
———. "Perspectives on the Eucharist in Ephrem the Syrian." *Worship* 61 (1987): 441–54.
———. "The Syriac *Vita* Tradition of Ephrem the Syrian." Ph. D. dissertation, Catholic University of America, 1988.
———. "An Unpublished *Karšunî* Arabic Life of Ephrem the Syrian." *LM* 106 (1993): 119–44.
Aprem, Mar. *Mar Aprem, Theologian and Poet, 301–373* A.D. Kerala, 1990.
Assemani, J. S. *Bibliotheca Orientalis Clementina-Vaticana.* 3 vols. Rome, 1719–28.
Bardy, G. "Le souvenir de saint Ephrem dans le haut moyen âge latin." *Revue du Moyen Age Latin* 2 (1946): 297–300.
Beck, E. "Asketentum und Mönchtum bei Ephräm." In *Il monachesimo orientale,* 341–62. *OCA* 153. Rome, 1958.
———. "Le Baptême chez St. Ephrem." *OS* 1 (1956): 111–36.
———. "Bardaisan und seine Schule bei Ephräm." *LM* 91 (1978): 271–333.
———. "Ein Beitrag zur Terminologie des ältesten syrischen Mönchtums." In *Antonius Magnus Eremita 356–1956,* 254–67. *SA,* no. 38. Rome, 1956.
———. "Besrâ (sarx) und pagrâ (sōma) bei Ephräm dem Syrer." *OC* 70 (1986): 1–22.
———. "Das Bild vom Sauerteig bei Ephräm." *OC* 63 (1979): 1–19.
———. "Das Bild vom Spiegel bei Ephräm." *OCP* 19 (1953): 5–24.
———. "Das Bild vom Weg mit Meilensteinen und Herbergen bei Ephraem." *OC* 65 (1981): 1–39.
———. *Dōrea und Charis.—Die Taufe. Zwei Beiträge zur Theologie Ephräms des Syrers. CSCO* 457. Louvain, 1984.
———. *Ephräm der Syrer. Lobgesang aus der Wüste.* Sophia, no. 7. Freiburg, 1967.
———. "Ephräms Brief an Hypatios übersetzt und erklärt." *OC* 58 (1974): 76–120.
———. "Ephräms des Syrers Hymnik." In *Liturgie und Dichtung. Festschrift für W. Dürig,* vol. 1, ed. H. Becker and R. Kaczynski, 345–79. St. Ottilien, 1983.
———. *Ephräms des Syrers. Psychologie und Erkenntnislehre. CSCO* 419. Louvain, 1980.

SELECT BIBLIOGRAPHY

———. *Ephräms Hymnen über das Paradies.* SA, no. 26. Rome, 1951.
———. "Ephräms Hymnus de Paradiso XV, 1-8." OC 62 (1978): 24–35.
———. *Ephräms Polemik gegen Mani und die Manichäer im Rahmen der zeitgenössischen griechischen Polemik und der des Augustinus.* CSCO 391. Louvain, 1978.
———. "Ephräms Rede gegen eine philosophische Schrift des Bardaisan übersetzt und erklärt." OC 60 (1976): 24–68.
———. *Ephräms Reden über den Glauben. Ihr theologischer Lehrgehalt und ihr geschichtlicher Rahmen.* SA, no. 33. Rome, 1953.
———. *Ephräms Trinitätslehre im Bild von Sonne/Feuer, Licht und Wärme.* CSCO 425. Louvain, 1981.
———. "Ephrem der Syrer." RAC 5 (1962): 521–31.
———. "Ephrem le Syrien." In DS 4, 788–800. Paris, 1960.
———. "Die Eucharistie bei Ephräm." OC 38 (1954): 41–67.
———. "Glaube und Gebet bei Ephräm." OC 66 (1982): 15–50.
———. "Die Hyle bei Markion nach Ephräm." OCP 44 (1978): 5–30.
———. "Die Mariologie der echten Schriften Ephräms." OC 40 (1956): 22–39.
———. "Philoxenos und Ephräm." OC 46 (1962): 61–76.
———. "Symbolum-Mysterium bei Aphraat und Ephräm." OC 42 (1958): 19–40.
———. "ΤΕΧΝΗ und ΤΕΧΝΙΤΗΣ bei dem Syrer Ephräm." OCP 47 (1981): 295–331.
———. *Die Theologie des Hl. Ephräm in seinem Hymnen über den Glauben.* SA, no. 21. Rome, 1949.
———. "Zur Terminologie von Ephraems Bildtheologie." In *Typus, Symbol, Allegorie bei den östlichen Vätern und ihren Parallelen im Mittelalter,* ed. M. Schmidt, 239–77. Eichstatt, 1982.
———. "Zwei ephrämische Bilder." OC 71 (1987): 1–23.
———. "Die zwei Paradoxa des Glaubens bei Ephräm." In *A Tribute to Arthur Vööbus,* ed. Robert H. Fischer, 169–75. Chicago, 1977.
Bestul, T. H. "Ephraim the Syrian and Old English Poetry." *Anglia* 99 (1981): 1–24.
Botha, P. J. "Antithesis and Argument in the Hymns of Ephrem the Syrian." *Hervormde Teologiese Studies* 44 (1988): 581–95.
———. "Christology and Apology in Ephrem the Syrian." *Hervormde Teologiese Studies* 45 (1989): 19–29.
Bou Mansour, T. "Analyse de quelques termes christologiques chez Ephrem." PdO 15 (1988/89): 3–20.
———. "Aspects de la liberté humaine chez Saint Ephrem le Syrien." ETL 60 (1984): 252–82.

SELECT BIBLIOGRAPHY xix

———. "La défense éphrémienne de la liberté contre les doctrines marcionite, bardesanite et manichéenne." *OCP* 50 (1984): 331–46.
———. "Étude de la terminologie symbolique chez Saint Ephrem." *PdO* 14 (1987): 221–62.
———. "La liberté chez Saint Ephrem le Syrien." *PdO* 11 (1983): 89–156, 12 (1984/85), 3–89.
———. *La pensée symbolique de Saint Ephrem le Syrien*. Bibliothèque de l'Université Saint Esprit, no. 16. Kaslik, 1988.
Bravo, C. *Notas introductorias a la noemática de San Efrén*. Rome, 1956.
Brock, S. P. "Clothing Metaphors as a Means of Theological Expression in Syriac Tradition." In *Typus, Symbol, Allegorie bei den östlichen Vätern und ihren Parallelen im Mittelalter*, ed. M. Schmidt, 11–40. Eichstatt, 1981.
———. "From Ephrem to Romanos." *SP* 20 (1989): 139–51.
———. *The Harp of the Spirit*. Studies Supplementary to Sobornost, no. 4. 2d ed. St. Alban and St. Sergius, 1985.
———. "Introduction to Syriac Studies." In *Horizons in Semitic Studies*, ed. J. H. Eaton, 1–33. University Semitics Study Aids, no. 8. Birmingham, 1980.
———. "Jewish Traditions in Syriac Sources." *JJS* 30 (1979): 212–32.
———. *The Luminous Eye: The Spiritual World Vision of St. Ephrem*. Rome, 1985. 2d ed., *CSS* 124. Kalamazoo, 1992.
———. "Mary and the Eucharist, an Oriental Perspective." *Sobornost/ECR* 1 (1979): 50–59.
———. "Mary in Syriac Tradition." In *Mary's Place in Christian Dialogue*, ed. A. Stacpole, 182–91. Slough, 1981.
———. "The Mysteries Hidden in the Side of Christ." *Sobornost* 7 (1978): 464–72.
———. "The Poet as Theologian." *Sobornost* 7 (1977): 243–50.
———. "The Poetic Artistry of St. Ephrem: An Analysis of H. Azym. III." *PdO* 6/7 (1975/76): 21–28.
———. "St. Ephrem on Christ as Light in Mary and in the Jordan (= Hymns on the Church, 36)." *ECR* 7 (1976): 137–44.
———. *St. Ephrem the Syrian: Hymns on Paradise*. Crestwood, 1990.
———. "An Unpublished Letter of St. Ephrem." *PdO* 4 (1973): 317–22.
———. "World and Sacrament in the Syrian Fathers." *Sobornost* 6 (1974): 685–96.
Bruns, P. "Arius hellenizans?—Ephraem der Syrer und die neoarianischen Kontroversen seiner Zeit." *ZKG* 101 (1990/91): 21–57.

Bundy, D. D. "Ephrem's Critique of Mani: The Limits of Knowledge and the Nature of Language." In *Gnosticisme et Monde Hellénistique*. *Actes du Colloque de Louvain-la-Neuve (11–14 mars 1980)*, ed. J. Ries et al., 289–98. Publications de l'Institut Orientaliste de Louvain, no. 27. Louvain-la-Neuve, 1982.
———. "Language and the Knowledge of God in Ephrem Syrus." *Dialogue and Alliance* 1 (1988): 56–64.
———. "Language and the Knowledge of God in Ephrem Syrus." *PBR* 5 (1986): 91–103.
———. "Marcion and the Marcionites in Early Syriac Apologetics." *LM* 101 (1988): 21–32.
Burkitt, F. C. S. *Ephraim's Quotations from the Gospels*. TS, no. 7, part 2. Cambridge, 1905.
Caquot, A. "Une homelie éthiopienne attribuée à saint Mari Ephrem, sur le séjour d'Abraham et Sara en Egypte." In *Mélanges Antoine Guillaumont*, ed. R. Coquin, 173–85. Geneva, 1988.
Cramer, W. *Die Engelvorstellungen bei Ephräm dem Syrer*. OCA, no. 173. Rome, 1965.
———. *Der Geist Gottes und des Menschen in frühsyrischer Theologie*. Münsterische Beiträge zur Theologie, no. 46. Münster, 1979.
Dalmais, I. "La vie monastique comme ascèse vigiliale d'après Saint Ephrem et les traditions liturgiques syriennes." In *Liturgie, Conversion et Vie Monastique*, ed. A. Triacca and A. Pistoia, 73–86. Paris, 1989.
Darling, R. A. "The 'Church from the Nations' in the Exegesis of Ephrem." In *OCA*, no. 229, 111–22. Rome, 1987.
de Halleux, A. "Une clé pour les hymnes d'Ephrem dans le ms. Sinai syr. 10." *LM* 85 (1972): 171–99.
———. "Ephrem le Syrien." *RTL* 14 (1983): 328–55.
———. "Mar Ephrem théologien." *PdO* 4 (1973): 35–54.
———. "La transmission des Hymnes d'Ephrem d'après le ms. Sinai syr. 10." In *OCA*, no. 197, 21–63. Rome, 1974.
El-Khoury, N. "Gen. 1,26 dans l'interprétation de Saint Ephrem, ou la rélation de l'homme à Dieu." In *OCA*, no. 205, 199–205. Rome, 1978.
———. "Hermeneutics in the Works of Ephrem the Syrian." In *OCA* 229, 93–110. Rome, 1987.
———. *Die Interpretation der Welt bei Ephräm dem Syrer*. Tübinger theologische Studien, no. 6. Tübingen, 1976.
———. "The Use of Language by Ephraim the Syrian." *SP* 16 (1985): 93–99.
———. "Willensfreiheit bei Ephräm der Syrer." *OKS* 25 (1976): 60–66.

SELECT BIBLIOGRAPHY

Féghali, P. "Un commentaire de la Genèse attribué à saint Ephrem." In *OCA* 226, 159–75. Rome, 1986.
———. "Commentaire de l'Exode par saint Ephrem." *PdO* 12 (1984/85): 90–131.
———. "Influence des Targums sur la pensée exégétique d'Éphrem?" In *OCA* 229, 71–82. Rome, 1987.
———. "Notes sur l'exégèse de S. Ephrem; commentaire sur le déluge (Gen. 6,1–9,17)." *PdO* 8 (1977/78): 67–86.
———. "Note sur l'influence de S. Paul sur les Carmina Nisibena de S. Ephrem." *PdO* 9 (1979/80): 5–25.
———. "Les premiers jours de la création, commentaire de Gn. 1,1–2,4 par Saint Ephrem." *PdO* 13 (1986): 3–30.
———. "Protologie et eschatologie dans l'oeuvre de S. Ephrem." *PdO* 9 (1979/80): 307–12.
Fiey, J.-M. "Les évêques de Nisibe au temps de saint Ephrem." *PdO* 4 (1973): 123–35.
———. *Nisibe: metropole syriaque orientale et ses suffragants des origines à nos jours*. *CSCO* 388. Louvain, 1977.
Fransen, P. "Les extraits d'Ephrem latin dans la compilation des XII pères de Florus de Lyon." *Revue Benedictine* 87 (1977): 349–71.
Froidevaux, L. "Sur un recueil arménien d'hymnes de saint Ephrem." *RSR* 51 (1963): 558–78.
Geerard, M. "Ephraem Graecus." In *Clavis Patrum Graecorum*, 2:366–468. Turnhout, 1974.
Gelineau, J. "Données liturgiques contenues dans les sept madroshé 'De la nuit' de S. Ephrem." *OS* 5 (1960): 107–21.
Gerson, D. "Die Commentarien des Ephraem Syrus im Verhältniss zur jüdischen Exegese. Ein Beitrag zur Geschichte der Exegese." *MGWJ* 17 (1868): 15–33, 64–72, 98–109, 141–49.
Graffin, F. "L'Eucharistie chez Saint Ephrem." *PdO* 4 (1973): 93–121.
———. "Hymnes inédites de saint Ephrem sur la virginité." *OS* 6 (1961): 213–42.
———. "Les hymnes sur la perle de saint Ephrem." *OS* 12 (1967): 129–50.
———. "La soghita du cherubin et du larron." *OS* 12 (1967): 481–90.
Gribomont, J. "Les hymnes de Saint Ephrem sur la Pâque." *Melto* 3 (1967): 147–82.
———. "La tradition liturgique des Hymnes Pascales de Saint Ephrem." *PdO* 4 (1973): 191–246.
———. "Le triomphe de Pâques d'après saint Ephrem." *PdO* 4 (1973): 147–89.

Griffith, S. H. "Ephraem, the Deacon of Edessa, and the Church of the Empire." In *DIAKONIA: Studies in Honor of Robert T. Meyer*, ed. T. Halton and J. P. Williman, 22–52. Washington, 1986.
_____. "Ephraem the Syrian's Hymns 'Against Julian': Meditations on History and Imperial Power." *VC* 41 (1987): 238–66.
_____. "Images of Ephraem: The Syrian Holy Man and His Church." *Traditio* 45 (1989/90): 7–33.
Guillaumont, A. "Un Midrash d'Exode 4, 24–26 chez Aphraate et Ephrem de Nisibe." In *A Tribute to Arthur Vööbus*, ed. R. H. Fischer, 89–95. Chicago, 1977.
Hanson, A.G.P. and L. Van Rompay. *Efrem de Syriër: Uitleg van het boek Genesis.* Kampen, 1993.
Hausherr, I. *Noms du Christ et voies d'Oraison.* OCA 157, 64–72. Rome, 1969.
Hemmerdinger-Iliadou, D. "Vers une nouvelle édition de l'Ephrem grec." *SP* 3 (1961): 72–80.
_____. "Saint Ephrem le Syrien: sermon sur Jonas." *LM* 80 (1967): 47–74.
_____. "Ephrem: versions grecque, latine et slave. Addenda et corrigenda." *Epeteris Hetairaias Buzantinon Spoudon* 42 (1975/76): 320–73.
Hemmerdinger-Iliadou, D. and J. Kirchmeyer. "Ephrem grec et latin." In *DS* 4, 800–822. Paris, 1960.
Hidal, S. *Interpretatio Syriaca. Die Kommentare des hl. Ephräm des Syrers zu Genesis und Exodus mit besonderer Berücksichtigung ihrer Auslegungsgeschichtlichen Stellung.* Coniectanea Biblica; Old Testament Series, no. 6. Lund, 1974.
Jansma, T. "Investigations into the Early Syrian Fathers on Genesis." In *Studies on the Book of Genesis*, ed. B. Gemser, et al. *Oudtestamentische Studien* 12 (1958): 69–181.
_____. "Ephraems Beschreibung des ersten Tages der Schöpfung." *OCP* 37 (1971): 295–316.
_____. "Ephraem's Commentary on Exodus: Some Remarks on the Syriac Text and the Latin Translation." *JSS* 17 (1972): 203–12.
_____. "Beiträge zur Berichtigung einzelner Stellen in Ephraems Genesiskommentar." *OC* 56 (1972): 59–79.
_____. "The Provenance of the Last Sections in the Roman Edition of Ephraem's Commentary on Exodus." *LM* 85 (1972): 155–69.
_____. "Ephraem on Genesis xlix 10. An Enquiry into the Syriac Text Forms as Presented in His Commentary on Genesis." *PdO* 4 (1973): 247–56.

———. "Ephraem on Exodus ii. 5: Reflections on the Interplay of Human Freewill and Divine Providence." *OCP* 39 (1973): 5–28.
———. "Weitere Beiträge zur Berichtigung einzelner Stellen in Ephraems Kommentäre zu Genesis und Exodus." *OC* 58 (1974): 121–31.
Kanjiramukalil, S. *Church and Eucharist in St. Ephrem*. Kerala, 1987.
Kechichian, P. "Bibliographie en langue arménienne sur St. Ephrem de Nisibe." In *Ephrem Hunayn Festival*, 279. Baghdad, 1974.
Kowalski, A. "'Rivestiti di gloria'. Adamo ed Eva nel commento di S. Efrem a Gen. 2,25 Ricerca sulle fonti dell'esegesi siriaca." *Cristianesimo nella storia* 3 (1982): 41–60.
Kronholm, T. *Motifs from Genesis 1–11 in the Genuine Hymns of Ephrem the Syrian with Particular Reference to the Influence of Jewish Exegetical Tradition*. Coniectanea Biblica, Old Testament Series, no. 11. Lund, 1978.
———. "The Trees of Paradise in the Hymns of Ephraem Syrus." *ASTI* 11 (1977/78): 48–56.
Lamy, T. J. "L'exégèse en orient au IVe siècle ou les commentaires de Saint Ephrem." *RB* 2 (1893): 5–25, 161–81, 465–86.
Lattke, M. "Sind Ephraems Madrāšē Hymnen?" *OC* 73 (1989): 38–43.
Lavenant, R., trans. *Ephrem de Nisibe: Hymnes sur le Paradis*. SC 137. Paris, 1968.
Leloir, L. "L'actualité du message d'Ephrem." *PdO* 4 (1973): 55–72.
———. "La Christologie de S. Ephrem dans son Commentaire du Diatessaron." *Handes Amsorya* 75 (1961): 449–66.
———. *Doctrines et méthodes de S. Ephrem d'après son Commentaire de l'Evangile concordant*. CSCO 220. Louvain, 1961.
———, trans. *Ephrem de Nisibe: Commentaire de l'Evangile Concordant ou Diatessaron*. SC 121. Paris, 1966.
———. "Ephrem et l'ascendance davidique du Christ." *SP* 1 (1957): 389–95.
———. "Ephrem le Syrien." In *DHGE* 15, 590–97. Paris, 1963.
———. "La pensée monastique d'Ephrem et Martyrius." In *OCA*, no. 197, 105–34. Rome, 1974.
———. "La pensée monastique d'Ephrem le Syrien." In *Memorial du Cinquantenaire 1914–64*, 193–206. Travaux de l'Institut Catholique de Paris, no. 10. Paris, 1964.
———. "Saint Ephrem, moine et pasteur." In *Théologie de la vie monastique*, 85–97. Paris, 1961.
———. "Symbolisme et parallelisme chez Ephrem." In *A la rencontre de Dieu. Mémorial Albert Gelin*, 363–74. Lyon, 1961.

Levene, A., ed. *The Early Syrian Fathers on Genesis, from a Syriac MS. on the Pentateuch in the Mingana Collection.* London, 1951.
McVey, K. "St. Ephrem's Understanding of Spiritual Progress: Some Points of Comparison with Origen of Alexandria." *The Harp* 1 (1988): 117–28.
_____, trans. *Ephrem the Syrian Hymns.* CWS. New York, 1989.
_____. "The Anti-Judaic Polemic of Ephrem Syrus' Hymns on the Nativity." In *Of Scribes and Scrolls: Studies in the Hebrew Bible, Intertestamental Judaism, and Christian Origins,* ed. H.W. Attridge, J.J. Collins, and T.H. Tobin, 229–40. Lanham, 1990.
Mahr, A. *Relations of Passion Plays to St. Ephrem the Syrian.* Columbus, 1942.
Martikainen, J. *Das Böse und der Teufel in der Theologie Ephraems der Syrer. Ein systematisch-theologische Untersuchungen.* Publications of the Research Institute of the Abo Akademi Foundation, no. 32. Abo, 1978.
_____. *Gerechtigkeit und Güte Gottes: Studien zur Theologie von Ephraem dem Syrer und Philoxenos von Mabbug.* Göttinger Orientforschungen, no. 20. Wiesbaden, 1981.
_____. "Some Remarks about the Carmina Nisibena as a Literary and a Theological Source." In *OCA,* no. 197, 345–52. Rome, 1974.
Mathews, E. G., Jr. "The Armenian Version of Ephrem's Commentary on Genesis." *forthcoming.*
_____, trans. *Ephrem the Syrian: Commentary on the Diatessaron.* Fathers of the Church. Washington, DC. *forthcoming.*
_____. "'On Solitaries': Ephrem or Isaac?" *LM* 103 (1990): 91–110.
_____. "St. Ephrem, *Madrāšê On Faith,* 81–85: Hymns on the Pearl, I–V." *SVTQ* 38 (1994): 45–72.
_____. "Three Mêmrê on Solitaries attributed to Ephrem the Syrian and Isaac the Teacher. Editions, Translations and Commentary with an Investigation into Their Place in the History of Syriac Asceticism." Ph. D. dissertation, Catholic University of America, *forthcoming.*
_____. "The *Vita* Tradition of Ephrem the Syrian, the Deacon of Edessa." *Diakonia* 22 (1988–89): 15–42.
Melki, J. "Saint Ephrem le Syrien, un bilan de l'édition critique." *PdO* 11 (1983): 3–88.
Molenberg, C. "Two Christological Passages in Ephrem Syrus' Hymns on Faith." *SP* 20 (1989): 191–96.
Murray, R. "The Characteristics of Earliest Christianity." In *East of Byzantium: Syria and Armenia in the Formative Period,* ed. N. G.

Garsoian, T. F. Mathews and R. W. Thomson, 3–16. Washington, 1982.
_____. "Der Dichter als Exeget." *ZKT* 100 (1978): 484–94.
_____. "Ephraem Syrus." In *Theologische Realencyklopädie* (1982), 9:755–62.
_____. "The Exhortation to Candidates for Ascetical Vows at Baptism in the Ancient Syriac Church." *NTS* 21 (1974/75): 59–80.
_____. "Features of the Earliest Christian Asceticism." In *Christian Spirituality: Essays in Honour of Gordon Rupp*, ed. Peter Brooks, 65–77. London, 1975.
_____. "A Hymn of St. Ephrem to Christ (= Hymns on Virginity, 31)." *Sobornost/ECR* 1 (1979): 39–50.
_____. "A Hymn of St. Ephrem to Christ on the Incarnation, the Holy Spirit and the Sacraments (= Hymns on Faith, 10)." *ECR* 3 (1970): 142–50.
_____. "The Lance Which Reopened Paradise." *OCP* 39 (1973): 224–34, 391.
_____. "Mary, the Second Eve in the Early Syriac Fathers." *ECR* 3 (1971): 372–84.
_____. "St. Ephrem Syrus." In *Catholic Dictionary of Theology* II, 220–23. London, 1967.
_____. "St. Ephrem the Syrian on Church Unity." *ECQ* 15 (1963): 164–76.
_____. "St. Ephrem's Dialogue of Reason and Love (= Hymns on the Church, 9)." *Sobornost/ECR* 2 (1980): 26–40.
_____. *Symbols of Church and Kingdom*. Cambridge, 1975.
_____. "The Theory of Symbolism in St. Ephrem's Theology." *PdO* 6/7 (1975/76): 1–20.
Noujaim, G. "Anthropologie et économie de salut chez S. Ephrem: autour des notions de ghalyātâ, kasyātâ et kasyâ." *PdO* 9 (1979/80): 313–15.
_____. "Essai sur quelques aspects de la philosophie d'Ephrem de Nisibe." *PdO* 9 (1979/80): 27–50.
Ogren, I. *The Paraenesis of Ephrem the Syrian: a Contribution to the History of the Slavic Translation*. Uppsala, 1989. [In Russian]
Ortiz de Urbina, I. "L'évêque et son role d'après saint Ephrem." *PdO* 4 (1973): 137–46.
_____. "Mariologos sirios en la estela de s. Efren." *Marianum* 41 (1979): 171–98.
_____. "Le Paradis eschatologique d'après Saint Ephrem." *OCP* 21 (1955): 467–72.
_____. "S. Efrem e il sangue redentore." In *Atti della Settimana Sangue e Antropologia Biblica nella Patristica*, Vol. II, 575–80. Rome, 1982.

———. "La vergine nella teologia di S. Efrem." In *OCA*, no. 197, 65–104. Rome, 1974.
Outtier, B. "La célébration du XVIe centennaire de la mort de St. Ephrem au Liban." *Irenikon* 47 (1974): 361–63.
———. "Contribution à l'étude de la préhistoire des collections d'hymnes d'Ephrem." *PdO* 6/7 (1975/76): 49–61.
———. "Le cycle d'Adam à Altamar et la version arménienne du Commentaire de S. Ephrem sur la Genèse." *REA* 18 (1984): 589–92.
———. "Les recueils arméniens et géorgiens d'oeuvres attribuées à S. Ephrem le Syrien." In *Actes 29e congrès international des Orientalistes: Orient Chrétien*, 53–58, Paris, 1975.
———. "Les recueils géorgiens d'oeuvres attribuées à S. Ephrem le Syrien." *Bedi Kartlisa* 32 (1974): 118–25.
———. "Saint Ephrem d'après ses biographies et ses oeuvres." *PdO* 4 (1973): 11–33.
Peral Torres, A. *Comentario al Genesis de San Efren*. Madrid, 1978.
Petersen, W. L. "The Dependence of Romanos the Melodist upon the Syriac Ephrem: Its Importance for the Origin of the Kontakion." *VC* 39 (1985): 171–85.
———. *The Diatessaron and Ephrem Syrus as Sources of Romanos the Melodist*. *CSCO* 475. Louvain, 1985.
Polotsky, H. J. "Ephraems Reise nach Aegypten." *Orientalia* 2 (1933): 269–74.
Renoux, C. "Les mēmrē sur Nicomédie d'Ephrem de Nisibe." *PdO* 4 (1973): 257–63.
———. "S. Ephrem de Nisibe. Pédagogie divine et charité." *Présence d'En Calcat* 37 (1973): 6–10.
———. "Vers le commentaire de Job d'Ephrem de Nisibe." *PdO* 6/7 (1975/76): 63–68.
Ricciotti, G. *San Efrem Siro: Biografia—Scritti—Teologia*. Torino-Roma, 1925.
Robson, P. "Ephrem as Poet." In *Horizons in Semitic Studies*, ed. J. H. Eaton, 34–38. University Semitics Study Aids, no. 8. Birmingham, 1980.
Rousseau, D. O. "La rencontre de saint Ephrem et de saint Basile." *OS* 2 (1957): 261–84; 3 (1958): 73–90.
Rouwhorst, G. A. M. "De Paashymnen van Efrem der Syrer." *Het christelijk Oosten* 37 (1985): 73–92.
———. "L'évocation du mois de Nisan dans les Hymnes sur la Résurrection d'Ephrem de Nisibe." In *OCA*, no. 229, 101–10. Rome, 1987.
———. *Les hymnes pascales d'Ephrem de Nisibe: analyse théologique et*

recherche sur l'evolution de la fête pascale chrétienne à Nisibe et à Edesse et dans quelques églises voisines au quatrième siècle. Supplements to *VC,* no. 7. Leiden, 1989.
Saber, G. *La théologie baptismale de Saint Ephrem. Essai de théologie historique.* Bibliothèque de l'Université Saint Esprit, no. 8. Kaslik, 1974.
———. "La typologie sacramentaire et baptismale de saint Ephrem." *PdO* 4 (1973): 73–92.
Samir, K. "L'Ephrem arabe. Etat des travaux." In *OCA,* no. 205, 229–42. Rome, 1978.
———. "Eine Homilien-Sammlung Ephräms des Syrers. Codex Sinaiticus arabicus Nr. 311." *OC* 58 (1974): 51–75.
———. "Note sur l'auteur du commentaire de la Genèse et ses recensions." In *OCA,* no. 226, 177–82. Rome, 1986.
———. "Le recueil ephrémien arabe des 52 homélies." *OCP* 39 (1973): 307–32.
Scher, A., ed. *Histoire nestorienne inédite (Chronique de Séert) PO* 4, 5. Paris, 1908.
Schmidt, M. "Die Augensymbolik bei Ephraem und Parallelen in der deutschen Mystik." In *Typus, Symbol, Allegorie bei den östlichen Vätern und ihren Parallelen im Mittelalter,* ed. M. Schmidt, 278–301. Eichstatt, 1982.
———. "Influence de saint Ephrem sur la littérature latine et allemande du début du moyen-âge." *PdO* 4 (1973): 325–41.
Sed, N. "Les hymnes sur le paradis de saint Ephrem et les traditions juives." *LM* 81 (1968): 455–501.
Segal, J. B. *Edessa "The Blessed City."* Oxford, 1970.
Serjuni, A. H. "On the Seven *Vahangs* of Joseph by St. Ephrem." *Sion* 47 (1973): 26–37, 137–44. [In Armenian]
Sims-Williams, P. "Thoughts on Ephrem the Syrian in Anglo-Saxon England." In *Learning and Literature in Anglo-Saxon England,* ed. M. Lapidge and H. Gneuss, 205–26. Cambridge, 1985.
Teixidor, J. "Muerte, cielo y Seol en San Efren." *OCP* 27 (1961): 82–114.
———. "Le thème de la déscente aux enfers chez Saint Ephrem." *OS* 6 (1961): 25–40.
———. "La verdad de la resurrección en la poesía de San Efren." *Annales del Seminario de Valencia* 1 (1961): 99–124.
Ter Petrossian, L. "Hymns of St. Ephrem the Syrian: Textual Studies." *HA* 92 (1978): 15–48. [In Armenian]
Tonneau, R. M. "Moise dans la tradition syrienne." In *Moise, l'homme de l'Alliance,* 252–54. Paris, 1955.
Treppner, M. *Ephraem der Syrer und seine Explanatio der vier ersten*

Kapitel der Genesis. Erganzungsheft zur Theologisch-Praktischen Monatschrift, no. 3. Passau, 1893.

Vaillant, A. "Le saint Ephrem slave." *Byzantinoslavica* 19 (1958): 279–86.

Van Vossel, V. *L'onction baptismale chez saint Ephrem.* Baghdad, 1984.

Vööbus, A. "Afrem and the School of Urhai." In *Ephrem Hunayn Festival,* 209–16. Baghdad, 1974.

———. "Beiträge zur kritischen Sichtung der asketischen Schriften die unter dem Namen Ephraem des Syrers überliefert sind." *OC* 39 (1955): 48–55.

———. *Celibacy, a Requirement for Admission to Baptism in the Early Syrian Church. PETSE,* no. 1. Stockholm, 1951.

———. *Einiges über die karitative Tatigkeit des syrischen Mönchtums. CBU,* no. 51. Pinneberg, 1947.

———. *History of Asceticism in the Syrian Orient. A Contribution to the History of Culture in the Near East.* Vol. I, *CSCO* 184. Louvain, 1958. Vol. II, *CSCO* 197. Louvain, 1960. Vol. III, *CSCO* 500. Louvain, 1988.

———. *A Letter of Ephrem to the Mountaineers: A Literary-Critical Contribution to Syriac Literature. CBU,* no. 25. Pinneberg, 1947.

———. *Literary, Critical and Historical Studies in Ephrem the Syrian. PETSE,* no. 10. Stockholm, 1958.

———. "Ein neuer Text von Ephraem über das Mönchtum." *OC* 42 (1958): 41–43.

———. "Origin of Monasticism in Mesopotamia." *CH* 20 (1951): 27–37.

———. "Les reflets du monachisme primitif dans les écrits d'Ephrem le Syrien." *OS* 4 (1959): 299–306.

———. "Selbstanklagen Ephräms des Syrers in griechischer überlieferung—Beobachtungen über ihre Herkunft." *OC* 41 (1957): 97–101.

———. "Sur le developpement de la phase cenobitique et la reaction dans l'ancien monachisme syriaque." *RSR* 47 (1959): 401–7.

———. *Syriac and Arabic Documents Regarding Legislation Relative to Syrian Ascetism. PETSE,* no. 11. Stockholm, 1960.

———. *Untersuchungen über die Authentizität einiger asketischen Texte überliefert unter dem Namen 'Ephraem Syrus.' CBU,* no. 57. Pinneberg, 1947.

Walsh, J. "The Syriac Tradition: St. Ephrem." *The Way* 20 (1980): 228–33.

Yousif, P. "An Approach to the Divine Reality in the Thought of St. Ephrem of Nisibis." In *The Church I Love: A Tribute to Rev. Placid*

SELECT BIBLIOGRAPHY   xxix

J. Podipara, CMI, ed. J. Madley and G. Kaniarakath, 54–69. Kottayam, 1984.

———. "Les controverses de S. Ephrem sur l'Eucharistie." *Euntes Docete* 33 (1980): 405–26.

———. "La croix de Jesus et la Paradis d'Eden dans la typologie biblique de Saint Ephrem." *PdO* 6/7 (1975/76): 29–48.

———. *L'Eucharistie chez Saint Ephrem de Nisibe. OCA,* no. 224. Rome, 1984.

———. "L'Eucharistie et le Saint Esprit d'après s. Ephrem de Nisibe." In *A Tribute to Arthur Vööbus,* ed. R. H. Fischer, 235–46. Chicago, 1977.

———. "Exégèse et typologie bibliques chez S. Ephrem de Nisibe et chez S. Thomas d'Aquin." *PdO* 13 (1986): 31–50.

———. "Foi et raison dans l'apologétique de saint Ephrem de Nisibe." *PdO* 12 (1984/85): 133–51.

———. "Histoire et temps dans la pensée de s. Ephrem de Nisibe." *PdO* 10 (1981/82): 3–35.

———. "Marie et les derniers temps chez saint Ephrem de Nisibe." *Études Mariales* 42 (1985): 31–55.

———. "Le repas fraternel ou l'agapé dans les memre sur la table attribués à S. Ephrem." *PdO* 9 (1979/80): 51–66.

———. "Le sacrifice et l'offrande chez S. Ephrem de Nisibe." *PdO* 15 (1988/89): 21–40.

———. "St. Ephrem on Symbols in Nature: Faith, the Trinity and the Cross (Hymns on Faith no. 18)." *ECR* 10 (1978): 52–60.

———. "Symbolisme Christologique dans la Bible et dans la nature chez S. Ephrem de Nisibe." *PdO* 8 (1977/78): 5–66.

———. "Le symbolisme de la croix dans la nature chez S. Ephrem de Nisibe." *OCA,* no. 205 (1978): 207–27.

———. "Typologie und Eucharistie bei Ephraem und Thomas von Aquin." In *Typus, Symbol, Allegorie bei den östlichen Vätern und ihren Parallelen im Mittelalter,* ed. M. Schmidt, 75–107. Eichstatt, 1982.

———. "La Vierge Marie et le disciple bien-aimé chez S. Ephrem de Nisibe." *OCP* 55 (1989): 283–316.

———. "La Vierge Marie et l'Eucharistie chez saint Ephrem de Nisibe et dans la patristique syriaque antérieure." *Études Mariales* 36/37 (1978/80): 49–80.

Secondary works concerning Ephrem's *Commentary on the Diatessaron* will be included in our translation to that work which is to appear in a subsequent volume of this series. More comprehensive bibliography for the study of Ephrem, and for general Syriac studies, can be found by consulting the following works:

Brock, S. P. "Syriac Studies 1961–1970, a Classified Bibliography." *PdO* 4 (1973): 393–465.
———. "Syriac Studies 1971–1980, a Classified Bibliography." *PdO* 10 (1981/82): 291–412.
———. "Syriac Studies 1981–1985, a Classified Bibliography." *PdO* 14 (1987): 289–360.
Moss, C. *Catalogue of Syriac Printed Books and Related Literature in the British Museum.* London, 1962.
Ortiz de Urbina, I. *Patrologia Syriaca.* 2d ed. Rome, 1965.
Roncaglia, M. P. "Essai de bibliographie sur saint Ephrem." *PdO* 4 (1973): 343–70.
Samir, K. "Compléments de bibliographie éphrémienne." *PdO* 4 (1973): 371–92.

GENERAL INTRODUCTION

GENERAL INTRODUCTION

The golden age of Syriac literature, which extended from the fourth to the eighth centuries, produced a number of important figures who merit more serious attention than they have heretofore received: Balai, Cyrillona, Aphrahat, Jacob of Sarug and Narsai, to name just a few. Unfortunately, due to the inaccessibility of their writings, knowledge of these authors is generally limited to Syriac specialists. The single writer from this period who has achieved any degree of recognition beyond the realm of the specialist is Ephrem the Syrian. Unquestionably the greatest writer in the history of the Syriac-speaking church, Ephrem stands as the pillar of Syriac Christian literature and culture. His works, which have survived in considerable quantity, have had an inestimable impact on all facets of subsequent Syriac literature. Known by his contemporaries as the "Harp of the Holy Spirit," Ephrem's renown extended from his native Syria throughout the ancient Christian world.[1]

(2) Scholars in his native Syriac-speaking tradition have always held Ephrem in the highest esteem, referring to him as the "Cicero" and even as the "Homer" of his own literary tradition.[2] Until recently however, Ephrem has been judged somewhat less sympathetically by many Western scholars. The great Cardinal Robert Bellarmine commented pejo-

---

1. See Y. Azema, ed., *Théodoret de Cyr, Correspondance III, SC* 111 (Paris, 1965) 190. Epiphanius, in his *Panarion,* 51.22.7, speaks of "Ephrem the wise man of the Syrians," K. Höll and J. Dummer, eds., *Epiphanius Panarion, GCS* 31, rev. ed. (Leipzig, 1985) 2:285. Jerome also speaks of how distinguished Ephrem's writings were in the churches. See E. C. Richardson, ed., *Hieronymus, Liber de Viris Inlustribus, TU,* no. 14 (Leipzig, 1896) 87. See also the discussion of Palladius, Sozomen and the *Apophthegmata Patrum,* below.

2. A. Mingana, "Remarks on the Text of the Prose Refutations of S. Ephrem," *JRAS* (1922): 523.

ratively that Ephrem "was obviously more pious than learned."[3] In the early part of this century the well-known British Syriacist F. C. Burkitt levelled such disparaging judgments as "[the popularity of Ephrem's works] shows a lamentable standard of public taste."[4] Some years later the same author added that "Ephrem is extraordinarily prolix, and when the thought is unravelled it is mostly commonplace, his poems make very heavy reading for us moderns."[5] More recently, J. B. Segal has wrily commented that Ephrem's work, "it must be confessed, shows little profundity or originality of thought, and his metaphors are labored. His poems are turgid, humorless, and repetitive."[6] The motivation behind such severe judgments as these may be traced to the frustration on the part of these scholars who were looking for more precise and concrete historical data concerning the events and figures of the early Syriac-speaking church.[7]

(3) Contemporary scholars are more willing to take Ephrem on his own terms. Sebastian Brock has called Ephrem "one of the great Christian poets of all times,"[8] while Simon Tugwell goes so far as to declare Ephrem to be "one of the great religious poets of the world."[9] Prevailing scholarly opinion is in general agreement with the assessment of Robert Murray who says, "Personally, I do not hesitate to evaluate Ephrem not only as the true ancestor of Romanos and therefore of the Byzantine Kontakion, but as the

---

3. Cited, with approbation, by R. Payne Smith, "Ephraim the Syrian," in *Dictionary of Christian Biography* (London, 1880) 2:140; and in "St. Ephraem, Doctor of the Church," in *Butler's Lives of the Saints,* ed. H. Thurston and D. Attwater, rev. ed. (New York, 1956) 2:574.
4. F. C. Burkitt, *Early Eastern Christianity* (London, 1904) 99.
5. F. C. Burkitt, "The Christian Church in the East," in *The Cambridge Ancient History* (Cambridge, 1939) 12:502.
6. J. B. Segal, *Edessa, "The Blessed City"* (Oxford, 1971) 89.
7. S. P. Brock, "The Poetic Artistry of St. Ephrem: An Analysis of H. Azym. III," *PdO* 6/7 (1975–76): 22.
8. S. P. Brock, "Dramatic Dialogue Poems," in *OCA,* no. 229 (Rome, 1987) 135.
9. S. Tugwell, *Prayer* (Dublin, 1974) 1:138.

greatest poet of the patristic age and, perhaps, the only theologian-poet to rank beside Dante."[10]

(4) In addition to this greater appreciation of Ephrem and his writings, there is also an increasing awareness of the importance of Syriac language and culture, both in its own right, and as it concerns a number of related disciplines.[11] Syriac is an Eastern dialect of Late Aramaic. During the fifth and fourth centuries BC, *Reichsaramäische*, or Imperial Aramaic, was spoken throughout the vast Persian Empire that ruled over the entire Near East at that time. An early dialect of Jewish Palestinian Aramaic was the language that Jesus himself most likely spoke.[12] From the fourth to the seventh centuries of our era, the Syriac dialect of Aramaic served as the *lingua franca* throughout a large part of the Middle East, and by the middle of the seventh century, Syriac-speaking Christian missionaries were clearly established in China and may have ventured as far east as the Mekong delta.[13]

(5) The heritage of Syriac-speaking Christianity continues to be represented by a number of Oriental churches. These churches are the Maronite, the Syrian Catholic, the Syrian Orthodox (also known as Jacobite), the Church of

10. See, for example, R. Murray, "Ephrem Syrus, St." in *A Catholic Dictionary of Theology* (London, 1967) 2:222; idem, *Symbols of Church and Kingdom* (Cambridge, 1975) 31; S. P. Brock, *The Harp of the Spirit*, Studies Supplementary to Sobornost, no. 4, 2d ed. (Fellowship of St. Alban and St. Sergius, 1983) 6; and idem, *The Luminous Eye: The Spiritual World Vision of St. Ephrem* (Rome, 1985; 2d ed., *CSS* 124. Kalamazoo, 1992) 145.

11. See S. P. Brock, "An Introduction to Syriac Studies," in *Horizons in Semitic Studies*, ed. J. H. Eaton, University Semitics Study Aids, no. 8 (Birmingham, 1980) 1–33.

12. For the phases of the Aramaic language, see J. A. Fitzmyer, S. J., *A Wandering Aramean: Collected Aramaic Essays*, Society of Biblical Literature Monograph Series, no. 25 (Missoula, Montana, 1979) especially 6–10, 57–84; and E. Y. Kutscher, "Aramaic," in *Current Trends in Linguistics*, ed. T. A. Sebeok, Linguistics in South West Asia and North Africa, (Paris, 1970) 6:347–412.

13. See Y. Saeki, *The Nestorian Documents and Relics in China*, 2d ed. (Tokyo, 1951); K. Enoki, "The Nestorian Christianism in China in Medieval Time according to Recent Historical and Archaeological Researches," in *L'Oriente cristiano nella storia della civiltà*, Accademia Nazionale dei Lincei, no. 341 (Rome, 1964) 45–77; P. Pelliot, *Recherches sur les chrétiens d'Asie centrale et d'extrême orient*

the East or Assyrian church (also known as Nestorian), and both the Syro-Malabar and the Syro-Malankar churches of India.[14] The Melkite church, more correctly known today as the Greek Catholic church, is of Syriac origin but adopted Byzantine liturgical practices beginning in the tenth century.[15] These churches have endured varying degrees of Latinization, which in some cases date back to the Crusades, and are now in the process of restoring their liturgies according to their authentic Syriac origins.[16]

(6) As for the origins of Syriac-speaking Christianity, because of the paucity of material available, nearly every aspect of the problem is still matter for debate among scholars with no easy solution forthcoming.[17] The existence of Christ-

---

(Leiden, 1973); and B. C. Colless, "The Traders of the Pearl," *Abr-Nahrain* 9 (1969–70): 17–38, 10 (1970-71): 102–21, 11 (1971): 1–21, 13 (1972–73): 115–35, 14 (1973–74): 1–16, 15 (1974–75): 6–17, 18 (1978–79): 1–18.

14. For a brief overview see Brock, "An Introduction to Syriac Studies," 30–33. See also J. Madey, *Die Kirchen des Ostens. Ein Einführung* (Freiburg, 1972).

15. See J. Nasrallah, "La liturgie des patriarcats melchites de 969 à 1300," *OC* 71 (1987): 156–81; and C. Charon, "Le rite byzantin et la liturgie chrysostomienne dans les patriarcats melkites," in *Chrisostomika: studi e ricerche intorno a S. Giovanni Crisostomo a cura del Comitato per il XVe centenario della sua morte* (Rome, 1908) 474–518.

16. See J. Vellian, ed., *The Romanization Tendency*, The Syrian Churches Series, no. 8 (Kottayam, 1975).

17. The best survey of the evidence and arguments involved is still Murray, *Symbols*, 4–24. Murray has also dealt with these questions in his later article, "The Characteristics of the Earliest Christianity," in *East of Byzantium: Syria and Armenia in the Formative Period*, ed. N. G. Garsoian, T. F. Mathews, and R. W. Thomson (Washington, 1982) 3–16. The most important earlier studies are J. Labourt, *Le christianisme dans l'empire perse sous la dynastie sassanide (224–632)* (Paris, 1904) 1–17; J. M. Fiey, *Jalons pour une histoire de l'église en Iraq*, CSCO 310 (Louvain, 1970) 32–65; W. Bauer, *Orthodoxy and Heresy in Earliest Christianity* (Philadelphia, 1971) 1–43; L. W. Barnard, "Origins and Emergence of the Church in Edessa during the First Two Centuries," *VC* 22 (1968): 161–75; idem, "Early Syriac Christianity," in *Studies in Church History and Patristics*, Analecta Blatadon, no. 26 (Thessalonica, 1978) 194–223, especially 197–201; J. B. Segal, "When Did Christianity Come to Edessa?" in *Middle East Studies and Libraries: A Felicitation Volume for Professor J. D. Pearson*, ed. B. C. Bloomfield (Mansell, 1980) 179–91. For the origins of the Church in the eastern parts of the Syriac speaking regions, see now M.-L. Chaumont, *La christianisation de l'em-*

ian communities in various regions of Syria and Mesopotamia can, however, be established with reasonable certainty before the third century. The reference in the canonical *Acts of the Apostles* to the presence of "Parthians and Medes and Elamites and residents of Mesopotamia"[18] at the first Pentecost suggests that at least by the year 80, the Apostolic church knew of Christian communities in these areas. Bardaisan, in his *Book of the Laws of Countries,* witnesses to Christian communities in the eastern regions of the Near East at the end of the second century.[19] In the mid-third century, Dionysius of Alexandria speaks of bishoprics in "the Syrias and Arabia . . . and in Mesopotamia."[20] Abercius, bishop of Hierapolis, c. 200, left on an inscription, discovered in 1883, an account of his journey to Rome, in which he describes "the plain of Syria and all the cities, even Nisibis, having crossed the Euphrates. And everywhere I had associates having Paul as a companion, everywhere faith led the way."[21]

---

pire iranien des origines aux grandes persecutions du 4ᵉ siècle, CSCO 499 (Louvain, 1988).

18. Acts 2.9. While some scholars want to dismiss this list as a common topos for "all the world" [see, for example, S. Weinstock, "The Geographical Catalogue in Acts II,9–11," *JRS* 38 (1948): 43–46; and J. Brinkman, "The Literary Background of the Catalogue of Nations," *CBQ* 25 (1963): 418–27], there is no reason to discount entirely any historical veracity in the verse. See Fiey, *Jalons pour une histoire de l'église en Iraq,* 34–35.

19. F. Nau, ed., *Bardesanes Liber Legum Regionum* (Brepols, 1907) 2.1:604–8. Bardaisan mentions Syria, Edessa, Parthia, Media, and Hatra, among others.

20. Letter to Stephen, bishop of Rome, preserved in Eusebius, *History of the Church* VII.5.2. The *Chronicle of Arbela,* chapters 1ff. [P. Kawerau, ed., *Die Chronik von Arbela, CSCO* 467–68 (Louvain, 1985)] alleges that there were bishops in that diocese beginning in the early second century, but this document suffers from much doubt as to its authenticity. Some scholars, e.g., J.-M. Fiey, "Auteur et date de la Chronique d'Arbèles," *OS* 12 (1967): 265–302, went so far as to consider this *Chronicle* the work of its editor, Alphonse Mingana. See S. P. Brock, "Alphonse Mingana and the Letter of Philoxenos to Abu 'Afr," *BJRL* 50 (1967): 199–206, for a refutation of these scholars and Chaumont, *La christianisation de l'empire iranien,* 29–38, for an overview of the problems.

21. Translation excerpted from J. Quasten, *Patrology* (Utrecht, 1975) 1:171–73. For the inscription see, W. Wischmeyer, "Die Aberkios inschrift als Grabepigramm," *JAC* 23 (1980): 22–47.

The *Chronicle of Edessa* records a flood that destroyed the Christian church of Edessa in 201.[22]

(7) Walter Bauer's now famous study, *Orthodoxy and Heresy in Earliest Christianity*, has demonstrated the tendentiousness of the old assumption that orthodox Christianity was the first to be established in cities and was only later perverted by the arrival of heretical teaching(s). His study has also opened the eyes of scholars to the problems of applying the anachronistic labels of orthodoxy and heresy to ancient Christian cultures. While the indications just reviewed tell us little of the nature of these early Syriac-speaking communities, there is little question that some form of Christianity existed very early in various regions of Syria and Mesopotamia.[23]

(8) The classic account that purports to tell of the coming of Christianity to Syria is the *Teaching of Addai*.[24] According to this document, King Abgar V Ukhāmâ of Edessa, having heard reports of how Jesus was performing miracles and great healings in Palestine sent missives imploring Jesus to come to Edessa and heal him of an uncertain malady.[25] Jesus responded by saying that He was unable to come in person

---

22. See L. Hallier, *Untersuchungen über die Edessenische Chronik, TU*, no. 9, part 1 (Leipzig, 1892) 146. See, however, the arguments of Bauer, *Orthodoxy and Heresy in Earliest Christianity*, 12–21, on this passage being an interpolation.

23. The so-called Bauer thesis has been called into question. For Edessa, see especially, T. A. Robinson, *The Bauer Thesis Examined: The Geography of Heresy in the Early Christian Church* (New York and Ontario, 1988) 45–59; and S. Gero, "With Walter Bauer on the Tigris: Encratite Orthodoxy and Libertine Heresy in Syro-Mesopotamian Christianity," in *Nag Hammadi, Gnosticism, and Early Christianity*, ed. C.W. Hedrick and R. Hodgson, Jr. (Peabody, 1986) 287–307. For a concise, if not always up-to-date, introduction to the history of early Christianity in Syria, see W. S. McCullough, *A Short History of Syriac Christianity to the Rise of Islam* (Chico, California, 1982).

24. For text and translation see G. Phillips, ed., *The Doctrine of Addai the Apostle* (London, 1876). The same text with a new translation appears in G. Howard, trans., *The Teaching of Addai* (Missoula, Montana, 1981).

25. According to the *Teaching of Addai*, this disease was a bad case of gout [Howard, trans., *The Teaching of Addai*, z (text), 15 (translation)], while Eusebius, *History of the Church* I.13, records that Abgar "was perishing from terrible suffering in his body, beyond human power to heal."

but that He would send one of His disciples after He had been raised up to His Father. Following the ascension of Jesus, the Apostle Thomas, before he went to India, commissioned his disciple Addai to go to Edessa and preach the Good News. After Addai arrived there he healed Abgar of his illness, and the king and his court were are all soon converted. The remainder of the book, as the title suggests, deals with the preaching of Addai to the newly converted Edessans.

(9) Some form of the *Teaching of Addai* already existed in the early fourth century, for Eusebius claims to have had in his possession a text translated from a Syriac copy reportedly found in the archives of Edessa.[26] Nevertheless, the *Teaching of Addai* in its present form cannot be dated prior to the early fifth century.[27] The ordination of Addai's disciple Palut by Serapion, bishop of Antioch, indicates, although anachronistically, a concern on the part of the final redactor to link the Church of Edessa to the greater church of the Byzantine empire.[28]

(10) Current scholarly opinion offers two theories concerning the origins of the *Teaching of Addai*. The first, expressed as early as 1903, argues that this document is an adaptation by the Christian community of Edessa of the account of the conversion of the royal house of Adiabene to Judaism recorded by the Jewish historian Josephus.[29] This theory of the origins of the *Teaching of Addai* is buttressed by the role played therein by Tobia bar Tobia, a Jew who lodged Addai in his house and served as the one who

26. The correspondence is cited in Eusebius, *History of the Church* I.13.
27. See Murray, *Symbols*, 4.
28. Serapion was bishop in Antioch during the years 199–211, thereby negating any possibility of having ordained Palut. Many scholars have used this fact to relocate the story in the reign of Abgar VIII the Great, who ruled Edessa from 177 to 212. See, for example, E. Kirsten, "Edessa," in *RAC* 3:569–70; and Segal, *Edessa, "The Blessed City"*, 70.
29. The legend is found in Josephus, *Jewish Antiquities* XX.17–48. This theory, first expounded in J. Marquart, *Osteuropäische und ostasiatische Streifzüge* (Leipzig, 1903) 300, was reiterated simultaneously by Segal, *Edessa, "The Blessed City"*, 67–69, and Murray, *Symbols*, 8–9.

brought Addai to Abgar. There are other indications that the earliest missionaries into the Syriac-speaking regions, taking literally the command of the Apostle Paul to go first to the Jew and then to the Greek (or, in this case, the pagan), followed paths that had already been trodden by itinerant Jews and were at that time dotted with established Jewish communities.[30] Support has also come from other studies that present compelling evidence that Christianity made greater advances into areas where the Jewish community was small or lacked unity, whereas in the case of a large or strong Jewish presence, the Christian missionaries made little or no progress.[31]

(11) A second theory on the origins of the *Teaching of Addai* has more recently been advanced by H. J. W. Drijvers,[32] who argues that because of many literary similarities to the activities of Mani and his disciples, one of whom was named Addai, the *Teaching of Addai* should be viewed as an orthodox version of the founding of the Church in Edessa based on an anti-Manichean polemic. While Drijvers has argued this point quite cogently, his theory still has not completely overturned the position repostulated by Segal and Murray. Even if his theory has not received full acceptance Drijvers has, nonetheless, drawn more careful attention to the importance of Mani in the Syriac-speaking church during this early period.[33]

(12) Recent discoveries, such as the documents at Qum-

---

30. See, for example, Rom 1.16, 2.10.
31. This was already the position of A. Harnack, *The Mission and Expansion of Christianity in the First Three Centuries* (New York, 1962) 1–18. See now the studies of Jacob Neusner, especially, "The Conversion of Adiabene," *JBL* 83 (1964): 60–66; *A History of the Jews in Babylonia*, Brown Judaic Studies, no. 62 (Chico, California, 1984) 1:180–83; and *Aphrahat and Judaism*, Studia Post-Biblica, no. 19 (Leiden, 1971) especially, 1–4. Josephus, *Antiquities*, XVIII.ix.1, already mentions Nisibis as one of the centers of Babylonian Jewry.
32. H. J. W. Drijvers, "Facts and Problems in Early Syriac-Speaking Christianity," *The Second Century* 2 (1982): 157–75.
33. In addition to the study just mentioned, see H. J. W. Drijvers, "Odes of Solomon and Psalms of Mani. Christians and Manichaeans in Third-Century Syria," in *Studies in Gnosticism and Hellenistic Religions presented to Gilles Quispel*,

GENERAL INTRODUCTION 11

ran and Nag Hammadi, and most notably the *Cologne Mani Codex*,[34] have significantly altered our knowledge of the origins of Syriac-speaking Christianity. It is now known that Syrian Christianity and various sects indigenous to the Syrian regions were not simply Hellenistic Christian missionary movements from Antioch as was heretofore thought,[35] but were rather part of a much more complex development of various Judeo-Christian sects that also produced diverse Christian and baptist sects such as the Elkasites, Mandeans, and others. While much still remains to be studied, it is becoming increasingly clear that the Essenes, the Elkasites, and other similar groups were separate developments of an ascetic Jewish sectarian ideology that exerted influence over much of the Near East. As Murray has pointed out, the strength of this theory lies in the sectarian "ascetical doctrine and practice; it is now clear that such asceticism was not alien to all forms of Judaism, but that in the extraordinary variety of the latter in the time of Christ the seeds of not merely temporary but permanent celibacy for spiritual combat were present."[36]

(13) Certainly, one fact that is agreed upon by scholars is that early Syriac-speaking Christianity, in all its manifestations, seems to have been based on strong ascetical tendencies. It was this same asceticism that underlay the encratism of Tatian, the asceticism of Mani, and that absolute sexual renunciation demanded by the *Acts of Thomas*.[37] This ascetic

---

ed. R. van den Broek and M. J. Vermaseren (Leiden, 1981), 117–30 [reprinted in H. J. W. Drijvers, *East of Antioch. Studies in Early Syriac Christianity* (London, 1984) Study X].

34. R. Cameron and A. J. Dewey, *The Cologne Mani Codex*, Society of Biblical Literature Texts and Translations: Early Christian Literature Series, no. 3 (Missoula, Montana, 1979).

35. See, for example, H. Lietzmann, "Die Anfänge des Christentums in Syrien und seinem Hinterland," in *Kleine Schriften, TU*, no. 67 (Berlin, 1958) 1:94–96.

36. Murray, *Symbols*, 17–18.

37. A. F. J. Klijn, *The Acts of Thomas*, Supplements to Novum Testamentum, no. 5 (Leiden, 1962). See also R. Murray, "Features of the Earliest Christian Asceticism," in *Christian Spirituality: Essays in Honour of Gordon Rupp*, ed. Peter

12   GENERAL INTRODUCTION

tendency affected not only the fringe sects but exerted strong influence as well on the more mainline community. It has even been suggested that as late as the beginning of the fourth century a vow of celibacy had actually been a prerequisite for baptism in the churches of Syria.[38] It is in this still nebulous period at the beginning of the fourth century that the figure of Ephrem appears.

Life

1. Sources and Legends

(14) There is certainly no dearth of sources for the the life of Ephrem. Already, less than half a century after Ephrem's death, historians began to recount the deeds of the great Syrian saint. Palladius, writing about 420, devoted an entire chapter to "Ephrem, the deacon of the church at Edessa. He had accomplished the journey of the Spirit in a right and worthy manner, never deviating from the straight path and he was deemed worthy of the gift of natural knowledge (γνῶσις φυσικὴ). The knowledge of God succeeded this, and finally blessedness. He always practiced the quiet life and edified those whom he met for many years. . . ."[39] Although Palladius knew that Ephrem was a deacon in Edessa, he shows no awareness that Ephrem actually lived nearly all of his life in Nisibis. The single event that Palladius does recount concerns Ephrem's efforts during a famine that afflicted Edessa in 373, a famine so severe, according to Palladius, that it caused Ephrem to leave his monastic cell to render his assistance to the city. It was largely through Ephrem's efforts that many Edessan citizens survived, though Ephrem himself died shortly after this effort.

(15) Less than a quarter of a century after Palladius

Brooks (London, 1975) 65–77; and idem, "The Characteristics of Earliest Christianity," 3–16.

38. See A. Vööbus, *Celibacy, A Requirement for Admission to Baptism in the Early Syrian Church*, PETSE, no. 1 (Stockholm, 1951); and R. Murray, "The Exhortation to Candidates for Ascetical Vows at Baptism in the Ancient Syriac Church," *NTS* 21 (1974–75): 59–80.

39. Palladius, *The Lausiac History*, 40, in *Palladio: La Storia Lausiaca*, ed. G. J.

GENERAL INTRODUCTION 13

wrote, the church historian Sozomen devoted a rather lengthy notice in his *History of the Church* to Ephrem, calling him:

> the greatest ornament of the Catholic Church . . . [who] devoted his life to monastic philosophy . . . although he received no instruction he became, contrary to all expectation, so proficient in the learning and language of the Syrians, that he comprehended with ease the most abstruse theorems of philosophy. His style of writing was so replete with splendid oratory and with richness and temperateness of thought that he surpassed the most approved writers of Greece.[40]

Sozomen adds much new detail and several anecdotes to the report of Palladius. He is the earliest source that we have that connects Ephrem with Basil of Caesarea, who was "universally confessed to have been the most eloquent man of his age . . . was a great admirer of Ephrem and was astonished at his erudition." Sozomen also provides the names of several of Ephrem's disciples.[41] In addition, Sozomen is the first to record that Ephrem composed his hymns as an antidote to the hymns of Bardaisan's son, who was perhaps a bit too appropriately named Harmonius. These hymns of Harmonius were not only charming the Syrian populace by their rhythms but were also infecting them with the doctrine of his father.[42] As does Palladius, Sozomen ends his notice with the famine that struck Edessa, for which reason Ephrem "quit the solitary cell in which he pursued philosophy," i.e., his monastic practices.

M. Bartelink (Verona, 1974) 206–8. English translation in R. T. Meyer, trans., *Palladius: The Lausiac History*, ACW 34 (New York, 1964) 116–17.

40. Sozomen, *History of the Church*, III.16, in *Sozomenus Kirchengeschichte*, ed. J. Bidez and G. C. Hansen, GCS 50 (Berlin, 1960) 127–31. English translation in C. D. Hartranft, trans., "The Ecclesiastical History of Salaminius Hermias Sozomenus," in *LNPF* 2d series (reprint, Grand Rapids, 1983) 2:295–97.

41. Sozomen names Abba, Zenobius, Abraham, Moses, Simeon, Paulonas, and Arad, but see B. Outtier, "Saint Ephrem d'après ses biographies et ses oeuvres," *PdO* 4 (1973): 20–21, for the differing traditions concerning Ephrem's disciples.

42. Ephrem himself confirms the role Bardaisan and his son played in early Syriac hymnography; see *Hymns against Heresies*, 1.17, 53.5.

(16) There is also a long *Encomium* on Ephrem that has come down to us under the name of Gregory of Nyssa.[43] This homily, delivered on the feast day of Ephrem, while recounting details found in Palladius and Sozomen, clearly derives information from an independent tradition. It was this *Encomium*, clearly a product of the Second Sophistic panegyrical tradition, that served Simeon Metaphrastes as the source for his *Life of Ephrem;* Simeon's *Life of Ephrem* in turn served as the source for two other short Byzantine lives of Ephrem.[44]

(17) The author of this *Encomium*, with great vividness, describes an Ephrem who:

reckoned the whole earth as foreign to himself and turned his back on material creation as an enemy for the sake of the unseen blessedness stored up in heaven. . . . [He] practiced incessant tears, a life of solitude, withdrawal from one place to another, flight from evils, fasting and vigils without measure, [used the] ground for a bed, [practised] an austerity of life beyond words and poverty and humility taken to the limit . . . [he] despised all worldly things . . . fled the world and the things of the world, and, as Scripture says, "he wandered far and dwelt in the desert," heedful of only himself and God and there received a lavish increase in virtue for he knew precisely that the eremitical life would free the one who desired it from the turmoil of the world and would provide silent converse with the angels.[45]

(18) While this *Encomium* served as the Byzantine prototype, Palladius and Sozomen became the primary sources

43. St. Gregory of Nyssa, *De Vita S. Patris Ephraem Syri, PG* 46, 820A–849D. A new edition of this work by A. Spira is in preparation. It will appear in W. Jaeger and H. Langerbeck, eds., *Gregorius Nyssenus Opera: Supplementum*, vol. 2. This work cannot be attributed to Gregory of Nyssa; see the discussion in A. Vööbus, *Literary, Critical and Historical Studies in Ephrem the Syrian, PETSE*, no. 10 (Stockholm, 1958) 41–45; and E. G. Mathews, Jr. "The *Vita* Tradition of Ephrem the Syrian, the Deacon of Edessa," *Diakonia* 22 (1988–89): 22–23.

44. For Simeon's *Life of Ephrem*, see Symeon Logotheta Metaphrastes, *Opera Omnia, PG* 114, 1253–68. The two other Byzantine *Lives of Ephrem* do not seem ever to have been edited. See discussion in Vööbus, *Literary, Critical and Historical Studies in Ephrem the Syrian*, 41–45.

45. St. Gregory of Nyssa, *De Vita S. Patris Ephraem Syri*, 824C–825A, 832D.

for Ephrem's biography in the Syriac and oriental traditions. In the middle of the seventh century, Ananišô, a monk from the monastery of Beth Abê, compiled in Syriac a large book about the history and sayings of the monks of Egypt.[46] In his work, which included a translation of Palladius, he combined the notice of Ephrem with two *apophthegmata* that he found told of Ephrem. This account of Ananišô then became the foundation for the Syriac *Life of Ephrem*. The *Chronicle of Seert*, which contains two long notices on Ephrem, survives in an Arabic version, but is clearly dependent on the same tradition as the Syriac *Life of Ephrem*.[47]

(19) This Syriac *Life of Ephrem* is the only real full-length work that we possess that can rightly be called a biography of Ephrem.[48] It alone provides such details as Ephrem was born of a Christian mother and of a father who was a pagan priest; he accompanied Jacob of Nisibis to the Council of Nicea; he spent eight years as a monk in Scetis during which time he met with the great Egyptian monk, Abba Bishoi; afterwards he sailed to Constantinople to meet with Basil the Great, and that after Ephrem's return to Syria, Basil attempted to ordain him as priest, only to be foiled by Ephrem who feigned madness before Basil's emissaries. Ephrem's connections with Scetis, the great center of Egyptian monasticism, and his own eremitic life on a mountain outside of Edessa are emphasized throughout the Syriac *Life*.

46. See E. A. Wallis Budge, *The Book of Paradise, Being the Histories and Sayings of the Monks and Ascetics of the Egyptian Desert, by Palladius, Hieronymus and Others* (London, 1904); and now R. Draguet, *Les formes syriaques de la matière de l'Histoire lausiaque, CSCO* 389–90, 399–400 (Louvain, 1978).

47. A. Scher, *Histoire nestorienne inédite (Chronique de Séert), PO* 4, 5 (Paris, 1908). For the *Chronicle*'s sources for its material on Ephrem, see Outtier, "Saint Ephrem d'après ses biographies et ses oeuvres," 24–26.

48. This text exists in three different recensions which have now been edited synoptically with English translations by J. P. Amar, "The Syriac *Vita* Tradition of Ephrem the Syrian," (Ph. D. diss., Catholic University of America, 1988). Previous editions by T. J. Lamy, ed., *Sancti Ephraem Syri Hymni et Sermones* (Machelen-lez-Deinze, 1886) 2:3–89; and P. Bedjan, ed., *Acta Martyrum et Sanctorum Syriace* (Paris, 1892), 3:621–65, not only reflected only a single recension but each offered a "corrected" version, with the result that neither edition accurately reflected the manuscript being edited.

(20) In 1933, H. Polotsky showed that the pericope concerning Ephrem's extended sojourn in Egypt and his meeting with Abba Bishoi was purely legendary and, moreover, betrayed a later tradition concerning the transferral of Ephrem's relics to the monastery of Abba Bishoi for protection from being desecrated by barbarian invasions.[49] Subsequent to Polotsky's article, Dom O. Rousseau published a long study that demonstrated that the several pericopes involving the meeting between Ephrem and Basil were also purely legendary. This meeting was actually fabricated from two brief references found in Basil's works, one to "a Syrian" and the other to "a certain Mesopotamian," which were then combined with the above-mentioned witness of Sozomen that Basil was an admirer of the works of Ephrem.[50] This meeting was subsequently further embellished in a spurious *Life of Basil*, attributed to Amphilochius of Iconium, which served as the source for the pericope in the *Life of Ephrem*. While these studies exposed the legendary nature of these particular pericopes, scholars continued for some time to consider the core of the Syriac *Life of Ephrem* as historical and even to maintain its claim to be the work of Ephrem's disciple, Simeon of Samosata.[51]

(21) In addition to these biographical works, there exists a number of texts from antiquity that lay claim to being autobiographical, the most important of which is the so-called

---

49. H. J. Polotsky, "Ephraems Reise nach Aegypten," *Or* 2 (1933): 269–74. See also the later Arabic legends in H. G. Evelyn White, *The Monasteries of the Wadi 'n Natrun* (New York, 1932) 2:114, 316, 420. For recent studies of the relation of Ephrem and Abba Bishoi, see M. Blanchard, "Coptic Heritage of St. Ephrem the Syrian," in *Proceedings of the Vth International Congress of Coptic Studies* (Rome, 1993); and idem, "Apa Bishoi and Mar Ephrem," in *Middle Eastern Christian Studies*, no. 1, *forthcoming*.

50. Basil, *Homilies on the Hexaemeron*, 2.6; and *Homilies on the Holy Spirit*, 29.74. See D. O. Rousseau, "La rencontre de saint Ephrem et de saint Basile," *OS* 2 (1957): 261–84; 3 (1958): 73–90. This legend must have existed already in the early sixth century as Severus of Antioch seems to have known of a meeting between Basil and Ephrem, see J. Lebon, ed., *Severi Antiocheni liber contra impium Grammaticum, CSCO* 102 (Louvain, 1933) 180.

51. Among the scholars who thought thus include E. Bouvy, "Les sources historiques de la vie de saint Ephrem," *RA* 2 (1903): 155–64; S. Schiwietz, *Das morgenländische Mönchtum* (Mödling bei Wien, 1938) 3:93–165; R. Duval, *La lit-*

GENERAL INTRODUCTION 17

Testament of Ephrem. This document survives in a Syriac as well as in a highly periphrastic Greek version.[52] This document purports to record Ephrem's deathbed instructions to his disciples. As in Palladius, there is no mention here of any Nisibene period of Ephrem's life. Finally, to these documents must also be added a number of Syriac ascetic texts that are attributed to Ephrem in the manuscript tradition. These texts depict an extreme eremitical lifestyle, not unlike that described in some of the lives of the Syrian monks written by Theodoret, fifth-century bishop of Cyr.[53]

(22) While all these sources may differ in details, they are all in accord in fostering the legend that Ephrem was a monk/hermit of nearly Antonine proportions.[54] This has been the traditional picture of Ephrem throughout the

---

térature syriaque (Paris, 1907) 329; A. Baumstark, *Geschichte der syrischen Literatur* (Bonn, 1922) 33–34, 66; J. B. Chabot, *La littérature syriaque* (Paris, 1935) 25; P. Peeters, *Le tréfonds oriental de l'hagiographie byzantine* (Brussels, 1950) 176; and I. Ortiz de Urbina, *Patrologia Syriaca* (Rome, 1965) 57.

52. The Syriac text of the *Testament* can be found in E. Beck, ed., *Des Heiligen Ephraem des Syrers Sermones IV, CSCO* 334 (Louvain, 1973) 43–69. The Greek text is in J. S. Assemani, *Sancti Patris Nostri Ephraem Syri Opera Omnia quae exstant graece, syriace, latine, in sex tomos distributa* (Rome, 1732–43), 2:230C–247A. There are also later versions in Arabic, Armenian, and Georgian, all listed in M. Geerard, *Clavis Patrum Graecorum* (Brepols, 1974) 2:397–98. In the introduction to the translation volume that accompanies his text [*Des Heiligen Ephraem des Syrers Sermones IV, CSCO* 335 (Louvain, 1973) xi–xiv], Beck demonstrates that this work is a late compilation containing many non-Ephremic features. See also A. Vööbus, *HASO* II, 70–73. Ephrem himself, in his *Hymns on Nisibis* 19.15, praised the bishops of Nisibis for not having left behind any such testament.

53. These texts are described in Vööbus, *Literary, Critical and Historical Studies in Ephrem the Syrian,* 59–86; and idem, *HASO* II, 1–10. Three of these texts have been edited, with German translations, by Beck, *Sermones IV,* 1–43 [English translation of "On Hermits and Desert Dwellers," by J. P. Amar, in *Ascetic Behavior in Greco-Roman Antiquity: A Sourcebook,* ed. V. Wimbush, Studies in Antiquity and Christianity, no. 6 (Minneapolis, 1990) 66–80]. Editions of the rest of these texts, with English translations, have been prepared in E. G. Mathews, Jr., "Three Mêmrê on Solitaries Attributed to Ephrem the Syrian and Isaac the Teacher. Editions, Translations and Commentary with an Investigation into Their Place in the History of Syriac Asceticism," (Ph. D. diss., Catholic University of America, *forthcoming*). See also idem, "'On Solitaries': Ephrem or Isaac?" *LM* 103 (1990): 91–110.

54. In addition to the studies just mentioned, see J. P. Amar, "Byzantine As-

Christian world, in literature, as the texts just enumerated demonstrate, as well as in Christian iconography.[55] The decree *Principi apostolorum Petro*, promulgated by Pope Benedict XV on 5 October 1920, declaring Ephrem to be a doctor of the universal Church, is largely based on the *Encomium* attributed to Gregory of Nyssa.[56] Therefore, one must acknowledge that this monastic-inspired picture of Ephrem has also contributed to his "official" biography as proclaimed by the Roman Catholic Church.

(23) Despite the importance of Ephrem to nearly every aspect of the fourth-century Syrian church and its subsequent development, no comprehensive study of his life was attempted until 1960. This surprising fact is no doubt due not only to the complex nature of the many biographical documents just mentioned but also to the immense number of writings in nearly all early Christian languages that claim to have been written by Ephrem. Arthur Vööbus was the first to attempt such an evaluation of the biographical tradition of Ephrem.[57] After having put all the material to critical scrutiny, he still could only conclude that:

> The historical details of Ephrem's life are very scanty, and in many points do not allow us to reach a conclusion with desirable certainty. For the stream of the tradition is demonstratively discolored by the media through which it passed. Therefore the student of his-

---

cetic Monachism and Greek Bias in the *Vita* Tradition of Ephrem the Syrian," *OCP* 58 (1992): 123–56.

55. See, for example, the study of J. R. Martin, "The *Death of Ephraim* in Byzantine and Early Italian Painting," *Art Bulletin* 33 (1951): 217–25, where Ephrem is always depicted at his death surrounded by a retinue of monks, hermits, and even stylites.

56. *Acta Apostolicae Sedis* 12 (1920): 457–73, translated by B. A. Hausman, S. J., in *The Papal Encyclicals*, ed. C. Carlen (Raleigh, NC, 1981) 3:195–201.

57. Vööbus, *Literary, Critical and Historical Studies in Ephrem the Syrian*. Much of this study reappears in idem, *HASO* II. More than a decade prior to the appearance of Vööbus' studies, R. Draguet had announced a project to study the tradition of the life of Ephrem [R. Draguet, *Les Pères du désert* (Paris, 1949) viii–ix] but was too detained by other duties ever to bring it to completion.

GENERAL INTRODUCTION 19

tory is faced with a complex problem: Ephrem quite different from the historical Ephrem.[58]

(24) Vööbus, predisposed to the life of Ephrem as depicted in the Greek tradition, went on to describe Ephrem as an athlete in asceticism whose ascetical practices were "equated with contempt for nature, subjugation of the body and killing bodily needs."[59] Vööbus was also the first to introduce into the discussion those Syriac texts, mentioned above, that deal with an ascetical lifestyle of the severity for which Syrian monks were well known in the fifth and sixth centuries.[60] Vööbus defended the attribution, found in the manuscript tradition, that these texts were written by Ephrem and, on the basis of his evaluation of the evidence, pronounced Ephrem to be the founder and foremost practioner of this solitary ascetic lifestyle that was lived entirely in the mountains or in the desert with no comforts other than what nature itself provided.[61]

(25) Vööbus seemed, therefore, to have defended the traditional biography of Ephrem. But, the work of two scholars was soon to change all that. At the same time that Vööbus was bringing his studies to completion, Dom Edmund Beck began what was to be a more than thirty-year

58. Vööbus, *Literary, Critical and Historical Studies in Ephrem the Syrian*, 46 and idem, *HASO* II, 84.
59. Vööbus, *HASO* II, 97.
60. For the lifestyle of these monks see, in addition to Theodoret, *History of the Monks of Syria*, cited above, A. Festugière, *Antioche païenne et chrétienne* (Paris, 1959); P. Canivet, *Le monachisme Syrien selon Theodoret de Cyr*, Théologie historique, no. 42 (Paris, 1977); P. R. Brown, "The Rise and Function of the Holy Man in Late Antiquity," *JRS* 61 (1971): 80–101 [Reprinted in idem, *Society and the Holy in Late Antiquity* (Berkeley and Los Angeles, 1982) 103–52]; and I. Pena, et al., *Les reclus syriens* (Jerusalem, 1980).
61. See the arguments and description of this lifestyle in Vööbus, *HASO* II, 1–41. Many of Vööbus' positions on Ephrem's life stem from his analysis of these texts rather than on the works of unquestionable authenticity, with the result that his picture is of the same "discoloration" as the traditional one from which he claimed to distance himself. On Vööbus' methods see, especially, J. Gribomont, "Le monachisme au sein de l'église en Syrie et en Cappadoce," *SM* 7 (1965): 9–12.

project of editing the Syriac works of Ephrem. Based on this critical text work, Beck began to notice discrepancies between the traditional image of Ephrem and the image of Ephrem that emerged from his genuine writings.

(26) In two extremely important articles, Beck laid the foundations for what would result in a complete reevaluation of the biography of Ephrem.[62] In the first of these articles, Beck demonstrated that such terms as ʾabîlê "mourners," bʾnay qʾyāmâ "covenanters," and most particularly, ʾihidāyê "solitaries," which were commonly used of monks and ascetics in later texts, were used very differently in the genuine writings of Ephrem as well as in those of his near contemporary Aphrahat. For example, Ephrem and Aphrahat used the term ʾihidāyâ simply to designate a celibate person rather than a solitary who lived alone in caves or the wilderness.[63] In the time of Ephrem and Aphrahat the persons designated by these terms were not only not monks in any formal sense, but were still very much involved in the day to day affairs of the life of the Church.

(27) Beck's research further revealed that in Ephrem's genuine Syriac works there is to be found no concern for any lifestyle or ascetic practice that can be labelled monastic or eremitic; Ephrem's overwhelming concern was to serve his local church community, and to help his bishops defend it against the influence of various heterodox groups. In several articles and monographs, Dom Louis Leloir has since lent further support to Beck's conclusions.[64]

(28) Subsequent to Beck's studies, Dom Bernard Outtier

---

62. See E. Beck, "Ein Beitrag zur Terminologie des ältesten syrischen Mönchtums," *SA* 38 (1956): 254–67, and idem, "Asketentum und Mönchtum bei Ephraem," in *Il monachesimo orientale, OCA*, no. 153 (Rome, l958) 341–62.

63. In the New Testament the term ʾihidāyâ translates the Greek term μονογενῆς; see John 1.14, 18; 3.16, 18; I John 4.9. The term was then transferred to that one who had a special relationship with Christ, *the ʾihidāyâ*, or "Only-Begotten." For the importance of this spirituality in the early Syrian church, see the study of Murray, "Features of the Earliest Christian Asceticism," 65–77; and, especially, G. Winkler, "The Origins and Idiosyncrasies of the Earliest Form of Asceticism," in *The Continuing Quest for God*, ed. W. Skudlarek (Collegeville, 1982) 9–43.

64. See, especially, L. Leloir, *Doctrines et méthodes de S. Ephrem d'après son*

was asked to give a reassessment of the biographical tradition of Ephrem at a conference celebrating the sixteenth centenary of Ephrem's death.[65] In this seminal study, Outtier subjected the biographical sources to a meticulous reevaluation. The result was that he exposed the tendentious nature of Palladius and Sozomen as sources. Palladius blindly pasted Evagrian labels on Ephrem. These Evagrian words that Palladius employed have been cited more than once to show how little Palladius knew of Ephrem.[66] The final sentence of Palladius' notice concludes that Ephrem "left some writings, too, most of which are worthy of attention." Such a comment does not give one the fullest confidence that Palladius knew anything of the real Ephrem.

(29) The account of Sozomen is such "un véritable panégyrique"[67] that it is doubtful in the extreme that it contains even a kernel of historicity. Some of the anecdotes Sozomen relates are also told of others. For example, Sozomen recounts the story of a woman whom Ephrem encountered. To Ephrem's rebuke to her for staring at him, she replied, "Wherefore should I obey your injunction, for I was born not of the earth, but of you." This same anecdote is told by Theodoret about Jacob of Nisibis.[68]

Commentaire de l'Evangile concordant, CSCO 220 (Louvain, 1961) 53–67; idem, "La pensée monastique d'Ephrem et Martyrius," in *OCA,* no. 197 (Rome, 1974) 105–34; idem, "Saint Ephrem, moine et pasteur," in *Théologie de la vie monastique* (Paris, 1961) 85–97; and idem, "La pensée monastique d'Ephrem le Syrien," in *Memorial du Cinquantenaire 1914–64,* Travaux de l'Institut Catholique de Paris, no. 10 (Paris, 1964) 193–206. Leloir, however, maintains that Ephrem did know of and yearned for that rigorous eremitical life that he considered as the highest form of life.

65. Outtier, "Saint Ephrem d'après ses biographies et ses oeuvres," 11–33.

66. Palladius' description of Ephrem being "worthy of the gift of natural knowledge, to which succeeded the knowledge of God, and finally blessedness," is taken verbatim from the prologue of Evagrius' *Praktikos;* see A. and C. Guillaumont, *Evagre le Pontique Traité pratique ou le moine* II, SC 171 (Paris, 1971) 492. See also, R. Draguet, "L'Histoire Lausiaque—une oeuvre écrite dans l'esprit d'Evagre," *RHE* 41 (1946): 321–64, 42 (1947): 4–9; Amar, "The Syriac *Vita* Tradition of Ephrem the Syrian," 9; and Mathews, "The *Vita* Tradition of Ephrem the Syrian, the Deacon of Edessa," 19–20.

67. Outtier, "Saint Ephrem d'après ses biographies et ses oeuvres," 19.

68. See Theodoret, *History of the Monks of Syria,* I.

(30) Outtier then went on to demonstrate that the Syriac *Life of Ephrem* is itself dependent on these same unreliable sources. In not a few places it can now be seen that the Syriac *Life* also includes pericopes from Theodoret's *Histories* and the *Life of Basil* of Ps.-Amphilochius, which the compiler of the *Life of Ephrem* adapted from the original context to highlight the role of Ephrem. It has thus been made clear that the Syriac *Life of Ephrem* is little more than a pastiche of earlier texts stemming from a very unreliable Greek hagiographical tradition and can in no way be considered to be a product of one of his disciples.[69]

(31) In striking contrast to this Greek biographical tradition of Ephrem there exists a native Syriac biographical tradition represented by, in addition to Ephrem's own genuine works, two noteworthy documents: the *Foundation of the Schools* by Bar Hadbešabbâ of Halwan (fl. s. VI)[70] and a *Mêmrâ on Mar Ephrem the Teacher* by Jacob of Sarug (d. 521).[71] Bar Hadbešabbâ preserves a tradition that knows of Ephrem only as a teacher who was appointed by Jacob of Nisibis as head of the school in that city. After Nisibis had been ceded to the Persians in 363, Ephrem went to Edessa and there opened another school where his commentaries were used until those of Theodore of Mopsuestia were translated into Syriac during the tenure of Qiyorê (fl. s. V) as head of the school.[72]

(32) A little more than a century after the death of Ephrem, Jacob of Sarug composed a panegyrical *mêmrâ*, entitled *On Mar Ephrem the Teacher*. The description of Ephrem provided by Jacob's *mêmrâ* is of particular value since Jacob

---

69. Further details can be found in Amar, "The Syriac *Vita* Tradition of Ephrem the Syrian," 9–32; and Mathews, "The *Vita* Tradition of Ephrem the Syrian, the Deacon of Edessa," 15–42.

70. A. Scher, ed., *Mar Barhadbšabba 'Arbaya cause de la fondation des écoles*, PO 4.4 (Paris, 1907).

71. Bedjan, ed., *Acta Martyrum et Sanctorum Syriace*, 3:665–79. A new edition of this important work with an English translation is in preparation by J. P. Amar.

72. For the history of the school of Nisibis, see A. Vööbus, *History of the School of Nisibis*, CSCO 266 (Louvain, 1965).

had studied in Edessa and later became bishop of Sarug, a town less than 25 miles south of Edessa.[73] Jacob therefore preserves reliable information about local Edessan traditions that concerned Ephrem. Although one must admit that we find little in the way of concrete data concerning Ephrem in this *mêmrâ*, one cannot but be struck by the fact that the sole picture Jacob paints is of Ephrem as a teacher. In the short space of 289 poetic lines Ephrem's teaching or teaching activity is explicitly mentioned nearly fifty times without a single mention or even a hint of any ascetical or monastic practices. Jacob says of him that he is "the chosen one, head and chief of the teachers . . . an athlete who conquered by the purity of his teaching."[74] In typical Syrian poetic fashion Jacob relates how Ephrem taught the Daughters of the Covenant (in Syriac, *b'nāt q'yāmâ*) to sing his hymns, which contain the true doctrine as well as an antidote to the poison of the heretics.[75] Ephrem is described as "the spring of new wine by whose songs the land is intoxicated so that it might rejoice in him."[76] Jacob has clearly depicted Ephrem as a teacher and a guide who guards the flock from the heterodox teaching of the "wolves," i.e., the followers of Mani, Marcion, and Bardaisan. We certainly cannot say that these concerns are not those of a monk, but the picture Jacob paints is clearly of one who is visibly and actively engaged in teaching and preserving the orthodoxy of the lay church community. It is this picture of Ephrem as teacher, with no mention of any monastic activity, that has been preserved in the early, native Syrian tradition.

(33) Recent scholarship, having recovered this native Syrian tradition, has thus demonstrated that the traditional biography of Ephrem is almost totally inaccurate; it presents not the Ephrem of history but an Ephrem who was the product of a complex process of Byzantine hagiographical

---

73. Baumstark, *Geschichte der syrischen Literatur,* 148–58; and W. Wright, *A Short History of Syriac Literature* (London, 1894) 67–72.
74. Bedjan, ed., *Acta Martyrum et Sanctorum Syriace,* 3:665.
75. Ibid., 668.
76. Ibid., 667.

embellishment. Ephrem's own life, insofar as we know it, reflects evangelical practices and concerns, not those of the anchorite. Ephrem lived his life as an unmarried disciple of Christ wholly engaged in helping and advising his bishops by preaching, teaching, writing, and fighting against heresies, all to keep careful guard over the whole flock of Christ.[77] Although the particular circumstances of this pastoral activity are unknown to us, it is clear that Ephrem's ministry was not congruent with the lifestyle of the ascetics described in any of those texts that have come out of the Greek tradition. It is particularly striking that Ephrem's service to the Nisibene hierarchy and his ministry to the Daughters of the Covenant were the very two things that monks were warned to avoid above all else, namely, bishops and women.[78]

(34) In light of these recent studies, the fact that Ephrem is not even once mentioned in Theodoret's *History of the Monks of Syria*, (written c. 440)[79] takes on much greater importance. This glaring absence is made all the more remarkable by two further observations. Theodoret did not include Ephrem in his *History* even though he did include Ephrem's bishop, Jacob of Nisibis.[80] Moreover, he omits any mention of Ephrem in spite of the notices of Palladius and Sozomen! Theodoret was an eyewitness to the development of monasticism in Syria and knew firsthand many of the traditions and legends. One would think that he certainly should have

77. See E. Beck, "Ephrem der Syrer," in *RAC*, 5:524; J.-M. Fiey, "Les évêques de Nisibe au temps de saint Ephrem," *PdO* 4 (1973): 123–35; and I. Ortiz de Urbina, L'évêque et son role d'après saint Ephrem," *PdO* 4 (1973): 137–46. *Hymns on Nisibis* 13–17, reveal how much Ephrem identified his theological vocation with his ecclesiastical service.

78. See J.-C. Guy, ed., *Jean Cassien, Institutions cénobitiques*, SC 109 (Paris, 1965) XI.18: "For neither [bishops nor women] will allow one who has once engaged in intercourse with God to take any further care for the quiet of his cell, or to remain with pure eyes in divine contemplation."

79. For the dating of this work, see R. M. Price, trans., *A History of the Monks of Syria by Theodoret of Cyrrhus*, CSS 88 (Kalamazoo, 1985) xiii–xv.

80. Theodoret paired Ephrem with Jacob in his *History of the Church*, L. Parmentier and F. Scheidweiler, eds., *Theodoret, Kirchengeschichte*, GCS 44 (Berlin,

included a monk in his *History* who was "the greatest ornament of the Catholic Church."[81] Therefore, despite what first appears to be a considerable number of source documents, after being subjected to critical evaluation, "the chief facts which remain are deducible from [Ephrem's] authentic writings."[82]

(35) In the paragraphs that follow we will attempt to trace out the history of Ephrem's life and the events in which he was involved insofar as these can be discerned with any degree of accuracy.

2. Period in Nisibis

(36) Although no source exists as verification, scholarly consensus places the birth of Ephrem at c. 309, in or around Nisibis. Contrary to the Syriac *Life of Ephrem* in which Ephrem is portrayed as being born to a father who was a priest of a pagan cult—one recension speaks of both his parents being idol worshippers—,[83] it is more likely, based on Ephrem's own admission, that he was born of two faithful Christian parents: "In the way of truth was I born even though as a child I did not yet perceive it,"[84] and "Your truth was in my youth; your truth is in my old age."[85] Ephrem seems to have had at least one sister, as later chroni-

---

1954) 2:26. Rev. B. Jackson, trans., "The Ecclesiastical History, Dialogues, and Letters of Theodoret," in *LNPF* 2d series (reprint, Grand Rapids, 1983) 3:91–92.
 81. Bidez and Hansen, eds., *Sozomen, Kirchengeschichte*, 127.
 82. Murray, *Symbols*, 30.
 83. Vat. MS. Syr. 117. See Amar, "The Syriac *Vita* Tradition of Ephrem the Syrian," 69 (text), 199 (translation).
 84. *Hymns against Heresies* 26.10.
 85. *Hymn on Virginity* 37.10. See also *Hymns against Heresies* 3:13, where Ephrem refers to his having been baptized in the name of the Trinity. According to the Paris recension of the Syriac *Life*, Ephrem was baptized by Jacob at age 18, and according to the Vatican recension, at age 28. See Amar, "The Syriac *Vita* Tradition of Ephrem the Syrian," 92 (text), 226 (translation). But both these recensions say that Ephrem's baptism occurred after he left Nisibis in 363! For the normal Syriac practice of baptizing young adults and not infants, see S. P. Brock, "Some Early Syriac Baptismal Commentaries," *OCP* 46 (1980): 20–61.

cles refer to Ephrem's nephew, Absimius, a son of Ephrem's sister.[86]

(37) Nisibis, which Ephrem identifies with ancient Akkad,[87] was an acknowledged center of political and commercial activity.[88] Long an object of great desire and contention between the Romans and Persians, Nisibis had been part of the Roman empire since 297, when Narses, King of Persia signed a treaty with the Emperor Diocletian ceding the Eastern frontier to the Roman empire. Diocletian then quickly built Nisibis into his strongest eastern fortress.[89] When the Sassanians overthrew the Parthians and came into power in Persia, it was their primary goal to reestablish the borders of the ancient Achaemenid empire.[90] The infant Shapur II ascended to the throne in 309, and during his reign, which spanned the entire life of Ephrem, the Sassanian empire reached its apex.[91] Under his leadership Persia was constantly engaged in trying to regain the eastern Roman territories. Thus, Ephrem's busy ecclesiastical involvement was from time to time interrupted by Persian attacks on Nisibis.

(38) In the beginning of the fourth century, Syrian territory enjoyed a certain measure of peace. Shapur was still an infant and the Edict of Milan brought a measure of relief from Roman persecution of Christians. During this period

---

86. See F. Nau, "Étude sur les parties inédites de la chronique ecclésiastique attribuée à Denys de Tell Mahré (†845)," *ROC* 2 (1897): 62; and J. B. Chabot, ed., *Chronique de Michel le Syrien*, 4 vols. (Paris, 1900–10) 4.169 (text), 2.9 (translation). Attempts to identify this Absimius with the early Syriac poet, Cyrillona, have not met with much approval.

87. *Commentary on Genesis*, VIII.1.

88. Nisibis had a virtual monopoly on the trade between Persia and Rome. See J. Sturm, "Nisibis," in *PWK* 17.714–57, and N. Pigulevskaja, *Les villes de l'état iranien aux époques parthe et sassanide* (Paris, 1963) 49–59.

89. See R. N. Frye, "The Political History of Iran under the Sasanians," in E. Yarshater, ed., *The Cambridge History of Iran* (Cambridge, 1983) 3.1:131–32; and Fiey, "Les évêques de Nisibe au temps de saint Ephrem," 123.

90. See A. Christensen, *L'Iran sous les Sassanides*, 2d ed. (Copenhagen, 1944).

91. For the reign of Shapur II, see Frye, "The Political History of Iran under the Sasanians," 116–80, especially 132–41.

Jacob, perhaps the first bishop of Nisibis, attended the Council of Nicea, bringing back to his native church the foundations of Nicean orthodoxy, though the report that Ephrem accompanied Jacob to the Council of Nicea is almost certainly to be rejected.[92] Ephrem would later look back on the careers of the various bishops he served and refer to Jacob as the one who gave birth to the Nisibene church, and as the one who weaned the flock in the faith, and gave milk to the infants.[93] It was Jacob who had the first church built in Nisibis during the years 313–20.[94] Although Ephrem worked closely with all the bishops whom he served, the Syriac *Life of Ephrem* preserves the tradition that Jacob was as influential in Ephrem's early formation as he was in rearing the church of Nisibis in the orthodox faith.[95]

(39) In 338, after the death of Constantine, Shapur II, now firmly in control of his own army, began his attempt to take back from Rome all that he considered Persian territory and laid siege to Nisibis. When the city repulsed his attack,[96] Shapur resorted to levying a double poll tax on all Christians living within the borders of his empire. Simeon bar Sabbae, bishop of Seleucia-Ctesiphon, stood forth on behalf of the Christians in his flock for whom this tax was an unbearable burden. Shapur responded by setting into mo-

92. See *Life of Ephrem*, 5, in Amar, "The Syriac *Vita* Tradition of Ephrem the Syrian," 82–83 (text), 214–16 (translation). For a discussion of the problem of the actual order of the first bishops of Nisibis, see J.-M. Fiey, *Nisibe: metropole syriaque orientale et ses suffragants des origines à nos jours*, CSCO 388 (Louvain, 1977) 21–33.
93. See *Hymns on Nisibis* 14.
94. Fiey, *Nisibe*, 23; and idem, "Les évêques de Nisibe au temps de saint Ephrem," 126–27.
95. See *Life of Ephrem*, 3–7, in Amar, "The Syriac *Vita* Tradition of Ephrem the Syrian," 73–89 (text), 203–23 (translation).
96. The sources confuse the roles of Jacob and Ephrem in the defense of the city. Jacob alone is involved in Theodoret, *History of the Monks of Syria*, I.11; Ephrem beseeches Jacob in idem, *History of the Church*, II.26; but in the *Life of Ephrem*, 6, Ephrem plays the dominant role. See Amar, "The Syriac *Vita* Tradition of Ephrem the Syrian," 84–88 (text), 217–22 (translation). For discussion, see P. Peeters, "La légende de saint Jacques de Nisibe," *AB* 38 (1920): 285–373; Canivet, *Le monachisme syrien*, 71–72, and Amar, "The Syriac *Vita* Tra-

tion a vicious persecution against the Christians of Persia in which many, including Bishop Simeon bar Sabbae, lost their lives.[97] Early Syriac literature is full of martyr acts that stem from these persecutions, although they may not all, in fact, be the work of Marutha of Maipherkat, their traditional author.[98] In 338 Jacob died and Babu succeeded him as bishop.[99]

(40) In May of 345, Constantius arrived in Nisibis, after having regained Adiabene from Shapur and the Persians, thus winning the title Adiabenicus.[100] Shapur attempted a second siege of Nisibis in 346, but was again repulsed. The ensuing truce lasted less than two years, at which time Shapur recommenced his efforts to regain Mesopotamia for the Persian empire. In 350 Shapur was again at the walls of Nisibis, this time followed by a convoy of elephants from India and accompanied by hosts of Persia's best archers.[101] When the elephants were slow to succeed, Shapur dammed up the Mygdonius River and then managed to breach the wall by unleashing the stored up water. Still, Shapur was unsuccessful in his attempt to take over the city as the Nisibenes were able to refortify the battered walls before the Persian forces could enter. Shortly after this defeat Shapur had to set aside this western campaign in order to stave off assaults from the Chionites, apparently a Hunnish people, who were making

---

dition of Ephrem the Syrian," 15–18. The *Life* also telescopes the siege of 338 and that of 350 into one single siege.

97. See account in Sozomen, *History of the Church*, II.9.

98. The Syriac acts are found in Bedjan, ed., *Acta Martyrum et Sanctorum Syriace*. For a study of the Syriac tradition of these Acts, see G. Wiessner, *Untersuchungen zur syrischen Literaturgeschichte: Zur Märtyrerüberlieferung aus der Christenverfolgung Schapurs*, 2 vols., Abhandlungen der Akademie der Wissenschaften in Göttingen, philologisch-historische Klasse, Dritte Folge, No. 67 (Göttingen, 1967). These persecutions are also recorded in Greek traditions; see H. Delehaye, ed., *Les versions grecques des Actes des martyrs persans sous Sapor II*, PO 2.4 (Brepols, 1905), and Sozomen, *History of the Church*, II.9–15.

99. Fiey, "Les évêques de Nisibe au temps de saint Ephrem," 122.

100. See A. Piganiol, *L'empire chrétien* (Paris, 1972) 84.

101. See Theodoret, *History of the Church*, II.26; Amar, "The Syriac *Vita* Tradition of Ephrem the Syrian," 84–88 (text), 217–22 (translation); and the relevant description in W. C. Wright, ed., *The Works of the Emperor Julian*, LCL (New York, 1913), 1:68–72.

GENERAL INTRODUCTION 29

incursions on the eastern borders in the region of the Caspian Sea.[102]

(41) This retreat of Shapur and his army once again left Nisibis in relative peace for a short period. Sometime shortly after Shapur's retreat, c. 350–52, Vologeses, who had now succeeded Babu as bishop, constructed a baptistery in Nisibis. This monument, the oldest Christian edifice in the entire East, is still in existence and has been called "the most beautiful Christian construction in the East."[103]

(42) Ephrem was now nearing fifty years of age, and had spent his entire life in service to the church of Nisibis and as a faithful servant to her three bishops: Jacob, Babu, and Vologeses. Tradition, beginning with Palladius, has nearly unanimously named Ephrem a deacon. The word Ephrem uses to describe his own position is ʿallānâ,[104] which is most often interpreted, with reference to the Greek tradition, as deacon. While ʿallāna is not the usual Syriac term to designate a deacon, there is little reason to doubt this tradition, although there is no source to locate his ordination in Nisibis or in Edessa. A little more problematic is the tradition that Jacob of Nisibis had appointed Ephrem as head or interpreter (in Syriac, m'paššqānâ) of the Christian school at Nisibis.[105] Even if one were to grant that the School of Nisibis existed this early and that Ephrem was involved in the early years of this school, still his exact role cannot be determined on the basis of the scanty evidence that has survived.[106] Of Ephrem's role as *defensor fidei*, there can be no doubt; Ephrem often assumed the role that he demanded of a good bishop.[107]

102. Frye, "The Political History of Iran under the Sasanians," 137.
103. Fiey, "Les évêques de Nisibe au temps de saint Ephrem," 129. For the Greek inscription on the baptistery, see J. Jarry, "Inscriptions syriaques et arabes inédites du Tur 'Abdin," *Annales Islamologiques* 10 (1972): 242–43.
104. *Hymns against Heresies* 56.10.
105. Scher, ed., *Mar Barhadbšabba 'Arbaya cause de la fondation des écoles*, 377.
106. For a negative judgment, see Vööbus, *History of the School of Nisibis*, 8–9; and idem, "Afrem and the School of Urhai," in *Ephrem Hunayn Festival* (Baghdad, 1974) 209–16.
107. See Ortiz de Urbina, "L'évêque et son role d'après saint Ephrem,"

(43) It was very likely during this period that Ephrem took the opportunity to reflect on the ecclesiastical life of his native city. He saw three periods in the history of the church of Nisibis, each corresponding to the guidance of the three bishops whom he served:

> Three illustrious priests, after the manner of the two great luminaries,
> have carried on and then handed down the See, the Authority and the Flock.
> To us who mourn so for the first two, this last one is wholly a consolation.
> He Who created two great luminaries chose for Himself these three lights,
> and set them in the three dark seasons of siege that have taken place here.
> When one pair of lights was dimmed the other shone wholly forth.
> These three priests were treasures who held in their faithfulness the key of the Trinity.[108]

(44) Although the chronology of Ephrem's writings is by no means clear,[109] a number of his hymns probably date from this period—most notably the *Hymns on Paradise*, many of the *Hymns on Nisibis*, and perhaps some of his liturgical hymns, particularly those anti-Jewish *Hymns on the Paschal Feast*. Nisibis had a large Jewish community in the fourth century and Ephrem composed many hymns that dealt with the Jews, which show him to be much more acerbic than was his younger contemporary, Aphrahat.[110] The *Chronicle of Seert* records that Ephrem left in Nisibis a liturgy

---

137–46. On Jacob's role as bishop, see now D. Bundy, "Jacob of Nisibis as a Model for the Episcopacy," *LM* 104 (1991): 235–49. See also R. Murray, "St. Ephrem the Syrian on Church Unity," *ECQ* 15 (1963): 164–76.

108. *Hymns on Nisibis* 13.1–3. Hymns 13–21 concern these three bishops. See also Fiey, "Les évêques de Nisibe au temps de saint Ephrem."

109. See E. Beck, *Ephräm der Syrer, Lobgesang aus der Wüste*, Sophia: Quellen östlicher Theologie, no. 7 (Freiburg im Breisgau, 1967) 14–17.

110. See Murray, *Symbols*, 41–68; and A. P. Hayman, "The Image of the Jew in the Syriac Anti-Jewish Polemical Literature," in *"To See Ourselves as Others See*

GENERAL INTRODUCTION   31

that he composed. This liturgy, which has not survived, remained in use until the reforms of Išōyab of Adiabene (c. 650).[111]

(45) Ephrem's activity in Nisibis reached its conclusion when Shapur II began his fourth, and what would prove to be his final and most successful, assault on the Roman empire. This time Shapur bypassed Nisibis in order to strike deeper into Roman territory. Repulsed in this effort, Shapur returned and besieged Amid. Victorious in this endeavor, he had all the inhabitants of this city either killed or sent to Khuzistan as slaves.[112] With the death of Constantius in 361 the pagan emperor Julian[113] succeeded to the throne and mounted a final assault against the Persian forces. But by the time Julian and his army marched forth Shapur had already taken Singara and Bezabdê.

(46) Julian's campaign against the Persians met with initial success and he regained certain outposts. Shapur, however, lured him deep into Persian territory, before the very walls of Seleucia-Ctesiphon, the Persian capital. Here the Roman army was thoroughly routed and Julian himself was slain. As the body of Julian was brought back to Nisibis on its way to Tarsus where he had requested to be buried, Ephrem noted the juxtaposition of the Persian flag flying on the ramparts of Nisibis and the slain corpse of the pagan emperor:

Us": Christians, Jews, "Others" in Late Antiquity, ed. J. Neusner and E. S. Frerichs (Chico, California, 1985) 423–41. Murray, *Symbols*, 19, points out, however, that "the Christians in Mesopotamia lived at the door of the Jews like poor relations not on speaking terms. Ephrem's bitterness is less surprising than Aphrahat's courtesy."

111. Scher, ed., *Histoire nestorienne inédite (Chronique de Séert), PO* 4, 83–85.
112. Frye, "The Political History of Iran under the Sasanians," 137.
113. Julian the Apostate was a popular figure in Syriac literature. See J. H. G. Hoffman, ed., *Julianos der Abtruennige. Syrische Erzaehlungen* (Leiden, 1880) [English translation in H. Gollancz, *Julian the Apostate* (Oxford, 1928)]. See also the texts, including Ephrem's hymns, translated in S. N. C. Lieu, *The Emperor Julian: Panegyric and Polemic*, 2d ed. (Liverpool, 1989). For modern studies, see R. Browning, *The Emperor Julian* (Berkeley and Los Angeles, 1976); G. Bowersock, *Julian the Apostate* (Cambridge, Massachusetts, 1978); and D. Bowder, *The Age of Constantine and Julian* (New York, 1978).

There I saw a foul sight:
the banner of the captor, which was fixed on the tower,
the body of the persecutor, which was lying on the bier.
Believe in "Yes and No," the word that is true,
I went and came, my brethren, to the bier of the defiled one
and I stood over it and I derided his paganism,
I said, "Is this he who exalted himself
against the living name and who forgot that he is dust?"
[God] has returned him to within his dust that he might know that he is dust.[114]

While Ephrem proclaimed the final victory over paganism, he was also forced to decry the sins and pagan practices of his native Nisibis that had brought on this catastrophe.[115]

(47) The emperor Jovian, who succeeded the slain Julian, saw that the Roman troops were much too depleted to continue fighting against the Persians. He was thus forced to conclude a treaty with Shapur II in 363 that ceded several eastern territories to Persia, including Nisibis, Singara and Bezabdê. That *ignobile decretum*[116] stated that Nisibis was to be Persian for 120 years, and the inhabitants were to be allowed to go to Amid freely and not to be forcibly relocated as the inhabitants of Amid had been just four years previously. Shapur had to content himself with destroying all the idols that had been reintroduced by Julian.

(48) The chronology concerning when Ephrem left Nisibis and went to Edessa remains very vague.[117] Ammianus Marcellinus relates that all the Christians were forced to

---

114. *Hymns against Julian* 3.3–4. Translation of Judith Lieu in S. N. C. Lieu, *The Emperor Julian: Panegyric and Polemic*, 118.

115. See *Hymns against Julian* 2.20–21. See also *Hymns on Nicomedia*, especially, hymns 10–11, where he exhorts the inhabitants of Nisibis to repent. Ironically, Julian had declined aid to Nisibis against the Persian assault on the grounds that Nisibis was wholly Christianized. See Sozomen, *History of the Church*, V.3.

116. J. C. Rolfe, ed., *Ammianus Marcellinus*, LCL (Cambridge, 1939) XXV.7.13.

117. *Hymns on Nisibis* 22–25 may deal with this period of Ephrem's life, but they are lost. See Beck, *Ephräm der Syrer. Lobgesang aus der Wüste*, 15.

leave Nisibis and went directly to Amid.[118] Contemporary scholars are generally in the habit of saying that Ephrem went very quickly to Edessa and spent the remaining ten years of his life there.[119] The little evidence that exists, however, does not support this presumption.[120] Ephrem's own writings, contrary to the witness of Ammianus Marcellinus (XXV.9.1–6), offer hints that he remained in Nisibis some time after the Persian-Roman treaty of 363 was signed.[121] Other evidence, albeit later and of more dubious trustworthiness, suggests that Ephrem went from Nisibis to Beth Garbāyê.[122]

3. Period in Edessa

(49) The city which was known to native speakers of Syriac as Urhai, was renamed Edessa, after the Seleucian capital in Macedonia, by its founder Seleucus I Nicator in 303/2 BC.[123] Ephrem, following a long-standing and widespread tradition, identifies Edessa as the city of Erekh that was built by Nimrod.[124] Edessa, like Nisibis, had been under Roman con-

118. Rolfe, ed., *Ammianus Marcellinus*, XXV.9.
119. See, most recently, K. McVey, *Ephrem the Syrian Hymns*, CWS (New York, 1989) 23; and S. P. Brock, *St. Ephrem the Syrian Hymns on Paradise* (Crestwood, 1990) 11.
120. A. Scher maintains that Ephrem did not leave Nisibis until 369. See his *Kaldu wa-Atur* II (Beirut, 1913) 47 (in Arabic).
121. *Hymns against Julian* 2.26–27, for example, suggests, contrary to Ammianus, that the Christians were not forced to leave as they had been in other cities.
122. See Amar, "The Syriac *Vita* Tradition of Ephrem the Syrian, 92 (text), 226 (translation).
123. The city, located in modern southeastern Turkey, is now called Urfa. During the time of Antiochus IV Epiphanes, Edessa was known as Antioch by the Callirhoe, or "beautiful flowing," referring to the river Daisan. See R. Duval, *Histoire politique, religieuse et littéraire d'Edesse jusqu'à la première croisade* (Paris, 1892); Segal, *Edessa "The Blessed City";* H. J. W. Drijvers, "Hatra, Palmyra und Edessa. Die Städte der syrischmesopotamischen Wüste in politischer, kulturgeschichtlicher und religionsgeschichtlicher Beleuchtung," in *ANRW* (Berlin-New York, 1977) 2.8:799–906; and idem, *Cults and Beliefs at Edessa*, Études préliminaires aux religions orientales dans l'empire Romain, no. 90 (Leiden, 1980) especially, 9–18.
124. Cf. *Commentary on Genesis* VIII.1. Muslim commentators later claimed that it was Edessa where Abraham offered his son Isaac up as sacrifice. See

trol since the time of Diocletian. A fortress of exceptional importance, Edessa had also long been an object of the struggles between Rome and both the Parthian and Sassanian dynasties of Persia.[125] Beginning in 132 BC, Edessa was ruled by a long line of Nabatean kings under whom it grew very prosperous due to its strategic position on the Roman silk route.

(50) When Ephrem arrived in Edessa he found a cosmopolitan city with a very syncretistic or, as H. J. W. Drijvers calls it, poly-interpretable,[126] culture. Cults of Nebo and Bel, Atargatis, Azizos and Monimos and Sin, Lord of the gods, were still thriving in Edessa, as well as other lesser known cults.[127] Edessa also had a certain reputation as a great center of learning, for which reason it came to be known as the "Athens of the East."[128] The writings of Bardaisan witness to a thriving Edessene tradition of classical philosophy.

(51) As mentioned above, Edessa had traditions that traced its Christian origins back to Apostolic times; it already venerated the letter of Jesus to Abgar which was purported to protect the city against invasion. The body of the Apostle Thomas was brought back from India and buried in the crypt of the "great church" of Edessa which bore his name.[129] Many martyrs are also associated with Edessa, the most famous being Shamona, Guria and Habib,[130] as well as Sharbil and Barsamya.[131]

Segal, *Edessa "The Blessed City"*, 1–4; and Duval, *Histoire politique, religieuse et littéraire d'Edesse*, 104.

125. Segal, *Edessa "The Blessed City"*, 115; and Drijvers, *Cults and Beliefs at Edessa*, 11.

126. Drijvers, *Cults and Beliefs at Edessa*, 17.

127. Ibid.

128. Ibid., 14.

129. The *Life of Ephrem*, 33, refers to a Church of St. Thomas (in Syriac, *hayklâ rabbâ d'Mar Tômâ*). The Spanish pilgrim Etheria came to Edessa exclusively to pray at his tomb; see H. Petre, ed., *Etherie, Journal de Voyage, SC* 21 (Paris, 1957) 158, and his comments on page 54.

130. F. C. Burkitt, *Euphemia and the Goth,* Text and Translation Society, no. 2 (Dublin and London, 1897). The *Life of Ephrem,* 35, claims that Ephrem wrote hymns in commemoration of these famous martyrs. If he did, they have not survived.

131. W. Cureton, *Ancient Syriac Documents* (London, 1864) 41–72, and R.

(52) Ephrem arrived in Edessa, some time after 363, to find the surviving Christian community to be a minority among many various heterodox groups and still thriving pagan cults. The Syriac *Life of Ephrem* specifies that Ephrem "found nine heresies . . . most notably those of Bardaisan, Arius, Mani and of Marcion."[132] Ephrem was also appalled to find that the members of the Christian community there who shared his adherence to the canons of the Council of Nicea were known as "Palutians," after a certain Palut, an early bishop of Edessa, while it was the community of the Marcionites who were known as the "Christians."[133] The Syriac *Life of Ephrem* emphasizes Ephrem's struggle against Bardaisan, although Ephrem waged constant battle against all these heterodox groups during the few remaining years of his life.[134]

(53) While details are few and imprecise, Ephrem's activity in Edessa was such that he is remembered in the biographical traditions either as a lifelong Edessan or at least as one who made no mark until his arrival there. As already mentioned, Palladius knew nothing of a Nisibene period of Ephrem's life. Sozomen mentions Nisibis as his birthplace, but only in passing. The author of the spurious *Testament of Ephrem* expresses concern only for the fortunes of Edessa; Nisibis is not mentioned once. The Syriac *Life* speaks at length of Jacob and various political events, but only after Ephrem leaves Nisibis is he baptized, and only after his arrival in Edessa did he begin his writing and his fight against the heretics. The *Encomium on Ephrem,* attributed to Gregory of Nyssa, most clearly expresses this traditional disparage-

---

Duval, "Les Actes de Scharbil et les actes de Barsamya," *JA* ser. 8, 14 (1889): 40–58. These martyrdoms are depicted as having taken place in the time of Trajan, but it is more likely that they belong to the period of the Decian persecution. See now S. A. Harvey, "The Edessan Martyrs and Ascetic Tradition," in *OCA*, no. 236 (Rome, 1990) 195–206.

132. See Amar, "The Syriac *Vita* Tradition of Ephrem the Syrian," 154 (text), 293 (translation). Ephrem himself enumerates a number of heresies in *Hymns against Heresies* 22.

133. See *Hymns against Heresies* 22.5.

134. For a brief overview, see D. Bundy, "Language and the Knowledge of God in Ephrem Syrus," *PBR* 5 (1986): 91–103.

ment toward Nisibis saying that Ephrem "came to the city of Edessa, for it was not right that the sun be hidden under the earth any longer."[135]

(54) Tradition relates that Ephrem undertook the writing of sacred songs as an antidote to the hymns of Bardaisan that were still being sung in the city. Ephrem gathered together the Daughters of the Covenant to sing his hymns. Scholars generally consider this Edessan period as the period in which Ephrem produced the greater part of his literary compositions; the majority of his surviving hymns and commentaries seem to stem from this period. Tradition also maintains that Ephrem set up a school in Edessa after the manner of the one he had directed in Nisibis. His biblical commentaries, probably written during this period, were long used as the standard commentaries in this school.[136]

(55) Perhaps the best known, and certainly the most documented, event of his life was also the last task that Ephrem was ever to accomplish. Recounted first by Palladius, less than 50 years after the death of Ephrem, it was repeated by Sozomen and then incorporated into the Syriac *Life of Ephrem*.[137] In the spring of 373, Edessa was beset with such a severe famine that the entire city was thrown into confusion. The rich of the city had large quantities of grain in their storehouses but were unwilling to part with any of it for fear of being cheated. Ephrem, therefore, offered himself as mediator between those well-fed rich and the rest of the city who were in dire straits. He distributed the grain and also saw to the needs of the sick and dying in what might have been Edessa's first emergency relief effort.

(56) Shortly after this effort, on 9 June 373, as recorded in the *Chronicle of Edessa*, Ephrem departed this life.[138] Ac-

---

135. St. Gregory of Nyssa, *De Vita S. Patris Ephraem Syri*, 833A.

136. Scher, ed., *Mar Barhadbšabba 'Arbaya cause de la fondation des écoles*, 381–82. Most of these commentaries, however, survive only in Armenian versions; see further, below.

137. Palladius, *The Lausiac History*, 40; Sozomen, *The History of the Church*, III.16; and Amar, "The Syriac *Vita* Tradition of Ephrem the Syrian," 184–87 (text), 327–31 (translation).

138. Hallier, *Untersuchungen über die Edessenische Chronik*, 149. In many ac-

GENERAL INTRODUCTION   37

cording to a tradition preserved in the Syriac *Life* as well as in the *Testament*, it was Ephrem's desire that he be laid to rest in the cemetery designated for strangers.[139] It was not too long afterwards, however, that the citizens of Edessa exhumed his body and moved it into a cave which was the burial ground traditionally reserved for the bishops of Edessa.[140]

Writings

(57) Much of Syriac Christian literature prior to the fourth century seems to have emanated from heterodox circles. The first of these, the *Book of the Laws of the Countries* (written c. 220–25) and almost certainly the same book Eusebius refers to as *On Fate*, was written by Phillip, a disciple of Bardaisan of Edessa.[141] The *Odes of Solomon*, which have heretofore defied efforts to find their original context, seem to come from around the same time as the *Book of the Laws of*

---

counts the date 378 appears as the year of Ephrem's death, see P. Peeters, *Bibliotheca Hagiographica Orientalis,* Subsidia Hagiographica, no. 10 (Brussels, 1910) 63. The general concensus now is to follow the *Chronicle of Edessa*. The Roman Church celebrates the feast of Ephrem on June 9, while the Greek Church celebrates it on January 18, and the Maronite Church on June 18. The June dates are probably more correct as the harvest normally took place in April/May; see W. Wright, ed., *The Chronicle of Joshua the Stylite* (Cambridge, 1882) XLIV, 40 (text), 34 (translation).

139. *Testament,* 297–98, in Beck, *Sermones IV,* 52. Amar, "The Syriac *Vita* Tradition of Ephrem the Syrian," 189 (text), 333–34 (translation).

140. According to the Paris recension; see Vööbus, *HASO* II, 91–92. The Vatican recension reads "beneath his [i.e., Ephrem's] church"; see Amar, "The Syriac *Vita* Tradition of Ephrem the Syrian," 189 (text), 333 (translation). This church became the Armenian monastery Dair Sargis, now Khidhir Elias; see Fiey, "Les évêques de Nisibe au temps de saint Ephrem," 135. The Vatican recension of the *Life of Ephrem* also records the presence of "a blessed retinue of hermits, stylites and monks" at his funeral; see Amar, "The Syriac *Vita* Tradition of Ephrem the Syrian," 189 (text), 333–34 (translation). This anachronistic picture was a favorite in Byzantine and Italian painting, see Martin, "The *Death of Ephraim* in Byzantine and Early Italian Painting," 217–25.

141. H. J. W. Drijvers, *The Book of the Laws of Countries, Dialogue on Fate of Bardaisan of Edessa* (Assen, 1965); idem, *Bardaisan of Edessa,* Studia Semitica Neerlandica, no. 6 (Assen, 1966); and studies XI–XIII in idem, *East of Antioch. Studies in Early Syriac Christianity.*

38   GENERAL INTRODUCTION

the Countries.[142] The apocryphal *Acts of Thomas* probably also date from the third century.[143] In the fourth century, however, we find a sudden proliferation of orthodox Christian literature in Syriac; in addition to the works of Aphrahat and of Ephrem there have survived collections of poems by Balai and Cyrillona, in addition to the slightly later *Book of Steps.*

(58) From nearly every one of our sources it is clear that Ephrem was a prolific writer; Sozomen, for example, numbered his writings at three million verses.[144] But, even more than the sheer quantity of his writings, Ephrem was known, even beyond his native Syria, for the beauty and divinely inspired teaching found in his compositions. One of several *apophthegmata* that was told of Ephrem gives some indication of the esteem in which he was held:

When the holy Mar Ephrem was a child he had a dream or vision which he related to people and which he also wrote about in his testament: A vine sprouted on his tongue and grew up, and everything under heaven was filled by it. It bore abundant clusters, and even the birds of the sky came and ate of its fruit. The more they ate, the more its clusters increased.[145]

---

142. J. H. Charlesworth, *The Odes of Solomon,* Society of Biblical Literature Texts and Translations, no. 13, Pseudepigrapha Series 7 (Chico, California, 1977). See also studies VII–X, in Drijvers, *East of Antioch. Studies in Early Syriac Christianity.* While scholars tend towards either a second century date (e.g., Charlesworth) or a third century date (Drijvers), dates ranging from 50 BC to 300 AD have been proffered. Also still unsettled are the questions of whether these *Odes* were originally written in Syriac or Greek (or Hebrew?) and whether they emanated from Christian, Jewish, Baptist, or Gnostic circles.

143. Klijn, *The Acts of Thomas.*

144. The figure "three hundred thousand" in the translation of Hartranft, trans., "The Ecclesiastical History of Salaminius Hermias Sozomenus," 295, is a mistranslation of the Greek. In addition to the works about to be discussed, in the liturgical books of all the Syrian churches, there are many prayers and writings attributed to Ephrem that have not yet begun to be sifted. Many may correspond to those that survive in Armenian; see St. Ephraem Syrus, *Alōt'k'* (Venice, 1879); and *Srobyn Ep'remi Matenagrut'iwnk',* vol. 4 (Venice, 1836).

145. From the Paris recension; see Amar, "The Syriac *Vita* Tradition of Ephrem the Syrian," 101 (text), 237 (translation) and his discussion, 7–10.

Theodoret of Cyr calls Ephrem the "lyre of the Spirit, who daily waters the Syrian nation with streams of grace."[146] Sozomen and Jerome both marvel that Ephrem's writings lost none of their beauty even in translation.[147]

(59) It is this very quantity and popularity of Ephrem's works, however, that has given rise to the considerable problems concerning his literary legacy. Ephrem wrote only in Syriac but translations were made, perhaps beginning even in his own lifetime, into nearly every language of the Christian world: Greek, Armenian, Latin, Arabic, Coptic, Ethiopic, Slavonic, Georgian, and Syro-Palestinian.[148] Of these, it is the Greek corpus which presents the greatest conundrum to scholars. The Greek works attributed to Ephrem are so numerous that even in the native Greek patristic tradition only the works of John Chrysostom exceed them. These Greek texts, which are primarily concerned with ascetical subjects, do not exist in Syriac, and are almost certainly not by Ephrem.[149] The origin of these works may perhaps be traced to disciples of Ephrem or to writers who somehow identified themselves with him. These Greek texts, and the ascetic circles out of which they came, have contributed in large part to the hagiographical picture of Ephrem in the Byzantine tradition, such as we find embodied in the *Encomium on Ephrem* attributed to Gregory of Nyssa.[150]

(60) With the exception of the Armenian corpus, nearly

---

146. See Azema, ed., *Théodoret de Cyr, Correspondance III, SC* 111 (Paris, 1965) 190. George Syncellus refers to Ephrem as "that tongue which pours forth like the ocean," A. Mosshammer, ed., *George Syncellus, Ecloga Chronographia* (Leipzig, 1984) 15.

147. Sozomen, *History of the Church* III.16; Jerome, *De Viris Inlustribus* 115.

148. See, especially, E. Beck, D. Hemmerdinger-Iliadou, and J. Kirchmeyer, "Ephrem le Syrien," in *DS*, 4:788–822; and other studies in bibliography, above.

149. See Geerard, *Clavis Patrum Graecorum*, 2:366–468; D. Hemmerdinger-Iliadou, "Ephrem grec et latin," in *DS*, 4:800–822; and A. de Halleux, "Ephrem le Syrien," *RTL* 14 (1983): 338–43.

150. St. Gregory of Nyssa, *De Vita S. Patris Ephraem Syri*. See discussion above. The author of this work was acquainted with many of the Greek texts attributed to Ephrem.

all of the texts that survive in languages other than Syriac can be traced back to this spurious Greek collection.[151] The Armenian corpus of works attributed to Ephrem constitutes an immense collection, comprising well over five volumes of edited text, with much still to be edited. Most of this Armenian corpus, consisting primarily of biblical commentaries and a small number of hymns, appears to be genuine.[152] Still, with the exception of the greater portion of the *Commentary on the Diatessaron* and small fragments of the *Hymns on Nicomedia*, no Syriac originals of these texts survive.

(61) The corpus of Ephrem's Syriac works has long existed in partial editions which were based on very faulty manuscripts. Due principally to the efforts of Dom Edmund Beck, begun in 1955, scholars now have available reliable critical texts of all Ephrem's genuine Syriac works.[153] Although there are complete translations in German and many in French, English translations of the works of Ephrem have, until recently, been much less numerous, and are scattered

151. J. Kirchmeyer, "Autres versions d'Ephrem," in *DS*, 4:819–22; and de Halleux, "Ephrem le Syrien," 338–43.

152. See the *Works of Saint Ephrem*, edited in four volumes by the Mechitarist Fathers in *Srobyn Ep'remi Matenagrut'iwnk'*. Ephrem's *Commentary on the Diatessaron* has been reedited by Dom L. Leloir. See L. Leloir, ed., *Saint Ephrem. Commentaire de l'évangile concordant, version arménienne*, CSCO 137, 145 (Louvain, 1953, 1954 [for the Syriac original, see idem, ed., *Saint Ephrem Commentaire de l'évangile concordant*, Chester Beatty Monographs, no. 8 (Dublin, 1963); idem, ed., *Saint Ephrem Commentaire de l'évangile concordant Texte Syriaque (Manuscrit Chester Beatty 709) Folios Additionnels*, Chester Beatty Monographs, no. 8 (Louvain, 1990)]. See also idem, trans., *Ephrem de Nisibe: Commentaire de l'Evangile Concordant ou Diatessaron*, SC 121 (Paris, 1966). To these volumes should be added L. Maries and C. Mercier, eds., *Hymnes de Saint Ephrem conservées en version arménienne*, PO 30.1 (Paris, 1961); C. Renoux, ed., *Ephrem de Nisibe Mêmrê sur Nicomédie*, PO 37.2–3 (Brepols, 1975), and several editions of short texts scattered in various journals. See also C. Renoux, "Vers le commentaire de Job d'Ephrem de Nisibe," *PdO* 6/7 (1975/76): 63–68; and E. G. Mathews, Jr., "The Armenian Version of Ephrem's Commentary on Genesis," *forthcoming*.

153. Each of these Syriac texts has an accompanying German translation. For list, see bibliography. For a review of the history of the editions of Ephrem's works, see J. Melki, "Saint Ephrem le Syrien, un bilan de l'édition critique," *PdO* 11 (1983): 3–88.

GENERAL INTRODUCTION 41

in journals not always accessible to the average reader.[154] The few collections of Ephrem's works that do exist in such series as *Library of Nicene and Post-Nicene Fathers*, are based on the unsatisfactory editions that existed prior to Beck's editions and are often so literal that one must have recourse to the original Syriac in order to decipher the English.[155]

(62) The genuine Syriac works of Ephrem fall into two basic categories: poetry and prose. The poetry, for which Ephrem was most famous, can be subdivided into *madrāše*, or hymns, and *mêmrê*, or metrical homilies.[156] The *madrāše*, which survive in a number of collections assembled by later compilers,[157] are varied in meter and are clearly a more proper vehicle for Ephrem's poetic genius. Utilizing more than 50 different syllable patterns, these *madrāše* comprise the greatest portion of Ephrem's genuine Syriac works. These *madrāše* have been edited under such headings as *On Faith, On Fasting, Against Heresies, On Virginity, On the Nativity, On the Church, On Paradise, Against Julian, On Nisibis, On Holy Week, On the Paschal Feast*, as well as the *Hymns on Abraham Kidunaya and Julian Saba*, which are of questionable authenticity.[158]

(63) The *mêmrâ*, composed of unvarying isosyllabic lines,

154. Many of these works can conveniently be found in Brock, *The Harp of the Spirit*, 87–88; see also bibliography, above.
155. "Selections Translated into English from the Hymns and Homilies of Ephraim the Syrian, and from the Demonstrations of Aphrahat the Persian Sage," in *LNPF*, 13:113–412. English translations of a selection of eighteen of Ephrem's hymns can be found in Brock, *The Harp of the Spirit*. The *Hymns On the Nativity, Hymns On Virginity* and the *Hymns against Julian*, have now appeared in McVey, *Ephrem the Syrian Hymns*. The *Hymns on Julian* have also been translated in Lieu, *The Emperor Julian*, 89–128. The fifteen *Hymns on Paradise*, perhaps Ephrem's most beautiful hymns, have now been translated in Brock, *Hymns on Paradise*. For Ephrem's *Hymns on the Pearl*, see E. G. Mathews, Jr., "St. Ephrem, *Madrāše On Faith*, 81–85: *Hymns on the Pearl*, I–V," *SVTQ* 38 (1994): 45–72.
156. E. Beck, "Ephräms des Syrers Hymnik," in *Liturgie und Dichtung*, ed. H. Becker and R. Kaczynski (St. Ottilien, 1983) 1:345–79.
157. See A. de Halleux, "Une clé pour les hymnes d'Ephrem dans le ms. Sinai syr. 10," *LM* 85 (1972): 171–99; idem, "La transmission des Hymnes d'Ephrem d'après le ms. Sinai syr. 10," in *OCA*, no. 197 (Rome, 1974) 21–63.
158. See the arguments of E. Beck in his accompanying translation volume.

was a favorite genre of many Syriac writers of the fifth–seventh centuries. Balai (d. c. 435) popularized a pattern of 5+5 syllables per line; Jacob of Sarug wrote in lines of 12+12 syllables. The 7+7 syllable pattern was known as the meter of Ephrem. While he no doubt wrote many such *mêmrê*, many that were written in this pattern came to be attributed to Ephrem; this is due perhaps to the stature of Ephrem and to his preeminent place in the history of Syriac literature, or simply to the ignorance or negligence of certain scribes. On the basis of Beck's editions and studies, though he edited six volumes of Syriac *mêmrê* attributed to Ephrem, very few can be held to be undoubtedly authentic.[159] As discussed above, the several ascetical *mêmrê*, whose authenticity Vööbus vigorously defended, have been shown to be of later origin.

(64) Ephrem's genuine Syriac prose works, with which this volume deals, can also be further subdivided into two groups: expository prose and rhetorical prose. The former category includes the *Commentaries on Genesis and Exodus*, Ephrem's famous *Commentary on the Diatessaron* (which survives in a complete version in Armenian only) and his *Prose Refutations of Mani, Marcion, and Bardaisan.*

(65) Ephrem was certainly a prolific commentator on the Bible. Both Syriac and Greek traditions remember Ephrem as having commented on all the books of the Bible. While the *Commentary on Genesis* is the only commentary to have been preserved in its entirety in Syriac, there is little doubt that Ephrem did in fact comment on most of the books of the Bible. Many of these commentaries survive in Armenian translation; there are also partial versions that survive in Syriac in fragments preserved in later Syriac commentaries and catenae.[160]

(66) In several of the works that purport to narrate the

---

159. See the remarks in Beck's editions of these *mêmrê*, *Sermones* I–IV, and also the warnings of S. P. Brock, "A Syriac Verse Homily on Elijah and the Widow of Sarepta," *LM* 102 (1989): 93, and especially, 98.

160. A partial list can be found in Ortiz de Urbina, *Patrologia Syriaca*, 61–64. See also T. J. Lamy, "L'exégèse en orient au IVe siècle ou les commentaires de Saint Ephrem," *RB* 2 (1893): 5–17. To date, these fragments have not undergone any critical study.

biography of Ephrem there appears the story of how Ephrem received a heavenly scroll from a choir of angels while he sat meditating in his cell on Mt. Edessa. In the Syriac *Life of Ephrem*, there immediately follows the fanciful account of how, on the very next morning after his reception of the scroll, Ephrem began "writing the commentary on the first book of Moses . . . and when he completed the first book, he began the second." When a fellow hermit showed these commentaries to the teachers in the Christian school of Edessa, they were "astounded and amazed at their teaching and wisdom."[161] Thus was Ephrem's renown as a biblical scholar and exegete remembered in later tradition.

(67) The *Life of Ephrem* refers to both the *Commentary on Genesis* and the *Commentary on Exodus* as *pušāqê*, although in the manuscript the two works are given different titles: Genesis is called a *pušāqâ*, "exposition" or "explanation," while Exodus is titled a *turgāmâ*, "interpretation" or "translation."[162] There seems to be nothing in either text, or in Ephrem's other writings, to suggest that he did not employ these two terms synonymously.[163]

(68) As both of the commentaries translated here bear witness, Ephrem's method of exegesis is not intended to provide a continuous, verse by verse, exposition of the biblical text. Rather, Ephrem dwells on texts that have a particular theological significance for him, or whose orthodox interpretation needs to be reasserted in the face of contemporary heterodox ideas. For example, the two accounts of creation together with the narrative concerning Adam and Eve in the garden occupy fully a third of the *Commentary on Genesis*. On the other hand, much of the Patriarchal nar-

---

161. Amar, "The Syriac *Vita* Tradition of Ephrem the Syrian," 102–3 (text), 238–39 (translation).
162. *Turgama* is cognate to the Hebrew term, *targum*, which designates the Aramaic translations—sometimes somewhat embellished—of the Hebrew Scriptures.
163. See, for example, E. A. Bevan and F. C. Burkitt, eds., *S. Ephraim's Prose Refutations of Mani, Marcion and Bardaisan* (London, 1921), 2:222.30–32, where the two terms are used interchangeably, and also the discussion in S. Hidal, *Interpretatio Syriaca* (Lund, 1974) 8–9.

ratives are treated summarily or not at all. In the *Commentary on Exodus* chapters 22 and 26–30 of Exodus are not treated at all and chapter 15, the Canticle of Moses, is merely paraphrased without comment.

(69) With respect to the other prose category, the rhetorical or artistic prose works are represented by only two compositions: The *Homily on Our Lord* and the *Letter to Publius*, both translated below. Although these two works are the only two surviving examples of this genre from Ephrem, other examples exist in early Syriac literature: in many of Aphrahat's *Demonstrations*, in parts of the *Acts of Thomas* and in sections of some of the *Acts of the Persian Martyrs*.[164]

(70) In the *Homily on Our Lord* and the *Letter to Publius* one finds elaborate rhetorical figures and stylistic devices joined with a Semitic love for both parallelism and paradox. With rhythmic cadences and elaborate chiastic structures, Ephrem succeeds in creating language and imagery nearly as striking as his poetry. Sebastian Brock provides a long list of passages which exemplify the stylistic features of the *Letter to Publius* together with short examples from the *Homily on Our Lord* and Aphrahat's *Demonstrations*. The following two samples, the first from the *Letter to Publius* and the second from the *Homily on Our Lord*, are taken from Brock's list:[165]

> lûqbal ḥewwārê 'akwatôn hāwyâ
> wəlûqbal 'ukkāmê badmûtôn ṣāḥmâ
> wəlûqbal sûmmāqê 'akwatôn sûmmāqâ
> wəlûqbal ṣappîrê 'akwatôn ṣāprâ
> wəlûqbal snî'ê 'akwatôn mkā'râ
>
> ṭaybûtâ qerbat ləpûmê məgaddpānê
> w'ebdat 'ennûn kinnārê məsabbḥānê
> meṭṭûl hānâ netlûn kûl pûmîn sûbḥâ
> ləhaw daklâ menhûn mêmar gûddāpâ

164. See R. Murray, "Some Rhetorical Patterns in Early Syriac Literature," in *A Tribute to Arthur Vööbus. Some Studies in Early Christian Literature and its Environment, Primarily in the Syrian East*, ed. Robert H. Fischer (Chicago, 1977) 109–31.

165. S. P. Brock, "Ephrem's Letter to Publius," *LM* 89 (1976): 263 (from *Letter*), and 264 (from *Homily on Our Lord*).

(71) Ephrem's writings show strong influence from both Jewish and his native Mesopotamian backgrounds.[166] In many of his hymns, especially in his *Hymns on Paradise,* Ephrem makes use of an haggadic style of interpretation and employs what undoubtedly were opinions of the Jewish community of his time.[167] From his native Mesopotamian tradition, Ephrem inherited important vocabulary items, such as *samm hayyê* ("medicine of life"), one of his terms for the Eucharist.[168] He also composed a number of dialogue poems, a genre of poetry that has been demonstrated to have early Mesopotamian origins.[169]

Theological Method

(72) Ephrem's renown as one of the world's preeminent religious poets is primarily due to the penetrating theological thought developed in his *madrāšē.*[170] It was as a poet that Ephrem himself saw his true vocation.[171] In his hymns Ephrem employs his favorite Semitic poetic devices with marvelous technical artistry and fashions a poetry that can at times be almost breathtaking.[172] Due to the nature of Ephrem's poetry, however, his theological method is not

---

166. See Brock, *The Luminous Eye,* 6–9.
167. See N. Sed, "Les hymnes sur le paradis de saint Ephrem et les traditions juives," *LM* 81 (1968): 455–501. We have also noted many parallels in the notes to our translations, below.
168. See *Homily on Our Lord,* 3, below and note *ad loc.*
169. See, especially, S. P. Brock, "The Dispute Poem: From Sumer to Syriac," *Bayn al-Nahrayn* 7 (1979): 417–26; idem, "Dialogue Hymns of the Syriac Churches," *Sobornost* 5 (1983): 35–45; and idem, "Dramatic Dialogue Poems," 135–47.
170. See, above all, E. Beck, *Die Theologie des hl. Ephräm in seinen Hymnen über den Glauben;* A. de Halleux, "Mar Ephrem théologien," *PdO* 4 (1973): 35–54; S. P. Brock, "The Poet as Theologian," *Sobornost* 7 (1977): 243–50; and T. Bou Mansour, *La pensée symbolique de Saint Ephrem le Syrien,* Bibliothèque de l'Université Saint-Esprit, no. 16 (Kaslik, 1988).
171. See *Hymns against Heresies* 56.10.
172. Ephrem gained his reputation on the basis of these lyrical hymns, yet the theological vision of Ephrem is by no means confined to the *madrāšē.* The artistic prose pieces translated below are representative of his method and con-

easily systematized. This is not to say that Ephrem had no system—much less that his thought was diffuse—it is only that his method does not conform well to standard Western models. Contrary to all that we associate with Western theology, Ephrem preferred to express his theology in poetry and, therefore, in images. Ephrem had the particular genius to comprehend that the vehicle of poetry was the least inaccurate way to describe the Christian mystery which is, as the term suggests, essentially beyond human understanding. To the thought of Ephrem, any theology which "constitutes itself into a system is always dangerous. It imprisons in the enclosed sphere of thought the reality to which it must open thought."[173] It is, therefore, extremely difficult to convey Ephrem's thought in short quotations from his work.[174] To appreciate Ephrem fully one must read extended selections of his writings very carefully; nevertheless some general characteristics of Ephrem's thought can be outlined in very broad strokes.[175]

(73) Ephrem's theological method consciously avoids the kind of "precision" that generally characterized contempo-

---

tain some of his most beautiful and sublime reflections. Although the commentaries tend to be literal exegesis of the text, parts of the *Commentary on the Diatessaron* reveal the same lyrical qualities found in the artistic prose pieces translated here.

173. This apt explication is borrowed from V. Lossky, *Orthodox Theology: An Introduction* (Crestwood, NY, 1978) 15. Many readers of Ephrem see this method as a revitalizing contrast to an ever increasing dogmatism—even legalism—in Western theology.

174. See I. H. Dalmais, "L'apport des églises syriennes à l'hymnographie chrétienne," *OS* 2 (1957): 251: "He who has the patience to follow the meandering courses will impregnate himself little by little with the mystery of faith which discloses itself in the discrete light of contemplation."

175. For general characteristics of Ephrem's poetry see Beck, "Ephräms Hymnik"; Brock, "The Poetic Artistry of St. Ephrem: an Analysis of H. Azym. III," 21–28; R. Murray, "The Theory of Symbolism in St. Ephrem's Theology," *PdO* 6/7 (1966–67): 1–20; P. Yousif, "La Croix de Jesus et la Paradis d'Eden dans la typologie biblique de Saint Ephrem," *PdO* 6/7 (1975–76): 29–48; idem, "Symbolisme Christologique dans la Bible et dans la Nature chez S. Ephrem de Nisibe," *PdO* 8 (1977–78): 5–66; Brock, *The Luminous Eye;* and Bou Mansour, *La pensée symbolique de Saint Ephrem le Syrien.*

rary theological inquiry informed by Hellenistic philosophical categories. His thought on a given subject remains fluid. It is perhaps for this reason that the theological writings of Ephrem continued to be used by Chalcedonians, Monophysites, and Nestorians alike. This fluidity has led some modern commentators to observe wryly that the distinct advantage of "doing theology" in Syriac lies in the fact that one's orthodoxy remains impenetrable.[176]

(74) Ephrem's emphasis on the obvious sense of the words of Scripture, and his treatment of the two economies of salvation and the two Adams places him in a position much closer to the Antiochian tradition of scriptural exegesis than to the Alexandrian which preferred the allegorical method.[177] Taking for granted the dynamic convergence of the Old and New Testaments, Ephrem shows his true genius by the way he draws out the full significance or the inner sense of the words and sets them in their typological context within the rest of the sacred text.[178] The bond that unites the two Testaments is so intimate that there is virtually no incident or detail in one which does not have its typological parallel in the other.[179]

---

176. See, for example, Brown, "The Rise and Function of the Holy Man in Late Antiquity," 92.

177. For a general overview of typology, see J. Daniélou, *Sacramentum Futuri. Études sur les origines de la typologie biblique*, Études de théologie historique (Paris, 1950); in English translation, idem, *From Shadows to Reality* (Westminster, MD, 1960).

178. For typology in Ephrem, see Leloir, *Doctrines et méthodes de S. Ephrem,* especially, 40–52; idem, "Symbolisme et parallelisme chez Ephrem," in *À la rencontre de Dieu. Memorial Albert Gelin* (Lyon, 1961) 363–74; idem, "La Christologie de S. Ephrem dans son Commentaire du Diatessaron," *HA* 75 (1961): 449–66; C. Bravo, *Notas introductorias a la noemática de San Efrén* (Rome, 1956); and Murray, *Symbols, passim.*

179. This position of Ephrem's is too integral to his method simply to say that he held it in opposition to Marcion. Nowhere in his writings does Ephrem show any concern for Marcion's amputated biblical canon. See F. C. Burkitt, "Introductory Essay," in *S. Ephraim's Prose Refutations of Mani, Marcion, and Bardaisan,* ed. E. A. Bevan and F. C. Burkitt, 2:cxvii; and H. J. W. Drijvers, "Marcionism in Syria: Principles, Problems, Polemics," *The Second Century* 8 (1987–88): 167.

(75) While Ephrem would accept many more biblical passages as historical than would the modern biblical exegete, he cannot at all be labelled a fundamentalist. In fact, Ephrem himself chides those who interpret Scripture in a rigid, literal fashion.[180] On the other hand, Ephrem recognized the symbolic nature of biblical discourse without having to turn to the allegorism of the Alexandrian school.

(76) Perhaps no other writer has ever made such creative use of typology. Nevertheless, to treat Ephrem's theology as merely typological would be a gross misrepresentation of his thought. His theological method, often labelled symbolic theology, is an intricate weave of parallelism, typology, names and symbols. In the creative application of these tools, Ephrem displays a genius admirably suited to express the various paradoxes of the Christian mystery. The formulation of Ephrem's theology clearly manifests his conception of the grand harmony that exists between God and all His creation. Types (in Syriac *tūpsê*, in Greek τύποι) and symbols (in Syriac *râzê*, in Greek σύμβολα)[181] can be found throughout all creation simply by reason of the fact that the world was created by God; they point both to His existence and to His activity as Creator.

(77) For Ephrem the Bible stands as part of this world and its history, but is, at the same time, the interpreter of the world's history. The types found in Scripture and the symbols found in nature all direct one to the truth (in Syriac *šrārâ*):

> In his book Moses
> described the creation of the natural world
> so that both nature and Scripture
> might bear witness to the Creator:
> nature, through man's use of it,

---

180. See, for example, *Hymns on Faith* 31.1, *Hymns on Paradise* 11.6–7, and *Commentary on the Diatessaron*, 22.3.

181. These Greek terms are only the most common parallels to the Syriac terms, they are in no way exact correspondences. For a discussion of these and other terms that Ephrem employs, see Bou Mansour, *La pensée symbolique*, 23–71.

Scripture, through his reading of it.
These are the witnesses
which reach everywhere,
they are to be found at all times,
present at every hour
confuting the unbeliever
who defames the Creator.[182]

In his *Hymns on Virginity*, Ephrem says more concisely: "Wherever you look, God's symbol is there; wherever you read, there you will find His types. For by Him all creatures were created, and He stamped all his possessions with His symbols when He created the world."[183] It is by the very reason that God created the world that these types and symbols can be found everywhere; they are pointers to His existence and to His creative activity.

(78) Another fundamental position of Ephrem's theology is his insistence on the unity of God and the absolute and unbridgeable gap between God and creature. God is the only true self-subsistent being (in Syriac, '*ituta*) and it is He who created all else that exists. Ephrem maintains this very rigid *creatio ex nihilo* position against Bardaisan and his followers, who claim that there are five eternal substances (in Syriac, '*ityê*) and against the Marcionites and the Manicheans, both of whom follow a teaching that all things come from *hūlê*, or eternal primal matter. Ephrem argues that the '*ityê* of Bardaisan and the *hūlê* of Mani and Marcion are nothing more than elements or created natures (in Syriac, *kyānê*), created by the sole Being who created all that is not Himself.[184]

(79) As noted above, Ephrem's method deliberately eschews any definition of the divine nature. Ephrem considers any attempt to define God as a setting of limits on that which is limitless, as confining that which cannot be con-

---

182. *Hymns on Paradise* 5.2. Translation by Brock, *Hymns on Paradise*, 102–3.
183. *Hymns on Virginity* 20.12. See also 6.7: "Creation gives birth to the symbols of Christ, as Mary gave birth to His limbs."
184. See *Hymns against Heresies* 14.7–10, and *passim*, and *Commentary on Genesis*, I.2, below, and notes *ad loc.*

fined. As one might expect, Ephrem's arguments for what can and cannot be said about God are nearly always formulated in apologetic contexts. Ephrem was continually defending the Christian faith against many heterodox teachings, but primarily against the teachings of Mani, Bardaisan, Marcion, and the Arians.[185]

(80) The challenge posed by Arian speculation on the Godhead caused Ephrem to insist even more vigorously on the absolute incomprehensibility of God, who is Creator, Eternal, and Spirit. No creature who is subject to time and corporeality can know anything of God in Himself. For a creature to presume to know that which is beyond the limited capacity of its nature to know is not only futile but blasphemous. The divine nature is completely incomprehensible to the human mind and should not be "pried into."[186] Those who engage in such intellectual "prying" or "investigating" show that they have "ceased to believe," that they have "renounced their faith and annulled their baptism."[187] Ephrem further says that these "priers" and "investigators" have succeeded the idolaters as the latest offensive of Satan.[188] He also accuses them of blindness, presumption, mental inflexibility, literalism and an inability to distinguish levels of discourse. Their rational scrutiny and argument lead only to disputes and quarrels, forcing great

---

185. See, especially, Ephrem's *Hymns against Heresies, Prose Refutations* and his *Hymns on Faith*. In *Hymns against Heresies*, 22.2–4, Ephrem enumerates also the Paulinians, Sabellians, Photinians, Borborians, Cathars, Audiens, and Messalians as enemies of the Nicean, Christian faith. See also Beck, *Die Theologie*, and idem, *Ephräms Polemik gegen Mani und die Manichäer im Rahmen der zeitgenössischen griechischen Polemik und der des Augustinus*, CSCO 391 (Louvain, 1978).

186. This word (in Syriac *bʿātâ*) is one of several terms that Ephrem employs, particularly in his *Hymns on Faith*, in a very pejorative sense, specifically to describe the Arian intellectual endeavor. The other most common terms Ephrem uses are: *bsātâ*, *ʿuqqābâ* and *drāšâ* —"search into," "investigate," and "dispute." For Ephrem and the Arians, see Beck, *Die Theologie*, and P. Bruns, "*Arius hellenizans?*—Ephräm der Syrer und die neoarianischen Kontroversen seiner Zeit," *ZKG* 101 (1990/91): 21–57.

187. See, for example, *Hymns on Faith* 9.10, 23.2.

188. See *Hymns on Virginity* 13.9, 14.2–3.

breaches of charity and bringing division into the body of Christ.[189]

(81) Ephrem is very insistent that only what God Himself has chosen to reveal to humanity (in Syriac, *galyātâ*) can now be an object of consideration by the human intellect—although still not to be defined, for these revelations remain only partial. Moreover, those things that God has not revealed but has kept hidden (in Syriac, *kasyātâ*), most particularly those things pertaining to His own nature, to the generation of the Son, and to the Holy Spirit, cannot be subjected to any human intellectual scrutiny.[190]

(82) God Himself, in His great goodness and love for humanity, chose to cross that ontological chasm which separates Him from His creation in order to reveal something of Himself. He left His perfect silence, as it were, to speak to humanity. Ephrem speaks of three primary means by which God chose to reveal Himself, all of which he refers to as "changes" (in Syriac, *šuḥlāpê*).[191] Ephrem is very careful to emphasize that none of these "changes" that God takes on nor the names by which He accepts to manifest Himself affects His essential nature in any way. God has willed to undergo these "changes" out of love for humanity and His awareness of human weakness. These "changes" served to dim the divine brightness for the sake of humanity, but God Himself loses absolutely nothing of His nature or His majesty. The first of these three means are the types and the symbols found in Scripture and in nature, discussed above. God has also allowed Himself to be called by certain names in the Scriptures, such as Creator, Father, Healer,

---

189. See, especially his *Hymns on Faith* and *Prose Refutations*, *passim*, and discussion in de Halleux, "Mar Ephrem Théologien."

190. *Hymns on Faith* 44.7: "If God had not wished to reveal Himself to us there would have been nothing in creation that would be able to say anything at all about Him." See also 19.7 and 51.2–3, and G. Noujaim, "Anthropologie et économie de salut chez S. Ephrem: autour des notions de ghalyâtâ, kasyātâ et kasyâ," *PdO* 9 (1979/80) 313–15.

191. See, especially, *Hymns on Virginity* 28.11, *Hymns on Faith* 5.7, 11.9, 31.5, and *Hymns on Paradise* 11.6–7.

etc.; these provide humanity with a certain revelation of God.[192]

(83) The greatest "change" to God was, of course, His taking on human flesh (in Syriac, *lbes̆ basrâ*).[193] This is the central mystery of the faith and the heart and pinnacle of God's revelation to humanity. Ephrem often marvels at the awesome paradox of God having condescended to take on human flesh. In one of his *madrāsē*, he says:

> Your mother is a cause for wonder: the Lord entered her
> and became a servant; He who is the Word entered
> —and became silent within her; thunder entered her
> —and made no sound; there entered the Shepherd of all,
> and in her He became the lamb, bleating as He came forth.
>
> Your mother's womb has reversed the roles:
> the Establisher of all entered in His richness,
> but came forth poor; the Exalted One entered her,
> but came forth meek; the Splendrous One entered her,
> but came forth having put on a lowly hue.
>
> The Mighty One entered, and put on insecurity
> from her womb; the Provisioner of all entered
> —and experienced hunger; He who gives drink to all entered
> —and experienced thirst: naked and stripped
> there came forth from her He who clothes all.[194]

It is here, in his theology of the Incarnation, that Ephrem demonstrates his greatest genius. He develops and refines a typology and a symbolism to such a degree that together they become a unique vehicle for proclaiming this Good

---

192. For a treatment of some of those names that apply to Jesus, see I. Hausherr, "La philosophie du nom chez Ephrem," in idem, *Noms du Christ et voies d'oraison, OCA*, no. 157 (Rome, 1960) 64–72; and Murray, *Symbols*, 159–204, especially 166–70.

193. The Syriac expression means literally, "to put on/clothe oneself in flesh." Ephrem develops this especially in *Hymns on Faith* 31.4, 32.8–13; *Hymns against Heresies* 30.4. See also S. P. Brock, "Clothing Metaphors as a Means of Theological Expression in Syriac Tradition," in *Typus, Symbol, Allegorie bei den östlichen Vätern und ihren Parallelen im Mittelalter*, ed. M. Schmidt (Eichstatt, 1981) 11–40.

194. *Hymns on the Nativity* 11.6–8. Translation from Brock, *The Luminous Eye*, 12.

News. Symbols and types, from both nature and Scripture, now operate for Ephrem on two distinct planes: the horizontal, between the Old and New Testaments, and the vertical, between this world and Paradise.[195] All these types and symbols find their fulfillment in Christ, the one who reveals their true meaning, whom Ephrem often calls "the Lord of the Symbols."[196] Nature and the two Testaments constitute three harps on which the Divine Musician plays.[197] In the vision of Ephrem these symbols are so plentiful that they can hardly be grasped for their multitude. In one place Ephrem, overcome with the quantity of these types and symbols, says in mock despair: "This Jesus has so multiplied His symbols that I have fallen into their many waves."[198] To list all the symbols that Ephrem uses or to treat any in detail would be beyond the limited scope of this brief introduction.[199] A few examples of Ephrem's use of symbol, however, should indicate something of the complexity of images that he is able to evoke.

(84) Ephrem's development of the theme of the new Adam and the new Eve leads him to some very interesting observations. For instance, Ephrem speaks of the Incarnation occurring when the Word entered into the ear of Mary as an antidote to the poison that the serpent had put into the ear of Eve. The word of life that Mary heard and accepted undid the word of death that Eve had previously heard and accepted.[200]

195. Murray, "The Theory of Symbolism."
196. This title occurs, among other places, in *Hymns on Faith* 9.11, *Commentary on the Diatessaron* 1.1, *Hymns on Virginity* 6.7, and in the refrain to *Hymns on Unleavened Bread* 3.
197. This theme occupies Ephrem in his *Hymns on Virginity* 27–30. See translations in McVey, *Ephrem the Syrian Hymns*, 382–97.
198. *Hymns on Nisibis* 39.17.
199. While he shares some images with other writers, Western as well as Eastern, Ephrem is without parallel among the Fathers in the broad range of symbols he employs. See Bou Mansour, *La pensée symbolique*. For a briefer, less technical, discussion of some of Ephrem's favorite images, see Brock, *The Luminous Eye*, 37–91.
200. See *Hymns on the Church* 49.7. See also R. Murray, "Mary, the Second Eve, in the Syrian Fathers," *ECR* 3 (1971): 372–84; and E. Beck, "Die Mariologie der echten Schriftum des Ephraems," *OC* 40 (1956): 29–34.

(85) Ephrem views the scene of Christ on the cross in a similar vein. At the very moment Christ was pierced with the lance there were removed from the Garden of Eden the cherub that had been placed there and the sword that he had wielded to prohibit anyone's reentry. It was at that moment that access into Paradise became possible once again for humanity.[201]

(86) Ephrem develops an elaborate exegesis of the garments of the old and new Adam. When Adam and Eve were banished from Paradise, they lost the garment of glory with which they had been clothed, but the new Adam restored that garment: "Blessed is He who took pity on the leaves of Adam and sent down a garment of glory to cover his nakedness."[202] This same fact is also indicated by the Gospel account that Christ abandoned His garments in the sepulchre upon His resurrection. Humanity will now be reclothed in the garment of glory that it had before the sin of Adam and Eve.[203] This reclothing of humanity also presents to Ephrem the only comprehensible solution to the problematic Gospel passage where Jesus curses the fig tree causing it to wither. To the thought of Ephrem, Jesus is rather showing His disciples that fig leaves will no longer be needed as humanity will be reclothed in glory.[204]

(87) Perhaps Ephrem's favorite and best known image is that of the pearl. In five of his *Hymns on Faith*, Ephrem "picked up a pearl . . . , [and] it became a fountain and from it [he] drank of the mysteries of the Son."[205] As he turned the pearl over in his hands it took on different hues.

---

201. See R. Murray, "The Lance Which Reopened Paradise," *OCP* 39 (1973): 224–34.
202. *Hymns on Fasting* 3.2.
203. See Brock, *The Luminous Eye*, 65–76.
204. *Commentary on the Diatessaron* 16.10. See S. P. Brock, *The Holy Spirit in the Syrian Baptismal Tradition*, The Syrian Churches Series, vol. 9 (Poona, 1979) 48–52.
205. *Hymns on Faith* 81.1. A French translation of all five of these beautiful hymns can be found in F. Graffin, "Les hymnes sur la perle de Saint Ephrem," *OS* 12 (1967): 129–49. A new English translation is found in Mathews, "St. Ephrem, *Madrāšē On Faith*."

Likewise, as Ephrem considered the Incarnation from different angles, he saw different and more profound facets to the meaning of the Incarnation.

(88) Another favorite image of Ephrem is the mirror.[206] The Gospel, with its proclamations and demands, is a mirror in which we can see ourselves as we truly are. In the *Letter to Publius* (see translation below), Ephrem develops that image to very profitable lengths; in the mirror, as an image of the Gospel, one can see with unsettling clarity the final destiny of those who have died. Ephrem also finds fruitful sources of contemplation in the olive tree and its various properties and products;[207] even the milk congealed into yogurt by a housewife symbolizes to Ephrem faith and its power to bring stability to the ever fickle human mind and heart.[208] Other images that he uses to great advantage are those related to clothing, medicine, and to conception and giving birth.

(89) The entire aim of Ephrem's poetry is not to explain the system of the universe nor to impose any rigid ideas of his own about the Christian message on others, but rather to give birth in God's creatures to that true worship of the Creator of all, to instill a desire to live the mystery of God's love toward humanity. Types and symbols are but a simple invitation to the one who perceives them to participate in the divine life offered to all; they are not proof texts to coerce the unbeliever. Grace is never forceful.[209] The believer should follow the Apostles and Prophets, who serve as the inns and milestones on the path of life, to seek the inner sense of Scripture.[210]

(90) The resultant growth in faith clears the eye of the seeker to see more symbols and to see them more clearly. As

---

206. See E. Beck, "Das Bild vom Spiegel bei Ephräm," *OCP* 19 (1953): 5–24.

207. See *Hymns on Virginity* 4–7.

208. See *Hymns on Faith* 5.20.

209. See *Hymns on Nisibis* 16.6.

210. See E. Beck, "Das Bild vom Weg mit Meilensteinen und Herbergen bei Ephraem," *OC* 65 (1981): 1–39.

light is necessary for sight, so is faith necessary for recognition of God's symbols. Faith thus leads one to a more profound sense of God's activity on behalf of humanity. This deeper sense of the divine economy engenders a wonder and awe before the goodness of God, and it is this awe that leads one to the only proper activity of a human being, which is to give praise. For Ephrem, the pinnacle of human activity is to live with God in an engagement of love and wonder which, all the while, leads one to render Him praise.

(91) As one prominent contemporary theologian and Syriacist states, "It is truly marvelous to us that such thought, so ingrained in its own time, so conditioned by an intellectual horizon that is today considered out-of-date, continues to speak with a voice so fresh and so contemporary. Perhaps, it is because one encounters the Eternal only in the concrete of the present moment and not in the abstractions of times long past."[211] It is no doubt for this reason that Ephrem has recently been recovered from the obscurity in which he had been cast for far too long.

211. de Halleux, "Mar Ephrem théologien," 38. See also L. Leloir, "L'actualité du message d'Ephrem," *PdO* 4 (1973): 55–72.

COMMENTARY ON GENESIS

INTRODUCTION

Ephrem's *Commentary on Genesis* stands at the head of a long history of Syriac literature that finds its source in this first book of the Bible. This literature comprises other narrative commentaries, several treatises in question and answer format, as well as numerous poetic treatments, by such figures as Narsai and Jacob of Sarug, that have themes from Genesis as their subject, e.g., Paradise, the Fall, Cain and Abel, etc. Ephrem's *Commentary* also serves as the starting point of a Syriac Hexaemeral tradition that includes such figures as Jacob of Sarug, Jacob of Edessa, Moshe bar Kêphâ and Emmanuel bar Shaharrê.[1]

(2) The book of Genesis was a book to which Ephrem returned on more than one occasion. He drank from that source not only here and in his *Hymns on Paradise*, but throughout his hymns. Ephrem found that "the book of creation is the treasure house of the Ark, the crown of the Law."[2] Genesis was such a treasure store to Ephrem that in the prologue to his *Commentary on Genesis*, he claims that he "had not wanted to write a commentary on the first book of Creation, lest we should now repeat what we had set down in the *madrāšē* and in the *mêmrê*. Nevertheless, compelled by the love of friends, we have written briefly on those things of which we wrote at length in the *madrāšē* and in the *mêmrê*."[3] If this prologue is genuine, this would most probably place the composition of the *Commentary on Genesis* during the short time at the end of his life when he dwelt in Edessa. Whether this be true or not, the account preserved in the

1. For a concise overview, see E. Ten Napel, "Some Remarks on the Hexaemeral Literature in Syriac," in *OCA*, no. 229 (Rome, 1987) 57–69.
2. *Hymns on Paradise* 6.1. Translation in Brock, *Hymns on Paradise*, 109.
3. *Commentary on Genesis*, Prologue 1.

Syriac *Life of Ephrem* that Ephrem wrote the *Commentary* while a hermit in the mountains outside of Edessa is completely anachronistic.[4]

(3) As this prologue indicates, Ephrem, on the whole, does not deal with the text in such depth, or in the same ways, as he did in his hymns. Throughout the entire *Commentary on Genesis*, Ephrem rarely engages in the typological or symbolic exegesis that so characterizes his hymns. Most of the *Commentary* is a close literal reading of the text. In fact, much of that portion of the *Commentary* that treats the text subsequent to Genesis 4 is simply a paraphrasing of the biblical text. The entire first half of the *Commentary on Genesis* is devoted to only three pericopes: the six days of creation; the fall of Adam and Eve; and the flood that occurred in the days of Noah.

(4) In independent studies, T. Jansma and A. Guillaumont have shown that Ephrem's entire account of the six days of creation, on the surface a very literal commentary, is a polemic aimed primarily against the teachings of Bardaisan.[5] Ephrem's polemic is centered on his position that God is a) the only self-subsistent being and b) the creator of everything else. To take any other position would, in Ephrem's view, be to make God an "arranger" and not "the Creator." This is the very teaching that Moses[6] had set down, "to set right once more those things that had become confused in Moses' generation, lest this evil tradition (i.e. considering created things to be gods) be transmitted through-

---

4. This account of the composition of the *Commentary on Genesis* is used by the two longer recensions, MS. Vat. 117, and MS. Par. 235, to explain the vision of the vine found in the *Apophthegmata Patrum*. See Amar, "The Syriac *Vita* Tradition of Ephrem the Syrian," 102–3 (text), 238–39 (translation) and introduction, above.

5. See T. Jansma, "Ephraems Beschreibung des ersten Tages der Schöpfung," *OCP* 37 (1971): 300–305; and A. Guillaumont, "Genèse 1,1–2 selon les commentateurs syriaques," in *IN PRINCIPIO: Interprétations des premiers versets de la Genèse, EA*, no. 152 (Paris, 1973) 115–32. This important observation also goes a long way toward explaining the disproportional time that Ephrem spends on the "primeval history" account.

6. See *Hymns against Heresies*, 48.2.

out the entire world."⁷ The distinction between Creator and creature was infinite and could not be traversed without committing blasphemy.⁸

(5) Bardaisan who, according to Ephrem, composed 150 hymns as did David,⁹ taught that there were five eternal principles (in Syriac, '*ityê*)¹⁰ each in its own region: light in the East, wind in the West, fire in the South, water in the North, while darkness inhabited the lower regions. The Lord of all (another '*ityâ*) occupied the region above. Due to some sort of mingling of these eternal elements chaos ensued, and from the mixture of the elements the Lord of all made the world and set it into order.¹¹

(6) While there is now little doubt that Ephrem is dealing here with the false teachings of Bardaisan, Ephrem's polemic extends also to the teachings of Marcion and Mani against all of whom Ephrem was engaged in constant battle.¹² The teaching of all three of Ephrem's primary protagonists contained the idea, in one form or another, that the world was fashioned out of various preexistent substances. Ephrem in several places calls Bardaisan the teacher of Mani, particularly vis-à-vis his cosmology. "Because Mani was unable to find another way out, he entered, though unwill-

7. *Commentary on Genesis*, Prologue, 2.
8. See *Prose Refutations* II, 219 (text), civ (translation); and T. Kronholm, *Motifs from Genesis 1–11 in the Genuine Hymns of Ephrem the Syrian*, Coniectanea Biblica Old Testament Series, no. 11 (Uppsala, 1978) 35–39.
9. See *Hymns against Heresies*, 53.6.
10. See *Commentary on Genesis* 1. 2, and note *ad loc.*, below, for a discussion of this term.
11. See *Hymns against Heresies*, 3.4, 41.7, and *Prose Refutations, passim*. For Bardaisan's myth, see Drijvers, *Bardaisan of Edessa*, 96–126, for Ephrem's treatment of Bardaisan, 133–43. See also E. Beck, "Bardaisan und Seine Schule bei Ephräm," *LM* 91 (1978): 271–333, especially 271–88; B. Ehlers, "Bardesanes—ein Syrische Gnostiker," *ZKG* 81 (1970): 334–51; studies XI–XIII in Drijvers, *East of Antioch. Studies in Early Syriac Christianity;* H. Kruse, "Die 'mythologischen Irrtümer' Bar-Daiṣāns," *OC* 71 (1987): 24–52; and most recently, though not most reliably, J. Teixidor, *Bardesane d'Edesse: La première philosophie syriaque* (Paris, 1992).
12. See, especially, *Hymns against Heresies* and *Prose Refutations I and II*, and references below.

ingly, by the door which Bardaisan opened."[13] To Ephrem, Mani was the "quintessence of heresy."[14] Mani's cosmology also included the eternal *hylē*, introduced first by Marcion "the first thorn, the firstborn of the briar of sin, the weed earliest to grow."[15] Apparently, both Bardaisan and Mani had to allegorize the biblical account of the creation to make it accord with their respective cosmologies.[16]

(7) From an exegetical viewpoint Ephrem, in his *Commentary on Genesis,* offers interpretations of many passages that are otherwise attested only, or primarily, in Jewish traditions. Particularly in Nisibis, Ephrem was engaged in heated debate with the Jews and it would be most unlikely that he had no more than a simple passing acquaintance with a Jewish tradition of exegesis. However, because of the nature of their sources, problems of dating the texts, etc., one cannot always pinpoint a precise source, but the parallels are too numerous to be dismissed.[17] In certain places in the *Commen-*

13. C. W. Mitchell, ed., *S. Ephraim's Prose Refutations of Mani, Marcion and Bardaisan* (London, 1912) 1:122 (text), xc (translation).

14. *Hymns against Heresies* 22.13–22, 41.8, 51.14. See also *Prose Refutations* I.9. For Mani's intricate cosmological myth see S. N. C. Lieu, *Manichaeism in the Later Roman Empire and Medieval China,* 2d ed. (Tübingen, 1992) 7–32. See also Beck, *Ephräms Polemik gegen Mani und die Manichäer;* D. Bundy, "Ephrem's Critique of Mani: The Limits of Knowledge and the Nature of Language," in *Gnosticisme et Monde Hellénistique. Actes du Colloque de Louvain-la-Neuve (11–14 mars 1980),* ed. J. Ries, et al., Publications de l'Institut Orientaliste de Louvain, no. 27 (Louvain-la-Neuve, 1982) 289–98; and idem, "Language and the Knowledge of God in Ephrem Syrus," 91–103.

15. *Hymns against Heresies* 22.17. For Marcion, see A. von Harnack, *Marcion: Das Evangelium vom Fremden Gott, TU,* no. 45 (Leipzig, 1924); E. C. Blackmann, *Marcion and His Influence* (London, 1948); R. J. Hoffman, *Marcion: On the Restitution of Christianity,* AAR Academy Series, no. 46 (Chico, California, 1984). See also E. Beck, "Die Hyle bei Markion nach Ephräm," *OCP* 44 (1978): 5–30; and D. Bundy, "Marcion and the Marcionites in Early Syriac Apologetics," *LM* 101 (1988): 21–32.

16. See H. J. W. Drijvers, "Mani und Bardaisan. Ein Beitrag zur Vorgeschichte des Manichäismus" in *East of Antioch,* and idem, "Edessa und das Jüdische Christentum, *VC* 24 (1970): 32–33. See also *Commentary on Genesis* I.1, below, where Ephrem strongly insists at the outset that there is nothing allegorical to be found in the first verse of Genesis.

17. For general studies of the Jewish background of Ephrem's method of

tary, Ephrem is reading a text that preserves Targumic traditions against the reading of the Peshitta version, the Syriac *textus receptus*.[18] In the notes to our translation, we have made many references to Jewish sources, particularly to those found in Louis Ginzberg, *The Legends of the Jews*. These should be taken simply as parallels *not* as indicating Ephrem's source. The primary purpose of these references are to highlight, by means of a readily available resource, the Jewish—and not Hellenistic—milieu out of which Ephrem wrote.[19] The attentive reader will also quickly note that Ephrem's very method of exegesis is much more close to Jewish Haggadah than to the more familiar exegesis of Western Christianity.

(8) The text of the *Commentary on Genesis* was published on the basis of a single manuscript: MS. Vat. Syr. 110, dated to the sixth century.[20] The text was first edited by Peter Mobarek, S.J., with Latin translation, in the great Roman edition of Ephrem's works.[21] In 1955, R. M. Tonneau, O.P.,

---

exegesis, see D. Gerson, "Die Commentarien des Ephraem Syrus im Verhältnis zur jüdischen Exegese: ein Beitrag zur Geschichte der Exegese," *MGWJ* 17 (1868): 15–33, 64–72, 98–109, 141–49; R. Tonneau, "Moïse dans la tradition Syrienne," in *Moïse, l'homme de l'Alliance* (Paris, 1955) 242–54; A. Guillaumont, "Un midrash d'Exode 4,24–26 dans Aphraate et Ephrem de Nisibe," in *A Tribute to Arthur Vööbus*, ed. R. Fischer, 109–31; Kronholm, *Motifs;* S. P. Brock, "Jewish Traditions in Syriac Sources," *JJS* 30 (1979); and P. Féghali, "Influence des Targums sur la pensée exégètique d'Ephrem?" in *OCA*, no. 229 (Rome, 1984) 71–82. A concise summary of the difficulties of detecting Ephrem's sources, albeit written with respect to his hymns, can be found in Sed, "Les hymnes sur le paradis de saint Ephrem," 455–501: "En général, les attaches judaiques des symboles d'Ephrem sont évidentes. La présence d'un ensemble de faits convergents constitue ici un indice probant. Cependant, nous ne trouvons jamais d'emprunts matériels, copies serviles de formules ou de sentences rabbiniques," 456.

18. See notes to translation below. See also Brock, "Jewish Traditions in Syriac Sources," 219; and Féghali, "Influence des Targums," 71–82.

19. A detailed study of the Jewish background of Ephrem's *Commentary on Genesis*, is being undertaken by the present translator.

20. This manuscript comes from the famous monastery of Our Lady of the Syrians in Egypt. See S. E. and J. S. Assemani, *Bibliothecae Apostolicae Vaticanae Codicorum manuscriptorumque Catalogus* (Rome, 1769) 1:3, 76.

21. J. S. Assemani, ed., *Sancti Patris Nostri Ephraem Syri Opera Omnia*

published a more reliable text based on the same manuscript together with a new Latin translation.[22] Subsequent to the publication of Tonneau's text, T. Jansma has published several articles with corrections and suggested emendations to both the text and translation of Tonneau.[23]

(9) Most modern scholars accept the *Commentary* as genuine Ephrem. P. Féghali, however, has made the claim that this text has the flavor of "'notes prises' ou d'une tradition qui demeura orale avant d'être consignée par écrit."[24] The text seems rather to be quite tightly written with an organized general purpose throughout. The text sustains the polemic against the heresies of Marcion, Bardaisan, and Mani into Section II on the Fall of Adam and Eve. Refutations of these figures were genuine ongoing concerns of Ephrem and such a sustained polemic would be unlikely in a collection of later notes. We have also attempted, throughout our translation of the *Commentary*, to make reference to Ephrem's hymns where he manifests similar exegesis and/or concerns. The large number of concurrences and the style argue for authenticity. On the basis of all these considerations, therefore, it is difficult to accept these remarks of Féghali.

(10) More recently, David Bundy has noted the discrepancy between this *Commentary* as found in MS. Vat. Syr. 110 and an early Armenian version, long thought to be simply a translation of the published Syriac text.[25] Bundy is quite

---

1:1–115. This six volume edition of Ephrem's works also contains three *madrāšē* on Genesis (2:316–29), but they cannot be by Ephrem.

22. R. M. Tonneau, *Sancti Ephraem Syri in Genesim et in Exodum Commentarii*, *CSCO* 152 (Louvain, 1955) 3–121.

23. Jansma, "Ephraems Beschreibung," 309–16; idem, "Beiträge zur Berichtigung einzelner Stellen in Ephraems Genesiskommentar," *OC* 56 (1972): 59–79; and idem, "Weitere Beiträge zur Berichtigung einzelner Stellen in Ephraems Kommentäre zu Genesis und Exodus," *OC* 58 (1974): 121–31.

24. Féghali, "Influence des Targums," 72. See also his "Notes sur l'exégèse de S. Ephrem; commentaire sur le deluge (Gen. 6,1–9,17)," *PdO* 8 (1977/78): 67–70.

25. D. Bundy, "Ephrem's Exegesis of Isaiah," in *SP* 18.4 (Kalamazoo/Leuven, 1990) 235–36 (he lists here all the scholars who hold the text as

right to point this out; the Armenian version, for all intents and purposes heretofore overlooked, is a different commentary.[26] The pervasive Judaic background underlying the Syriac *Commentary* also argues in favor of Ephrem's authorship. Syria underwent substantial Hellenization after the death of Ephrem and it is unlikely a later commentary would not reflect that movement. These factors, coupled with those observations noted above in regard to the comments of Féghali, preclude Bundy's too hasty, in the opinion of this translator, conclusion that this Syriac text is spurious.[27] Until further study has been done on the Armenian and the other Syriac versions, however, judgment must wait.[28]

(11) Outside of the very periphrastic Latin version of Mobarek and the more recent Latin translation of Tonneau, complete translations of Ephrem's *Commentary on Genesis* exist only in Spanish and Dutch.[29] Apart from these, only short excerpts have been translated into modern languages:

---

genuine). Bundy also notes here that certain other manuscripts, still unedited, contain Syriac texts of a *Commentary on Genesis*, attributed to Ephrem, which diverge from the Syriac text as found in MS. Vat. Syr. 110. An Arabic version, similar to these unedited Syriac versions, is edited in J. Tabet, *Tafsir li-sifr al takwin* (Kaslik, 1982). For further comments on this text, see P. Féghali, "Un commentaire de la Genèse attribué à saint Ephrem," in *Actes du deuxième Congrès international d'études arabes chrétiennes*, ed. K. Samir, S. J., OCA 226 (Rome, 1986) 159–75.

26. The position of G. Zarp'analean, *Matenadaran haykakan t'argmanut'eanc' naxneac'* [*Catalogue of Ancient Armenian Translations*] (Venice, 1889) 444, that the Armenian version is based on a Syriac epitome, which he claims Ephrem himself was wont to do with his works, is completely untenable; the work is in no way a simple epitome and there exists no source that tells of Ephrem's epitomizing his own works.

27. Féghali, "Un commentaire de la Genèse attribué à saint Ephrem," 159–75, demonstrates that the Arabic version, to which Bundy makes appeal, is rather a work of Cyril of Alexandria.

28. The only edited text of the Armenian version, based on a single manuscript, is found in the *Srobyn Ep'remi Matenagrut'iwnk'* (Venice, 1836) 1:1–131. A new edition of the Armenian *Commentary on Genesis* attributed to Ephrem with a translation and a study of its relationship to all the extant oriental versions claiming to be Ephrem's *Commentary on Genesis* is being undertaken by the present translator.

29. A. P. Torres, *Comentario al Genesis de San Efren* (Madrid, 1978); A. G. P.

the Prologue and Section I have been translated into French,[30] while Section II has recently been rendered into English.[31] The emendations suggested by Jansma and all of these translations have also been consulted in the present translation.

Hanson and L. Van Rompay, *Efrem de Syriër: Uitleg van het boek Genesis* (Kampen, 1993).

30. P. Féghali, "Les premiers jours de la création, commentaire de Gn. 1,1–2,4 par Saint Ephrem," *PdO* 13 (1986): 3–30.

31. Brock, *Hymns on Paradise*, 197–224. On p. 233 of this work, Brock notes that there is on deposit in the Bodleian Library at Oxford an unpublished M. Litt. thesis, by Katharine Refson, which contains an English translation of the *Commentary on Genesis*.

COMMENTARY ON GENESIS

Commentary of Ephrem on the First Book of the Torah

Prologue

HAD NOT WANTED to write a commentary on the first book of Creation, lest we should now repeat what we had set down in the metrical homilies and hymns. Nevertheless, compelled by the love of friends, we have written briefly of those things of which we wrote at length in the metrical homilies and in the hymns.[1]

2. The reason that Moses[2] wrote [this book] is as follows: the Creator had been manifest to the mind of the first generations, even up until the [generation of] the Tower.[3] The fact that creatures were created was also publicly taught. Moreover, from [the generation of] the Tower to [the generation of] Moses, there was no lack of men among the sons of Shem to preach these things. But, when the sons of Abram went astray in Egypt and deserved to become godless along with the entire world, they too became estranged from those noble commandments that are fixed in our nature and they considered substances, which had come into being out of nothing, to be self-existent be-

---

1. See Kronholm, *Motifs*, for a discussion of Gen 1–11 in the genuine hymns of Ephrem. For the two types of poetry mentioned here, see general introduction above.

2. Here, as in *Hymns on Paradise* 1.1, 4.3, 5.2, etc., Ephrem specifically designates Moses as author of the Pentateuch. On occasion, Ephrem will say "Scripture says." In most places, however, Ephrem simply writes "he/it says," leaving the subject to be supplied. In our translation we have supplied Moses as subject even in places where it could just as reasonably be translated "as Scripture says" as does Brock, *Hymns on Paradise, passim*.

3. That is, the Tower of Babel. See Gen 11.1–9.

ings,[4] and they called created things that had been made out of something[5] "gods." Still, God willed to set right once more, through Moses, those things that had become confused in Moses' generation, lest this evil tradition[6] be transmitted throughout the entire world.

3. Therefore [God] sent Moses to the Egyptians so that where error had arisen he might blunt its edge with the bright rays of true knowledge. [God] wrought through the hand [of Moses] mighty works and miracles lest they be in any doubt about what [Moses] was going to write down. On account of these things He enlightened him and . . .[7] Moreover, Moses was also anointed with a radiance so that the radiance of his face would manifest the Spirit who spoke with his tongue.[8]

4. After the mighty works [of God that occurred] in Egypt, both in the sea and in the desert, [Moses] wrote about the substances that were created out of nothing so that [the descendants of Abraham] might know that they were falsely called self-existent beings. And [Moses] wrote about the creatures that were made out of something[9] and were erroneously worshipped as gods. He wrote that God, who had been set up alongside thousands and myriads, is One.[10] He wrote about the mysteries of the Son that were inscribed when creatures were created. He also inscribed the types [of the Son] that were depicted in the just ones who preceded Him as well as the allegorical and symbolic[11] meanings that were signified by the works of his

4. I.e., 'ityê. See note 26, below.
5. Read here *mdm* for *qdm*, as Jansma, "Ephraems Beschreibung," 311.
6. Read here *mšlmnut'* for *mšlmut'*, as Jansma, "Weitere Beiträge," 122.
7. There is a lacuna in the manuscript at this point.
8. Cf. Exod 34.35.
9. Delete here the negative particle *l'*, as Jansma, "Ephraems Beschreibung," 311.
10. Cf. Dan 7.10.
11. These two words are supplied to fill a lacuna in the text—only the first has been conjectured by Tonneau. Ephrem's use of allegory here is not to be equated with that more highly developed form of allegorical interpretation associated with the School of Alexandria. For Ephrem's use of the term, see Bou Mansour, *La pensée symbolique*, 52–57.

staff.¹² He wrote about the true commandments that had become forgotten, while adding those that were necessary for the infantile state of the [Jewish] people.

5. [Moses] then wrote about the work of the six days that were created by means of a Mediator who was of the same nature and equal in skill to the Maker. And after [Moses] said, "This is the book of the generations of heaven and earth,"¹³ he turned back and recounted those things that he had left out and not written about in his first account. He spoke of the origin of the house of Adam and of their dwelling in Paradise, of the coming of the serpent, of his deceit, of their rashness concerning the tree which had been forbidden them, and of their being cast out from there as punishment.

(2) He spoke of the offering that Cain and Abel brought, of the murder of Abel, of the curses that were decreed against Cain, the story of their seven generations reaching unto the words that Lamech, the son of Cain, spoke to his wives.

(3) He spoke of the ten generations from Adam unto Noah.

(4) He spoke of the wickedness that the two tribes cultivated in Noah's generation.¹⁴

(5) He spoke of the construction of the ark and of the preservation of everything that had been created.

(6) After these things [Moses] spoke of their departure from the ark and about Noah's offering and about the bow in the clouds that was granted him for the covenant of peace.¹⁵

(7) After these things [Moses] spoke of the vineyard that Noah planted, how he became drunk, fell asleep and was uncovered, and of the curse of Canaan and the blessings of his brothers.

12. Cf. Exod 4.2ff., 7.9ff., 8.5ff., 10.13, 14.16, 17.5–9.
13. Gen 2.4.
14. That is, the tribe of Cain and the tribe of Seth.
15. This phrase "covenant of peace" is often used in the Bible to designate the covenant between God and Noah. See, for example, Num 25.12, Isa 54.10, Ezek 34.25, 37.26.

(8) After these things [Moses] spoke of the seventy-two sons who were born to the sons of Noah, of the building of the Tower, of the tongues that they received,[16] and how they were scattered from there throughout the entire earth.

(9) After these things [Moses] spoke of the next ten generations from Shem unto Abraham.

(10) After these things [Moses] spoke of Abraham's departure from Ur, of his dwelling at Haran, his settling in the land of Canaan and of Sarah being led to Pharaoh's house and being returned on account of the plagues that came upon Pharaoh's household.

(11) After these things [Moses] spoke of Lot's separation from Abraham, of Lot's being taken captive along with the Sodomites, and of his deliverance by Abraham who was blessed by Melchizedek when he gave him a tenth of all the goods that he had rescued.

(12) After these things [Moses] spoke of [Abraham's] faith in his seed, of his asking to know how his seed would inherit a land that was already full of inhabitants, and of his offering and the covenant of peace that God established with him on that very day.

(13) After these things [Moses] spoke of how Abraham was persuaded by Sarah to enter into Hagar, how after Hagar had conceived, she held her mistress contemptible in her eyes, despised her and fled, how an angel saw her and sent her back to serve her mistress.

(14) After these things [Moses] spoke of the covenant of circumcision that God gave to [Abraham] and of how [Abraham] circumcised Ishmael and all the sons of his household.

(15) After these things [Moses] spoke of the vision that came to [Abraham] while he was sitting in the doorway of his tent, of the coming of the angels who came in the guise of strangers, of how they promised Isaac to Sarah, and how she laughed within herself.

(16) After these things [Moses] spoke of the [angels']

---

16. Read here *dqblw* for *dhblw*, as Jansma, "Beiträge," 62.

going to Sodom, of Abraham's intercession for [the Sodomites], of the [angels'] going into Lot's house, of the mob of Sodomites, of the departure of Lot and his daughters, and of the punishment that the Sodomites received for their effrontery.

(17) After these things [Moses] spoke of Lot's daughters who made their father drink wine and sleep with them without knowing it.

(18) After these things [Moses] spoke of Abimelech who took Sarah and how God did not allow him to touch her.

(19) After these things [Moses spoke] of the birth of Isaac, of his circumcision, of his weaning, and of the departure of the handmaid and her son because he had laughed at the son of the free woman.

(20) After these things [Moses] spoke of the covenant that Abimelech established with Abraham.

(21) After these things [Moses] spoke of the testing of Abraham, of how he raised up Isaac upon the altar, of Isaac's deliverance from heaven, and of the ram in the tree that became the sacrifice in Isaac's stead.

(22) After these things [Moses] spoke of the death of Sarah and her burial in the double cave of the sons of Hem.[17]

(23) After these things [Moses] spoke of the oath that Abraham made Eliezer swear, of [Eliezer's] journey to Mesopotamia, of the prayer of his servant at the well, and of his bringing Rebekah back to the house of Abraham to become Isaac's wife.

(24) After these things [Moses] spoke of Rebekah's barrenness, of how Isaac prayed and she conceived, of how she inquired of the Lord and it was told to her, "Two nations are in your womb and the elder shall serve the younger."

(25) After these things [Moses] spoke of the birthright of Esau which was sold to Jacob.

(26) After these things [Moses] spoke of the covenant

---

17. Concerning this cave, Ephrem consistently refers to it as belonging to the sons of Hem and not to the sons of Heth, or the Hittites, as do all the versions.

that the king of the Philistines established with Isaac just as he had done with Abraham.

(27) After these things [Moses] spoke of how Jacob, with the counsel of his mother, seized the blessings of Esau.

(28) After these things [Moses] spoke of Jacob's going down to the house of Laban and of the vision of the ladder that he saw while he slept.

(29) After these things [Moses] spoke of how Jacob became betrothed to the one woman of his desire and ended up marrying three others whom he did not desire.

(30) After these things [Moses] spoke of [Jacob's] return to his father's house, of Laban's coming in anger, of how God restrained him from doing Jacob any harm, and of their covenant of peace on the mountain of Gilead.

(31) After these things [Moses] spoke of the host of angels that met him.

(32) After these things [Moses] spoke of the ambassadors of peace whom [Jacob] sent to Esau, of the offering that he sent ahead to Esau, of Jacob's struggle with the angel, of how the angel touched his hip joint and it became dislocated, and of how Esau, his brother, joyfully received him.

(33) After these things [Moses] spoke of [Jacob's] dwelling in Shechem, of the force [with which Shechem] took their sister, of how [Jacob's sons] destroyed the whole city by fraud, and of how displeasing this was to their father.

(34) After these things [Moses] spoke of the death of Rachel near Ephratha, of Jacob's coming to his father, and of the death and burial of Isaac.

(35) After these things [Moses] spoke of the descendants of Esau and of the kings who reigned in Edom before a king reigned in the house of Israel.

(36) After these things [Moses] spoke of the dreams of Joseph.

(37) After this [Moses] spoke of Tamar's marriage, of the violent death of her husbands, how she beguiled and deceived Judah, how, in his first judgment, Judah condemned her to the fire but, in his final judgment, reversed [his decision], acquitted her and raised her to greater honor than himself.

(38) After these things [Moses] spoke of how Joseph was sent out with his brothers, of how they cast him into a pit, of his being sold to Arabs, of his going down to Egypt, of his flight from his mistress, of his being cast into prison, of how he interpreted dreams for Pharaoh's servants and even for Pharaoh, of the dignity that he attained, of the corn he gathered in the seven years of plenty, and of the great quantity of money he collected during the years of famine.

(39) After these things [Moses] spoke of how Joseph's brothers came to him, of how he was concealed from them and how he tormented them, of how he then revealed himself to them and kissed them.[18]

(40) After these things [Moses] spoke of their telling Jacob the good news about Joseph, of the seventy souls who went down with him to Egypt, of Joseph's coming out to meet his father, his bringing Jacob in to Pharaoh, [Jacob's] blessing of Pharaoh, of how Pharaoh settled [Joseph's] brothers in the best part of the land of Egypt, of how Joseph bought all the land of Egypt for Pharaoh with the exception of the lands belonging to the priests.

(41) After these things [Moses] spoke of the illness of Jacob and of the blessings he gave to Joseph's sons, making the younger Ephraim greater than Manasseh, his older brother.

(42) After these things [Moses] spoke of the blessings with which Jacob blessed his own sons, of how, after he had finished his words, he straightened up his feet in the bed and was gathered to his people. [Moses then spoke of] how Joseph took Jacob up and buried him where Abraham and Isaac were buried.

(43) After these things [Moses] spoke of the death of Joseph and of how he made his brothers swear to take up his bones with them to the land of their inheritance.

(44) All these things Moses wrote down in the first book of Creation and to begin his discourse he said:

---

18. Ephrem here plays on the words *šnq*—"torment," and *nšq*—"kiss."

Section I

1. *In the beginning God created the heavens and the earth,*[19] that is, the substance of the heavens and the substance of the earth.[20] So let no one think that there is anything allegorical in the works of the six days.[21] No one can rightly say that the things that pertain to these days were symbolic, nor can one say that they were meaningless names or that other things were symbolized for us by their names. Rather, let us know in just what manner heaven and earth were created in the beginning. They were truly heaven and earth. There was no other thing signified by the names "heaven" and "earth." The rest of the works and things made that followed were not meaningless significations either, for the substances of their natures correspond to what their names signify.[22]

19. Gen 1.1.

20. In the Peshitta text of Gen 1.1, the particle *yat*, as it does in the early Targums, precedes both "heaven" and "earth." In the thirteenth century, the Jacobite polymath Bar Hebraeus pointed out that *yat*, preserved only here in the Syriac version of the Old Testament, is the Palestinian Aramaic equivalent to *l(a)* in Syriac, i.e., a marker to designate the direct object, like *'et* in Hebrew [M. Sprengling and W. C. Graham, eds., *Barhebraeus' Scholia on the Old Testament. Part I: Genesis–II Samuel* (Chicago, 1931) 5]. This observation, together with the fact that the rabbis interpreted *'et* of the Hebrew text as indicating "substance," has caused commentators to say that Ephrem is interpreting the particle in similar fashion. Though this interpretation is no doubt philologically correct, it seems more in line with Ephrem's literal reading of the text to understand that he is reading *yāt* as the construct (the genitive construction in Syriac) of the Syriac word *yātâ*—"essence, substance," and is simply interpreting this term for his readers. This interpretation subsequently became the standard exegesis of this passage in Nestorian tradition, see T. Jansma, "Investigations into the Early Syrian Fathers on Genesis," in *Studies on the Book of Genesis*, ed. B. Gemser et al., Oudtestamentische Studien, no. 12 (New York, 1958) 101.

The word *yātâ*, derives from *'it* [for the background of which, see J. Bethune-Baker, *Nestorius and His Teaching* (Cambridge, 1908) 212–17], a root which is of fundamental importance for Ephrem's polemics and his whole theological outlook. See Beck, *Die Theologie*, 5–13; and N. El-Khoury, *Der Interpretation der Welt bei Ephraem dem Syrer* (Tübingen, 1976) 42–46. Also, see I. 2, below and note *ad loc.*

21. See El-Khoury, *Der Interpretation der Welt bei Ephraem*, 49–62; and Kronholm, *Motifs*, 41–43. *Hymns on the Nativity* 26 is a meditation on the work of the six days in their relation to the Incarnation.

22. In the thought of Ephrem, for something to have a name is to have a

COMMENTARY ON GENESIS 75

2. *In the beginning God created heaven and earth.*[23] At this point these comprised the only things that had been made, for there was nothing else created along with heaven and earth. Even the elements[24] that were created on that day had not yet been created. If the elements had been created along with heaven and earth, Moses would have said so. But he did not, lest he give the names of the elements precedence over their substances. Therefore, it is evident that heaven and earth came to be from nothing because neither water nor wind had yet been created, nor had fire, light or darkness been given their natures, for they were younger than[25] heaven and earth. These things were created things that came after heaven and earth and they were not self-subsistent beings[26] for they did not exist before [heaven and earth].[27]

---

qnōmâ, or substance, and that name designates just what that substance is. See *Hymns on Faith* 16.2: "in the names are the substances"; *Hymns against Heresies* 48.2: "the name Creator testifies to God who created everything"; *Sermons on Faith* 2; and El-Khoury, *Der Interpretation der Welt bei Ephraem*, 45. See also I.12, below.

23. Gen 1.1.

24. This Syriac word, *kyānê*, is the same word just translated "natures" in the previous paragraph. See the discussion of Beck, *Die Theologie*, 13–15, and idem, *Ephräms Reden über den Glauben. Ihr theologischer Lehrgehalt und ihr geschichtlicher Rahmen*, SA, no. 33 (Rome, 1953) 4–8, for the various usages of this word in Ephrem.

25. To designate age is the normal manner in Syriac to express posteriority or priority. These five elements that Ephrem enumerates are those elements that Bardaisan postulated as *'ityê*, or self-subsistent beings [see next note]. See Jansma, "Ephraems Beschreibung," 300–305; and Drijvers, *Bardaisan*, 96–126.

26. I.e., *'ityê*. For Ephrem the term *'ityâ* (and its derivative *'itûtâ*), denoting self-subsistent being, can be used only of God. He is the only *'itûtâ*, or "Being." To give to a created thing the name *'ityâ* is, to Ephrem, more blasphemous than any idol-worshiping that was committed in the Old Testament. See *Hymns against Heresies* 53, devoted specifically to this subject, especially 11–12: "Moses witnessed to us that he called no other by the name of *'itûtâ*. They were called gods but not *'ityê*... [God] revealed to Moses his name. He called himself *ehyeh* (cf. Exod 3.14) for that is the name of *'itûtâ*." See also *Hymns against Heresies* 16.9; and Beck, *Die Theologie*, 11–13. For the question of Ephrem's treatment of Bardaisan in his hymns, see also Beck, "Bardaisan und Seine Schule," 271–333.

27. Here, as throughout this first section, Ephrem is emphasizing, against the teachings of the Bardaisanites, Marcionites, and Manicheans, that everything that exists was created by God. His argument here centers on the water,

3. After this [Moses] spoke not of the things that were above the firmament, but rather of those things that were between the firmament and the earth which is within [the womb].[28] [Moses] wrote about [the things within the firmament] for us, although he did not write about everything for us, for he did not record for us the day on which the spiritual beings were created.[29]

(2) [Moses] then goes on to write that *the earth was tohu and bohu*,[30] that is, void and desolation. This is to show that even the void and desolation were older than[31] the elements. I am not saying that the void and desolation were something. Rather [I am saying] that the earth, which does exist, was known [to exist] in something which does not exist, for the earth existed alone without any other thing.[32]

---

wind, fire, light, and darkness, Bardaisan's eternal principles [see Drijvers, *Bardaisan*, 96–126]; for Ephrem they were the fundamental elements (*kyānê*), which were created by God. Ephrem's arguments that water, wind, fire and light were in fact created elements and that darkness had no real existence of its own (see I.16, below) completely undermine Bardaisan's cosmology.

This position is the focal point of Ephrem's polemic in this commentary; see introduction above. He stresses the same points in his hymns, especially in his *Hymns against Heresies*. "Out of nothing God created everything," *Hymns against Heresies*, 28.8. See also *Hymns against Heresies* 3, which is devoted specifically to the subject of *creatio ex nihilo*, against Bardaisan. See also Hidal, *Interpretatio Syriaca*, 76–78; and El-Khoury, *Die Interpretation der Welt bei Ephraem*, 65–81.

28. See I.17, below.

29. Although according to *Hymns on the Nativity* 26.5, the angels had been created by the second day, it is possible that here Ephrem betrays acquaintance with the Jewish debate over whether the angels were created on the second day or on the fifth day of creation. See *Genesis Rabbah* 1.3. Whether Ephrem was aware of this debate or not, his point is that the angels were also created and they were created after heaven and earth. See W. Cramer, *Die Engelvorstellungen bei Ephraem dem Syrer*, OCA, no. 173 (Rome, 1965) 112, 170; Hidal, *Interpretatio Syriaca*, 67; and El-Khoury, *Die Interpretation der Welt bei Ephraem*, 64–65.

30. Gen 1.2. The words *toh* and *boh* of the Hebrew text are here transliterated in the Peshitta. In the later Nestorian tradition, it is the vocabulary of the Greek tradition, i.e., ἀόρατος καὶ ἀκατασκεύαστος, that becomes the focal point of the standard exegesis of this passage. See Jansma, "Investigations," 102–3.

31. See above, note 25.

32. Ephrem here asserts that even something that may or may not have any existence in and of itself preceded those elements that Bardaisan calls '*ityê*, or

COMMENTARY ON GENESIS 77

4. After [Moses] spoke about the creation of heaven and earth and showed that the waste and desolation preceded the elements that were created by the length of that moment that followed [their creation],[33] he turned to write about those elements saying, *Darkness was upon the face of the abyss.*[34] For the abyss of waters was created at that time. But how was it created on the day on which it was created? Even though it was created on this day and at this moment, Moses does not tell us here how it was created. For now, we should accept the creation of the abyss as it is written, while we wait to learn from Moses how it was created.

(2) As for the darkness that was upon the face of the abyss, some posit that it was a cloud of heaven. Now, if the firmament had been created on the first day they would speak rightly. If the upper heavens were similar to the firmament, then there would have been a thick darkness between the two heavens, for the light had not been created nor affixed there to dissipate the darkness by its rays. But if the place between the two heavens is light as Ezekiel,[35] Paul,[36] and Stephen[37] bear witness, then how could the heavens, which had dissipated the darkness with their lights, spread darkness over the abyss?

5. Because everything that was created was created in those six days,[38] whether it was written down that it was creat-

---

eternal principles. He may, however, also be alluding to still another of Bardaisan's false teachings. Bardaisan placed great importance on the concept of space, a material substance which contained and enclosed everything, including God. Ephrem considers this to be a restriction of the nature of God, see *Prose Refutations* 1:129–33 (text), xciv–xcvi (translation), 2:16 (text) iv–viii (translation), with Burkitt's remarks, 2:cxxiii–cxxiv. See also Drijvers, *Bardaisan*, 136.

33. Again Ephrem insists on the creation of everything. There was a length of time between the creation of heaven and earth and the creation of the first elements. See *Hymns on Faith* 26.2, where Ephrem implies that time began when God began the creation, and discussion in Hidal, *Interpretatio Syriaca*, 76–78.

34. Gen 1.2.
35. Cf. Ezek 1.1, 22.
36. Cf. Acts 9.3, 22.6; 26.13.
37. Cf. Acts 7.55–56.
38. See *Hymns on the Nativity* 26; and El-Khoury, *Der Interpretation der Welt bei Ephraem*, 49–62.

ed or not, the clouds must also have been created on the first day, just as fire was created along with wind, although Moses did not write about the fire as he did about the wind. Thus, the clouds were created along with the abyss although Moses did not write that the clouds were created along with the abyss, just as he did not record the creation of fire along with that of the wind when he wrote about the creation of the wind.

(2) It was necessary that everything be known to have its beginning in those six days. The clouds were surely created along with the abyss, for how many times were these brought forth from the abyss? Elijah saw a cloud rising up out of the sea.[39] Solomon also said, *By his knowledge the depths broke forth and the clouds sprinkled down dew.*[40] It was not only because of their substance that they should have been created at this point, but they were created on that first night because they also rendered service on that first night. Just as the clouds covered Egypt for three days and three nights,[41] clouds were spread over all of Creation on the first night and on the first day. If the clouds had been dispersed, light would not have been required on the first day because the brightness of the upper heavens would have been sufficient to fill the place of the light that was created on the first day.

6. After one night and one day were completed, the firmament was created on the second evening and henceforth its shadow rendered service for all subsequent nights. Therefore, heaven and earth were created on the evening of the first night. Along with the abyss that was created, there were also created those clouds which, when they were spread out, brought about the requisite night. After their shadow had served for twelve hours, light was created beneath them and the light dispersed their shadow that had been spread over the waters all night.

7. After Moses spoke of the darkness that was spread over the face of the abyss, he then said, *the wind of God was hovering over the face of the waters.*[42] Because Moses called it *the wind*

---

39. Cf. 1 Kings 18.44.
41. Cf. Exod 10.22.
40. Prov 3.20.
42. Gen 1.2.

of God and said *it was hovering,* some posit that this is the Holy Spirit[43] and, because of what is written here, associate it with the activity of creation. Nevertheless, the faithful[44] do not make this connection, for these things cannot be so related. Rather, by those things that are truly said about it, they associate it with that element,[45] just as, on the basis of the names employed, they cannot posit the Spirit as maker,[46] for it is said that an evil spirit of God consumed Saul.[47]

    43. The Syriac word *rūhâ,* as does the Hebrew cognate *ruāh,* can mean either "wind" or "spirit." For a discussion of this wind/spirit in Ephrem's hymns, see Kronholm, *Motifs,* 43–44.

    44. I.e., the orthodox, Nicene Christians, who were probably a small but growing minority at this time. See Bauer, *Orthodoxy and Heresy in Earliest Christianity,* 1–43; and H. J. W. Drijvers, "Rechtgläubigkeit und Ketzerei im ältesten syrischen Christentum," in *Symposium Syriacum 1972, OCA,* no. 197 (Rome, 1974) 291–308.

    45. I.e., the natural wind. *Targum Onkelos* also interprets this as the natural wind [see M. Aberbach and B. Grossfeld, *Targum Onkelos to Genesis* (Denver, 1982) 21, n. 4.]. This interpretation of Ephrem may again be in consideration of Bardaisan's teaching. According to Ephrem, Hymns against Heresies 55, Bardaisan taught that the Spirit bore two daughters: "the shame of dry land" and the "image of the waters." In the same hymn, Ephrem accuses Bardaisan of "dishonoring the beautiful name of the Holy Spirit who is too pure even for a mirror." See discussion in Drijvers, *Bardaisan,* 143–52.

    46. See also *Hymns against Heresies* 50.8, where "the wind hovers over the water *kyāna'īt*—"naturally." See also the discussion of the history of interpretation of this passage in Syriac tradition in Jansma, "Investigations," 104–6. In the *Hymns on Epiphany* 8.15, Ephrem seems to maintain the very opposite position, but see Beck's remarks on the authenticity of these hymns in E. Beck, ed., *Des Heiligen Ephraem des Syrers Hymnen de Nativitate (Epiphania), CSCO* 187 (Louvain, 1959) viii–xiii. In any case, it is certain that the Ephrem who wrote this commentary cannot be that "certain Syrian" from whom Basil got his information on the meaning of the Syriac word here. Recently, S. Giet, ed., *Basile de Césarée, Homélies sur l'Hexaéméron, SC* 26bis (Paris, 1968) 169, n. 3, seems to have opted for Ephrem by default. This long-debated question of Basil's source has finally been resolved in favor of Eusebius of Emesa, through the intermediary of Diodore of Tarsus. See J. Pouchet, "Les rapports de Basile de Césarée avec Diodore de Tarse," *BLE* 87 (1986): 243–72, especially, 260–68; and L. Van Rompay, "L'informateur Syrien de Basile de Césarée. A propos de Genèse 1,2," *OCP* 58 (1992): 245–51.

    47. Cf. 1 Sam 16.14. Here the Peshitta reads *mdyb'*—"consume" against the Hebrew or Greek text. This reading does survive in some targumic passages. See, for example, A. Sperber, *The Prophets according to the Codex Reuchlinianus* (Leiden, 1969) 63–64.

(2) It is indeed said that *it was hovering*, but what came forth from the waters on the first day when [the wind] was hovering over the waters? If on the day that it was written that *it was hovering over the waters* nothing came out of the waters, and then on the fifth day when the waters brought forth reptiles and birds, it was not written that the wind *was hovering*, how then can anyone say that this wind took part in the activity of creation? For, although Scripture said *it was hovering*, it did not say that anything came out of the waters on the day that it was hovering.

(3) Just as through the service of the clouds, that is, the shadow of the first night, we infer the creation of the clouds that came to be on the first day, so too through the service of the wind, which is its breeze,[48] Moses wished to make known to us the creation [of the wind]. For just as clouds do not exist without a shadow, neither does wind exist without a breeze. It is in their service then that we infer those things that are not otherwise made apparent to us. Therefore that wind was blowing because it was created for this purpose. After it blew and manifested its creation through its service on the first night, it once again became calm on the first day just as the clouds were once again dispersed on the first day.

8. After [Moses] spoke of heaven and earth, of the darkness, the abyss and the wind that came to be at the beginning of the first night, he then turned to speak about the light that came to be at dawn of the first day. At the end of the twelve hours of that night, the light was created between the clouds and the waters and it chased away the shadow of the clouds that were overshadowing the waters and making them dark. For Nisan was the first month; in it the number of the hours of day and night were equal.

(2) The light remained a length of twelve hours so that each day might also obtain its [own] hours just as the darkness had obtained a measured length of time. Although the light and the clouds were created in the twinkling of an eye, the day and the night of the first day were each completed in twelve hours.

---

48. On the breezes as ministers in Paradise, see *Hymns on Paradise*, 9.7–13.

(3) The light then was like a bright mist over the face of the earth. Whether it was like the dawn or like the pillar that gave light to the people in the wilderness,[49] it is obvious that it would have been unable to chase away the darkness that was spread over the face of everything, unless it had spread out completely over everything, either by its substance or by its brightness. The light was released so that it might spread over everything without being fastened down. It dispersed the darkness that was over everything although it did not move. It was only when [the light] went away and when it came that it moved, for when [the light] went away the rule was given to the night and at [the light's] coming there would be an end to [the night's] rule.

9. After the brightness [of the light] rendered its service for three days,[50] lest, like nothing, it return to nothing, God bore clear witness that the light *was very good*.[51] Although God did not [actually] say that the works that preceded the light were very good, He did [in fact] say it about them, for although He did not say it of them in the beginning when only these things had come into existence out of nothing, He did say it of them after everything else had come into existence; for [Moses] included all that had been made together with all that was created in six days, when he said on the sixth day: *God saw everything that he had made, and behold, it was very good.*[52]

(2) Because that first light was indeed created good, it rendered its service by its brightness for three days and it also served, as we say,[53] for the conception and the birth of everything that the earth brought forth on the third day. The sun was in the firmament in order to ripen whatever had sprouted under that first light. It is said that from this light, now diffused, and from fire, which were both created on the first day, the sun, which was in the firmament, was

---

49. Cf. Exod 13.21.
50. See *Hymns on Virginity* 51.2: "For three days the light rendered its service and [then] was hidden."
51. Gen 1.4.
52. Gen 1.31.
53. Read ’*amrnn* for ’*amryn*, as Jansma, "Weitere Beiträge," 122.

fashioned, while the moon and the stars also came to be from that same first light.

(3) Just as the sun, which rules the day by the fact that *it gives light to the earth*,[54] actually causes the fruits of the earth to ripen, so too does the moon, which rules the night and tempers the strength of the night by its brightness, also bring forth, according to its first nature, fruits and vegetation. For Moses speaks in his blessings of *the yield which the moon brought forth*,[55] along with the other things on account of which the light was created, although they say that, for the sake of the things that were to come forth, the light was created on the first day. After the earth brought forth everything during the course of the third day, then [the moon] came to be in the manner of the light on the fourth day, so that through the moon, as well as through the light, all fruit would have its beginning, and then through the sun all vegetation would become ripe.

10. Thus, through light and water the earth brought forth everything. While God is able to bring forth everything from the earth without these things, it was His will to show that there was nothing created on earth that was not created for the purpose of mankind or for his service.[56]

(2) The waters that the earth drank on the first day were not salty.[57] Even if these waters were like the deep on the surface of the earth, they were not yet seas. For it was in the seas that these waters, which were not salty before being gathered together, became salty. When they were sent throughout the entire earth for the earth to drink they were sweet, but when they were gathered into seas on the third

---

54. Gen 1.17.

55. Cf. Deut 33.14. The manuscript here reads Jacob where Moses is clearly intended. The text Ephrem cites differs from both the Hebrew and the Greek text.

56. Ephrem is at great pains to emphasize that everything that has been made has been made for the sake of humanity; see *Hymns on Nisibis* 38.9 and *Hymns on Paradise* 6.6. See also discussion of Kronholm, *Motifs,* 67.

57. See *Genesis Rabbah* 5.3, where it is argued that these waters were sweet. The question whether these waters were sweet or salty seems not to have been a concern of Christian exegetes.

day, they became salty, lest they become stagnant due to their being gathered together, and so that they might receive the rivers that enter into them without increasing. For the quantity that a sea requires for nourishment is the measure of the rivers that flow down into it. Rivers flow down into seas lest the heat of the sun dry them up. The saltiness [of the seas] then swallows up [the rivers] lest they increase, rise up, and cover the earth. Thus the rivers turn into nothing, as it were, because the saltiness of the sea swallows them up.[58]

11. The seas had been created when the waters were created and were hidden in those waters, and although the seas became bitter, the waters above them were not bitter. Just as there were seas in the flood, but they were covered over [by those waters], they were not able to change into their bitter nature the sweet waters of the flood which came from above. If these waters had been bitter, how would the olives and all the plants have been preserved in them? How did those of the house of Noah and those with them drink from them?

(2) Although Noah had commanded that all sorts of food be brought for himself and those with him because there would be no food anywhere, he did not allow water to be brought because those who had entered the ark would be able to take from the water outside of the ark to drink. Therefore, just as the waters of the flood were not salty while the seas were hidden within them, neither were the waters that were gathered on the third day bitter even though the seas below them were bitter.

12. Just as the gathering of the waters did not precede that word which said, *"Let the waters be gathered and let the dry land appear,"*[59] neither did the seas exist until that moment when *God called the gathering of water "seas."*[60] When they received their name they were changed.[61] In their [new] place the [waters] attained that saltiness that had not been theirs

58. Cf. Eccles 1.7.
60. Gen 1.10.
59. Gen 1.9.
61. See note 22 above.

[even] outside of their [old] place. For [their place] became deep at that very moment when [God] said, *"Let the waters be gathered into one place."* Then either the land [under] the sea was brought down below the [level of the] earth to receive within it its own waters along with the waters that were above the entire earth, or the waters swallowed each other so that the place might be sufficient for them, or the place of the sea shook and it became a great depth and the waters quickly hastened into that basin. Although the will of God had gathered these waters when the earth was created, a gate was opened for them to be gathered into one place. Just as in the gathering of the first and second waters there was found no gathering place because there was no place from which they might go out, so now do these waters come down with all the rains and showers and are gathered into seas along paths and roads which had been prepared for them on the first day.

13. The upper waters, because they had been separated on the second day from the lower waters by the firmament set between them, were also sweet like the lower waters. (The upper waters are not those that became salty in the seas on the third day, but are those that were separated from them on the second day.) They were not salty, therefore, because they would not have become stagnant, for they had not been left on the land to become stagnant. The air there does not serve to cause [things] to be born or to swarm, nor do rivers flow into them to keep them from evaporating for there is no sun there to generate heat that would cause them to evaporate. They remain there for the dew of blessing and are kept there for the floodgates of wrath.[62]

(2) The waters that are above the firmament do not move about because something made does not move about within something that is not made, nor does something move about within nothing. Something that is created within something[63] possesses, at its creation, all of that thing; that

---

62. See Deut 33.28, where the "dew of heaven" is used in context of a blessing (in Gen 27.39, for curse) and Gen 7.11, for the floodgates of wrath.

63. Delete negative particle *l'* as Jansma, "Ephraems Beschreibung," 312–13.

is, that thing moves, rises and falls within that thing in which it was created. But nothing surrounded the upper waters. Therefore, the upper waters were unable either to turn or to move about because they had nothing in which they might turn or move about.

14. Heaven, earth, fire, wind, and water were created from nothing as Scripture bears witness, whereas the light, which came to be on the first day along with the rest of the things that came to be afterwards, came to be from something. For when these other things came to be from nothing, [Moses] said, *God created heaven and earth.* Although it is not written that fire, water, and wind were created, neither is it said that they were made.[64] Therefore, they came to be from nothing just as heaven and earth came to be from nothing.

15. After God began to make [things] from something, Moses wrote, *God said, "Let there be light,"* and so on. Although Moses did say, *God created the great serpents,* nevertheless *"let the waters swarm with swarming things"* had been [said] prior to that. Therefore those five created things were created from nothing and everything else was made from those [five] things that came to be from nothing.

(2) Fire was also created on the first day, although it is not written down that it was created. Since [fire] had no existence in and of itself but existed in something else, it was created together with that thing in which it came to be. It is not possible that a thing which does not exist of itself can precede that thing which is the cause of its existence. That [fire] is in the earth, nature bears witness, but that it was not created together with the earth, Scripture affirms, when it said, *In the beginning God created heaven and earth.*[65] Fire too then, since it does not exist of itself, will remain in the earth, even if the earth and the waters have been commanded at every moment to bring forth fire from their wombs along with the waters and the wind and the clouds.

---

64. Ephrem distinguishes (though not with rigid consistency) the term *brʾ*, meaning "to create," i.e., from nothing, from the term *ʿbd* meaning "to make," i.e., out of existing materials.

65. Gen 1.1.

16. Darkness, too, is neither a self-subsistent being[66] nor a created thing; it is a shadow, as Scripture makes clear. It was created neither before heaven nor after the clouds, for it was with the clouds and was brought forth from the clouds. [Darkness] also exists in another [thing], for it has no substance of its own. When that in which it exists vanishes, the darkness likewise vanishes with it. For whatever comes to an end along with another thing when it vanishes is without its own existence, because that other thing is the cause of its existence.[67]

(2) So, how could darkness, whose existence is due to the clouds and to the firmament and not to the first light or to the sun, exist of itself? It is [a thing] which one thing brings forth by its cover and another destroys by its brightness. If one thing creates it and causes it to become something while another thing turns it back into nothing, how can it be a self-subsistent being? The clouds and the firmament, which were created at the beginning, bring it forth and the light that was created on the first day brings it to an end. If one created thing can create something and another created thing can destroy it—for subsequent to that, one thing can bring it into visibility at any moment—and another, at that very moment that it itself returns to nothing, turns it back into nothing, it is under the compulsion of that [one thing] which causes it to begin and [that other thing] that causes it to go away. If created things cause it to come into existence and also cause it to vanish then it is a created from created things. [The darkness then] is but a shadow of the firmament and it vanishes in the presence of another thing, as it disappears before the sun. Some teachings[68] posit that

---

66. I.e., an ’*ityâ*, as Bardaisan held. In fact, Ephrem will show that it is not even a created thing. In *Prose Refutations* 1:52, Ephrem claims that Bardaisan had said that it was the assault of darkness on the other ’*ityê* that introduced disorder into the universe.

67. On the non-existence of darkness, see also *Prose Refutations* 1:98–100 (text) and lxxvii–lxxviii (translation), and *Hymns against Heresies* 11.2, 16.20, 17.1ff., 21.5, 41.7.

68. Or, "sects." Féghali, "Les premiers jours de la creation," 22, n. 36, identifies this as the teaching of Mani. See also, Lieu, *Manichaeism*, 12–15; and G.

this [darkness], which is at all times subject to created things, is an adversary of creatures, and they make that thing which has no substance of its own a self-existent being.

17. After [Moses] spoke of those things that came to be on the first day, he began to write about those things that came to be on the second day, saying, *And God said, "Let there be a firmament between the waters and let it separate the waters below the firmament from the waters above the firmament."*[69] The firmament between the waters was pressed together from the waters.[70] It was of the same measure as the waters that were spread out over the surface of the earth. Then if, in its origin, [the firmament] was above the earth (for the earth, water, and fire were beneath it, while water, wind, and darkness were above it), how do others posit that this [firmament], which is enveloped like an embryo in the uterus within the womb, is the womb of everything created between everything?

(2) For if the firmament had been created between everything, light, darkness, and wind, which were above the firmament when it was created, would have been confined above the firmament. If the creation [of the firmament] had occurred at night, the darkness and wind would also have remained there together with the waters which remained there. But if the creation [of the firmament] had occurred in the day, the light and the wind also would have remained there along with the waters. And if they had remained there then the [wind, water, and lights] that are here would be different things. When, then, could they have been created? But if they did not remain there, how did those elements that were above [the firmament] when they were created move down below it?

18. The firmament was created on the evening of the sec-

Widengren, *Mesopotamian Elements in Manichaeism* (Uppsala, 1946) 31–51. It should not, however, be restricted to Mani, as Bardaisan held a similar position.

69. Cf. Gen 1.7–8.

70. That is, the firmament was composed of the solidified water. Cf. Job 38.30. See also *Genesis Rabbah* 4.2, Josephus, *Antiquities*, I.30. See *Hymns on the Nativity* 26.5. This interpretation was also preserved in later Nestorian tradition; see Jansma, "Investigations," 114–16.

ond night, just as the heavens came to be on the evening of the first night. But when the firmament came into existence, the covering of clouds that had served for a night and a day in the place of the firmament dissipated. Because [the firmament] had been created between the light and the darkness, no darkness remained above it, for the shadow of the clouds was dispelled when the clouds themselves were dispelled. Nor did any of this light remain there, for its alotted measure of time had come to an end and so it sank into the waters that were beneath [the firmament].[71]

(2) The wind could not have remained there either because it did not even exist there. For, it was on the first night that [Moses] said *it hovered* and not on the second night. If the firmament had been created on the first night when [the wind] was blowing there could then be some debate. But, since it is not written that [the wind] was blowing when the firmament was created, who would say that the wind was there when Scripture does not say so?

19. After the wind hovered on the first day, manifested its service by its blowing and returned to its stillness, then the firmament came to be. It is evident, therefore, that [the wind] neither remained above nor descended below, for how can one seek in any position or place for something whose very substance only exists at the moment of its service and whose service comes to an end when it ceases to blow? The wind underwent three things on the day of its creation: it was created from nothing, it blew in and through something, and it reverted to being hidden in its stillness.

20. After the wind had undergone these three things, the firmament was created on the evening of the second day. There was then nothing that rose along with it, because there was nothing that remained above it. It made a separation between the waters that it was commanded to separate, but not between the light, the wind, or darkness, for this had not been commanded.

---

71. For the lights sinking into water in Jewish tradition, see L. Ginzberg, *Legends of the Jews* (Philadelphia, 1939) 1:25.

(2) There was no light, therefore, on the first night. On the night of the second and third day, it sank into the waters beneath the firmament and rose up as we said [above]. But on the fourth day, when the waters were gathered into one place, they say that [the firmament] was formed and that the sun, the moon, and the stars were formed from [the firmament] and from fire, and there were places set apart for the lights. Therefore, the moon would rise in the west of the firmament, the sun in the east, and at that same moment, the stars were dispersed in orderly fashion throughout the entire firmament.

(3) Although God said that the light which came to be on the first day *was very good*, He did not say this about the firmament which came to be on the second day, because the firmament had not yet been finished, neither in its structure nor in its adornment. The Creator delayed until the lights came to be so that when [the firmament] was adorned with the sun and the moon and the stars, and the strength of the darkness that was weakened by the lights that shone from it, He would then say of [the firmament], included with the rest [of creation], that *it was very good.*[72]

21. After [Moses] spoke of the firmament that came to be on the second day, he then turned to write about the gathering of the waters and about the grass and the trees that the earth brought forth on the third day, saying, *And God said, "Let the waters under the heavens be gathered together into one place, and let the dry land appear."*[73] From the fact that He said, *"Let the waters be gathered into one place,"* it is evident that it is the earth that supports the seas and that the abysses beneath the earth do not stand on nothing. Although the waters, by the word of God, were gathered in the night, the surface of the earth still became dry in the twinkling of an eye.

22. After these two things had occurred, God commanded the earth to bring forth at dawn grass and herbs of every

---

72. Gen 1.31.
73. Gen 1.9.

kind and all the various fruit-bearing trees.⁷⁴ Although the grasses were only a moment old at their creation, they appeared as if they were months old. Likewise, the trees, although only a day old when they sprouted forth, were nevertheless like [trees] years old as they were fully grown and fruits were already budding on their branches.⁷⁵

(2) The grass that would be required as food for the animals who were to be created two days later was [thus] made ready. And the new corn that would be food for Adam and his descendants, who would be thrown out of Paradise four days later, was [thus] prepared.

23. After [Moses] spoke about the gathering of the waters and about the sprouting of the vegetation on the earth on the third day, he turned to write about the lights that were created in the firmament saying, *And God said, "Let there be lights in the firmament of the heavens to separate the day from the night,"* that is, "one to rule over the day and the other [to rule] over the night."⁷⁶

(2) That [God] said, *"Let them be for signs,"* [refers to] measures of time, and *"let them be for seasons,"* clearly indicates summer and winter. *"Let them be for days,"* are measured by the rising and setting of the sun, and *"let them be for years,"*⁷⁷ are comprised of the daily cycles of the sun and the monthly cycles of the moon.⁷⁸

(3) Indeed [Moses] said, *God made the two great lights, the greater light to rule the day, and the lesser light to rule the night; and [He made] the stars.*⁷⁹ Although all that was done before the fourth day was begun in the evening, the works on the fourth day were fashioned at dawn. Because the third day had been completed, in that [Moses] said, *It was evening and it was morning; day three,*⁸⁰ God did not create the two lights

---

74. Cf. Gen 1.11–12.
75. For the trees being created fruit-bearing in Jewish tradition, see Ginzberg, *Legends*, 1:59, 5:107.
76. Gen 1.14, 16.   77. Gen 1.14.
78. Compare *Genesis Rabbah* 6.1.
79. Gen 1.16.
80. Gen 1.13.

in the evening lest night be changed into day and morning be given priority over evening.

24. Because the days followed the same order in which the first day was created, the night of the fourth day, like that of the other days, preceded its day. And if its evening preceded its dawn, the lights were not created in the evening, but rather at dawn. But to say that one of them was created in the evening and the other at dawn cannot be allowed for Moses said, *"Let there be lights,"* and *God made the two great lights.*[81] If they were great when they were created and they were created at dawn, then the sun would have stood in the east and the moon opposite it in the west. The sun would have been set very low because it was created in the place where it set out over the earth, whereas the moon would have been set higher because it was created in the place where it stands on the fifteenth day. Indeed, at the moment the sun appears over the earth, the lights see each other and the moon sinks. From the position of the moon, from its size and from the light it produced, it is clear, then, that it was fifteen days old when it was created.

25. Just as the trees, the vegetation, the animals, the birds, and even mankind were old, so also were they young. They were old according to the appearance of their limbs and their substances, yet they were young because of the hour and moment of their creation. Likewise, the moon was both old and young. It was young, for it was but a moment old, but was also old, for it was full as it is on the fifteenth day.

(2) If the moon had been created a day old or even two, it would have given no light; because of its proximity to the sun, it would not even have been visible. If it had been created about four days old, although it might have been visible, it would still not have given any light. This would have rendered false the verse *God created the two great lights*,[82] as well as *He said, "Let there be lights in heaven to give light upon the*

---

81. Gen 1.14, 16.
82. Gen 1.16.

earth."[83] Therefore, the moon had to be fifteen days old. The sun, although it was only one day old, was nevertheless four days old, for it is according to the sun that each day is counted and will be reckoned. Accordingly, those eleven days, by which the moon was older than the sun, that were added to the moon at that first moment are also added to it each year, for these [days] are used in the lunar reckoning.

(3) There was nothing lacking in that year for Adam and his descendants, for any deficiency in the measure of the moon had been filled in when the moon was created. Thus, Adam and his descendants learned from this year that, henceforth, eleven days were to be added to every year. Clearly then, it was not the Chaldeans who arranged the seasons and the years; these things had been arranged before [the creation of] Adam.

26. After Moses spoke about the lights that came to be in the firmament, he turned to write about the swarming things, the birds, and the serpents that were created from the waters on the fifth day, saying, *And God said, "Let the waters cause living things to swarm, and let the birds fly above the earth." And God created the great serpents and every living creature with which the waters swarmed according to their kind.*[84]

(2) When the waters were gathered, which had been ordered on the second day, there appeared rivers as well as springs, lakes, and ponds. At the word of God these waters dispersed throughout Creation and brought forth swarming things and fish from within them; the serpents were created in the abysses and the birds soared in flocks out of the waves into the air.[85]

(3) As for the great serpents that were created, although the Prophets said that Leviathan dwelt in the sea,[86] Job said that the Behemoth dwelt on dry land.[87] David too, speaking

---

83. Gen 1.14.
84. Gen 1.20–21.
85. Compare Ginzberg, *Legends,* 1:28, where "the birds are fashioned out of marshy ground saturated with water."
86. Cf. Isa 27.1; Ps 74.13–14, 104.26.
87. Cf. Job 40.15.

of this beast, said that *on a thousand mountains is Behemoth's pasture land,*[88] that is, *his place of repose.* Perhaps it was after they were created that their places were separated so that Leviathan should dwell in the sea and Behemoth on dry land.[89]

27. After [Moses] spoke about the creation of the swarming things and of the birds and the sea serpents on the fifth day, he turned to write about the creeping things and the animals and the beasts that were created on the sixth day, saying, *And God said, "Let the earth bring forth living creatures according to their kinds: cattle and reptiles and beasts."*[90] Although the entire earth was swarming with swarming things, nevertheless the cattle and the beasts were set along the border of Paradise so that they might dwell near Adam.[91]

(2) Therefore, the entire earth stirred with creeping things as had been commanded. [The earth] also brought forth the beasts of the field as companions to the wild beasts, and it brought forth as many beasts as would be suitable for the service of that one who, on that very day, was to transgress the commandment of his Lord.

28. After [Moses] spoke about the reptiles, the beasts and the cattle that were created on the sixth day, he turned to write about the creation of that man who was fashioned on the sixth day, saying, *"And God said. . . ."*[92] But to whom was God speaking? Here, as in every place where He creates, it is

---

88. Cf. Ps 50.10. Jansma, "Beiträge," 60, wants to read '*bry*'—"in Hebrew." This version of Ps 50.10 does occur in the Hebrew text, but this emendation would constitute the only time that Ephrem makes a reference to the Hebrew text. See discussion in Hidal, *Interpretatio Syriaca,* 71. I find this reading in no extant Targum.

89. It was a widespread Jewish tradition that the great serpents were to be equated with Leviathan and Behemoth, see Ginzberg, *Legends,* 1:26–29, *Genesis Rabbah* 7.4. The Targums also witness to this tradition. At Gen 1.21, *Targum Neofiti* reads, "And the Lord created the *two* great monsters, "while *Targum Pseudo-Jonathan* reads, "God created the great sea monsters, *Leviathan and his companion.*" See also 1 Enoch 60.7–8, and 2 Bar 29.4.

90. Gen 1.24.

91. Cf. *Hymns on Paradise* 3.4

92. Gen 1.26.

clear that He was speaking to His Son.[93] The Evangelist said about Him that *everything came to be through Him and without Him not one thing came to be.*[94] Paul too confirms this when he said, *In Him all things were created, in heaven and on earth, all that is visible and all that is invisible.*[95]

29. *And God said, "Let us make man in our image."*[96] According to what has been the rule until now, namely, if it pleases God He will make it known to us, Moses explains in what way we are the image of God, when he said *"Let them have dominion over the fish of the sea, and over the birds, and over the cattle, and over all the earth."*[97] It is the dominion that Adam received over the earth and over all that is in it that constitutes the likeness of God who has dominion over the heavenly things and the earthly things.[98]

(2) Then [Moses] said, *male and female He created them,*[99] to make known that Eve was inside Adam, in the rib that was drawn out from him. Although she was not in his mind she was in his body, and she was not only in his body with him, but she was also in soul and spirit with him, for God added nothing to that rib that He took out except the structure and the adornment. If everything that was suitable for Eve, who came to be from the rib, was complete in and from that rib, it is rightly said that *male and female He created them.*[100]

---

93. For Ephrem, the Son was clearly the intermediary for all creation; see *Hymns on Faith* 6.6–16, *Sermons on Faith* 1.75–77, *Hymns on the Nativity* 26, *Commentary on the Diatessaron* I.6, and also discussion in Kronholm, *Motifs,* 39–43.

94. John 1.3.
95. Col 1.16.
96. Gen 1.26.
97. Gen 1.26.

98. See also II.10, below. Dominion over the earth constituting the divine image was particularly characteristic of Jewish and Antiochene Christian tradition. See, for example, John Chrysostom, *Homilies on Genesis* 2, 8; Severus of Gabala, *On the Creation of the World,* 5; and Theodoret of Cyr, *Questions on Genesis,* 20. For summary, see M. Alexandre, *Le commencement du livre Genèse I–V* (Paris, 1988) 175–88, especially 184; and J. Barr, "The Image of God in the Book of Genesis," *BJRL* 51 (1968): 11–26.

99. Gen 1.27.

100. Gen 1.27. For Eve being in Adam at his creation, see *Hymns on the Church* 45.2, *Hymns on Nisibis* 48.10, and *Hymns against Heresies* 8.5, and discussion of Kronholm, *Motifs,* 81–83. See also II.12, below.

30. *And God blessed them and said to them, "Be fruitful and multiply, and fill the earth and subdue it; and have dominion over the fish of the sea, over the birds and over every animal that crawls upon the earth."*[101] They were blessed on this earth, as if this dwelling place had been prepared for them before they sinned. Although they had not yet sinned, [God] knew that they were about to sin.

(2) *Be fruitful and multiply and fill,* not Paradise, but *the earth,* and *have dominion over the fish of the sea and the birds and over all the beasts.*[102] But how was Adam to rule over the fish of the sea unless he were to be in proximity to the sea? And how was he to rule over the birds that fly throughout every region unless his descendants were to dwell in every region? And how was Adam to rule over every beast of the earth unless his offspring were to inhabit the entire earth?

31. Although Adam was created and was blessed to rule over the earth and over everything that was created and blessed therein, God had indeed made him to dwell within Paradise. God truly manifested His foreknowledge in His blessing and manifested His grace in the place where He set Adam to dwell. Lest it be said that Paradise was not created for [Adam's] sake, [God] set him there in Paradise to dwell. And lest it be said that God did not know that Adam would sin, He blessed him on this earth. And everything with which God blessed Adam preceded the transgression of the commandment, lest by the transgression of him who had been blessed, the blessings of Him who gave the blessings be withheld and the world be turned back into nothing on account of the folly of that one for whose sake everything had been created.[103]

(2) Therefore, God did not bless Adam in Paradise, because that place and all that is in it is blessed. But God blessed him on the earth first so that by that blessing with which [His] grace blessed beforehand, the curse of the earth, which was about to be cursed by [His] justice, might [thus] be diminished. But even though the blessing was one

101. Gen 1.28. 102. Gen 1.28.
103. See note 56 above.

of promise, in that it was fulfilled after his expulsion from Paradise, His grace, nevertheless, was of actuality, for on that same day, [God] set [Adam] in the garden to dwell, clothed him with glory[104] and made him ruler over all the trees of Paradise.

32. After Moses spoke about the reptiles, the cattle, and the beasts, about mankind and about their blessing on the sixth day, he turned to write about God's rest that took place on the seventh day saying, *Thus heaven and earth were finished, and all their host. And God rested on the seventh day from all His work which He had done.*[105]

(2) From what toil did God rest? For the creatures that came to be on the first day came to be by implication,[106] except for the light which came to be through His word. And the rest of the works which came to be afterwards came to be through His word. What toil is there for us when we speak one word, that there should be toil for God due to the one word a day that He spoke?[107] If Moses, who divided the sea by his word and his rod, did not tire and Joshua, son of Nun, who restrained the luminaries by his word, did not tire, then what toil could there have been for God when He created the sea and the luminaries by [His] word?

33. It was not because He rested on [that day] that God, who does not weary, blessed and sanctified the seventh day, nor because He was to give it to that people, who did not understand that since they were freed from their servitude, they were to give rest to their servants and maidservants. He gave it to them so that, even if they had to be coerced, they would rest. For it was given to them in order to depict by a temporal rest, which He gave to a temporal people, the mystery of the true rest which will be given to the eternal people in the eternal world.

(2) Also because a full week was required, God exalted by

---

104. Ps 8.5, Peshitta. See General Introduction above and notes *ad loc.*
105. Gen 2.1–2.
106. In Syriac, *remzâ*. That is, the creation of these creatures is implied and not explicitly stated in the account of creation for the first day.
107. Compare *Genesis Rabbah* 10.9, 12.10.

His word that seventh day which His works had not exalted so that, because of the honor accorded that day, it might be united to its companions, and that the reckoning of the week, which is required for the service of the world, might be completed.

Section II

1. After Moses spoke of the sabbath rest, of how God blessed and sanctified this day, he returned to the account of how the Creation was first fashioned, briefly passing over those things of which he had already spoken, while recounting in detail those things that he had left out. He then began to write about the creation account a second time, saying, *These are the generations of heaven and earth when they were created. In the day that God made heaven and earth, when no tree of the field existed and no vegetation had sprouted—for God had not brought down rain upon the earth and Adam was not there*[108] *to till the earth; but a spring rose up and watered the whole face of the earth.*[109]

2. Understand, O hearer, that although the days of creation were finished and [God] had blessed the Sabbath day which was sanctified and he had completed [his account], Moses still returned to tell the story of the beginning of Creation even after the days of creation had been finished.

(2) *These are the generations of heaven and earth,*[110] that is, this is the account of the fashioning of heaven and earth on the day when the Lord made heaven and earth for as yet *no tree of the field existed and no vegetation had sprouted.*[111] Even if[112] these things were not actually created on the first day—for

---

108. Whereas in Hebrew the word Adam could mean either "man" or "anyone" as well as indicating a proper name [see R. S. Hess, "Splitting the Adam: the Usage of *'ādām* in Genesis i–v," in *Studies in the Pentateuch*, ed. J. A. Emerton, Supplement to Vetus Testamentum, no. 41 (Leiden, 1990) 1–15], when one finds it in Syriac it can only be taken as a proper name. Similarly, Adam occurs as a proper name at Gen 2.5 in *Targum Neofiti*.
109. Gen 2.5–6.
110. Gen 2.4.
111. Gen 2.5.
112. Read *'pn* for *'p* with Jansma, "Beiträge," 62.

they had been made on the third day—still [Moses] did not rashly introduce, on the first day, the report of those things that were created on the third day.

3. For [Moses] said, *no trees existed and no vegetation had sprouted—for the Lord had not brought down rain upon the earth; but a spring rose up out of the earth and watered the whole face of the earth.*[113] Because everything that has been born and will be born from the earth [will be] through the conjunction of water and earth, [Moses] undertook to show that no tree nor vegetation had been created along with the earth, because the rain had not yet come down. But after the great spring rose up from the great abyss and watered the whole face of the earth, and after the waters had been gathered together on the third day, then the earth brought forth all the vegetation.

(2) These waters, then, over which the darkness had been spread on the first day are the same ones that rose up from the spring and, in the blink of an eye, covered the entire earth. This was also the [same spring] that was opened in the days of Noah and that covered the surface of all the mountains on the earth. This spring did not rise up from below the earth but out of the earth, for [Moses] said, *the spring rose up* not from below the earth but, *out of the earth.* The earth itself, which bears these waters in its womb, bears witness that these waters were not prior to the earth.[114]

(3) *The spring* then *rose up out of the earth,* as Scripture says, *and watered the whole face of the earth.* Thus [the earth] produced trees, grasses, and plants. It was not that God was unable to bring forth everything from the earth in any other way. Rather, it was His will that [the earth] should bring forth by means of water. [God] began the creation [of the vegetation] this way right from the beginning so that this procedure would be perpetuated until the end of time.

4. After [Moses] spoke about those things that had been

---

113. Gen 2.5–6.
114. Ephrem seems to be basing his interpretation here on such biblical passages as Ps 24.2, where the Lord "founded the earth upon the seas."

omitted and that had not been recounted on the first day, he turned to write about how Adam was fashioned saying, *Adam was not there to till the earth.* Obviously, Adam did not exist in the days that preceded the sixth day, since he was created on the sixth day. *Then, on the sixth day the Lord formed Adam from the dust of the earth and blew into his nostrils the breath of life; and Adam became a living being.*[115] Even though the beasts, the cattle, and the birds were equal [to Adam] in their ability to procreate and in that they had life, God still gave honor to Adam in many ways: first, in that it was said, *God formed*[116] *him with His own hands and breathed life into him;*[117] God then set him as ruler over Paradise and over all that is outside of Paradise; God clothed Adam in glory; and God gave him reason and thought so that he might perceive the majesty [of God].[118]

5. After Moses spoke of how Adam was so gloriously fashioned, he turned to write about Paradise and Adam's entry therein saying, *The Lord had previously planted Paradise in Eden and there He placed Adam whom He had fashioned.*[119]

(2) Eden is the land of Paradise and [Moses] said *previously*[120] because God had [already] planted it on the third day. He explains this by saying, *the Lord caused every tree that is*

---

115. Gen 2.7.
116. The Syriac verb used here, *gbl*, is used of forming something from existing material, such as a sculpture. See *Hymns against Heresies* 48.2.
117. Gen 2.7. This divine breath is what distinguishes humanity from the animals, a theme which Ephrem develops more fully in his hymns; see Kronholm, *Motifs*, 57–67.
118. The special love and care that God took for Adam, evident throughout this section of the *Commentary,* is also prominent in Ephrem's hymns. In *Hymns on Faith* 67.19, Ephrem says that "from the very beginning God opened up the treasury of His Mercy when He formed Adam." For the great importance of God's special love for Adam in Ephrem's hymns, see also discussion in Kronholm, *Motifs,* 57–81.
119. Gen 2.8.
120. The Syriac word *qdm* can also mean "in the East," but Ephrem's comments here clearly militate against this translation. The normal English rendering "of old," would also be unsuitable here. In Jewish tradition, Paradise was also created "previously," on the third day; see *Genesis Rabbah* 15.3, 21.9; and Ginzberg, *Legends,* 1:18–20.

pleasant to the sight and good for food to sprout forth from the earth.[121] And to show that he was talking about Paradise, [Moses] said, *and the tree of life was in the midst of Paradise, and the tree of the knowledge of good and evil.*[122]

6. After [Moses] spoke about Paradise and about which day it had been planted, about Adam's entry therein, and about the tree of life and its companion, he turned to write about the river that flowed out from Paradise and which, once outside of it, divided into four distinct sources, saying, *A river flowed out of Eden to water Paradise.*[123]

(2) Here too Moses calls that delightful land of Paradise *Eden*. If that river had indeed watered Paradise, it would not have divided into the four rivers outside it. I would suggest that it was perhaps due to convention that it is said *to water*, since the spiritual trees of Paradise had no need of water. But if [someone should say that] because they are spiritual, they drink from the blessed and spiritual waters there, I would not quarrel over this.

(3) The four rivers that flowed from that river were not similar in taste to the head spring. For if the waters of our lands vary, all being placed under the sentence of a curse, how much more distinct should the taste of the blessed land of Eden be from the taste of that land which had been placed under the curse of the Just One due to Adam's transgression of the commandment?[124]

(4) The four rivers, then, are these: the Pishon, which is the Danube;[125] the Gihon, which is the Nile; and then the

---

121. Gen 2.9.

122. Gen 2.9. In *Hymns on Paradise* 3.2, all the other trees bowed down to the tree of life for it was "the captain of the host and the king of the trees." In 3.3, the tree of knowledge of good and evil was "endowed with awe and hedged with dread so that it may serve as a boundary to the inner edge of Paradise." See also 12.15, and *Hymns on Faith* 6.14.

123. Gen 2.10.

124. Ephrem has a particularly descriptive passage concerning the fragrances of Paradise in his *Hymns on Paradise* 11.9–15.

125. The identification of the Pishon with the Danube is fairly common in Syriac commentaries. It is found, for example, in Severus of Antioch and the commentaries of Mošê bar Kêphâ and of Išoʿdad of Merw as well as in Severian

COMMENTARY ON GENESIS   101

Tigris and the Euphrates, between which we dwell.[126] Although the places from which they flow are known, the source of the spring is not [known]. Because Paradise is set on a great height,[127] the rivers are swallowed up again and they go down to the sea as if through a tall water duct[128] and so they pass through the earth which is under the sea into this land.[129] The earth then spits out each one of them: the Danube, which is the Pishon, in the west; the Gihon in the south; and the Euphrates and the Tigris in the north.

7. After [Moses] spoke about Paradise and the rivers that were divided outside of it, he turned to speak about Adam's entry into Paradise and about the law that was laid down for him saying, *The Lord God took Adam and put him in the Paradise of Eden to till it and to guard it.*[130]

(2) But with what did Adam till the garden since he had no tools for tilling? How could he have tilled it since he was not capable of tilling it by himself? What did he have to till since there were no thorns or briars there? Moreover, how could he have guarded it as he could not possibly encompass it? And from what did he guard it since there were no thieves

---

of Gabala. For an overview of various Greek interpretations, see Alexandre, *Le commencement*, 259–60.

126. In his hymns, Ephrem is more inclined to interpret these rivers in more typological fashion; see, for example, *Hymns on Virginity* 4.14, and *Hymns on Faith* 48.10, where the Gospels are compared to these four rivers.

127. Ephrem conceived of Paradise as a mountain higher than all other mountains (see *Hymns on Paradise* 1.4), perhaps deriving his imagery from such passages as Isa 2.2, Ezek 28.13–14, and Ps 15.1, 24.3. See Brock, *Hymns on Paradise*, 49–57; Sed, "Les hymnes sur le paradis de saint Ephrem," 457–59; and, for the importance of the Near Eastern mytho-religious background of this concept, see G. A. Anderson, "The Cosmic Mountain: Eden and its Early Interpreters in Syriac Christianity," in *Genesis 1–3 in the History of Exegesis*, ed. G. A. Robbins (Lewiston, 1988) 187–224.

128. This loan word, in Greek, κάνθαρος, normally means "a drinking cup," "a beetle," or "a boat." The translation *cantharus* of R. Tonneau, *In Genesim et Exodum*, 21, is, therefore, not satisfactory. Kronholm, *Motifs*, 70, n. 81, suggests *aquaeductus, canalis*, which is closer to the meaning required here.

129. Thus, the earth receives blessing and healing from Paradise; see *Hymns on Paradise* 11.11.

130. Gen 2.15.

to enter it? Indeed, the fence that was erected after the transgression of the commandment bears witness that as long as Adam kept the commandment, no guard was required.

(3) Adam had nothing to guard then except the law that had been set down for him. Nor was any other "tilling" entrusted to him except to fulfill the commandment that had been commanded him. But if [someone were to say that Adam] had or would have these two things [to perform] along with the commandment, I would not oppose this [interpretation].[131]

8. After he spoke about Adam's entry into Paradise and why he had been put there, [Moses] turned to write about the law that was set down for him, saying, *and the Lord God commanded Adam, saying, "You may eat of every tree that is in Paradise; but of the tree of the knowledge of good and evil you shall not eat, for on the day that you eat of it you shall surely die."*[132]

(2) This commandment was an easy one, for God gave to Adam all of Paradise and withheld from him only one tree. If a single tree were sufficient to provide nourishment for someone and many were withheld, [that single tree] would offer relief from the torment [of hunger] by providing nourishment for one's hunger. But if God gave Adam many trees instead of a single one which would have been sufficient for him, any transgression would be due not to any constraint but to disdain.[133]

(3) [God] withheld from Adam a single tree and set death around it, so that if Adam would not keep the law out of love for the One who had set down the law, then at least the fear of death that was set around the tree would frighten him away from overstepping the law.

131. The idea that Adam was to "till" the commandment plays on the double meaning of *plh*—"to till, labor; to serve, worship." The word *šmr*—"to guard, keep"—more readily lends itself to Ephrem's interpretation. See *Hymns on Paradise* 3.16, 4.1–5. This same interpretation of this verse is also found in Jewish tradition. See Ginzberg, *Legends*, 1:70, 5:92, n.54, and *Genesis Rabbah* 16.5. For this verse, the texts of *Targum Neofiti* and *Targum Pseudo-Jonathan* specifically state the objects "the law" and "the commandments."

132. Gen 2.16–17.

133. Compare *Hymns against Heresies* 11.7, where Ephrem makes clear that God did all he could for Adam.

9. After he spoke about Adam's entry into Paradise and about the law that had been set down for him, Moses turned to write about the names that [Adam] gave to the animals saying, *the Lord formed out of the ground every beast of the field and every bird of the sky and brought them to Adam to see what he would call them.*[134]

(2) They were not really *formed,*[135] for the earth brought forth the animals and the water the birds.[136] When he said, *"He formed,"* [Moses] wished to make known that every animal, reptile, beast, and bird comes into being from the conjunction of earth and water.

(3) That [Moses] said, *He brought them to Adam,* is so that God might make known the wisdom of Adam and the harmony that existed between the animals and Adam before he transgressed the commandment. The animals came to Adam as to a loving shepherd. Without fear they passed before him in orderly fashion, by kinds and by species. They were neither afraid of him nor were they afraid of each other. A species of predatory animals would pass by with a species of animal that is preyed upon following safely right behind.

10. Adam thus began his rule over the earth when he became lord over all on that day according to the blessing he was given.[137] The word of the Creator came to pass in actuality and His blessing was indeed fulfilled on the same day that he was made ruler over everything, even though he would soon rebel against the Lord of everything. For God gave Adam not only rule over everything, which had been promised to him, but He also allowed him to bestow names [on the animals], which had not been promised to him. If then God did for Adam even more than he had expected, how could God have deprived Adam of these things unless Adam had sinned?

(2) For someone to give a few names to be remembered

---

134. Gen 2.19.
135. I.e., not in the same sense that Adam was "formed" by God's hands. See above II.4, and note *ad loc.*
136. Cf. Gen 1.20, 24.
137. See Kronholm, *Motifs,* 67–81, for the theme of Adam's lordship.

is not a great thing, but it is too large and too great a thing for any human being to bestow thousands of names in a single moment, without repeating any. It is possible for someone to bestow many names on many kinds of insects, animals, beasts, and birds, but never to name one kind by the name of another belongs either to God or to someone to whom it has been granted by God.[138]

(3) If God did indeed give Adam ruling authority, make him a participant in creation, clothe him with glory, and give him a garden, what else should God have done that Adam heed the commandment but did not do?[139]

11. After he spoke of the formation of the animals and of the names they received, [Moses] turned to write of Adam's sleep and of the rib that was taken from him and made into a woman, saying, *But for Adam there was not found a helper like him.* Moses called Eve *helper* because even though Adam had helpers among the beasts and animals he still required one like him of his own kind. Inside,[140] Eve was very diligent; she was also attentive to the sheep and cattle, the herds, and droves which were in the fields. She would also help Adam with the buildings, pens, and with any other task that Adam was capable of doing. The animals, even though they were subservient, were not able to help him with these things. For this reason God made for Adam a helper who would be solicitous for everything for which he was [solicitous] and who would indeed help him in many things.[141]

12. *And the Lord cast sleep upon Adam and he slept. God took*

---

138. The naming of all the animals without a single repitition was the sign of Adam's divine wisdom in Jewish tradition; see *Genesis Rabbah* 17.4, *Numbers Rabbah* 19.3; and Kronholm, *Motifs*, 80, n. 103 for other references. There is also a tradition, found in Ginzberg, *Legends*, 1:63, whereby it was by his inability to name any creatures that Satan was cast out of the heavenly court.

139. Compare *Hymns against Heresies* 20.8 (read ʿbd for ʿbr), *Armenian Hymns* 42.9–11, *Hymns on Faith* 62.2, and *Hymns on the Church* 48.9, where Ephrem is again amazed at Adam's fall after God did so much to make him happy.

140. I.e., within the gates of Paradise. The contrast here is inside and outside of Paradise as the animals were not permitted inside the gates of Paradise. See *Hymns on Paradise* 3.4.

141. See Kronholm, *Motifs*, 83–84.

one of his ribs and closed up its place with flesh. And the Lord fashioned the rib which He had taken from Adam into a woman and brought her to Adam.[142] That man, awake,[143] anointed with splendor, and who did not yet know sleep, fell on the earth naked and slept. It is likely that Adam saw in his dream what was done to him as if he were awake. After Adam's rib had been taken out in the twinkling of an eye, God closed up the flesh in its place in the blink of an eyelash. After the extracted rib had been fashioned with all sorts of beautiful things to adorn it, God then brought her to Adam, who was both one and two. He was one in that he was Adam and he was two because he had been created male and female.[144]

13. After he spoke of Adam's sleep, of the rib that had been taken out, and of the woman who had been fashioned from it and brought to [Adam], [Moses] wrote that *Adam said, "This time she is bone of my bones and flesh of my flesh. This one shall be called woman because she was taken out of man."*[145]

(2) *This time*—that is, this one who came after the animals was not like them for they were from the earth, but this one *is bone of my bones and flesh of my flesh.* Adam said this either as a prophecy or because he had seen it and knew it from the vision in his dream, as we just said above.

(3) Just as each animal had received from Adam the name of its species on that day, Adam did not call the rib that was fashioned [into the woman] *Eve,* by her own name, but named her *woman,* the name that was set down for all her kind. Then [Adam] said, *Let the man leave his father and his mother and cling to his wife so that they might be joined and the*

---

142. Gen 2.21–22.
143. The word used here, ʿirâ, is also the early Syriac word for "angel, watcher," that is, one who is always wakeful and watchful. For etymology, see R. Murray, "The Origin of Aramaic ʿir," *Or* 53 (1984): 303–17.
144. Cf. Gen 1.27. This thought is also amply represented in Jewish tradition; see Kronholm, *Motifs,* 81, n. 106, for references.
145. Gen 2.23. The word-play in Hebrew, 'îš—"man" from 'iššâ—"woman," does not work in Syriac nor in English.

two might become one[146] without division as they were from the beginning.

14. After these things Moses said, *The two of them were naked and were not ashamed.*[147] That they were not ashamed does not mean that they did not know what shame was. If they were children, as [the pagans][148] say, [Moses] would neither have said, *They were naked and were not ashamed,* nor, *Adam and his wife,* if they had not been young adults.[149] The names that Adam bestowed should be sufficient to convince us of [the level of] his wisdom. And the fact that [Moses] said, *he will till it and keep it,* should make known to us Adam's strength. The law that was set for them testifies to their full maturity and their transgression of the commandment should bear witness to their arrogance.

(2) It was because of the glory with which they were clothed that *they were not ashamed.* It was when this glory was stripped from them after they had transgressed the commandment that they were ashamed because they were naked.[150] The two of them then hastened to cover themselves with leaves—not their entire bodies but only their shameful members.

15. After [Moses] spoke of how their nakedness had been adorned with a heavenly garment and was no cause for shame, he turned to write about the cunning of the serpent, saying, *and the serpent was more cunning than any beast of the*

---

146. Gen 2.24.
147. Gen 2.25.
148. Syriac *brāyê* = Greek οἱ ἔξω "those outside," i.e., "those not of our party." The term could refer to pagans, heretics, Jews, or even Jewish Christians. I have not been able to discern exactly who is meant here.
149. In his hymns, Ephrem uses the same term, in Syriac, *šbry,* as he uses here, but he seems to be referring to the innocence of their minds rather than to their physical ages; see *Hymns on the Nativity* 26.8, *Hymns on Virginity* 12.12, and *Hymns on the Church* 46.7. The Jewish tradition is that Adam and Eve were born 20 years old. See Ginzberg, *Legends,* 1:59, 5:78, n.21.
150. For the importance of the garment of glory in the thought of Ephrem, see Brock, "Clothing Metaphors," 11–40; idem, *The Luminous Eye,* 65–76; and idem, *Hymns on Paradise,* 66–72. The vocabulary stems from Ps 8.6, Peshitta.

*field that the Lord had made.*¹⁵¹ Although the serpent was cunning, it was [only] more cunning than the dumb animals that were governed by Adam; it is not true that because [the serpent] surpassed the level of animals in cleverness, it was immediately raised up to the level of mankind. It was [only] more clever than those animals that lack reason and was [only] more crafty than the animals that had no mind. For, it is clear that the serpent, who did not have the mind of man, did not possess the wisdom of mankind. Adam was also greater than the serpent by the way he was formed, by his soul, by his mind, by his glory, and by his place.¹⁵² Therefore, it is evident that in cunning also Adam was infinitely greater than the serpent.¹⁵³

(2) Adam, who was set up as ruler and governor over all the animals, was wiser than all the animals. He who set down names for them all is more clever than any of them. Just as Israel, without a veil, was unable to look upon the face of Moses,¹⁵⁴ neither were the animals able to look upon the splendor of Adam and Eve;¹⁵⁵ when the beasts passed before Adam and they received their names from him, they would cast their eyes downwards, for their eyes could not endure Adam's glory. Although the serpent was more clever than all the animals, before Adam and Eve, who were the rulers over the animals, it was a fool.

16. After he spoke of the cleverness of the serpent, Moses turned to write about how that deceitful one came to Eve, saying, *the serpent said to the woman, "Did God truly say, 'You shall not eat of any of the trees of Paradise'?"*¹⁵⁶ As for the ser-

151. Gen 3.1.
152. I.e., Paradise, outside of which the serpent had to dwell. See note 140, above.
153. Similar emphasis on the serpent's relative lack of intelligence vis-à-vis Adam and Eve is found in *Hymns on the Church* 46.10, 47 *passim*, and 48.1. For the considerable attention that Ephrem gives to the cunning of the serpent in his hymns, see Kronholm, *Motifs*, 86–94.
154. Cf. Exod 34.33–35.
155. Literally, "the house of Adam," but, of course, Adam and Eve were the only two human beings alive at this time.
156. Gen 3.1. See also note 75 above.

pent's speech, either Adam understood the serpent's own mode of communication, or Satan spoke through it, or the serpent posed the question in his mind and speech was given to it, or Satan sought from God that speech be given to the serpent for a short time.[157] The words of the tempter would not have caused those two to be tempted to sin if their avarice had not been so helpful to the tempter. Even if the tempter had not come, the tree itself, by its beauty, would have caused them a great struggle due to their avarice. Their avarice then was the reason that they followed the counsel of the serpent. The avarice of Adam and Eve was far more injurious to them than the counsel of the serpent.[158]

17. For [Moses] said, *when the woman saw that the tree was good to eat and that it was a delight to the eyes, and that the tree was desirable to look at, she took of its fruit and she ate.*[159] Indeed, she was overcome by the beauty of the tree and by desire for its fruit. She was not overcome by the counsel that came into her ear; rather, she succumbed to the avarice that came from within herself.

(2) Because a commandment had been set down for those who were to be tempted, it was fitting that the tempter come along soon after. Because God, in his goodness, had given Adam all that was in Paradise and all that was outside of Paradise, demanding nothing of him, either by reason of his being created or because of the glory with which God had clothed him.

(3) God, in His justice, withheld one tree from that one

---

157. Despite these unresolved choices, at II.19, below, and in his hymns, Ephrem presumes that it was Satan who spoke through the serpent. In *Hymns on Paradise* 15.14, "the serpent is the instrument of the Evil One." In *Hymns against Heresies* 20.1, the serpent is "the harp on which Satan's melodies were played." See also *Hymns on Paradise* 3.4, 15.13; *Hymns on Nisibis* 77.6; *Hymns against Heresies* 11.7, 21.6–11, 43.1–6; and *Prose Refutations* 1:88. See discussion in Kronholm, *Motifs*, 86–95, and Ginzberg, *Legends*, 1:95, where Satan persuaded the serpent to be his vessel.

158. The Syriac text is confusing here, but the sense seems to be as translated.

159. Gen 3.6.

to whom He, in His goodness, had given everything in Paradise, on the earth, in the air, and in the seas. For, when God created Adam, He did not make him mortal, nor did He fashion him immortal, so that Adam, by either keeping or transgressing the commandment, might acquire from one of the trees, the [life] that he preferred.[160]

(4) God created the tree of life and hid it from Adam and Eve. This was so that the tree would not cause any great struggle with them by its beauty and thus double their agony. In addition, it was not right that they heed a commandment from Him who could not be seen for the sake of a reward that was before their eyes.[161]

(5) Even though God, in His goodness, had given them everything else, He wanted, in His justice, to give them immortal life that was to be conferred by their eating from the tree of life. Therefore, God set down for them a commandment. It was not a great commandment relative to the great reward that He had prepared for them; He withheld from them one tree, only enough for them to be under a commandment. God gave them all of Paradise so that they would be under no constraint to transgress the law.

18. As I said above, a tempter was required. For this purpose, however, Satan was not permitted to send any of the angels, nor any of the seraphim nor any of the cherubim. Nor was Satan himself permitted to come to Adam in the garden, neither in human appearance nor in a divine vision, as he came to our Lord on the mountain.[162] Neither did Behemoth or Leviathan, the giant beasts of renown, come nor did any of the other beasts nor any of the clean animals come, lest any of these be the reason that Adam and Eve transgressed the commandment. Rather, a serpent was allowed to come to them which, albeit cunning, was utterly despicable and hideous.

160. I.e., a life of mortality or a life of immortality. God created the tree of knowledge of good and evil as Adam's judge; see *Hymns on Paradise* 3.10, 13, 16; 12.15, 17.
161. See *Hymns on Paradise* 3.9, 17; 15.2, for the tree of life being hidden from Adam and Eve.
162. Cf. Matt 4.1–11, and parallels.

(2) And when the serpent came, it performed no signs that could be trusted nor did it fashion some deceitful vision, but it came alone, lowly, eyes cast down because it was unable to look upon the splendor of that one who would be tempted by it. Out of fear it did not go to Adam but went rather to Eve so that it might make her eat more quickly from the tree from which she was commanded not to eat. Prior to this she had tasted nothing from the thousands and millions [of trees] that were permitted her. That she had not yet tasted from them was not because she was fasting, but rather that hunger had not yet exerted any power over her for she had just been created at that very moment.

(3) The serpent was completely unhindered from coming in all haste because even the serpent's haste [worked] against the serpent. For, since Eve had just been created, she did not yet know what hunger was, nor had she yet been engaged in any inner struggle caused by the beauty of the tree. Therefore, because she was neither fasting nor had been engaged in any contest due to the tree, the serpent was completely unhindered from coming to tempt her.

(4) If [Eve] had been victorious in that momentary battle, in that brief contest, the serpent and that one who was in the serpent would [still] have received the punishment that they received, while she, together with her husband, would have eaten of the tree of life and would have lived for ever. Along with this promised life that [Adam and Eve] would have acquired, they would also have had by Justice all that had previously been given to them by Grace.

(5) The tempter, then, came in haste and was not hindered so that because it came, as tempter, at the time the commandment was given, [Adam and Eve] might know that it was the tempter and they might take precautions against his cunning. Then that one who was unable to give himself even the smallest of names offered them great counsel.[163]

19. That one who was in the serpent then spoke to the

---

163. See II.10, above, for Adam's bestowal of the names of all the animals, and note *ad loc.* for the underlying Jewish tradition of Satan's inability to bestow a single name.

woman, through the serpent, saying, *"Did God truly say, 'You shall not eat of any of the trees of Paradise'?"* We ought to understand here that if they had been commanded [not to eat] from all the trees, as the serpent said, then the commandment would have been great. The fact is, they had been commanded just the opposite; it was hardly a commandment at all, because it was so small, and it had been given to them for only that short time before the tempter departed from them.

(2) Eve responded and *said to the serpent, "We may eat of the fruit of the trees in Paradise; but [God] said, 'You shall not eat from the fruit of the tree which is in the middle of Paradise, neither shall you draw near to it, lest you die.'"* [164] When the serpent and that one who was in the serpent heard that [Adam and Eve] were permitted to eat from any of the trees of Paradise and that only one had been withheld from them, they seemed covered in shame for they saw no opportunity to offer their counsel.

20. The tempter then turned its mind to the commandment of Him who had set down the commandment, that [Adam and Eve] were not only commanded not to eat from one single tree, but they were not even to draw near to it. The serpent then realized that God had forewarned them about even looking at it lest they become entrapped by its beauty.[165] With this in mind, the serpent said, enticing Eve to look upon it, *"You will surely not die. For God knows that when you eat from it your eyes will be opened and you will be like God, knowing good and evil."*[166] But Eve failed to discern the import of the words of the serpent, who as tempter, had said the opposite of what God had said. She also failed to respond to

---

164. Gen 3.2–3. The Syriac word *qrb*, can also mean to touch, as it is normally translated in English texts of this passage. As is clear, however, from Ephrem's ensuing comments, he means they were not even to draw near the tree.

165. The tempter's apprehension of the meaning of this commandment is more fully developed in Ephrem's hymns; see *Hymns on Paradise* 3.5, 12.2–3, and discussion in Kronholm, *Motifs*, 97–98, especially n. 31, for Jewish parallels.

166. Gen 3.4–5.

the serpent by saying, "How can my eyes be opened when they are not closed? How will I, by eating of the fruit, come to know between good and evil when, even before I have eaten, they are here in my presence?"[167] But she neglected these things that she ought to have said to the serpent and, just as the serpent desired, she directed her eyes away from the serpent who was before her and began to look upon the tree to which she had been commanded not to draw near.

(2) The serpent remained silent, for it perceived immediately that Eve was about to succumb. It was not so much the serpent's counsel that entered her ear and provoked her to eat from the tree as it was her gaze, which she directed toward the tree, that lured her to pluck and eat of its fruit. She could have said to the serpent, "If I cannot see, how is it that I see all that is to be seen? And if I do not know between good and evil, how can I discern whether your counsel is good or evil? How will I come to know whether the divinity is good or that having [my] eyes opened is good? And whence am I to discern that death is evil? If I already possess these things, why have you come to me? Your coming unto us is testimony that we have these things. Therefore, by the sight that I possess and by the ability to discern between good and evil that I have, I will examine your counsel. And if I do possess these things that you counsel me, where is all your craftiness that is unable to disguise your deceit?" She, however, said none of these things to the serpent so as to overcome it, but instead fixed her gaze on the tree and thus quickly brought about her own defeat.[168]

(3) She then went after that which her eyes desired and, being enticed by the divinity that the serpent had promised her, she stole away from her husband and ate. Afterwards, she gave some to her husband and he ate with her. Because she believed the serpent she ate first, thinking that she would be clothed with divinity in the presence of that one

---

167. Compare *Hymns on the Church* 47.3: "She did not ask it 'Are you a servant or a freeman? A heavenly being, a beast, or an angel?'" See also 48.3; and *Hymns on Paradise* 3.6.

168. See *Hymns on the Church* 47.3, 48.3; and Kronholm, *Motifs*, 99 ff.

from whom she, as woman, had been separated.[169] She hastened to eat before her husband that she might become head over her head, that she might become the one to give command to that one by whom she was to be commanded and that she might be older in divinity than that one who was older than she in humanity.

21. After she ate, Eve neither grew nor did she shrink, nor were her eyes opened. She neither received the divinity for which she had been looking, nor did she find that the opening of [her] eyes had taken her to Paradise. She then brought the fruit to her husband and made him eat after much entreaty, even if it is not written that she had to persuade him. After Eve ate, she did not surely die, as God had said, nor did she find divinity, as the serpent had said. And, if Eve had been stripped naked Adam would have been afraid and would not have eaten. Although Adam would not have been guilty, since he had not eaten, he would not have been victorious, either, for he would not really have been tempted. It would have been the nakedness of his wife that made him desist from eating and not the love or fear of his Commander. Thus, Adam was to be tested immediately by the seductive pleas of Eve who, having been tested by the counsel of the serpent, had drawn near and eaten, but had not become naked.

22. Then, after [Eve] had enticed Adam into eating, Scripture says, *the eyes of both of them were opened and they knew that they were naked.*[170] The opening of their eyes was not so that they would become like God as the serpent had said but so that they would see their nakedness as that enemy had expected.

(2) Before, their eyes had been both open and closed: open in that they could see everything, but closed in that they could see neither the tree of life nor their own naked-

---

169. That is, on the sixth day when Eve was made from the rib extracted from Adam. See *Hymns on Nisibis* 75.8, where the same verb is used to express the rib being extracted from Adam.

170. Gen 3.7.

ness.[171] The enemy was also jealous because [Adam and Eve] were richer in glory and reason than any other creature on the earth and because they alone had been promised the eternal life that is given by the tree of life.[172] The enemy, jealous of Adam and Eve both for the things that belonged to them and also for the things that they were soon to receive, set its traps, and in a momentary battle took from [Adam and Eve] those things they ought not to have lost even in a great battle.

23. If the serpent had been rejected along with sin, Adam and Eve would have eaten from the tree of life and the tree of knowledge would not have been withheld from them; from the one they would have gained infallible knowledge and from the other they would have received immortal life. They would have acquired divinity with their humanity, and if they had acquired infallible knowledge and immortal life, they would have possessed them in those same bodies. Thus, by its counsel, the serpent brought to nought everything that was soon to have become theirs. The serpent made them think that they would receive these things when they transgressed the commandment so that the transgression would be committed and they would not receive what they would have received if they had kept the commandment.[173] Thus, the serpent, through the divinity that he promised them, prevented them [from receiving] divinity. The serpent also brought it about that those to whom it had been promised that their eyes would be opened by the tree of knowledge, would not have their eyes opened by the promise of the tree of life.

(2) If Adam and Eve had sought to repent after they had transgressed the commandment, even though they would

---

171. Compare *Hymns on Paradise* 3.6.

172. As he does in his hymns, Ephrem here maintains that Satan's fall is due to his jealousy at humanity's exalted position in creation; see *Hymns on the Church* 11.1, *Hymns on Faith* 50.5–6, *Hymns on the Nativity* 21.15, and *Hymns on Nicomedia* 10.22, and discussion in Kronholm, *Motifs*, 90–92. See also II.26, 32, below.

173. Compare *Hymns on Paradise* 3.12.

not have regained that which they had possessed before their transgression of the commandment, they would have escaped from the curses that were decreed on the earth and upon them. God tarried in coming down to them for the sole reason that they might admonish each other and so plead for mercy when the judge came to them. The coming of the serpent had not been delayed lest their trial be too great when they looked upon the sight of that beautiful tree, whereas the judge delayed His coming to them so that He might give them an occasion to prepare their entreaty. But the haste of the tempter did not help them, even though its haste was for the purpose of helping them, nor did they benefit by the delay of the Judge, although His delay was for this same reason.

24. *And they heard the sound of the Lord walking in Paradise in the cool of the day and they hid themselves from the presence of the Lord among the trees in Paradise.*[174] It was not only by the patience He exhibited that God wished to help them, He also wished to benefit them by the sound of His feet. God endowed His silent footsteps with sound so that Adam and Eve might be prepared, at that sound, to make supplication before Him who made the sound. But since they did not come before Him in supplication, neither because of His delay nor because of the sound that was sent before Him, God then made a sound with His lips, just as He had made a sound for His footsteps and said, *"Where are you, Adam?"*[175] But Adam, instead of confessing his folly and asking for mercy before the judgment came upon him, said, *"I heard the sound of your [feet] in Paradise and I was afraid because I saw that I was naked and I hid myself."*[176] Now the sound of feet that went before God, who would soon reveal Himself in the punishment upon the house of Adam, prefigured the voice of John, who was to come before the Son, holding a winnowing fork in his hands in order to clean out His granaries,

---

174. Gen 3.8.
175. Gen 3.8.
176. Gen 3.10.

burning the straw in fire and purifying the wheat to bring into His granaries.[177]

25. *"I heard the sound of your [feet] and I hid myself."* When did you hear any sound from Him as you did now? For when He formed you, brought you into Paradise, cast sleep on you, took out your rib, formed and brought to you a woman, you did not hear any sound from Him. If you heard a sound from Him now for the first time, understand that the sound of His steps was bestowed for the purpose of a supplication from your lips. Speak to God now, before he asks you about the coming of the serpent and about the transgression that you and Eve committed. Perhaps then, the confession of your lips will absolve you from the sin of [eating] the fruit that your fingers plucked. But Adam and Eve refused to confess that thing which they had done and they related to Him who knows all only what had been done to them.

26. *"Where are you, Adam?"* In the divinity that the serpent promised you? Or in subjection to the death that I decreed for you? Would that you had considered the fruits![178] Suppose, Adam, that instead of a serpent, the most despicable creature of all, an angel or some other god had come to you? Would you have despised the commandment of Him who gave you all these things, heeding instead the counsel of one who had not yet done you any good? Would you have considered evil the one who formed you from nothing and made you a second god over Creation while considering good the one who gave you only a verbal promise of some good?

(2) If another god were to come to you in power, should you not have rejected his advice? How much more then in the case of a serpent who came to you with no power, with no wonderous deeds but with only the empty word that it

---

177. Cf. Matt 3.11–12, and parallels.
178. See *Hymns on Heresies* 26:4 where Ephrem says, "The fruit is the goal of the right way that runs from this tree to the Cross." These trees were two crowns in Adam's contest. See *Hymns on Paradise* 3.10, 9.1, 12.17–18; *Hymns on the Church* 19.7; *Hymns on Nisibis* 68.3; *Hymns against Heresies* 21.6; *Sermons on Faith* 3.1–38.

spoke to you? You have been unfaithful to your God and you have believed your betrayer. You have denied Him who has done good things for you, who made you ruler over everything, and you have put your faith in that crafty one who, by its cunning, has taken away your rule completely.[179]

(3) If the serpent had been withheld from coming to test Adam, those who complain about its having come would now complain about its being hindered from coming. For they say that it was out of jealousy that the serpent was hindered from coming so that [Adam], after a momentary trial, might acquire eternal life. Those who say that if the serpent had not come Adam would not have erred would now be saying that if the serpent had come, Adam and Eve would not have erred; just as those who say that if the serpent had not come Adam would not have sinned, would now think they are all the more right when they say, "If the serpent had come, Adam and Eve would not have gone astray." For who would have believed, if it had not actually happened, that Adam would listen to Eve[180] or that Eve would be persuaded by a reptile?

27. *"I heard the sound of [your feet] and I was afraid and hid myself."* Because Adam forgot what was required of him and said instead that which was not required—for, instead of confessing what he had done, which would have helped him, he related what had been done to him, which did not help him at all—*God said to him, "Who told you that you were naked? Have you then eaten of the tree of which I commanded you not to eat?"*[181] Did you see that you were naked with the sight bestowed on you by that tree, from which you were promised that glorious divine sight?"

(2) Adam again failed to confess his folly and blamed the woman who was like him, saying, *"The woman whom you set*

---

179. That Adam and Eve rejected God so quickly and without reflection is also found in *Hymns on the Church* 48.3–9, *Hymns on the Nativity* 5.5, *Hymns on Nisibis* 35.4, and *Hymns against Heresies* 11.7.
180. Read *hwʾ*—"Eve" for *hwyʾ*—"serpent," which would make no sense here, as Jansma, "Beiträge," 63.
181. Gen 3.11.

with me gave me of the tree and I ate.[182] I neither drew near to the tree myself nor did I dare to stretch out my hand towards the fruit." It is for this reason the Apostle said, *Adam did not sin but Eve transgressed the commandment.*[183] If God gave you the woman, O Adam, He gave her to you to help you, not to cause you harm, and as one to be commanded, not one to give command.[184]

28. Since Adam did not wish to confess his folly, God came down to question Eve *and said to her, "What is this that you have done?"*[185] Eve too, instead of making supplication with her tears and bearing the fault herself so that mercy might take hold of both her and her husband responded, not by saying, "The serpent counseled or seduced me," but simply said, *"The serpent deceived me and I ate."*[186]

29. When the two of them had been questioned and were both found to be wanting in remorse or true contrition, God went down to the serpent, not to make inquiry but to render punishment. For where there is opportunity for repentance, it would be right to inquire, but to one who is a stranger to repentance judgment is fitting. It is so that you might know that the serpent is not capable of repentance, that when *God said to it, "Because you have done this, cursed are you above every beast,"*[187] the serpent did not say, "I did not do it," because it was afraid to lie, nor did it say, "I did it," because it was a stranger to repentance.

(2) *"Cursed are you are above every beast,"* because you deceived those who rule over all the beasts. Instead of being more clever than all the beasts you will be more cursed than all the beasts and *"on your belly shall you go,"*[188] because you brought birth pangs upon the race of women. And *"dust you*

182. Gen 3.12.
183. 1 Tim 2.14.
184. Compare Ginzberg, *Legends,* 1:77, where an attempted reversal of roles is depicted as the reason for Eve's taking the fruit.
185. Gen 3.13.
186. Gen 3.13.
187. Gen 3.14.
188. Gen 3.14. Compare *Hymns on Paradise* 3.15; see also Kronholm, *Motifs,* 113, n. 72.

shall eat all the days of your life,"[189] because you deprived Adam and Eve from eating of the tree of life. *"I will put enmity between you and the woman and between your seed and her seed,"*[190] for in your pretence of love you have deceived and subjected to death both her and her offspring.

(3) Then [God] made known the enmity that was put between the serpent and the woman and between its seed and her seed when He said, *"He will tread on your head,"* that is, that one who wishes to escape the subjection of her seed [to death], *"and you will strike him,"* not in his ear, but *"in his heel."*[191]

30. Even though the punishment decreed against the serpent was justly decreed—because to the place where folly begins, the punishment also returns—the entire reason God began with this impious creature was so that, when Justice appeased its anger on this creature, Adam and Eve should grow afraid and repent so that there might be a possibility for Grace to preserve them from the curses of Justice.[192] But when the serpent had been cursed and Adam and Eve had still made no supplication, God came [to them] with punishment. He came to Eve first, because it was through her that the sin was handed on to Adam.

(2) God then rendered his judgment against Eve saying, *"I will greatly multiply your pains and your conceptions. With pangs you shall bring forth children."*[193] Even though she would have given birth because she had received the blessing of birth along with all the animals, she would not have given birth to many, for those to whom she would have given birth would have remained immortal. She would have been preserved from the pangs of their births, from the ignominy of having to raise them, and from wailing over their deaths. *"You shall turn toward your husband,"* to be counseled and not

---

189. Gen 3.14.
190. Gen 3.15.
191. Gen 3.15. See also Kronholm, *Motifs,* 112–18.
192. See *Hymns on the Church* 45.33, where "God had compassion on Adam and gave him opportunity for conversion."
193. Gen 3.16.

to give counsel and *"he shall rule over you,"*[194] because you thought that by eating of the fruit you would then rule over him.

31. After God had set down His judgment against Eve and still no repentance had risen up in Adam, He then turned to him, too, with punishment and said, *"Because you listened to the voice of your wife and were deceived into eating of the tree of which I said to you, 'You shall not eat of it,' cursed is the ground because of you."*[195] Although the earth, which had committed no folly, was struck on account of Adam, [God] still made Adam, who could suffer, suffer by the curse of [the earth], which could not suffer. For it was in that earth, which received the curse, that he, who did not receive the curse, was, in fact, cursed.

(2) Adam did not escape direct punishment by the fact that the earth received this curse. God also decreed against him, saying, *"All the days of your life you shall eat in pain,"*[196] that which, had you kept the commandment, you would have eaten without pain. *"Thorns and thistles it shall bring forth to you,"*[197] after the sin; had there been no sin, it would not have brought forth these things. *"You shall eat the plants of the field,"*[198] because on account of a trifling enticement on the part of your wife you have rejected the most pleasing fruits of Paradise. *"In the sweat of your brow you shall eat bread,"*[199] for you were not pleased to enjoy yourself in the garden without toil. These things will come upon you *"until you return to the earth from which you were taken,"*[200] because you have despised the commandment which now could have given you eternal life through the fruit of the tree of life which would have been lawful for you to eat. Because *"you are from the dust,"*[201] and have forgotten yourself, *"you shall return to your dust,"*[202] so that, through your state of humiliation, you shall come to know your true essence.[203]

194. Gen 3.16.
195. Gen 3.17.
196. Gen 3.17.
197. Gen 3.18.
198. Gen 3.18.
199. Gen 3.19.
200. Gen 3.19.
201. Gen 3.19.
202. Gen 3.19.
203. In Syriac, *qnōmutʾ*. See Beck, *Reden*, 8–14.

32. Even Satan, who was created, along with his deep abyss, within those six days, was fair until the sixth day, like Adam and Eve who were fair until they transgressed the commandment. Satan, who secretly became Satan on that sixth day, was, on that same day, secretly judged and condemned. For God did not wish to make known Satan's condemnation in the presence of those who had not even perceived that he was the tempter. Remember, the woman said, *"the serpent,"* and not Satan, *"deceived me."*[204]

(2) Therefore, Satan was judged in secret and all his hosts were condemned along with him, because the sin was a great one and to condemn any of them alone would have been too small a punishment. Therefore, just as pangs were decreed against Eve and her daughters, and thorns and death against Adam and his posterity, and just as it [was decreed] against the serpent that he and all his seed were to be trod upon, so it was also decreed against him who was in the serpent that he go to the fire together with all his hosts. For our Lord revealed in the New Testament that which had been hidden in the Old Testament when He said that *"concerning the judgment of the ruler of this world, this one is condemned."*[205]

33. After he spoke of the punishments that both the tempter and the tempted received, Moses wrote, *the Lord made for Adam and for his wife garments of skin, and clothed them.*[206] Were these garments from the skins of animals or were they created like the thistles and thorns that were created after the other works of creation had been completed? Because it was said that *the Lord made . . . and clothed them,* it seems most likely that when their hands were placed over their leaves they found themselves clothed in garments of skin. Why would beasts have been killed in their presence? Perhaps, it was so that by the animal's flesh Adam and Eve might nourish their own persons, and that with the skins they might cover their nakedness, and also so that by the

204. Gen 3.13.
205. John 16.11.
206. Gen 3.20.

death [of the animals] Adam and Eve might see the death of their own bodies.

34. After he finished these things [God] said, *"Behold, Adam has become like one of us, knowing good and evil."*[207] Even though by saying, *"He has become like one of us,"* he symbolically reveals the Trinity, [the point is] rather that [God] was mocking Adam in that Adam had previously been told, *"You will become like God knowing good and evil."*[208]

(2) Now, even though after they ate the fruit Adam and Eve came to know these two things, before [they ate] the fruit they had perceived, in reality, only good and they heard about evil only by hearsay. After they ate, however, a change occurred so that now they would only hear about good by hearsay, whereas in reality they would taste only evil. For the glory with which they had been clothed passed away from them, while pain and disease which had been kept away from them now came to hold sway over them.

35. *"And now, lest he put forth his hand and take also of the tree of life, and eat, and live forever. . . ."*[209] If Adam had rashly eaten from the one tree he was commanded not to eat, how much faster would he hasten to that one about which he had not been so commanded? But it was now decreed that they should live in toil, in sweat, in pains, and in pangs. Therefore, lest [Adam and Eve], after having eaten of this tree, live forever and remain in eternal lives of suffering, [God] forbade them to eat, while they were clothed with a curse, that which He had been prepared to give them before they incurred the curse and when they were still clothed with glory.

(2) [God did this,] lest this life-giving gift that they would receive through the tree of life become misery, and thus bring worse evil upon them than what they had already obtained from the tree of knowledge. From the latter [tree] they obtained temporal pains, whereas the former [tree] would have made those pains eternal. From the latter they

---

207. Gen 3.22.
208. Gen 3.5.
209. Gen 3.22.

obtained death which would cast off from them the bonds of their pains. The former [tree], however, would have caused them [to live] as if buried alive, leaving them to be tortured eternally by their pains. [God], therefore, withheld from them the tree of life. It was not right either that a life of delights be allowed in the land of curses or that eternal life be found in a transitory world.

(3) If they had eaten, however, one of two things would have occurred. Either the decree of death would have become a lie, or the life-giving capacity of the tree of life would have been denied. Therefore, lest the decree of death be loosed or the life-giving capacity of the tree of life become false, God took Adam far away from there lest he also incur loss from the tree of life just as he had been harmed by the tree of knowledge. *He sent him then to till the earth from which he was taken,*[210] so that he who had been harmed in the leisure of the garden might be aided by the toil of the earth.[211]

36. Then, after Adam was cast out from Paradise [Moses] wrote, *[God] set in the east of the Paradise of Eden a cherub and a sharp sword*[212] *to go about in every direction and to guard the way to the tree of life.*[213] That fence was a living being[214] who itself marched around to guard the way to the tree of life from any one who dared try to pluck its fruit, for it would kill, with the edge of its sword, any mortal who came to steal immortal life.[215]

---

210. Gen 3.23.
211. Compare *Hymns on Paradise* 1.10: "In His Grace, God granted Adam the low ground near Paradise, settling him in the valley below the foothills of Paradise." See also 12.15.
212. The Peshitta, *Targum Neofiti,* and *Targum Pseudo-Jonathan* all read "sharp" here instead of "fiery". See M. Alexandre, "L'épée de flamme (Gen 3,24): Textes chrétiens et traditions juives," in *Hellenica et Judaica. Hommage à V. Nikiprowetsky,* ed. A. Caquot et al. (Louvain-Paris, 1986) 403–41. For the importance of this sword in Ephrem's view of salvation history, see R. Murray, "The Lance," 224–34, 491.
213. Gen 3.24.
214. In Syriac, *hayyā.* See Ginzberg, *Legends,* 1:83–84, where angels are distinguished from "the holy Hayyot."
215. See *Hymns on Paradise* 2.1, 4.1–6, 11.3.

Section III

1. After Moses spoke of Adam's expulsion from the garden, of the cherub and of the sharp sword by which Paradise was enclosed, he turned to write about the birth of Cain and Abel and about their offerings, saying *Adam knew Eve, and she bore Cain and she said, "I have gotten a man,"*—not by Adam who knew her, but—*"by the Lord,"*[216] who had formed him in the womb. *She again gave birth, to Abel, and Abel became a shepherd and Cain a tiller of the earth. And it happened after some time,* that is, after they were reared or while they were shepherding or tilling, *that Cain brought to the Lord an offering of the fruits of the earth and Abel brought of the firstborn of his flock and of their fat portions.*[217]

2. Abel was very discriminate in his choice of offerings, whereas Cain showed no such discrimination. Abel selected and offered the choicest of his first born and of his fat ones, while Cain either offered young grains or [certain] fruits that are found at the same time as the young grains. Even if his offering had been smaller than that of his brother, it would have been as acceptable as the offering of his brother, had he not brought it with such negligence. They made their offerings alternately; one offered a lamb of his flock, the other the fruits of the earth. But because Cain had taken such little regard for the first offering that he offered, God refused to accept it in order to teach Cain how he was to make an offering. For Cain had bulls and calves and an abundance of animals and birds that he could have offered. But he offered none of these on that day when he offered the first fruits of his land.[218]

(2) What would have been the harm if he had brought ripe grains or if he had chosen the fruits of his best trees? Although this would have been easy, he did not do even

---

216. Gen 4.1.
217. Gen 4.2–4.
218. For Cain's negligent offering in Jewish tradition, see *Genesis Rabbah* 22.5, Philo, *On the Sacrifices of Abel and Cain,* XIII.52, and Ginzberg, *Legends,* 1:107–8. See also V. Aptowitzer, *Kain und Abel in der Agada, den Apokryphen, der hellenistichen, christlichen und muhammedanischen Literatur* (Leipzig, 1922).

this. It was not that he had other intentions for his best grains or his best fruits; it was that, in the mind of the offerer, there was no love for the One who would receive his offering. Therefore, because Cain brought his offering with negligence, God despised it on that account, lest Cain think either that God did not know of Cain's negligence, or that God preferred the offerings rather than those who were offering them.

3. Thus, God despised Cain's offering not only because of what he had done, but also because of what he was about to do. He was cruel toward his parents and bitter toward his brother and gave no honor to God. Abel's offering was accepted, therefore, because of his discrimination whereas that of Cain was despised because of his negligence.

(2) *Cain was very angry*,[219] not because his offering had been despised, for he could have satisfied with a choice offering that One whom he angered with his negligent offering; nor was it due to the fact that he had been despised that *his face became gloomy*,[220] for it would have been easy for him to offer a prayer.

(3) Whether the offering that Cain had chosen to bring was accepted or not, Cain had already made known his will, and whether he had been persuaded to offer a prayer or not, God had already seen his true request. Since Cain did not bring a choice offering in the place of his negligent one which was despised, nor did he offer a prayer on account of the contempt that he had shown to God, it became clear that *he was angry. He was angry* because the offering of his brother had been accepted. Cain became *angry* on account of the fire that had come down and distinguished between the offerings. *His face became gloomy* because there was laughter in the eyes of his parents and his sisters when his offering was rejected. They had seen that Cain's offering had been placed in the midst of the fire and yet the fire did not touch it.

219. Gen 4.5.
220. Gen 4.5.

4. *God said to [Cain], "Why are you angry and why is your face gloomy?"*[221] Instead of being filled with anger you ought to be filled with distress. Instead of your face being gloomy tears ought to be flowing from your eyes. *If you do well, I will accept it."*[222] Notice then, that it was not because of the small size of Cain's offering that it was rejected; it was not accepted because of his spitefulness and his lack of virtue.

(2) *"If you do well, I will accept it,* even though I did not accept it before, and it will be accepted along with the chosen offering of your brother even though it was not accepted before. *But if you do not do well, sin is couching at the first door."*[223] Abel will hearken to you through his obedience, for he will go with you to the plain. There you will be ruled over by sin, that is, you shall be completely filled with it.

(3) But, instead of doing well so that the offering which had been rejected might be credited to him as acceptable, Cain then made an offering of murder to that One to whom he had [already] made an offering with negligence.

5. *And Cain said to Abel, "Let us go out to the field."*[224] That he said, *"Let us go out to the field,"* [means] either that they dwelt on a mountain on the outskirts of Paradise[225] and that Cain led Abel down to the field, or that Abel was grazing his flocks on a mountain and [Cain] went up and brought him down to a field, which was more suitable for him because of its standing grain and its soil. For in the standing grains Cain killed Abel and in the earth he easily hid him. For [Moses] said *when they were in the field, Cain rose up against his brother Abel and killed him.*[226]

(2) After Cain had killed his brother, he persuaded his parents with lies that Abel had entered Paradise because he was pleasing to God, and that his offering was accepted bore witness to his entry; that it was by keeping the commandment that he entered Paradise just as by transgressing the commandment you were cast out from there. Then, just

221. Gen 4.6.
222. Gen 4.7.
223. Gen 4.7.
224. Gen 4.8.
225. See note 127, above, for geography of Paradise.
226. Gen 4.8.

when Cain thought that he had deceived his parents and that there would be no one to seek vengeance for Abel, God appeared to Cain and *said to him, "Where is Abel your brother?"*[227]

6. God appeared to Cain with kindness so that if he repented, the sin of murder that his fingers had committed might be effaced by the compunction on his lips. If he did not repent, however, there would be decreed on him a bitter punishment in proportion to his evil folly. But Cain was filled with wrath instead of compunction. To Him who knows all, who asked him about his brother in order to win him back, [Cain] retorted angrily and said, *"I do not know, am I my brother's keeper?"*[228]

(2) *[God] then spoke to him again, saying, "What have you done?"*[229] If you do not know where Abel is because you are not his keeper, tell Him who asked you what you have done. Why should He ask someone else concerning what you have done? Confess, therefore, what have you done to Him who would not have asked about what you did unless He knew what you had done. Then, when Cain refused to recount what he had done, his knowledge and his shame were exposed when *[God] said, "Your brother's blood is crying to me from the earth."*[230]

7. What then would you say, Cain? Should Justice take vengeance for the blood which cried out to it or not? Did it not delay so that you might repent? Did it not alienate itself from its own knowledge and ask you as if it did not know, so that you might confess? Did what it said to you not please you that you came to that sin to which it had warned you beforehand not to come? *"Cursed are you from all the earth,"*[231] because you have grieved Adam and Eve, the parents of all the earth. *"Cursed are you from the face of all the earth,"* because

---

227. Gen 4.9.   228. Gen 4.9.
229. Gen 4.10.
230. Gen 4.10. While the supplied subject of the Biblical quote is undoubtedly God, the verb is feminine, suggesting that Ephrem had in mind a personified attribute of God, such as Justice. See next section.
231. Gen 4.11.

you opened the gate of Sheol before the entire earth.[232] *"When you till the earth, it shall no longer yield to you its strength,"*[233] because you wished that you alone should eat of its strength. *"You shall wander about on the earth in fear,"*[234] because you have walked on it in arrogance and in haughtiness.

8. At the very moment that these curses [were decreed], the matter of the curses was fulfilled in him who, before the curses, had said in his pride, *"Am I my brother's keeper?"* After the curses, when his anger had subsided due to the trembling and wandering that had been laid upon him, Cain said, *"My offence is greater than I can bear."*[235] This was not accepted as repentance, for he said it after it had been sought from him. Now, he said it as if under constraint, as if he said it due to his terror and wandering.

(2) But Cain, instead of seeking God's longsuffering kindness so that he might persuade Justice by his petition, said, either out of fear or of cunning, *"You have driven me away from the face of the earth,"*[236] in that you cursed me from the earth and henceforth *from your face I will be hidden.*[237] I will no longer be able to stand before you because I spoke impudently before you and said that I am not my brother's keeper. Because I have become *one who is to wander about the earth in fear, it will be that whoever finds me will kill me."*[238]

(3) O Cain, are you asking for death or are you afraid of death? How can these things that were decreed against you be fulfilled if you die? If your life is dear to you even among these miseries, how much more dear was it to Abel who was far from these things?

(4) Although some say that Cain begged not to die, still others say that he asked for death, on account of which *God said to him, "It will not be as you say* concerning the killers who come after you.[239] Although the killers who come after you

---

232. In *Hymns on Nisibis* 39.16, Death says, "Through the sword of Cain I was glad for the first time." See also Kronholm, *Motifs*, 142–45.

233. Gen 4.12.   234. Gen 4.12.
235. Gen 4.13.   236. Gen 4.14.
237. Gen 4.14.   238. Gen 4.14.
239. Cf. Gen 4.15.

COMMENTARY ON GENESIS

will die the moment they are found, still *Cain shall be avenged sevenfold*,"[240] that is, because Cain sought death so that no one would mock his lowly state, seven generations would come and see his lowly state and then he would die.

9. Some say that the seven generations were those of his tribe who died with him. This [interpretation], however, cannot be maintained. For, even if the flood overtook them, it overtook that seventh generation. And if that one generation perished with [Cain], how can they say that seven generations perished with Cain when they cannot even show that the flood occurred in the seventh generation of Cain's descendants?[241]

(2) Scripture says that Cain begot Enoch and Enoch begot Edar[242] and Edar begot Mehujael and Mehujael begot Methushael and Methushael begot Lamech and Lamech begot Jabal.[243] *Jabal was the father of those who dwell in tents and have cattle.*[244] Those who dwell in tents and have cattle were not preserving their virginity in their tents. How aptly then does Scripture say, *All flesh had corrupted its path.*[245]

(3) If then there are found to be nine generations from Cain to the descendants of those who dwell in tents and have cattle and the flood had still not come, how can we assent to [the notion that] seven generations perished with Cain? Rather, it has been determined that there were nine generations that passed away, as we just said, and still the flood had not occurred. Therefore it was rightly stated that the shame of Cain, who had sought from that first day to flee from shame by a death, was spread out over seven generations.

(4) That Cain remained alive until the seventh generation is clear. First, because it had been so decreed concerning him and secondly, the length of the lives of those first

---

240. Gen 4.15.
241. See Ginzberg, *Legends*, 1:163, where Cain is numbered among the victims of the flood. Compare another Jewish tradition about the death of Cain in n. 257, below.
242. RSV, Irad. The letters *r* and *d* are easily confused in Syriac.
243. Cf. Gen 4.17–20. 244. Gen 4.20.
245. Gen 6.12.

generations also testifies to it. For if his father Adam remained alive until the ninth generation, that of Lamech, and was gathered from the world in the fifty-sixth year of Lamech, it is no great thing that Cain should remain until the seventh generation.

10. Because Cain sought to escape from reproach, he did not escape from reproach as he sought and, further, a sign which he had not expected was added to the first punishment. For [Moses] said, *The Lord put a sign on Cain lest anyone who finds him should kill him.*[246] Those who would find him were the sons of Seth who were compelled to seek revenge for the blood of Abel, their uncle. They cut themselves off from Cain and did not intermarry with him because of his reproach and because of their fear of him, but they did not dare to kill him because of his sign.

11. After Cain received the punishment and the sign had been added to it (although we spoke of why it was necessary, we will not speak here of what it was, for that is not necessary), [Moses] said that *Cain went away from the presence of the Lord and dwelt in the land of Nod, east of Eden.*[247] Cain, therefore, separated himself from his parents and his kin because he saw that they would not intermarry with him. The land of Nod is so called because it was the land in which Cain wandered about in fear and trembling.[248] But [the land] also received a second curse, when *God said, "When you till the earth it shall no longer yield to you its strength."*[249]

Section IV

1. *After Cain knew his wife and she conceived and bore Enoch, he built a city and he named it after his son, Enoch.*[250] He did this lest this city, too, be named after his wandering in fear, that is the city of Nod.[251] And to Enoch was born Edar. And Edar begot Mehujael and Mehujael begot Methushael and

---

246. Gen 4.15.   247. Gen 4.16.
248. In *Hymns on Paradise* 1.11, the land of Nod is "a place lower still than that of Seth and Enosh."
249. Gen 4.12. The earth had already received a curse in Gen 3.17.
250. Gen 4.17.   251. "Nod" means "wandering."

Methushael begot Lamech. And Lamech took two wives. He begot Jabal through Adah, and Jabal became the father of those who dwell in tents and of those who possess cattle. The name of his brother was Jubal. Jubal became the father of all those who play the lyre and the pipe. And Zillah bore Tubal-Cain, an artisan in every craft of bronze and iron, and the sister of Tubal-Cain was Naamah.[252]

(2) *And Lamech said to his wives, "Hear my voice because I have slain a man for wounding me and a young man for striking me. Because Cain was avenged sevenfold, Lamech [will be avenged] seventy-seven fold."*[253]

2. There are some who say, concerning Lamech's words to his wives, that his wives were daughters of Seth and they were exhorting him to do well, and he said to them, "What have you seen in me that is detestable or similar to my father Cain? For I, like Cain, have killed a man for wounding me. Just as he struck the cheeks of Abel as [one would] a youth and so killed him, so have I also killed a youth for beating me. If I have done as Cain did and Cain was avenged seven times, then I decree that I should be avenged seventy-seven times."

(2) Others, because they think that Cain was avenged for seven generations, say that Lamech was evil, because God had said, *"All flesh has corrupted its path,"*[254] and also because the wives [of Lamech] saw that the line of their generation would be cut off. They were giving birth not to males but to females only, for [Moses] said that it was *when men multiplied on the earth and daughters were born to them.*[255] When these wives saw the plight of their generation, they became fearful and knew that the judgment decreed against Cain and his seven generations had come upon their generation.

(3) [Lamech] then, in his cleverness, comforted them, saying, *"I have killed a man for wounding me and a youth for striking me."*[256] Just as God caused Cain to remain so that seven

252. Gen 4.17–22.
253. Gen 4.18–24.
254. Gen 6.12.
255. Gen 6.1.
256. Gen 4.23.

generations would perish with him, so [God] will cause me to remain, because I have killed two, so that seventy-seven generations should die with me. Before the seventy-seven generations come, however, we will die, and through the cup of death that we taste we will escape from that punishment which, because of me, will extend to seventy-seven generations."

3. Still others say that Lamech, who was cunning and crafty, saw the plight of his generation: that the Sethites refused to intermingle with them because of the reproach of their father Cain, who was still alive, and that the lands would become uncultivated from the lack of ploughmen and their generation would thus come to an end. Lamech, therefore, moved by zeal, killed Cain together with his one son whom he had begotten and who resembled him lest, through this one son who resembled him, the memory of his shame continue through their generations.[257]

(2) When he killed Cain, who had been like a wall between the two tribes to keep them from tyrannizing each other, [Lamech] said to his wives as if in secret, "A man and a youth have been killed but take and adorn your daughters for the sons of Seth. Because of the murders that I have committed and because of the adornment and beauty of your daughters, those who refused to be married to us in the past six generations might now consent to marry with us in our generation."

(3) Their daughters then adorned themselves for the sons of Seth, and Jabal enticed them with the choice portions of the flesh of animals and Jubal captivated them with the sweet sounds of his lyres. Then the sons of Seth yielded and, because of these things, they forgot that noble covenant that had been established by their father and they came down from their place, for it was higher than where the descendants of Cain dwelt. Thus, Lamech, by his cunning ploys, intermarried those tribes so that when "God takes pity

---

257. For a Jewish version of the tradition that it was Lamech who slew Cain, see Ginzberg, *Legends*, 1:116–17.

COMMENTARY ON GENESIS   133

on the tribe of Seth, who have mixed with us, so that it not perish, God might also have mercy on us so that we might escape from the punishment of murder on account of those who are married to us, for they have committed no murder."

Section V

1. Then after he had finished writing about the tribes of the descendants of Cain and had completed the story of the words of Lamech to his wives, [Moses] turned to record the generations of the house of Seth, beginning from Adam, saying that *when Adam had lived one hundred thirty years, he begot a son in his own likeness according to his image.*[258] In Seth, who was like Adam in all things, was depicted the likeness of the Son, who was sealed by the Father his progenitor[259] just as was Seth by Adam his begetter.[260]

(2) After Seth begot Enosh, [Moses] wrote *at that time he began to call on the name of the Lord.*[261] Because Seth had separated himself from the house of Cain, the Sethites were called by the name of the Lord, that is, the just people of the Lord.[262]

2. After Adam begot Seth and Seth Enosh and Enosh Kenan and Kenan Mahalalel and Mahalalel Jared and Jared Enoch,[263] [Moses] wrote about Enoch who was pleasing to God and *was not.*[264] Some say that while Adam was looking at him God transported him to Paradise lest [Adam] think that Enoch was killed as was Abel and so be grieved. This

258. Gen 5.3.
259. Cf. John 6.27.
260. In *Hymns against Heresies* 5.11–12, Ephrem says that God restored the image of God, undone by Cain, in Adam's son Seth. This restoration of the divine image is what suggests the parallel between Seth and Christ. See also *Hymns on the Nativity* 1.21, and discussion in Kronholm, *Motifs*, 150–54.
261. Gen 4.26.
262. This curious interpretation, moving from the active "call on" to the passive "called by," is also found in Eusebius of Emesa and Didymus of Alexandria. See S. D. Fraade, *Enosh and His Generation*, Society of Biblical Literature Monagraph Series, no. 30 (Chico, California, 1984).
263. Cf. Gen 5.3–18.
264. Gen 5.24.

was also so that [Adam] might be comforted by this just son of his and that he might know that for all who were like this one, whether before death or after the resurrection, [Paradise] would be their meeting-place.²⁶⁵

(2) Enoch begot Methuselah and Methuselah begot Lamech and Lamech begot Noah and Lamech prophesied about his son and said, *"This one shall bring us relief from our work and from the toil of our hands and from the earth which the Lord cursed,*²⁶⁶ by his offering which will be pleasing to God who, because of the sin of its inhabitants, will destroy in the waters of wrath the buildings that we have made and the plants over which our hands have toiled."

Section VI

1. After recounting the ten generations from Adam to Noah, [Moses] said, *Noah was five hundred years old and begot Shem and Ham and Japhet.*²⁶⁷ During this entire time Noah was an example to his sons by his virtue, for he had preserved his virginity for five hundred years among those of whom it was said, *All flesh corrupted its path.*²⁶⁸

2. After he spoke of the virtue of Noah, [Moses] turned to speak about the evil desire that was working in the children of his generation saying, *and it came to pass that when men increased and daughters were born to them. . . .*²⁶⁹ For he called those of the house of Cain *men,* and said that daughters were born to them to show that the line of their generation had been cut off as we said above.²⁷⁰

3. *And the sons of God saw that the daughters of men were beautiful and they took to wife such of them as they chose.*²⁷¹ He called the sons of Seth *sons of God,* those who, like the sons of Seth,

---

265. In *Hymns on the Church* 11.1, Ephrem says that it was because of Enoch's "love for the new life" that he was the first to defeat death. For the prominent place that Enoch plays in Ephrem's hymns, see Kronholm, *Motifs,* 154–63.
266. Gen 5.29. "Noah" means "relief" in Hebrew and in Syriac.
267. Gen 5.32. 268. Gen 6.12.
269. Gen 6.1. 270. See IV.2, above.
271. Gen 6.2. See also *Hymns on Paradise* 1.11–12.

had been called "the righteous people of God."²⁷² The beautiful daughters of men whom they saw were the daughters of Cain who adorned themselves and became a snare to the eyes of the sons of Seth. Then Moses said, *they took to wife such of them as they chose*, because when they took them, they acted very haughtily over those whom they chose. A poor one would exalt himself over the wife of a rich man and an old man would sin with one who was young. The ugliest of all would act arrogantly over the most beautiful.

(2) The sons of Cain were interested in neither the wealth nor the appearance of those women; they were seeking ploughmen for their lands that had been left uncultivated. Although this thing began because of the licentious and poor men—the licentious being driven by beauty and the poor being attracted to wealth—the entire tribe of Seth followed suit and was stirred to a frenzy over them.

(3) Because the sons of Seth were going into the daughters of Cain, they turned away from their first wives whom they had previously taken. Then these wives, too, disdained their own continence and now, because of their husbands, quickly began to abandon their modesty which up until that time they had preserved for their husbands' sake. It is because of this wantonness that assailed both the men and the women, that Scripture says, *all flesh corrupted its path*.²⁷³

4. Then the Lord said, *"My spirit shall not abide in man for ever, for he is flesh, but his days shall be one hundred and twenty years.*²⁷⁴ This generation will not live nine hundred years like the previous generations, for it is flesh and its days are filled with the deeds of flesh. Therefore, their days will be one

---

272. See V.1, above. In his hymns, Ephrem argues strongly against the identification of the "sons of God" being angels or heavenly creatures, as commonly held by many other traditions. See *Hymns on the Nativity* 1.48, *Hymns on Faith* 46.9, and *Hymns against Heresies* 19.1–8. The sons of Seth are explicitly called "sons of God" in *Hymns on Nisibis* 1.4, and *Hymns on Paradise* 1.11. For discussion, see Kronholm, *Motifs*, 166–68. Compare also Ginzberg, *Legends*, 1:151–52, where the sons of Seth descend the mountain and act wantonly with the daughters of Cain.

273. Gen 6.12.   274. Gen 6.3.

hundred and twenty years. If they repent during this time they will be saved from the wrath that is about to come upon them. But if they do not repent, by their deeds they will call down [the wrath] upon themselves." Grace granted one hundred and twenty years for repentance to a generation that, according to Justice, was not worthy of repentance.[275]

5. After these things [Moses] wrote of the offspring produced from the union of the daughters of Cain and the sons of Seth saying, *There were mighty men in those days; and also afterward, because judges went into the daughters of men, they bore the mighty men who were of old, the mighty men of renown.*[276] The mighty men who were born were born to the feeble tribe of Cain and not to the mighty tribe of Seth. The house of Cain, because the earth had been cursed so as not to give them its strength, produced small harvests, deprived of its strength, just as it is today that some seeds, fruits, and grasses give strength and some do not. Because, at that time, they were cursed and sons of the cursed and were dwelling in the land of curses, they would gather and eat produce that lacked nutrition, and those who ate these were without strength just like the food that they ate. As for the Sethites, on the other hand, because they were the descendants of the blessed [Seth] and were dwelling in the land along the boundary of the fence of Paradise, their produce was abundant and full of strength. So too were the bodies of those that ate that produce strong and powerful.

(2) Therefore, these mighty sons of Seth went into the daughters of Cain, that fearful wanderer, and they begot for the descendants of Cain *mighty men of renown*. [Moses] adds *of old,* because those thus born to the descendants of Cain were like Seth and Enosh, the first mighty men of renown.

---

275. See Ginzberg, *Legends,* 1:153, where God, in His mercy, granted this same time for the repentance of the sinners.

276. Gen 6.4, Peshitta. "Judges" here is another reading that occurs in the Peshitta and *Targum Neofiti*—both here and at Exod 22.7. This is also the interpretation found in *Genesis Rabbah* 26.5. For a history of this interpretation, see P. Alexander, "The Targumim and Early Exegesis of 'Sons of God' in Genesis 6," *JJS* 23 (1972): 60–71.

6. After Moses spoke about the mighty men who were born into the tribe of Cain, whose women, even though beautiful, were nevertheless smaller than the sons of Seth, he then said, *the Lord saw that the wickedness of man was great in the earth, and that every inclination of the thoughts of their hearts was always evil,*[277] for in the years given to them for repentance they had increased their sins. *The wickedness of mankind was great in the earth,* that is, evil extended and spread throughout both those tribes. *The inclination of the thoughts of their hearts was always evil,* for their sins were not committed only occasionally, but their sins were incessant; night and day they would not desist from their wicked thought.

7. Because of all this evil they committed, *the Lord said, "I will blot out [everything] from man to beast to reptile and bird, for I am sorry that I have made them."*[278] *God was sorry* does not mean that God did not know that they would come to this, but rather that He wished to make their great wickedness manifest before the generations to come, that they had committed such wantonness that they even brought to remorse God, who does not feel remorse. In addition, God defended His justice; He did not drown them in the flood without reason. That Nature that does not feel remorse humbled Itself to say, *"I am sorry,"* so that that rebellious generation might hear and quake in fear, and so that remorse might be sown in those whose heart rebelled against remorse.[279]

(2) If there had been any blemish in the works of God, He would have created a new world and would not have preserved in the ark anything that had caused remorse to Him

---

277. Gen 6.5.
278. Gen 6.7.
279. God took on this remorse and other "human characteristics due to human weakness." See *Hymns on Faith* 31.1–4, *Hymns against Heresies* 20.1, 30.2, 36.13 (and Beck's note *ad loc.*). It was the Marcionites, "the children of the left hand," who understood these verses anthropomorphically; see *Hymns on Virginity* 29.6. See discussion in Kronholm, *Motifs*, 204–6; and Hidal, *Interpretatio Syriaca*, 93–100.

who made it. Notice that by saying, *"I am sorry,"* He shows that He was not sorry. If God were sorry on account of the sinners, why would He be sorry concerning the beasts and the reptiles and the birds that had committed no sin? And if He were not sorry concerning them, why did He say, *"I am sorry,"* when He was not sorry? This remorse which, on account of the offenders, was extended to those who committed no evil vindicates God who said, *"I am sorry,"* for it was out of love for those sinners who were to perish that He said it and not because He was announcing His ignorance. That they should perish in their deeds was a great sorrow to that Grace that had made them, but if they did not perish, future generations would have been corrupted because of them.

8. But when they showed no fear and did not repent, neither when their lives had been shortened nor when He said, *"I am sorry,"* [God] then said to Noah, *"Because the end of all flesh is before me, make yourself an ark of gopher wood: three hundred cubits in length, fifty cubits in width and thirty cubits in height and finish it to a cubit above. Make it three stories and daub it with pitch on the outside."*[280] [God] brought that difficult task to this just man in the hope that He would not have to bring the flood upon them.

(2) Where was Noah to get gopher wood? pitch? iron? or rope? With the assistance of what craftsmen would he construct [the ark] and where would he procure laborers to help? Who, in that generation in which *all flesh corrupted its path,* would listen to him? If he and the sons of his household were to make the ark, who of all those who saw it would not mock it? Noah began the ark in the first year that was allowed that generation for repentance and he finished it in one hundred years.

9. Although Noah was an example to that generation by his righteousness and had, in his uprightness, announced to

---

280. Gen 6.13–16. In general, Ephrem uses the Syriac word *qbūtâ* for the ark in this *Commentary,* whereas in his hymns he uses the word *kewêlâ.* See Kronholm, *Motifs,* 183, for precise references.

them the flood during that one hundred years, they still did not repent.²⁸¹ So Noah said to them, "Some of all flesh will come to be saved with me in the ark." But they mocked him [saying], "How will all the beasts and birds that are scattered throughout every corner of the earth come from all those regions?" *His Lord then said to him, "Go into the ark, you and all your household, for I have seen that you are righteous in this generation. Take with you seven pairs of all clean animals and two pairs of the animals that are unclean."* ²⁸² He called the gentle animals *clean* and the vicious ones *unclean*, for even in the beginning God had multiplied the clean ones. [Hoping] that something visible might persuade those whom words could not persuade, *"in seven days I will send rain upon the earth for forty days and nights and I will blot out all that I have made."* ²⁸³

(2) On that same day elephants came from the east, apes and peacocks approached from the south, other animals gathered from the west, and still others hastened to come from the north. Lions came from the jungles and wild beasts arrived from their lairs. Deer and wild asses came from their lands and the mountain beasts gathered from their mountains.

(3) When those of that generation gathered [to see] this novel sight, it was not to repent, but rather to amuse themselves. Then, in their very presence, the lions began to enter the ark and the bulls, with no fear, hurried in right on their heels to seek shelter with the lions. The wolves and the lambs entered together and the hawks and the sparrows together with the doves and the eagles.²⁸⁴

10. When those of that generation were still not persuaded, neither by the gathering of all the animals at that time nor by the love that instantly grew between [the animals],

---

281. See *Hymns on Faith* 56.2. In 2 Pet 2.5, Noah is called "the herald of righteousness."
282. Gen 7.2.
283. Gen 7.4.
284. In Ephrem's hymns, this peace on the ark is sign of a new beginning, of a pre-fall state, and is thus also a type of the Church. See Kronholm, *Motifs*, 186–90, for references.

the Lord said to Noah, *"In seven days, I will blot out everything that I have made."*²⁸⁵

(2) He who granted one hundred years while the ark was being made to that generation, and still they did not repent, who summoned beasts that they had never seen and still they showed no remorse, and who established a state of peace between the predatory animals and those who are preyed upon and still they did not fear, delayed yet seven more days for them, even after Noah and every creature had entered the ark, leaving the gate of the ark open to them. This is a wonderous thing that no lion remembered its jungle and no species of beast or bird visited its customary haunt! Although those of that generation saw all that went on outside and inside the ark, they were still not persuaded to renounce their evil deeds.²⁸⁶

(3) This long-suffering patience of one hundred and twenty years was foremost so that they might repent and that the righteous among them might remain so that by them that generation might be judged, and so that the righteous might complete their lives lest it be said, "Why did He not leave those who did not sin?" Because God had already endured the trial of that generation for one hundred years, He subtracted twenty years. But the seven days which He delayed after the beasts had entered [the ark] were more than the twenty years He subtracted from them because of the signs [done in them].²⁸⁷

11. If they did not repent because of the signs done in those seven days, it was clear that they would not have repented in the twenty years in which there would have been no signs. Therefore God sent off, with many fewer sins, those whose lives He had shortened by twenty years.

(2) For this reason, *at the end of the seven days, in the six*

---

285. Gen 7.4.
286. See *Hymns on Nicomedia* 5.95–114.
287. The idea that God gave that evil generation more than sufficient time to repent is deeply rooted in Jewish tradition. See Ginzberg, *Legends*, 1:154 (where the extra week is out of regard for the memory of Methuselah), and further references in Kronholm, *Motifs*, 185, 191.

hundredth year of Noah's life, in the second month, on the seventeenth day of the month, the springs of the great abyss burst forth and the flood gates of heaven were opened. The Lord shut the door before Noah,[288] lest those left behind come at the time of the floods and break down the gate of the ark. The deluge came and *God blotted out all flesh. Only Noah was left and those that were with him in the ark.*[289] The springs of the abyss and the flood gates of heaven were open forty days and forty nights[290] and *the ark was afloat for one hundred fifty days.*[291]

12. *But after one hundred fifty days the waters began to subside and the ark came to rest on Mt. Qardu.*[292] *In the tenth month the tops of the mountains were seen. In the six hundred and first year, in the first month, the first day of the month, the waters were dried from off the earth. In the second month,* that is, Iyor, *on the twenty-seventh day of the month, the earth was dry.*[293] Therefore, Noah and those with him had been in the ark three hundred sixty-five days, for from the seventeenth of the second month, that is, Iyor, until the twenty-seventh of the same month the following year, according to the lunar reckoning, there were three hundred sixty-five days.[294] Notice then that even the generation of the house of Noah employed this reckoning

---

288. Gen 7.11, 16.
289. Gen 7.23.
290. Cf. Gen 7.12. See *Hymns on Nicomedia* 5.145–46, where Ephrem also echoes Jewish exegesis that the flood waters came from beneath the earth as well as from the skies. See also A. Levene, *The Early Syrian Fathers on Genesis* (London, 1951) 82–83, 186.
291. Cf. Gen 7.24, 8.3–4.
292. Following the Peshitta, Josephus, *Antiquities* I.3, 5–6, *Genesis Rabbah* 33.4, the Targums on this verse; see *Pseudo-Jonathan* at 2 Kings 19.37 and Isa 37.38, Ephrem locates the resting of the ark not on Ararat but on Mt. Qardu, in northern Iraq. See Kronholm, *Motifs,* 201. For the history of the tradition of the resting place of the ark, see L. R. Bailey, *Noah: The Person and the Story in History and Tradition* (Columbia, South Carolina, 1989) 61–82, especially, 65–68; and Ginzberg, *Legends,* 5:186, n.48.

For Ephrem, the landing of the ark on Mt. Qardu signaled the final and complete separation of humanity from Paradise. See *Hymns on Paradise* 1.10.

293. Gen 8.3–5, 13–14.
294. Compare the chronology of the various stages of the flood found in Ginzberg, *Legends,* 1:163.

of three hundred sixty-five days in a year. Why then should you say that it was the Chaldeans and Egyptians who invented and developed it?[295]

(2) *Then God said to Noah, "Go out, you and your wife and your sons and your sons' wives."*[296] Those whom he had brought in *one by one* in order to maintain chastity on the ark, he brought out *two by two* so that they might *be fruitful and multiply in creation.*[297] Even with respect to the animals that had preserved their chastity in the ark *[God] said, "Bring forth with you every animal that is with you of all flesh that they might breed on the earth and be fruitful and multiply on it."*[298]

13. After Noah and all those with him went out, *[Noah] took of every clean animal and offered up a whole burnt offering on an altar.*[299] Now, either every clean bird and beast was completely obedient to Noah after they came out, or on the day that they went out from the ark, [Noah] took from all the clean flesh and offered an acceptable sacrifice to God and so made the flood pass away from the earth.

(2) *The Lord smelled,*[300] not the smell of the flesh of animals or the smoke of wood, but He looked out and saw the simplicity of heart with which [Noah] offered the sacrifice from all and on behalf of all. And his Lord spoke to him, as He desired that Noah hear, *"Because of your righteousness, a remnant was preserved and did not perish in that flood that took place. And because of your sacrifice that was from all flesh and on behalf of all flesh, I will never again bring a flood upon the earth."*[301] God thus bound Himself beforehand by this promise so that even if mankind were constantly to follow the evil thoughts of their inclination, He would never again bring a flood upon them.

295. Ephrem makes the same point in *Hymns on the Crucifixion* 6.18.
296. Gen 8.16.
297. For the animal's preservation of chastity on the ark, see VI.2, above, the *Commentary on the Diatessaron* II.6, *Hymns on Nisibis* 1.9, *Hymns on the Nativity* 28.1. See also Ginzberg, *Legends*, 1:166, for this same celibacy in Jewish tradition. Although Ephrem does not mention it here, Noah also kept chastity on the ark. See *Hymns on the Nativity* 1.22, *Armenian Hymns* 4.13, *Hymns on Nisibis* 1.4.
298. Gen 8.17.
299. Gen 8.20.
300. Gen 8.21.
301. Cf. Gen 9.11–15.

COMMENTARY ON GENESIS 143

(3) And because there was neither planting nor harvest during that year and the seasonal cycles had been disturbed, God restored to the earth that which had been taken away in His anger and then said, *"All the days of the earth, planting and harvest, cold and heat, summer and winter, day and night shall not cease from the earth."*[302] For throughout the entire forty days of rain it had been night, and throughout the entire year, until the earth dried up, winter, with no summer, had been upon them.

14. [God] also blessed Noah and his sons that they might be fruitful and multiply and that fear of them should fall upon all flesh both in the sea and on dry land.[303] *"Only you shall not eat flesh with its life,"*[304] that is, you shall eat no flesh that has not been slaughtered and whose blood, which is its life, has not been drained. God established three covenants with Noah: one, that they should not eat blood; one of retaliation, that God will require the blood of animals; and one that a murderer is to be put to death.[305]

15. *"I will require your blood from every beast and from the hand of man."*[306] He requires it now and in the future. He requires it now in the case of a death that He decreed for a murderer, and also a stoning with which a goring bull is to be stoned.[307] At the end, at the time of the resurrection, God will require that animals return all that they ate from the flesh of man.

(2) God said, *"From the hand of a man and of his brother I will require the life of a man,"*[308] just as satisfaction for the blood of Abel was required from Cain, that is, *whoever sheds the blood of man, by man shall his blood be shed.*[309] The phrase *in the image of God He made . . . ,*[310] concerns his authority for, like God, he has the power to grant life and to kill.

(3) After these things God made a covenant with Noah and with all those who came out of the ark with him, saying,

302. Gen 8.22.
303. Cf. Gen 9.1–2.
304. Gen 9.4.
305. Cf. Gen 9.5–7.
306. Gen 9.5.
307. Cf. Exod 21.28.
308. Gen 9.5.
309. Gen 9.6.
310. Gen 9.6.

"*All flesh shall never again perish in the waters of a flood. I will set my bow in the clouds and it shall be a sign of the eternal covenant between God and all flesh that is on the earth.*"[311]

Section VII

1. After these things [Moses] wrote of how Noah *planted a vineyard and drank of its wine, got drunk, fell asleep, and lay uncovered in his tent. Ham saw the nakedness of his father and told his two brothers outside.*[312] Noah's drunkenness was not from an excess of wine but because it had been a long time since he had drunk any wine. In the ark he had drunk no wine; although all flesh was going to perish Noah was not permitted to bring any wine onto the ark. During the year after the flood Noah did not drink any wine. In that [first] year after he left the ark, he did not plant a vineyard, for he came out of the ark on the twenty-seventh of Iyor, the time when the fruit should be starting to mature and not the time for planting a vineyard. Therefore, seeing that it was in the third year that he planted the vineyard from the grape stones that he brought with him on the ark, and that it was three or even four years before they would have become a productive vineyard, there were, then, at least six years during which the just one had not tasted any wine.

2. Another indication that it was the long absence of wine that had caused Noah to become so drunk is when Moses said, *Ham went out into the street and told his brothers.*[313] How could there be a street there, unless they had built a village for themselves? If they had built a village it would have taken them several years to build. Therefore the building of a village and the laying out of its streets also bear witness that it had been many years, as we said, since the old man had drunk any wine, and that is the reason he became so drunk.[314]

---

311. Gen 9.13.   312. Gen 9.21–22.
313. Gen 9.22. "Into the street" is the reading in the Peshitta and *Targum Pseudo-Jonathan*.
314. Here, and in *Hymns on Nisibis* 57.5, Ephrem goes to great lengths to ensure that no guilt is impugned to Noah. See, however, *Hymns on Virginity*

(2) The brothers of [Ham], knowing the nobility of their father and that he, like Jacob, was protected by angels both while awake and while asleep, hid his nakedness, trembling all the while; their faces did not see his nakedness.[315]

3. *When Noah awoke and realized everything that his youngest son had done to him*[316]—for Noah had been both sleeping and awake. He was sleeping in that he had not perceived his nakedness, but awake in that he had been aware of everything that his youngest son had done to him. [Noah] cursed Canaan, saying, *"Cursed be Canaan. A slave of slaves shall he be to his brothers."*[317] But what sin could Canaan have committed even if he had been right behind his father when Ham observed the nakedness of Noah?

(2) Some say that because Ham had been blessed along with those who entered the ark and came out of it, Noah did not curse Ham himself, even though his son, who was cursed, grieved him greatly. Others, however, say that from that the fact that Scripture says, *Noah knew everything that his youngest son had done to him,* it is clear that it was not Ham, for Ham was the middle son and not the youngest. For this reason they speak of the youngest son, who was Canaan, and say that Canaan the youngest told of the nakedness of the old man. Then Ham went out into the street and jokingly told his brothers. For this reason then, even though it might be thought that Canaan was cursed unjustly, in that he did what he did in his youth, still he was cursed justly for he was not cursed in the stead of another. For Noah knew that unless Canaan was to deserve the curse in his old age, he would not have been cursed in his youth.

(3) Ham was justly withheld from both the blessing and from the curse. If he had been cursed even because of his laughter, he would have been cursed justly, but had he been

---

1.10, where "wine exposed and cast down Noah, the head of families." By impugning no guilt to Noah Ephrem differs from Jewish tradition. See Ginzberg, *Legends,* 1:167–68, and *Genesis Rabbah* 26–32, *passim.*

315. See also *Hymns on Faith* 9.2. For a more typological interpretation, see *Hymns on the Nativity* 1.23.

316. Gen 9.24.   317. Gen 9.25.

cursed, all the sons of Ham who had taken no part in the jesting or the laughing would have been cursed along with Ham. Therefore, Canaan was cursed because of his jesting and Ham was deprived of the blessing because of his laughter.

4. After Ham had been cursed through his one son, [Noah] blessed Shem and Japhet and said, *"May God increase Japhet and may He dwell in the tent of Shem, and let Canaan be their slave."*[318] Japhet increased and became powerful in his inheritance in the north and in the west. And God dwelt in the tent of Abraham, the descendant of Shem, and Canaan became their slave when in the days of Joshua bar-Nun, the Israelites destroyed the dwelling-places of [Canaan] and pressed their leaders into bondage.[319]

Section VIII

1. After those things, [Moses] wrote about the nations that came from Noah. From and including Japhet there were fifteen nations. From and including Ham there were thirty nations, apart from the Philistines and the Cappadocians who later came from them. From and including Shem there were twenty-seven nations, a total of seventy-two nations. Each of these nations dwelt in its own distinct place with its own people and [spoke] its own tongue.[320]

(2) Concerning Nimrod, [Moses] said, *He was a mighty hunter before the Lord,*[321] because, according to the will of the Lord, it was he who fought with each of these nations and chased them out from there so that they would go out and settle in the regions that had been set apart for them by God. *Therefore it is said, like Nimrod a mighty hunter before the Lord.*[322] One used to bless a chief or a ruler by saying, "May

---

318. Gen 9.27.   319. Cf. Josh 17.13.
320. See *Hymns against Heresies* 7.7, and *Sermones* II.2.484ff.
321. Gen 10.9.
322. Gen 10.9. For Ephrem's view of Nimrod in relation to other Christian traditions, see P. W. van der Horst, "Nimrod after the Bible," in idem, *Essays on the Jewish World of Early Christianity*, Novum Testamentum et Orbis Antiquus, no. 14 (Fribourg-Göttingen, 1990) 220–32.

you be like Nimrod, a mighty hunter who was victorious in the battles of the Lord." *Nimrod reigned in Erech,* which is now Edessa, *and in Accad,* which is now Nisibis, and *in Calah,* which is now Seleucia-Ctesiphon, *Rehoboth,* which is now Adiabene, *Calah,*[323] which is now Hatra, and *Resen, the great city* (that is, at that time),[324] which is now Reshaina.

2. Then Moses said, *the whole earth had one language, and they said, "Let us build a city and a tower with its top in the heavens, and let us make a name for ourselves, lest we be scattered over the face of the earth."*[325] For what purpose would those who had nothing to fear build a fortified city or a tower that reaches to heaven, since they had a firm covenant that there would be no flood? They said, *"Lest we be scattered over the face of the whole earth."* But who else was there, apart from themselves, to scatter them? From the fact that they said, *"Let us make a name for ourselves,"* it is clear that their vainglory and their unity, which built both the city and the tower, were brought to nought because of the division that came upon them.

3. *And the Lord came down to see the city,*[326] that is, the Lord saw the work of their mad folly *and said, "Nothing that they propose will be impossible for them,"*[327] that is, they will not escape punishment, for the opposite of that which they said, *"lest we be scattered,"* will befall them. *"Come, let us go down and there confuse their languages."*[328] Here, God was not speaking to one, for this *"Come, let us go down,"* would be superfluous [if only said] to one. He said it both to the Son and to the Spirit so that neither the ancient nor the more recent languages[329] be given without the Son and the Spirit.

(2) *"Let us confuse their tongues, so that they will not understand one another's language."*[330] It is likely that they lost their

---

323. For the two Calah's, see Jansma, "Investigations," 164. For similar equations, compare *Genesis Rabbah* 37.4.
324. Gen 10.10–12.
325. Gen 11.1, 4.
326. Gen 11.5.
327. Gen 11.6.
328. Gen 11.7.
329. Ephrem perhaps has in mind here the "new tongues" of Mark 16.17, or Acts 2.4.
330. Gen 11.7.

common language when they received these new languages, for if their original language had not perished their first deed would not have come to nought. It was when they lost their original language, which was lost by all the nations, with one exception, that their first building came to nought. In addition, because of their new languages, which made them foreigners to each other and incapable of understanding one another, war broke out among them on account of the divisions that the languages brought among them.

4. Thus, war broke out among those who had been building that fortified city out of fear of others. And all those who had been keeping themselves away from [the city] were scattered throughout the entire earth.

(2) It was Nimrod who scattered them. It was also he who seized Babel and became its first ruler. If Nimrod had not scattered them each to his own place, he would not have been able to take that place where they all [had lived before].

Section IX

1. After these things, [Moses] once again began to enumerate the generations from Noah to Abraham saying that Noah begot Shem and his brothers and Shem begot Arpachshad, and Arpachshad Shelah, and Shelah Eber, and Eber Peleg, and Peleg Reu, and Reu Serug, and Serug Nahor, and Nahor Terah, and Terah Abraham, Nahor, and Haran. Haran begot Lot and Milcah and Iscah, that is, Sarah, who was called Iscah for her beauty.[331] These two [married] their uncles.[332]

2. *And Terah took Abraham his son, Lot his grandson, and Sarah his daughter-in-law out of Ur of the Chaldees and he went and dwelt in Haran.*[333] *God appeared to Abram*[334] *and said to him,*

---

331. For the various interpretations of the name Iscah in Syriac tradition, see Jansma, "Investigations," 164–65. This identification of Iscah with Sarah is commonplace in Jewish tradition. Sarah was held to be so beautiful that even the most beautiful women were as apes in comparison. See Ginzberg, *Legends*, 1:60, 203, 222, 287.

332. Cf. Gen 11.10–29.   333. Gen 11.31.

334. Although Ephrem makes nothing of the change in Abraham's name,

"*Go out from your father's house to the land that I will show you. And I will make of you a great nation.*"[335] So Abraham left his parents who did not wish to go out with him and took Lot who believed the promise made to him. Since [God] had not made [Lot] a joint heir [with Abraham], neither did He allow the descendants of Abraham to enter into the inheritance with the descendants of Lot. Abraham then took Sarah and Lot and went to Canaan.[336]

3. *And there was a famine in the land and Abram went down to Egypt and said to Sarah, "When the Egyptians see you and say to you, 'She is his wife,' say 'I am his sister,' so that my life may be spared because of you.*"[337] Abraham gave a human reason as human beings do. Nevertheless, because Sarah thought it was Abraham who was sterile, she was taken to the palace: first, so that she might learn that it was she who was barren;[338] secondly, so that her love for her husband might be seen, for she did not exchange [her husband] for a king while she was a sojourner; and [lastly], so that the mystery of her descendants might be depicted in her. Just as she had no love for the kingdom of Egypt, they would not love the idols, the garlic, or the onions of Egypt. Just as the entire house of Pharaoh was struck by Sarah's deliverance, so too would all Egypt be struck down by the deliverance of her descendants.[339]

(2) Pharaoh's household was struck down because they honored [Sarah] above [Pharaoh], and because they de-

---

he preserves the form Abram wherever the Peshitta text does. Therefore, our translation reads Abram on each occasion that Ephrem does.

335. Gen 12.1–2.   336. Cf. Gen 12.5.
337. Gen 12.10–13.
338. Compare *Hymns on Virginity* 1.9: "Sarah was chaste in the bosom of Pharaoh." See also *Hymns on Virginity* 22.16–17. Jewish tradition also held Sarah to have been saved from this impurity; see *Genesis Rabbah* 53.6. A *mêmrâ*, later attributed to Ephrem, develops this idea further. See S. P. Brock and S. Hopkins, "A Verse Homily on Abraham and Sarah in Egypt: Syriac Original with Early Arabic Translation," *LM* 105 (1992): 87–146; and, for a later version of the same *mêmrâ*, A. Caquot, "Une homélie éthiopienne attribuée à saint Mari Ephrem sur le séjour d'Abraham et Sara en Egypte," in *Mélanges Antoine Guillaumont* (Geneva, 1988) 173–85.
339. Cf. Exod 14.26–28.

sired [Pharaoh] to marry her. Pharaoh was also struck down because he forced her to become his wife, although she was unwilling. Only to avoid their killing her and her husband would she have yielded in this matter.

Section X

1. *And a quarrel arose between the herdsmen of Abram and the herdsmen of Lot.*[340] Justice sent the contentious servants of Lot to the quarrelsome Sodomites to be chastised along with them and so that Lot might be delivered from them. Although the land had been promised to Abraham, he allowed Lot to choose the land of the Jordan, that is, all the land of Sodom, which was watered by the Jordan.

2. *After Lot had departed, the Lord appeared to Abram and said to him, "Rise, walk through the land, its length and its width, for I will give it to you."*[341] Here the cross is clearly delineated. Thus that land promised to the forefathers through the mystery of the cross, because of the cross, repudiated any other heirs.

Section XI

1. After these things, Chedorlaomer, the king of Elam, came with three allied kings to wage war against the king of Sodom and his four allies. The king of Sodom and his allies fled, and those with Chedorlaomer seized all the goods of Sodom as well as Lot and his goods and went off. Then Abraham led his 318 servants along with Aner and two of his companions, who were his allies. Abraham overtook them, routed them, and brought back the spoil and their goods and Lot his nephew and his goods.[342] But, because the goods of the Sodomites had been intermingled with those of the kings, Abraham refused [to take] any plunder from the kings.

2. *Melchizedek, the King of Salem, brought out bread and wine. He was a priest of God Most High. And he blessed [Abram] and*

340. Gen 13.7.
341. Gen 13.11, 13–14.
342. Cf. Gen 14.1–2, 10–16.

COMMENTARY ON GENESIS 151

said, "Blessed is the Lord who has delivered your enemies into your hand." And Abram gave him a tenth of everything.[343]

(2) This Melchizedek is Shem, who became a king due to his greatness; he was the head of fourteen nations.[344] In addition, *he was a priest*. He received this from Noah, his father, through the rights of succession. Shem lived not only to the time of Abraham, as Scripture says, but even to [the time of] Jacob and Esau, the grandsons of Abraham. It was to him that Rebekah went to ask and was told, *"Two nations are in your womb and the older shall be a servant to the younger."*[345] Rebekah would not have bypassed her husband, who had been delivered at the *high place*, or her father-in-law, to whom revelations of the divinity came continually, and gone straight to ask Melchizedek unless she had learned of his greatness from Abraham or Abraham's son.

(3) Abraham would not have given him a tenth of everything unless he knew that Melchizedek was infinitely greater than himself. Would Rebekah have asked one of the Canaanites or one of the Sodomites? Would Abraham have given a tenth of his possessions to any one of these? One ought not even entertain such ideas.

(4) Because the length of Melchizedek's life extended to the time of Jacob and Esau, it has been stated, with much probability, that he was Shem. His father Noah was dwelling in the east and Melchizedek was dwelling between two tribes, that is, between the sons of Ham and his own sons. Melchizedek was like a partition between the two, for he was afraid that the sons of Ham would turn his own sons to idolatry.

343. Gen 14.18–20.
344. *Contra* Heb 7.3. Ephrem makes the same identification of Melchizedek with Shem in *Armenian Hymns* 9.11–12 (mistranslated by Mariès because he did not realize Ephrem made this equation; see n.125 on p. 249). For Jewish background, see Ginzberg, *Legends*, 1:233, 314 (where he is consulted by Rebekah); s.v. "Shem" in *Encyclopedia Judaica* 5:225–26, and discussion in Hidal, *Interpretatio Syriaca*, 116–18. Epiphanius, *Panarion* 55.6, claims that it was the Samaritans who made the identification of Shem and Melchizedek.
345. Gen 25.22–23. Jewish tradition also holds that Sarah consulted Melchizedek. See Ginzberg, *Legends*, 1:314, and *Genesis Rabbah* 45.10.

Section XII

1. *After these things, God appeared to Abraham in a vision and said to him, "Your reward will be very great,"*[346]—because of your righteous action toward the captives whom you rescued. *But Abraham said, "What will you give me, for I continue to be childless and a slave born in my house will become my heir?" God brought Abraham outside and said to him, "Look toward heaven and number the stars if you are able to number them." Then God said, "So shall your descendants be." Abraham believed and this too was reckoned to him as great righteousness.*[347] Because he believed in a matter that was so difficult that few would have believed, it was reckoned to him as righteousness.

(2) At that same moment that God praised Abraham for his faith, *God said to him, "I am the Lord who brought you from Ur of the Chaldeans, to give you this land to possess." But Abraham said, "How shall I know that I am to possess this land?"*[348]

2. There are those who say that it was because Abraham doubted this that it was said to him, *"Know of a surety that your descendants will be sojourners in a land that is not theirs."*[349] But let those who say this know that at that same time Abraham believed his descendants would become like the sand.[350] If Abraham believed a matter so great as that from one old sterile woman his descendants would become like the sand, would he have any doubts, then, about such a little matter as that of land?

(2) If Abraham, who had not doubted about that great matter, was in doubt [about this small matter], why did [God] say to him, *"Take a three-year old goat, a three-year old ram, a turtledove and a pigeon"?*[351] Abraham was told these things in the night and then he did them in the day. From dawn to evening Abraham stood before his offering and chased away all the birds that wished to feed on his sacrifice.[352] After the fire had come down upon Abraham's acceptable sacrifice

---

346. Gen 15.1.
347. Cf. Gen 15.2–6; and Rom 4.3, 22.
348. Gen 15.7–8.   349. Gen 15.13.
350. Cf. Gen 13.16.   351. Gen 15.9.
352. Gen 15.11.

COMMENTARY ON GENESIS 153

that evening, God appeared to him and spoke to him.[353] If God had spoken to Abraham as if to punish him, He would not have accepted his sacrifice, nor would He have established a covenant with him on that day, nor would He have promised him that ten nations would become servants to his descendants, nor would it have been said that he would be buried at a ripe old age.[354]

(3) If all these good things came to him on that day because *he believed and it was accounted to him as righteousness*, then how can anyone say that on the very same day a man became worthy of great rewards because of his faith, his seed received punishment because of his lack of faith?

3. In that difficult matter, Abraham believed that a world of people would pour forth from the dead womb of Sarah. With respect to the matter of the land, Abraham did not question *if* it would come to pass but asked *how* it would come to pass. Abraham had seen the land of Canaan with its kings and its armies and had seen how populated it was, filled with its inhabitants. He had also heard, at that time, that the land was to be given not to him but rather to his seed. Abraham wished, therefore, since this was not to occur in his days, that God let him know how it would come about that his seed would enter and possess it.

(2) Abraham thought, "Perhaps these kings will destroy each other or other peoples might rise up and destroy them and empty out the land for us. Perhaps my seed will become strong and will go and slay its inhabitants and possess it, or maybe the land will swallow [its inhabitants] because of their deeds. Perhaps, the [inhabitants] might go into exile into another land because of hunger or rumor or some such reason. Abraham sought to know which of these [would happen], but he had no doubts whatsoever.

(3) Then God, who knew what he sought, showed him what he did not seek in addition to what he did seek. For by the offering that Abraham made [when] the birds came down and he chased them away, God clearly showed him

353. Gen 15.17.
354. Gen 15.18–20.15.

that his descendants would sin and be oppressed but would be saved through the prayers of their righteous ones. And by the pot of fire that came down, God made known that even if all their righteous ones should come to an end, deliverance from heaven would come to them. By the three-year old calf and the three-year old ram and the three-year old goat [God showed him] that either they would be delivered after three generations or that kings, priests, and prophets would soon arise from among his descendants. By the limbs of the animals that Abraham cut in two [God] depicted their many tribes, and by the bird that Abraham did not cut in two [God] signified their unity.

4. After He showed him these things *[God] said to [Abraham], "You will surely know"* what you desired to know, *"that your descendants will be sojourners in a land that is not theirs."*[355] But they will not go down as if into captivity; they will go down with cattle and oxen that will be sent after them, and *"they will become slaves for four hundred years,"*[356] for they will not be persuaded to go unless they have been enslaved. *"But I will bring judgment on the nation who will enslave them and they shall come out with great possessions and, as for yourself, you will be gathered to your fathers at a ripe old age and the fourth generation shall return here."*[357]

(2) The verse *the iniquity of the Amorites is not complete*[358] is to show that not until the full measure of their sins would they receive their just punishment by the sword.

5. And [Moses] said, *Sleep fell upon Abram.*[359] It was the same deep sleep that fell upon Abimelech. The sleep fell upon Abraham when God appeared to him and established a covenant with him that ten nations would become slaves to his descendants and that God would give his descendants the land from the River of Egypt to the Euphrates River as an inheritance.[360]

355. Gen 15.13.
357. Gen 15.14–16.
359. Gen 15.12.

356. Gen 15.3.
358. Gen 15.16.
360. Gen 15.18–20.

Section XIII

1. In that same year when Sarah saw that she was barren she said to Abraham, *"Behold, the Lord has prevented me from bearing children. Go into my maid that perhaps I may be comforted by her."*[361] After Abraham counseled her to be patient and she refused, [Moses] wrote that *Abraham hearkened to the voice of his wife,*[362] and she gave him Hagar, the Egyptian, whom Pharaoh had given her along with all the other things he gave her when he had taken her as a wife.

2. *And when Hagar conceived, she looked with contempt on her mistress,*[363] for Hagar thought that it would be her seed that would enter and possess the promised land. Although Sarah could have taken her and punished her, she saw that, even though Hagar had been her maid up to the time that Sarah gave her to her husband, she had now become her rival wife. Then, lest she disgrace Abraham by showing contempt to his concubine, *Sarah said to him, "My wrong be upon you;*[364] I did not exchange you for a king, yet now you prefer a maid to me. Hagar, whom I gave to you for the sake of the comfort that might come to me, instead of announcing to me that my prayer had been heard and that she had conceived, has rendered me evil instead of the good that I did to her, for she has made me a bitter reproach in the eyes of all her fellow servants."

3. When Hagar, who trusted in Abraham, saw that he took and handed her over to her mistress, after Sarah had been made an object of reproach, she took fright and fled. An angel found her and said to her, *"Return to your mistress and submit to her, for your descendants will multiply so that they cannot be numbered for their multitude, because the Lord has given heed to your servitude,"* that you have given yourself up to return and serve your mistress. *"You shall bear a son and you shall name him Ishmael. He shall be a wild ass of a man because he will dwell in the wilderness and, like a wild ass, he will not enter inhabited land. His hand will be against every one,"* to do them vi-

---

361. Gen 16.2.
363. Gen 16.4.
362. Gen 16.2–3.
364. Gen 16.5.

olence *"and everyone's hand will be against him,"* for he will strike at all peoples and all peoples will strike at him. *"He shall dwell along the border of all his kinsmen,"*[365] that is, the sons of Sarah and Keturah, for the inheritances have been divided among the sons of Shem.

4. Hagar heard that Abraham was to have many sons, but not from her. Hagar was convinced that Abraham would not again come into her, for she knew that he would only have intercourse with her until it was known that she had conceived. After that he would not touch her again. Abraham went into her to do the will of Sarah, so that Sarah might have a little comfort from Hagar until God should make her joyful with fruit from her own womb.

(2) *Hagar said, "You are a God of seeing,*[366] *who truly condescends to appear to those who worship you."* Then she added, *"I have seen a vision after you saw me,"*[367] because, prior to this, an angel had appeared to her in silence so that she would not be afraid. Then after the angel spoke with her there appeared to her a vision within the vision, that is, God in the angel. *Therefore she called the well "the well of the Living One has seen me."*[368]

5. Then Hagar went and sought her mistress. When Hagar recounted to Abraham and Sarah the vision that she had seen and that the angel had said that her son *would dwell at the boundary of his kinsmen,* the grief that had afflicted Sarah was now blotted out by the good news that she brought to Sarah. *Then Hagar gave birth and Abraham named his son Ishmael as he had been instructed by Hagar.*[369]

Section XIV

1. *When [Abraham] was ninety-nine years old, the Lord appeared to him and said, "Be blameless in the covenant that I am about to make with you and I will multiply you and will set you up as many nations,"* that is, tribes. But it was also fulfilled concerning the sons of Esau, the sons of Keturah, and Ishmael

365. Gen 16.7–12.
366. Gen 16.13.
367. Gen 16.13.
368. Gen 16.14.
369. Gen 16.15.

who became nations. *"And kings shall come forth from you,"* that is, from the house of Judah and Ephraim and the Edomites. But *"this is my covenant: you shall circumcise every male in the flesh of the foreskin."*³⁷⁰

2. *And God said to Abraham, "I will give you a son from Sarah, and I will bless him and he will become nations." Then Abraham fell on his face and laughed, and said to himself, "Can a child be born to a man who is a hundred years old? Can Sarah, who is ninety years old, bear a child?" And he said, "O that Ishmael might live in your sight!"*³⁷¹

(2) Now Abraham was not guilty of any doubt by his laughter, for he showed his love towards Ishmael in what he said. He had clung to this hope for twenty-five years. Abraham had manifested his faith in every vision that had come to him. However great his contest with barrenness became, he manifested the victory of his faith. But when old age was added to the barrenness he laughed in his heart. That his Lord would do these two things for him was a marvel to him. For [God] had said to him, *"Truly, Sarah, your wife, will bear you a son; I would in no wise test you, [to see] whether you would also believe in something that I would not do for you. As for Ishmael, I have heard you, behold, I have blessed him and multiplied him."*³⁷²

3. For if Abraham had had the smallest doubt, God would not have sworn to him in truth, nor would He have heeded him concerning Ishmael, nor would He have announced to Abraham that in another year a son would be born to him. [God] would have brought censure and reproof upon him. Then [God] said concerning Ishmael, *"He shall become the father of twelve princes,"*³⁷³ for he became twelve Arab tribes, like Jacob who became twelve tribes. *Then, on that very day, Abraham circumcised himself and his son Ishmael and all the males of his household.*³⁷⁴

(2) Because the Giver had committed himself to give Abraham the gift the following year, Abraham began to re-

---

370. Gen 17.1–2, 6, 10.
372. Gen 17.19–20.
374. Gen 17.23.

371. Gen 17.16–18.
373. Gen 17.20.

flect on when he would be blessed and when the closed womb of Sarah would be opened. Would this occur in a vision or not? While he was reflecting on this, *the Lord appeared to him while he was sitting at the door of his tent in the heat of the day*.[375] But, while Abraham was seeking to fill the eyes of his heart with this revelation, God took Himself up from him.

4. Then, while Abraham was considering why God had appeared and then hid Himself without speaking to him, *he looked, and behold, he saw three men standing above him*. He forgot his thoughts *and ran from the tent door to meet them*.[376]

Section XV

1. Although Abraham ran from the tent toward them as if toward strangers, he ran to receive those strangers with love. His love for strangers was thus proved by the haste with which he ran to meet those strangers. Therefore, the Lord, who had just appeared to him at the door of the tent, now appeared to Abraham clearly in one of the three.

(2) Abraham then fell down and worshipped Him, seeking from Him in whom majesty dwelt that He vouchsafe to enter his house and bless his dwelling. *"If I have found favor in your sight, do not pass by your servant."*[377] God did not oppose him, for *He said, "Do as you have said."* Then Abraham ran to Sarah [telling her] to make three measures of wheat and then he ran to the herd to get a fatted calf.[378]

2. The bread and meat, which was in abundance, was not to satisfy the angels, but rather so that the blessing might be distributed to all the members of his household. After the angels had washed and sat down beneath a tree, *Abraham brought and set before them what he had prepared;* he did not dare recline with them, but like a servant *stood apart from them*.[379]

(2) After they had eaten, *they inquired about Sarah*. She,

---

375. Gen 18.1.
376. Gen 18.2. *Armenian Hymns* 31–32 are devoted to this pericope. See also *Armenian Hymns* 44.1–14; 45.
377. Gen 18.3.   378. Cf. Gen 18.6–7.
379. Gen 18.8.

who even in her old age had preserved her modesty, came out from inside the tent to the door of the tent.[380] From Abraham's haste and from the silence that Abraham imposed on everyone with his gestures, those of his household knew that these who, because of the man of God, allowed their feet to be washed like men were not men.

3. *Then [God] said of Sarah, "At this time I will return to you and Sarah will have a son."* But Sarah, even though Abraham was standing behind her to strengthen her, *laughed to herself and said, "After I have grown old shall I [again] have youthfulness? My husband is also old."*[381] A sign would have been given her if she had asked to hear or to see and then believe: first, because she was a woman, old and barren; and secondly, because nothing like this had ever been done before. God then gave a sign specifically to her who had not asked for a sign, and said, *"Why did you laugh Sarah, and say, 'Am I, who am old, to bear a child?'"*[382] But Sarah, instead of accepting the sign that was given to her, persisted, by this falsehood, in denying the true sign that had been given to her. Even though she had denied it because she was afraid, nevertheless, in order to make her know that a false excuse did not convince Him, God said to her, *"But you did laugh*[383] in your heart; lo, even your heart is denying the foolishness of your tongue."

Section XVI

1. After the three men promised Sarah fruit, *they arose and they looked toward Sodom.*[384] It was not revealed to Sarah that they were going to Sodom lest, on the same day that they had given her joy in the promise that a son was to be hers, she be grieving over her brother on account of that sentence of wrath decreed on Sodom and the nearby villages. They hid this from Sarah lest she never cease weeping, but they revealed it to Abraham[385] so that he not cease praying, and so that it be announced to the world that nowhere in

380. Gen 18.9–10.
381. Gen 18.10–12.
382. Gen 18.13.
383. Gen 18.15.
384. Gen 18.16.
385. Gen 18.17–19.

Sodom was there found a single just man for whose sake it might be saved.

(2) *The cry against Sodom and Gomorrah was great and their sins were very grave.*[386] (The cry just mentioned is explained by the sins which he recounts below.) Then *God said, "I have come down to see if they have done altogether according to the outcry that has come to me and if not, I will know."*[387] It was not that God, who had just said, *their sins were very grave,* did not know that they had sinned. This was an example to judges not to prejudge a case, even based on very reliable hearsay. For if He who knows all set aside His knowledge lest He exact vengeance without full knowledge before the trial, how much more should they set aside their ignorance and not effect judgment before the case is heard.

2. Then two angels set out for Sodom and they went directly to the gate where Lot was sitting to receive strangers who came there. Lot rose to meet them as if to meet strangers, but when he drew near to them there appeared in the second angel the same vision that Abraham had seen in the third, and *Lot bowed himself with his face to the ground.*[388]

(2) Even to the Sodomites they appeared in a favorable aspect, for He said, *"I have come down to see."* For this *"I have come down to see,"* [means] "I have come down to test them." If they had not run after the vision they saw with such rabid fury, even though their former sins would not have been forgiven, they still would not have received the punishment that they were about to receive.

3. Lot then hastened to bring them inside before the Sodomites gathered and caused them any offence, but [the angels] kept stalling on various pretexts so that the Sodomites would come and be tested by them. In the case of Abraham, they had not tarried because they were not in any way testing him; they had come down to give him a reward for his test. Since they had come down to test Sodom, *they said* to Lot, who was pressing them to enter, *"No, we will spend the night in the street."*[389]

386. Gen 18.20.
388. Cf. Gen 19.1.
387. Gen 18.21.
389. Gen 19.2.

4. But Lot urged them more strongly and so they entered and ate, but *before they lay down to sleep, the men of Sodom surrounded the house and said to Lot, "Bring out to us the men who came to you in the night, that we may know them."*[390] Notice that the angels had entered during the night, which obscures appearances, and not during the day, in which forms can be clearly seen. They spread a veil, so to speak, over the sight of the Sodomites with the darkness that lay over their appearance. Although they had entered at night so that, by their being invisible, they might make more manageable the test of those who were to be tried, still the Sodomites took no benefit even from this for they had been preparing themselves to do them harm whether it was day or night.

5. After Lot had begged the Sodomites and they still refused, he promised them his two daughters. But the Sodomites would not take them, and they then threatened to do more harm to Lot than to the angels and they drew right up to the door to break it down.[391] Then the men brought Lot inside with them and the Sodomites outside were afflicted with blindness. But even by this they were not admonished, for after this they wore themselves out groping for the door. Then the men said to Lot, "Take your in-laws, your sons, your daughters, and any one else that belongs to you out of this place for we are about to destroy it."[392] Lot's sons-in-law are here called "sons," for Lot was soon to marry them to his daughters.

6. Lot went out and spoke with his sons-in-law and, although the Sodomites were gathered there, they neither saw him leave nor enter. When he returned, having been ridiculed even by his sons-in-law, *the men seized him and his wife and his two daughters by the hands and brought them out.*[393] The Sodomites did not see them, even though they went out as a group among them.

(2) Because the women [of Lot's household] had not been tested in Sodom, they were to be tested by a law set down for them when they left Sodom. Lot begged that Zoar

---

390. Gen 19.3–5.
391. Cf. Gen 19.7–9.
392. Cf. Gen 19.10–13.
393. Gen 19.16.

be preserved so that he might enter there because it was nearer. [One of the angels] *said to Lot, "Behold, I grant you this favor also, that I will not overthrow the city of Zoar;*[394] it shall be given to you on account of the dishonor of your two daughters."

7. When Lot entered Zoar, *the Lord brought down upon Sodom brimstone and fire from before the Lord from heaven,*[395] that is, the angel, in whom the Lord had appeared, brought down from before the Lord, who is in heaven, fire, and brimstone upon Sodom.

(2) Lot's wife then disregarded the commandment that had just been given as a test, and she became a pillar of salt.[396] Because Lot's wife thus remained behind, she doubled the trial of Lot and of his two daughters. But not even by this did they succumb to lay aside the command of the angel.

8. Because the young women were afraid to dwell in a desolate city on a mountain, and because they thought that all Creation had come to an end in a flood of fire as the generation of Noah did in a flood of water, *the elder said to the younger, "Behold, our father is old and there is not a man on earth to come into us. Let us make our father drink wine that we may preserve seed from him*[397] and there might descend, even from us, a third world like the second from Noah and the first from Adam and Eve."[398] Although there was wine for them, because everything in Zoar had been left for their possession, there was not a man in Zoar for at the very moment the angel said to Lot, *"Behold, I grant you this favor also, that I will not overthrow the city,"*[399] Zoar swallowed up its inhabitants. But all its goods were left so that through those who had possessed these [goods] the Just One, whom they had pro-

394. Cf. Gen 19.16–22.
395. Gen 19.24.
396. Cf. Gen 19.26.
397. Gen 19.31–32.
398. See *Hymns on Virginity* 38, where Ephrem excuses Lot for getting drunk as well as the behavior of his two daughters on the grounds that they thought themselves to be the last persons on earth. See also *Hymns on Virginity* 1.11. See also same tradition in *Genesis Rabbah* 51.8.
399. Gen 19.21.

voked by their deeds, might be appeased and through the goods that it left behind, the righteous Lot who had lost all he had in Sodom might be consoled.

9. Then the daughters began to bring forward various pretexts. "We were afraid to sleep because of visions." "Our mother comes and stands before us like a pillar of salt and we see the Sodomites burning with fire." "We hear the voices of women crying out from the midst of the fire and young children writhing in the midst of the conflagration appear to us." "So for the sake of your daughters' comfort do not sleep, but amuse yourself with wine that we might rob the night with a vigil that is free from terror."

(2) After they saw that his mind had been stolen by the wine and that a deep sleep had spread over his limbs, the elder went in and stole seed from the sleeping farmer, without his perceiving anything. Then this elder daughter, who had found success the previous day, enticed her sister also to become a "bride of the moment" and to take on a life in widowhood.

10. When the younger had thus been persuaded she too went in and departed without Lot perceiving her. Then, after the child within the daughters became evident, the younger complained to the elder saying, "It would have been better for us to be barren than to die of disgrace, to remain with our father without children than that our father be alone without daughters. For what excuses can we make to him when he judges us? And what answer shall we give when he is about to kill us [saying,] 'I said that no man knew my daughters in Sodom. Who then is the one who has known them on this mountain?' Should we say that we are bearing a spirit? When we reach the point of childbirth what will we do?"

11. Then, while they were fretting over these things, their father summoned them and said to them, "For days now I have been secretly watching your stomachs and day by day you confirm the suspicion of adultery that I have concerning you. Tell me then, whence has this pregnancy within you come about? When? How? By whom were you raped?"

(2) The elder answered her father and said, "Our betrothed pressed our mother to conceal them from you but to show us to them. Although nature made us their brides, your lack of sons made us their sisters. These, who had come to us in the likeness of brothers, when our mother was compelled to go out for some reason or another, then rose against us and subdued us like tyrants. When our mother returned and saw us, she threw those wanton ones out of her house with the disgrace they deserved. But she consoled us [saying,] "They were your betrothed and not adulterers; you have received the seed of your ploughmen even though you were, in all truth, raped."

12. Their father accepted their explanations since these things they related about the Sodomites were relatively minor things. For it was nothing that those who had assailed both each other and angels from on high would rape and disgrace, before the time of marriage, those to whom they were betrothed.

13. *The elder gave birth and she named him Moab*[400] and he became a nation because he was a son of Lot. *The younger, too, gave birth and named him Bar-ammi,*[401] that is, he is the race of my father because he is from my father. Because the two daughters had yielded to two disgraces their two sons became two nations; because the two daughters had been offered in the place of the two angels, their two offences were forgiven them. The young women could no longer be with Lot [as wives], because he was their father, nor could they belong to any others, for the husband of their youth was still alive. These two thus condemned themselves and, because they rashly did what was not right, deprived themselves of what they ought to have had. By this last solemn modesty, however, their previous rashness was greatly pardoned.

---

400. Gen 19.37.
401. Gen 19.38. The Syriac equivalent of the Hebrew "Ben-ammi," literally, "son of my people."

Section XVII

1. After these things Abraham went to the territory of the Philistines and, because he was afraid, said that Sarah *"is my sister."* Abimelech, king of Gadar, summoned Sarah to be brought before him. Because she had been tested by Pharaoh, even more because she had conceived Isaac, and because Abraham was praying very diligently, sleep quickly fell upon Abimelech when he fell into bed, just as it had upon Adam. *Then God said to Abimelech in a dream, "Behold, you are a dead man, because of the woman whom you have taken; for she is a man's wife." And Abimelech said, "Will you slay an innocent people? In the integrity of my heart and the innocence of my hands I have done this." And God said to him, "Because of this I did not let you touch her, lest you sin against me."*[402]

2. Abimelech rose early, summoned Abraham and reproved him for bringing this sin upon him. *Abraham said, "I was very afraid and called her my sister. But even about this I did not lie, for she is my sister, the daughter of my father but not the daughter of my mother."*[403] Sarah was indeed the sister of Abraham: from his father because she was the daughter of his father's brother, but not from his mother, for none of her sisters had been married to Haran the son of Terah. Another woman, a foreigner, was married to Haran. This one, who loved her tribe more than her children, remained with her family and refused to go out and accompany Lot, her son, or Sarah and Milkah, her daughters.

3. *And Abimelech said to Sarah, "Behold, I have given your brother a thousand pieces of silver and am returning you to him with a gift, because you have veiled the eyes of all those with me and you have reproved me concerning everything."*[404] *"You have veiled the eyes of all my people,"* because you brought all of his people to shame with the manifest reproof with which you reproved

---

402. Cf. Gen 20.1–6.
403. Gen 20.8–9, 12. See also *Hymns on Virginity* 22.16–18, and *Hymns on the Nativity* 20.4.
404. Gen 20.16, Peshitta.

him before them all. Sarah saw, in the deep sleep that He suddenly threw upon [Abimelech], that God was her help. So she said in a loud voice before everyone, "It is not right that you transgress the legal custom concerning your wife by [committing] adultery, not even by the taking of another wife."

(2) Unless Sarah received renewed youth in the seed that she had received, Abimelech would not have desired a woman ninety years old. *Then Abraham prayed and God healed Abimelech, his wife, and his female slaves so that they bore children,* because from the time [Abimelech] had decided to marry Sarah until he returned her, pangs of childbirth struck all the women in his household; they would kneel down, but they could not give birth.[405]

Section XVIII

1. Then the time came for Isaac to be born and milk flowed in the breasts of the old woman. On the day of the great feast that Abraham prepared when he circumcised and weaned Isaac, Sarah noticed Ishmael snickering.[406] But Sarah also saw how much Ishmael shared the characteristics of his mother, for just as Sarah was despised in the eyes of Hagar so too did Ishmael snicker at her son, and she thought, "If he acts thus to my son while I am still alive, perhaps [Abraham] will make him coheir with my son when I die and even give him two parts according to [the laws of] the firstborn."[407]

(2) Then Sarah, who showed no envy in any matter that concerned herself, became envious in this matter concerning her son. She was not envious of Hagar whom she had given to her husband. Since it was a matter of God's promise, and the son of the concubine thought that he would be coheir with the son of the freewoman, Sarah said, *"Cast out the slave woman and her son*[408] because it is not just

---

405. Gen 20.17–18.   406. Cf. Gen 21.4–9.
407. Compare Ginzberg, *Legends,* 1:263–64, where Sarah exhibits this same concern against Ishmael sharing in Isaac's inheritance.
408. Gen 21.10.

that a son of a handmaid should have any inheritance together with that son of the promise, to whom it was promised by God. It is not right that you be opposed to God and make an heir him whom God has not made an heir."[409]

2. As for Abraham, who had determined to do [what Sarah feared] because he made no distinction between his sons, [Moses] wrote that *the thing was very displeasing in the eyes of Abram on account of his son.* Then God said to him, "*All that Sarah says to you, heed her voice, for through Isaac shall your descendants be named. I will also make a great nation of the son of the slave woman, because he is your offspring.*"[410]

3. So Abraham rose early and gave Hagar and the child bread and water and sent them off. [Hagar] went and wandered in the wilderness and *an angel called from heaven to Hagar and said to her, "Behold, God has heard the cry of the child, so hold him fast with your hands; for I will make him a great nation." Then God opened her eyes and she saw a well of water and she filled [her skin] and gave the child a drink.*[411]

Section XIX

1. After these things, Abimelech and Phicol, the commander of his army, spoke to Abraham, for they saw that God was with him and had helped him in the wars of the kings and had also promised him the land of the Canaanites. They also feared that after Abraham destroyed the Canaanites he would also destroy their own land, so they hastened to make a covenant with him and the two of them made a covenant with Abraham.[412]

Section XX

1. *God again tested Abraham and said to him, "Take your son and go to the land of the Amorites and offer him up as a burnt offering on one of the mountains of which I shall tell you.*"[413] But lest it

---

409. See the fragmentary *Hymns on the Nativity* 20, which is devoted to this theme.
410. Gen 21.11–13.   411. Cf. Gen 21.14, 17–18.
412. Cf. Gen 21.22–24.
413. Gen 22.1–2. For the Aqedah in Syriac tradition, see S. P. Brock,

be said that God had greatly alarmed Abraham, God detained him for three days.

(2) Abraham rose early, cut some wood, and took two of his slave boys and Isaac and went out. But he did not inform Sarah because he had not been commanded to inform her. She would have persuaded him to let her go and participate in his sacrifice just as she had participated in the promise of his son. And he also [did not inform her] lest the inhabitants of his house stand against him and the women wail in mourning in his tent, and lest those who dwelt in that place gather together and snatch the youth from him or make him put off the day of his sacrifice. If he did not inform those two whom he took with him but did not bring up the mountain because he was afraid, how much more would he, who out of fear was unwilling to reveal it to those two, have been afraid [to inform] many?

2. While they were climbing Isaac inquired about the sacrifice. Abraham then made the same prophecy while they were ascending the mountain that he had made to the servants whom he left behind at the base of the mountain. Then, when he had bound Isaac, set him on the altar, and drawn out his knife, the angel of the Lord restrained him.[414]

(2) Lest Abraham think that [his sacrifice] was lacking anything and had thus been rejected, *the angel said to Abraham, "Now I know that you fear God,* for in this one who is more beloved to you than anything, your love toward the Lord of all is made known."[415]

(3) In two things then was Abraham victorious: that he killed his son although he did not kill him and that he believed that after Isaac died he would be raised up again and would go back down with him. For Abraham was firmly con-

---

"Sarah and the Aqedah," *LM* 87 (1974): 67–77; idem, "Genesis 22 in Syriac Tradition," in *Mélanges Dominique Barthélemy*, ed. P. Casetti *et al.*, Orbis Biblicus et Orientalis, no. 38 (Fribourg-Göttingen, 1981) 2–30; and idem, "Two Syriac Verse Homilies on the Binding of Isaac," *LM* 99 (1986): 61–129.

414. Cf. Gen 22.7–11.
415. Cf. Gen 22.12.

vinced that He who said to him, *through Isaac shall your descendants be named*,⁴¹⁶ was not lying.

3. *Then Abraham saw a ram in a tree, took it, and offered it upon the altar in place of his son.*⁴¹⁷ The question that Isaac had asked about the lamb attests to the fact that there had been no ram there. The wood that was on Isaac's shoulders proves that there had been no tree there. The mountain spit out the tree and the tree the ram,⁴¹⁸ so that in the ram that hung in the tree and had become the sacrifice in the place of Abraham's son, there might be depicted the day of Him who was to hang upon the wood like a ram and was to taste death for the sake of the whole world.

(2) *Then the angel spoke to him a second time, "By myself I have sworn," says the Lord, "that I will indeed multiply your seed and all the nations of the earth shall be blessed in your seed,"*⁴¹⁹ who is Christ.

Section XXI

1. After these things, Sarah died in Hebron, one hundred and twenty-seven years old, and Abraham buried her in the cave that he had bought from the Hittites.⁴²⁰

2. After three years, *Abraham said to his eldest servant, "Put your hand under my thigh and I will make you swear that you will not take a wife for my son from the daughters of the Canaanites."*⁴²¹ Abraham made him swear by the covenant of circumcision. Because God saw that the two heads of the world had dishonored this member, He set the sign of the covenant on it so that that member which was the most despised of all the limbs would now be the most honored of all the limbs. The

---

416. Gen 21.12.

417. Gen 22.13. Ephrem reads "tree" here against the Peshitta, which reads "bush." This reading, "tree," is also found in Targums *Onkelos, Neofiti,* and *Pseudo-Jonathan.* See B. Levy, *Targum Neophyti 1. A Textual Study* (New York, 1986) 1:164–66.

418. See Ginzberg, *Legends,* 1:282, where the ram "was created in the twilight of Sabbath eve in the week of creation."

419. Cf. Gen 22.15–18.   420. Cf. Gen 23.1–2, 19–20.

421. Gen 24.2–3.

sign of the covenant that was set on it bestowed on it such great honor that those who take oaths now swear by it and all those who administer oaths make them swear by it.

3. The servant swore the oath to his master and went off with many choice gifts. He sat beside a well, prayed, and asked for a sign. Even though he rejoiced in the sign that came to him, he still waited to see whether she was from [Abraham's] tribe. When he learned that she was the daughter of Bethuel, the son of Nahor,[422] he praised God and went and stayed in their house.[423]

4. When the servant told them about the oath that his master had made him swear and how the prayer that he prayed at the well was in fact fulfilled,[424] Bethuel and Laban said to him, *"This matter of yours and of your master has come from the Lord. Behold, Rebekah is before you. Take her and go."*[425]

(2) Then they called the young woman to learn from her [whether she would return with him or not]. Because she heard about the oath that Abraham had made him swear, and about the prayer that the servant had prayed at the well and about the sign for which he had asked and which had been granted to him, she feared to say "I will not go," because she knew that it was the will of the Lord that she go. So she went and became Isaac's [wife]. By the joy [which he received] from Rebekah, who came three years later, Isaac was comforted from the mourning of his mother with which he had been shrouded for three years.[426]

Section XXII

1. Because no law concerning virginity or chastity had been set down, lest desire ever make a stain in the mind of that just man, because it had been told him, *"Kings of nations shall come forth from you,"*[427] and because God had said about him, *"I know that Abraham will command his children and his grandchildren to keep my commandments,"*[428] Abraham took for

---

422. Cf. Gen 24.47.
424. Cf. Gen 24.34–49.
426. Cf. Gen 24.57–67.
428. Gen 18.19, Peshitta.

423. Cf. Gen 24.9–32.
425. Gen 24.50–51.
427. Gen 17.6.

himself a concubine after the death of Sarah, so that through the uprightness of his many sons who were to be scattered in lands throughout the entire earth, knowledge and worship of the one God would be spread. Abraham then had sons from Keturah and he sent them eastward with gifts. Abraham died one hundred and seventy-five years old and was buried next to Sarah, his wife.[429]

Section XXIII

1. *God blessed Isaac*[430] and Isaac prayed for Rebekah who was barren and after twenty years God heard him and she conceived. Her sons struggled together within her womb. She went to inquire of the Lord and it was told her, *"Two nations are in your womb,"* that is, the Edomite and Hebrew nations. As to whom she went to inquire it was to Melchizedek that she went to inquire, as we mentioned above in the genealogy of Melchizedek. She returned quickly because of the pangs that were striking her and she gave birth to Esau and Jacob.[431]

2. Jacob saw that the right of the firstborn was despised by Esau and he contrived to take it from him, trusting in God who had said, *"The elder shall serve the younger."*[432] Jacob boiled some lentils and *Esau came home famished after hunting, and said to Jacob "Let me eat some of that red pottage,"* that is, "Let me eat some of your lentils." *Jacob said to him, "Give me your birthright and you may take all of them." After Esau swore to him and sold him his birthright, Jacob then gave Esau [the lentils].*[433] To show that it was not by reason of his hunger that Esau sold his birthright, Scripture says, *After he had eaten he arose and went away and Esau despised his birthright.*[434] Therefore, Esau did not sell it because he was hungry but rather, since it had no value to him, he sold it for nothing as if it were nothing.

429. Cf. Gen 25.1–7, 10.
430. Gen 25.11.
431. Gen 25.21–26.
432. Gen 25.23.
433. Gen 25.29–34. Read here *l'esaw* for *wal'saw* as Tonneau, *In Genesim et Exodum*, 86, emends; see also Jansma, "Beiträge," 61.
434. Gen 25.34.

Section XXIV

1. *And there was a famine in the land and Isaac sowed and reaped in that same year a hundred measures.* Then, because Abimelech the king was afraid of that sojourner, he went to him with Phicol, the commander of his army, and said to him, "We see that the Lord is with you just as he was with your father in that you have reaped a hundred measures, as well as in many other things, so we say, Let us make a covenant between us and you, that you will do us no harm when you increase in number, just as we did not harm you when you were still few." Each swore an oath to the other and they departed in peace.[435]

Section XXV

1. *When Isaac was old and his eyes were dim, he said to Esau, "Go hunt some game and make me some stew that I may eat and that I myself may bless you before I die." And Esau went out to hunt some game.*[436] When Rebekah heard this, she went and counseled Jacob lest the birthright of Esau be contrary to the word of God which said that *the elder shall serve the younger.* Jacob, however, refused for he was afraid that instead of blessings he would receive curses.[437]

2. After Rebekah took upon herself the curses, *Jacob did [as she bid] and took [the two kids] and brought them in. And he called to his father and his father said to him, "Who are you?" He said, "I am Esau. I have done as you told me."* But Isaac was in doubt about the voice for he was afraid lest the blessings as well as the birthright elude [Esau]. *So Isaac said to him, "Come near, that I may feel you."* After the true voice had been disguised by reason of the false feel of his hands and he had been blessed and had departed, Esau came back, made [a stew] and called to his father. Isaac was stupefied when he saw how, in the name of Esau, the treasury of his blessings had also been stripped from him.[438]

(2) "Who was it then who hunted game and brought it to me

---

435. Gen 26.1, 12, 26–31.   436. Gen 27.1–5.
437. Cf. Gen 27.5–12.
438. Cf. Gen 27.13–14, 18–33.

and I have blessed him?—and indeed he shall be blessed."[439] For Isaac was unable to alter his blessings, first, because he knew that the will of the Lord had been accomplished just as it had been told to Rebekah, and secondly, since he had said to Jacob, *"Cursed be those who curse you,"*[440] he feared to curse [Jacob] lest, by his curses he harm not Jacob, who was blessed, but that the curse of his lips turn back on himself.[441]

3. *And Esau cried out and wailed bitterly,*[442] not because he lost his spiritual blessings but because he was now deprived of the bountiful produce of the blessed earth; not because he was no longer able to be righteous but because he would not be able to make his brother his servant; not because he would not inherit eternal life but because the land of the Canaanites would not be his portion. Since Esau had such spite for his brother that he wished to kill him, Rebekah persuaded Jacob to go to the house of Laban lest they kill each other in their strife, and she be bereft of both of them at the same time.[443]

Section XXVI

1. Then [Rebekah] spoke to Isaac and [Isaac] blessed Jacob and sent him to Haran for a wife. The day came to an end and he spent the night there [where he was]. In place of the pillows that had always been set out for him in his mother's tent, he set down a rock for his pillow. Full of self-pity, he fell asleep. *He saw in his dream a ladder set up on the earth and the top of it reached to heaven and angels were ascending and descending on it and the Lord was standing above it.*[444]

(2) The ladder that he saw, he saw because of the ascending and descending of the angels. Also, by the angels who were ascending and descending around him while he was sleeping, God clearly showed what great care He took toward Jacob, that he was being watched not only when he was awake, but even in his sleep there were angels who were

---

439. Gen 27.33.
441. Compare *Genesis Rabbah* 67.3.
443. Cf. Gen 27.41–45.
440. Gen 27.29.
442. Gen 27.34.
444. Cf. Gen 28.1–13.

commanded to ascend and descend around him to protect him. Thus, in the dream of the ladder, God clearly made manifest to Jacob the secret care that [He exerted] on his behalf. When Jacob had gone to sleep, he thought he was sleeping in a place that was very remote from God, but when he awoke and saw what care God was taking toward him in the desert, he said, "I have slept as if in the house of God and have reclined as if before the gate of heaven."[445]

2. To show him that the angels were ascending and descending to protect him, *God said to Jacob, "Behold, I am with you and will keep you wherever you go, and I will bring you back to this land; for I will not leave you until I have done what I have said to you." And Jacob said, "Surely the Lord is in this place to protect me and I did not know it."*[446]

(2) As for the oil that Jacob poured upon the pillar,[447] he either had it with him or he had brought it out of the village. In the oil that he poured upon the stone, he was depicting the mystery of Christ who was hidden inside it.

3. *Jacob named that place Bethel,*[448] which means *the house of God,* as he had just called it.[449] He then made a vow on the stone saying, *"If God will be with me, and will give me bread and clothing, this stone shall be God's house and of all that you give me I will give a tenth to you."*[450] In the rock the mystery of the church is also represented, for it is to her that the vows and offerings of all the nations were soon to come.[451]

Section XXVII

1. Jacob continued on and turned aside to a well where he saw Rachel the shepherd girl who, with her bare feet, her mean clothing, and her face burned from the sun, could not be distinguished from charred brands that come out of the fire. Jacob knew that He who had provided the beautiful Rebekah at the spring now provided Rachel in her mean

---

445. Cf. Gen 28.17.
447. Cf. Gen 28.18.
449. Cf. Gen 28.17.
446. Gen 28.15–16.
448. Gen 28.19.
450. Gen 28.20–22.
451. For the rich image of the rock as Christ and Church in Syriac literature, see Murray, *Symbols,* 205–38.

clothing at the well. Then he performed a heroic deed in her presence for, through the Son who was hidden in it, he rolled away a stone that even many could raise only with great difficulty.[452] When he betrothed her to God through this marvelous deed, Jacob then turned and married himself to her with a kiss.[453]

2. Jacob served seven years for Rachel but when those days came to an end Laban deceived him and brought him Leah instead of Rachel. Laban carried out this cunning scheme [not only] because of the ugliness of Leah, whom in the seven years of Rachel's betrothal, no man had married, but [he did it] even more because he saw how much his flock had been blessed during the seven years that Jacob had tended it. Laban, therefore, contrived that Jacob would work for him as shepherd a second time so that in the next seven years when he worked for Rachel[454] he would redouble the flock that he had gained in those first seven years.

3. *Laban* then contrived excuses because of the people of that country and *said, "It is not so done in our country to give the younger before the elder,"* and then he put forth his intentions, saying to him, *"Complete the wedding feast of this one and I will give you Rachel also for the service you will render me for another seven years,"*[455] and Laban gathered the men of the place around him and thus convinced [Jacob].[456] Therefore, lest Jacob turn the seed of the Just One to heathenism, while Leah remained in the house of Laban the heathen, and lest he deceive Rachel his wife (for the betrothed of a man is his wife), he took the one lest he deceive her and the other lest he sin against her or his seed. If Laban had not withheld Rachel from Jacob and said to him, *"Work for me seven years in exchange for Leah,"* he would not have been persuaded to

---

452. Cf. Gen 29.10. See also Ginzberg, *Legends,* 1:354, where "with his two arms alone [Jacob] accomplished what usually requires the united forces of a large assemblage of men."

453. Cf. Gen 29.11.   454. The text reads here "Leah."

455. Gen 29.26–27.

456. See Ginzberg, *Legends,* 1:360, where Laban makes all his friends take a pledge not to betray Laban's deceitful plan.

work seven days for her, not because she was ugly but because he hated to be the husband of two wives.

Section XXVIII

1. Leah bore Reuben, Simeon, Levi, and Judah and then ceased giving birth, whereas Rachel was barren. Because she heard Jacob say that Abraham had prayed over the barren Sarah and was heard, and that Isaac had also prayed for Rebekah and was answered, she thought that it was because Jacob had not prayed for her that her closed womb had not been opened. For this reason, she said in anger and in tears, *"Give me children, or I shall die!"* [457]

(2) Although he was angry with her because she said, *"Give me children,"* instead of saying, "Pray that children be given me," Jacob persuaded Rachel that "even if my fathers were answered, nevertheless Abraham was heard only after one hundred years and Isaac after twenty." [458] When she learned from him that she, who had become extremely despondent, ought to have great patience, she said to him, *"Then go into my handmaid, she shall bear on my knees and I shall be comforted by her,"* [459] following [the example] of Abraham, who took Hagar and did the will of Sarah because he loved her. "But you will not be persuaded by me because you hate me." So, lest she nag him, asking him every day for children, Jacob, who was sent from his parents to take a daughter of Laban, agreed to take the foreign woman. But it was also so that the sons of maidservants might become joint heirs with sons of freewomen that Jacob took both maidservants and freewomen. So he took Bilhah and she conceived and bore Dan and Naphtali. [460]

2. *When Leah saw that she had ceased bearing children, she too urged Jacob to go into her maidservant.* [461] When he tried to dissuade her, saying "There is comfort for you; you have chil-

---

457. Gen 30.1.
458. In *Hymns on the Nativity* 8.14, Ephrem compares this demand of Rachel with the docility of Mary, the mother of Christ.
459. Gen 30.3.　　　　　　　460. Cf. Gen 30.4–9.
461. Gen 30.9.

dren," she said to him, "It is not right that my maidservant should perform the duties of a handmaid for her fellow servant, and you have now made me a rival wife of Rachel's handmaid. Make Rachel also a rival wife to my maidservant." Then, lest he grieve Leah and cause a schism between the sisters, [Jacob] agreed, for the sake of peace in his dwelling, to go into Zilpah also. Zilpah conceived and bore Gad and Asher.[462]

3. After these things *Reuben found mandrakes in the field and brought them to Leah.*[463] Some say that the mandrake is a plant whose fruit resembles apples, which have a scent and are edible. So by means of these mandrakes, with cheerfulness seasoned with faith, Leah made Jacob take her that night.

(2) Then [Moses] wrote that *God heard Leah and she conceived and bore Issachar. Leah said, "God has given me my wage because I gave my maid to my husband."*[464] Unless it had been by the will of God that Jacob took Zilpah, no wage would have been rendered to Leah on behalf of Zilpah. Leah conceived and bore Issachar and Zebulun and Dinah their sister.[465]

(2) *Then God remembered Rachel* also *and she bore* Joseph *and she said, "I have learned that the Lord, and not my husband, will increase me."*[466]

Section XXIX

1. *After Joseph was born, Jacob said to Laban, "Give me my wives and my children for whom I have served you and let me go." Then Laban, who loved not Jacob but himself, said, "I know from experience that the Lord has blessed me because of you, so separate your wage from mine and I will grant it."*[467] Jacob consented because he had not yet received permission from God to depart. God, who saw that Laban had cheated from his wages that one to whom He had promised, *"I will go down with you and I will raise you up from there,"* made Jacob

---

462. Gen 30.10–13.
464. Gen 30.17–18.
466. Cf. Gen 30.22–24.
463. Gen 30.14.
465. Cf. Gen 30.18–21.
467. Gen 30.25–28.

rich from Laban's own flock without doing any harm to Laban.

2. It was to test Laban that the hornless and spotted lambs increased in his flock, so that he might know that God was with Jacob and cease doing evil to him. But then the sons of Laban also defrauded Jacob just as Laban had, and they said concerning that one who had also made them rich, *"From what is our father's he has become rich."*[468] And that one who had said, *"I know from experience that the Lord has blessed me because of you,"* changed both in heart and countenance toward [Jacob].

(2) God then appeared to Jacob and told him to return to the house of his father.[469] *Jacob called to Rachel and Leah and said to them, "Your father whom I have served with all my strength has changed my wage ten times, but God did not permit him to harm me, in that all his cunning wiles have been turned against him. If he agreed that the hornless lambs were mine, because he thought the flock would not bear any hornless, many of the lambs became hornless; but if he agreed that the spotted lambs [would be mine], because he thought that few spotted ones would be born to him, the whole flock bore spotted ones."*[470]

3. And Rachel and Leah said to him, *"There is no portion for us in our father's house, for he gives all that he has to his sons. He has sold us and has consumed our money, just as he has consumed your strength for the fourteen years that you served him on our behalf. Now, do whatever God has said to you, for we are ready to go with you whenever He sends you."*[471]

4. Jacob stole the heart of Laban and Rachel his gods and they went to the mountain of Gilead. But Laban pursued and overtook him. *The Lord appeared to Laban in a dream and said to him, "Take heed that you do not speak to Jacob, either great or small."*[472] But *Laban* was unable to suppress his stubbornness and *said, "It is in my power to do you evil but last night the*

---

468. Gen 31.1.
469. Cf. Gen 31.2–3.
470. Gen 31.4–8.
471. Gen 31.14–16.
472. Gen 31.24. Ephrem reads here "great or small" versus the Peshitta and Hebrew which read "good or bad."

God of your fathers forbade me. But why did you steal my gods together with my daughters and flee?"[473]

(2) Jacob loved Rachel very much for she loved his God and despised the idols of her father. She despised them as being useless things, not only by the fact that she stole them, but also in that, when they were being sought, she was using them as a seat while she was menstruating.[474]

(3) But this did not satisfy Laban, for he had risen early and sought his gods at dawn after the God of truth had appeared to him in the evening. He also retracted his statement, "You have made me rich because the Lord has blessed me on account of you," when he said, *"The flocks are my flocks and all that you see here is mine. Come now, let us make a covenant, and let it be a witness between us."*[475]

5. Because they had been blaming each other, *Jacob saying, "God saw that you have cheated my toil and the labor of my hands and He appeared to you last night,"*[476] and *Laban saying, "The flocks are my flocks and all that you see is mine,"*[477] they then said that all these things that preceded this covenant would be forgotten.

(2) So *Jacob took up a stone and set it up as a pillar* and each man brought a stone *and they made a great heap*[478] [saying,] "This heap, made up of many [stones], will bear witness, as if from the mouth of many, against anyone who would change one thing from the covenant that we are establishing before many. Behold, this heap testifies, to the same degree that those who made this heap are witnesses, that neither you nor I shall change one thing from the covenant that we have established by amassing this heap.

6. In order to make it known that the heap was built solely as a witness that from that time on neither of them should turn against the other, [Moses] said, *Jacob swore by the fear of his father Isaac,* and Laban said, *"The God of Abraham and the God of Nahor judge between us."*[479]

---

473. Gen 31.19–30.
475. Gen 31.43–44.
477. Gen 31.43.
479. Gen 31.53.

474. Cf. Gen 31.34–35.
476. Gen 31.42.
478. Gen 31.45–46.

Section XXX

1. After Jacob and Laban had parted from each other, *angels of God met Jacob*[480] to make known to him that if Laban did not obey God, who had appeared to him in the evening, he and those with him would be destroyed at dawn at the hands of those angels who protect him. Just as God had shown Jacob the angels that accompanied him when he went down, He also showed him angels when he was going up to make him know that the word was true which God had spoken to him: *"I will go down with you and I will bring you up from there."*[481] The army of angels[482] that God had shown Jacob was so that he would not fear Esau, for there were many more [angels] with Jacob than were with Esau.

2. After these things [Jacob] sent messengers to his brother Esau, apologizing for his delay. When he heard that [Esau] was coming to meet him with four hundred men, [Jacob] became afraid. While he prayed to God to remember the covenant He made with him when he was going down, [Jacob] still sent his brother an offering of good will so that [Esau] would not remember the offense that he committed against him on the day he stole his blessings.[483]

3. That night an angel appeared to [Jacob] and wrestled with him.[484] He both overcame the angel and was overcome by the angel so that [Jacob] learned both how weak he was and how strong he was. He was weak when the angel touched the hollow of his thigh and it became dislocated,[485] but he was strong, for *the angel said to him, "Let me go."* It was to show how long they had been contending with each other that [the angel] said, *"Behold, the dawn is rising."*[486] Then Jacob sought to be blessed in order to make known that it was in love that they had laid hold of each other.

---

480. Gen 32.1.
481. This verse actually occurs at Gen 46.4. Ephrem is perhaps confusing Jacob's later trip to Egypt with this earlier one to find a wife. Cf. Gen 28.15, where God also promised Jacob to be with him always.
482. Cf. Gen 32.2.
483. Cf. Gen 32.3–21.
484. Cf. Gen 32.22–24.
485. Cf. Gen 32.25.
486. Gen 32.26.

Then the angel blessed him to show that he was not angry that an earthly being had prevailed over him.[487]

4. God did all that He had promised Jacob. He made him rich as He had told him. He went down with him and brought him up as He had promised him. He also rescued him from Laban, and delivered him from his brother. But instead of performing the promised vow, which he had vowed to God when he went down,[488] Jacob elected, out of fear, to send [an offering] to Esau. Therefore, because he had gone back on his word, his hip joint was displaced. So he, who at one moment was equal in strength to a fiery angel, was now standing before Esau lame, but without pain.

Section XXXI

1. After these things Jacob went and dwelt in Shechem. When Shechem, the son of Hamor, saw Dinah, the daughter of Jacob, he seized her and disgraced her. The sons of Shechem persuaded the sons of Jacob to give her to them as a wife. But the sons of Jacob deceived the sons of Shechem into being circumcised before they would give her to them. Then, when the pain [of the sons of Shechem] was at its height, the sons of Jacob fell upon them, without their father [knowing], and slew all the males, captured their women, and plundered their wealth.[489]

Section XXXII

1. After those things *God said to Jacob, "Rise, go up to Bethel, and make an altar to the God who appeared to you when you fled from before your brother." And Jacob said to his sons, "Put away those foreign gods that you have taken as plunder from Shechem,"* and they brought him the molten idols and the rings of gold that were set in the ears of their idols and they buried them beneath the oak lest they be a stumbling block for Jacob's descendants. And *Jacob went to Isaac, his father,* at He-

---

487. Cf. Gen 32.26–29.
488. Cf. Gen 28.20–22.
489. Cf. Gen 33.18, 34.1–29.

bron and after twenty-three years *Isaac died, a hundred and eighty years old. His sons, Jacob and Esau, buried him.*[490]

Section XXXIII

1. Joseph was shepherding the flock with the sons of his father's concubines and brought an ill report of them to their father. Because Joseph had exposed them in their deed they hated him.[491]

(2) Joseph dreamed dreams: the first of sheaves; and the second of the sun, the moon and eleven stars, bowing down to him. His brothers hated him all the more because of his dreams. They ridiculed his dreams and said, "How will Rachel, who is dead, come and bow down to him?" Because it is said, "A man and his wife are one flesh," Jacob, symbolized by the sun, bowed down on the head of his staff, and with him, Rachel, symbolized by the moon, bowed down, although she did not [in fact] bow down.[492]

2. Then Jacob sent Joseph to the flock that he might bring back to him a report on his brothers.[493] But the brothers, by means of the cloak that was bespattered with blood, sent Jacob a report on Joseph.[494] With no mercy they cast him into a pit in the desert[495] but they wept over him with tears in the house. They sold him naked to the Arabs[496] but wept over him and wailed in the presence of the Canaanites. They put irons on his hands and feet and sent him on his way but composed lamentations over him in the village. Joseph went down to Egypt and was sold; within a few days he had changed owners twice.[497]

Section XXXIV

1. After these things, Judah took a wife and by her begot Er, Onan, and Shelah. Er, his firstborn, took Tamar as a wife. But because he was evil before the Lord, that is, because he

---

490. Cf. Gen 35.1–5, 27–29.
491. Cf. Gen 37.1–4.
492. Cf. Gen 37.5–11.
493. Cf. Gen 37.13–14.
494. Cf. Gen 37.32–33.
495. Cf. Gen 37.24.
496. Cf. Gen 37.28.
497. Cf. Gen 37.36.

was wicked before the Lord, the Lord slew him.[498] Even though his brother took Tamar out of love for her, because of his hatred towards his brother, Onan did not wish to raise up offspring for his brother. When God also slew the second son because of the cruel stratagem that he had contrived, it was thought that it was due to the sins of Tamar that her two husbands had died. Judah then sent her to her father's house and assured her that when Shelah grew up she would be given to him.[499]

2. When Shelah had become a young man and Judah did not wish to bring her back to his house,[500] Tamar thought, "How can I make the Hebrews realize that it is not marriage for which I am hungering, but rather that I am yearning for the blessing that is hidden in them? Although I am able to have relations with Shelah, I would not be able to make my faith victorious through Shelah. I ought then to have relations with Judah so that by the treasure I receive, I might enrich my poverty, and in the widowhood I preserve, I might make it clear that I did not desire marriage."

3. Because Tamar was afraid lest Judah find out and kill her in vengeance for his two sons of whose deaths she was accused, she, like Eliezer,[501] asked for a sign saying, "Let Your knowledge not condemn me for this act of desire, for You know that it is for what is hidden in the Hebrews that I thirst. I do not know whether this thing is pleasing to you or not. Grant that I may appear to him in another guise lest he kill me. [Grant] also that an invitation to lie with him[502] might be found in his mouth, so that I may know that it is acceptable to you that the treasure, which is hidden in the circumcised, might be transmitted even through a daughter of the uncircumcised. May it be that, when he sees me, he will say to me, 'Come, let me come into you.' "[503]

---

498. Cf. Gen 38.1–7.
499. Cf. Gen 38.8–11, and Jubilees 41.6.
500. Cf. Gen 38.14.
501. Cf. Gen 24.12–14.
502. Literally, "a word of fornication."
503. Gen 38.16.

4. While Tamar was making supplication to God for these things, behold, Judah came out and saw her. The prayer of Tamar inclined him, contrary to his usual habit, [to go] to a harlot.[504] When she saw him she was veiled for she was afraid. After the word of the sign for which she had asked had been spoken, she knew that God was pleased with what she was doing. Afterwards, she revealed her face without fear and even demanded remuneration from the lord of the treasure.[505]

5. After she stripped the man of his staff, his signet ring, and his cord and took for herself these three witnesses that they might testify to the third [person] that was to be generated from her, she had intercourse with him and returned to her father's house.[506] After three months it was reported to Judah that Tamar had committed harlotry and, as a result of her harlotry, had conceived. When he summoned her and learned that she had no defense, he commanded that she be burned.[507]

(2) When the inhabitants of Hebron assembled to follow her who was going out to be burned, she brought out her witnesses and, through some of her relatives, she sent a message to her father-in-law. *"By the man to whom these belong, I have conceived."*[508] When Judah saw his pledges, he marvelled at the faith of that woman. As he extended his hand to take them back, he reflected on the time that he had given them to her.

6. He then said, *"She is more innocent than I,"* that is, "She is more righteous than I. What great sinners my sons were. *Because of this, I did not give her to my son Shelah.*[509] She is innocent of that evil suspicion that I held against her and [for which] I withheld my son Shelah from her." She who had

---

504. Compare *Genesis Rabbah* 85.
505. The righteous "deceit" of Tamar due to her trust in God is a favorite theme of Ephrem. See *Hymns on Virginity* 22.19–20, and *Hymns on the Nativity* 1.12, 9.8.
506. Cf. Gen 38.16–19. 507. Cf. Gen 38.24.
508. Gen 38.25.
509. Cf. Gen 38.26, Jubilees 41.19.

been cheated out of marriage was justified in her fornication, and he who sent her out on account of his first two sons brought her back for the sake of his last two sons. *He did not lie with her again*[510] because she had been the wife of his first two sons, nor did he take another wife for she was the mother of his last two sons.[511]

Section XXXV

1. After Joseph had been sold to Potiphar[512] and this one had become rich because of Joseph, just as Laban had because of Joseph's father, Potiphar's mistress fell in love with Joseph and said, *"Lie with me."*[513] But when he would not submit to her and she tired of trying to catch him by guile, she cleverly maneuvered him into the bedchamber in an effort to subdue him. But after she had caught him by his clothing, he left it in her hand and fled outside. Because she thought she would become a laughingstock in the eyes of her servants, she cried out in a loud voice and those of her household assembled to be her witnesses, not to that which she wanted to do, but to that which she had prepared to say.[514]

2. But Joseph, who could have fled and, by doing so, have gone to his father's house, detested this flight which would have spared him from shame. He rather persevered until he saw how the dreams that he had seen would turn out.

3. Joseph's master came home and heard the words of his mistress and of the witnesses who corroborated what she said. Potiphar saw that Joseph's garment also [bore witness] against Joseph and so he threw Joseph into prison[515] without his garment just as [his brothers] had cast him into the pit in the desert without his cloak.

(2) That peace that had come to his master's servants while Joseph was in his master's house now came to the prisoners while he was confined in prison.[516] He also interpreted

510. Gen 38.26.
512. Cf. Gen 39.1.
514. Cf. Gen 39.11–18.
516. Cf. Gen 39.21–23.
511. Cf. Gen 38.27–30.
513. Gen 39.7.
515. Cf. Gen 39.19–20.

there two dreams for two of Pharaoh's servants; one was hung as Joseph told him and the other "placed the cup in Pharaoh's hand" as Joseph had interpreted for him. Joseph then sought from the chief butler to be remembered before Pharaoh but that "remember me," that Joseph had told him made him forget for two years.[517]

4. Pharaoh then saw twin dreams, one of ears of grain and one of cows. Although they are easily interpreted by every one, for the sake of Joseph they were hidden even from the wise men of Pharaoh. Then, after two years the chief butler remembered Joseph before Pharaoh and Pharaoh summoned him to be brought to him; the hair that had grown in his grief, joy then cut, and the filthy garments with which sorrow had clothed him, cheerfulness stripped from him.[518]

5. When Joseph came and heard the dreams of Pharaoh and saw what calamity was about to come upon the Egyptians, he told them the true interpretation and, in addition, gave them some beneficial counsel. *"Let Pharaoh select a wise man and set him in authority over all of Egypt to gather the grain of the good years to reserve a supply for the seven bad years so that no one in Egypt perish in the famine."*[519]

(2) When Joseph said, *"Let Pharaoh select a man,"* he spoke about himself. He, out of modesty, did not say it openly in his own name, but he would not give it to another, for he knew that no one else would be able to make suitable provision for the great scourge that was coming upon them. Joseph became great in the eyes of Pharaoh through his interpretation of Pharaoh's dreams but even more through the beneficial counsel that his mind had devised.[520]

6. Pharaoh then gave Joseph authority over all his territory and even added the signet ring with which the treasuries of his kingdom were sealed. This ring, which had never been placed on the hand of a non-Egyptian, was taken from the hand of Pharaoh and, with special honor, set on the fin-

---

517. Cf. Gen 40.1–23.
519. Cf. Gen 41.15–36.
518. Cf. Gen 41.1–14.
520. Cf. Gen 41.37–45.

ger of Joseph. With the ring that he was given, [Joseph] was given rule over everything.[521]

(2) *"I, Pharaoh, command that without you[r consent], no one shall lift up a hand or a foot in all the land of Egypt."*[522] Included among those who were to be subservient to him were all the army commanders and the princes of the king.

7. Joseph's [former] master was there when the dreams of Pharaoh were being interpreted. When [Potiphar] saw that only in respect to the throne was [Joseph] less than Pharaoh, he returned quickly to his house. In his haste to go to tell his wife of [Joseph's] greatness, he closely resembled his wife when she had come out to meet him to accuse Joseph. Potiphar said to [his wife], "Joseph, our servant, has become our master. He whom we sent to prison without clothing, Pharaoh has now clothed with a garment of fine white linen. He whom we cast prostrate into prison now sits upon the chariot of Pharaoh. He whom we had bound in irons now has a gold necklace set on his neck . . . How then can I look again upon him whom my eyes are unable to look upon?"

8. Then she said to him, "Do not fear Joseph to whom you did no evil, for he knows that the disgrace that came upon him in our domicile, whether justly or not, came upon him from my own hands. Go, then, without fear with the princes and army commanders who follow behind his chariot lest he think that the royal dignity he has received is an affliction to us. To show you that he is not evil, I will now speak the truth which is contrary to my previous lie. I was enamored of Joseph when I falsely accused him. I made assault on his clothing because I was overcome by his beauty. If he is just, it is I whom he will bring to grief and not you. And if he is [truly] just he will not bring me to grief, either, because if he had not been wronged he would not have been imprisoned. If he had not been imprisoned he would not have interpreted the dreams of Pharaoh and he would

---

521. Cf. Gen 41.37–42.
522. Gen 41.44.

not have come to this royal dignity of which you just informed me. Although we did not actually exalt him, it is as if we did exalt him, for it was due to our afflicting him that he has been accorded such honor and has become second to the king."

9. Then Joseph's [former] master went and, with those who were higher in rank than he, followed Joseph's chariot through the streets of Egypt. But Joseph did him no evil because he knew that it was God who had permitted his brothers to throw him into the pit in the desert, and [who had delivered him] from the pit, in order to send him in irons to Egypt, and who had permitted his master to send him to prison so that from that humble seat He might set him upon the chariot of Pharaoh.

Section XXXVI

1. Joseph went out to gather in the grain, and he laid it up in every city in which there was enough to store up in that year.[523] Then at the end of the good years, when those of famine came, Joseph took special care of the orphans, widows, and every needy person in Egypt so that there was no anxiety in Egypt.[524]

2. If this famine had been only in Egypt, Egypt would have had no fear, because of the grain Joseph [had stored up]. However, there was famine throughout the entire world and because the entire earth stood in need of [the grain in] Egypt, the grain supply quickly dwindled and became expensive even for the Egyptians. The Egyptians would have consumed the grain at little expense, because of its abundance, if the entire earth had not come down to buy grain there. To make known that the entire earth hungered, [Moses] said, *The entire world came to Egypt to buy grain from Joseph, because the famine was severe over all the earth.*[525]

3. When the famine prevailed even over the house of Jacob, *Jacob said to his sons, "Do not fear. Behold, I have heard*

---

523. Cf. Gen 41.48–49.   524. Cf. Gen 41.53–57.
525. Gen 41.57.

that there is grain in the land of Egypt. Go down and buy grain for us, that we may live and not die."[526] When Jacob said, *"Do not fear,"* he made known how much they did fear and [when he said,] *"I have heard that there is grain,"* that the grain was being consumed throughout the earth and [when he said,] *"buy grain for us that we may live and not die,"* that they had resigned themselves to perishing from the famine along with the entire land of Canaan.

4. Then the brothers of Joseph came and bowed down before him with their faces on the ground, and [Joseph] recognized them.[527] Prior to this he had been apprehensive about when they would come down to procure some grain, for he knew that they, along with all of Canaan, were afflicted with torment. When he saw them, however, he acted deceitfully while doing business with them and said, *"You are spies."*[528]

(2) They answered and said, "We do not even know the Egyptian language so that, by speaking Egyptian, we might escape notice and deceive the Egyptians. That we dwell in the land of Canaan you can learn from our offering. Moreover, there are twelve of us and it is impossible that we should all have the same evil purpose of spying. We have come of our own will to stand before you. That we are completely ignorant of the Egyptian language and do not wear the garb of Egyptians also testifies to our truthfulness. It is clear that we are not spies, for we are twelve. We are recognized everywhere because of our race and our number. *Behold, one of our brothers is with our father and another is no more.*"[529]

5. But Joseph, who saw that his dreams had not yet been fulfilled, for he had seen eleven stars bowing down to him but here were [only] ten,[530] kept himself hidden from them lest, by revealing himself, he be the one to render his

---

526. Gen 42.2.
527. Gen 42.6–7.
528. Gen 42.9.
529. Gen 42.13.
530. The fact that the sons of Jacob had just confessed to be "twelve" may be a scribal "correction" due to the traditional number of Jacob's sons. As the text stands, the "ten" here and the "twelve," above, cannot be reconciled.

dreams false. And *he said, "By this you shall be tested whether you are truly brothers, if you send for your youngest brother and bring him back to me."* Then *he threw them in prison for three days* so that they might have a taste of the suffering of him who had been imprisoned there for several years.[531]

6. Then, after [Joseph] carefully considered his dreams in which he had seen [his brothers] bow down to him twice, in the sheaves and in the stars, he knew that, after the second, he ought to reveal himself to them. So *he took and bound Simeon before their eyes*,[532] to learn from him how they had convinced their father about [the death of] Joseph. [Joseph] also knew that Simeon's sons and wife would urge Jacob to send Benjamin to him as quickly as possible.

(2) Perhaps, Simeon had been particularly malicious toward Joseph when they bound and sold him. But Joseph was not seeking vengeance from them, for when he was revealed to them he kissed them. When that one was bound who, more than any of them, had urged that Joseph be bound, they would know that it was a just restitution. *They even admitted, "In truth we deserve to endure these things, for we have looked upon the suffering of our brother when he beseeched us but we did not heed him."*[533]

(3) When Reuben[534] had spoken of those things, both those that had been carried out in Joseph's presence and [those things that had transpired] without him after they had thrown him into the pit, Joseph remembered *and wept*,[535] not because of what his brothers did to him but because God had raised him from that place to his present position.[536]

---

531. Cf. Gen 42.15–17.
532. Gen 42.24.
533. Gen 42.21.
534. Ephrem, following the Peshitta, consistently reads "Reubel" for "Reuben."
535. Gen 42.24.
536. Literally, "from where to where."

Section XXXVII

1. After they had loaded their supplies, the [brothers] went up and related to their father the evils that they had endured on this trip and how they had become objects of ridicule in Egypt, having been falsely accused of spying in Egypt, and that they would not have escaped this suffering had it not been for Benjamin. While some of them were recounting these things to their father, the others were emptying their sacks and behold, each one found his money in the opening of his sack.[537]

2. Jacob was full of grief because of all that had happened to them, but even more because of Simeon who was imprisoned. Although the brothers implored him daily to send Benjamin with them, Jacob would not assent because of his fear due to [what had happened to] Joseph.[538] Then, when their grain had run out and all the children of his household were languishing from hunger, all his sons drew near and said to Jacob, "Spare Simeon for the sake of his children and be without your youngest son for a few days lest Simeon's wife be widowed of Simeon."

3. Then Jacob was constrained by the famine, whether he was willing or not, to send Benjamin with them. So he gave them supplies and sent them off with blessings and said, "Just as I was bereaved of Rachel so am I now bereaved of Rachel's children."[539] Judah comforted his father and said, *"If I do not bring back Benjamin and set him before you then let me bear the blame forever."*[540] Then they took some of the choice fruits of the land: gum, pistachio nuts, which are berries, and so forth. They then went down and stood before Joseph. Joseph commanded his steward to give them lodging in his house.[541]

4. But when the [brothers] saw Joseph's servants hurrying to unburden their beasts and to bring in their baggage, they said to themselves, grieving, "We have bereaved our fa-

---

537. Cf. Gen 42.29–35.
538. Cf. Gen 42.36–38.
539. Cf. Gen 43.14.
540. Gen 43.9.
541. Cf. Gen 43.15–16.

ther of Benjamin and we shall never again see the face of our father. It was with treachery that our money was put into the openings of our packs, so that if we escape [the charge of] spying they might seize us and make us slaves [on the charge] of theft. Let us confess to the steward about the money before he begins to accuse us so that our brother Benjamin might free us from [the charge of] spying and the confession of our lips from [the charge of] theft."[542]

5. Then the [brothers] approached Joseph's steward and said to him, "When we returned the first time we opened our sacks and behold, there was each one's money in the opening of his sack. We are now returning it to you because it is not right that we take the money for the grain together with the grain."[543] But when the steward saw how terrified they were, he consoled them and said, "Rest assured, do not be afraid. It is not because of the money, which I received, that we are bringing you into this house.[544] We have eagerly awaited you because of the truth that is found among you. You are not going to be condemned for something that you did not take. You have been summoned to recline and be seated before our master, for he is just and by the honor that he has reserved for you this second time, he wishes to make you forget the disgrace that you endured the first time."

6. When Joseph entered the house, his brothers brought him an offering and bowed down to him trembling. He inquired about their welfare and they took heart. He asked if their father was alive and they were put at ease. He asked whether that one was their brother and he blessed him and said, "God be gracious to you, my son," and all fear was taken from their mind.[545] It was in the Egyptian language that Joseph blessed Benjamin and it was through an interpreter that they heard these initial [exchanges].

7. Joseph's affection for his brothers began to show and he went out to give them a respite, and wept within his

---

542. Cf. Gen 43.18.
544. Cf. Gen 43.23.
543. Cf. Gen 43.20–22.
545. Cf. Gen 43.26–29.

chamber. [Joseph] sat off by himself to eat and he made the Egyptians sit down. He began to make his brothers sit down as if around his [divining] cup;[546] the elder according to his status as elder and the youngest according to his youth.[547] It is amazing that his brothers did not recognize him: not by the money in their provisions when they went home the first time, not when Joseph had Simeon bound, not when he asked about his old father when they brought Benjamin back, not when they were accused of cheating, not from the fact that he made them stay in his house and blessed Benjamin, not even from the fact that he knew the names of all of them. This was all the more [amazing] since even his appearance was so similar. Even if his majesty had deluded them his dreams should have jarred their memory. Although they did not recognize Joseph because of his majesty, his rank, and his angry tongue, it was, nevertheless, because of the Lord that he remained hidden from them until his dreams should be fulfilled in them who had sold him in order to render them false.

Section XXXVIII

1. After the [brothers] ate, drank, and became inebriated, they rose early and departed, with a cup having been placed in Benjamin's sack and, again, with each one's money in his sack. Joseph's steward went out and overtook them and he poured into their ears the threats that he had been commanded by his master to say.[548]

2. *The [brothers], confident in their own trustworthiness, said, "With whomever the cup is found, let him die, and let all of us become slaves."*[549] These men then hastened to take down

---

546. The word that Ephrem uses here, a transliterated form of the Greek σκύφος, is found in the Peshitta only at Gen 44.5. A divining cup, in Aramaic *kasah*, and other divining paraphernalia are used in conjunction with the sons' seating arrangement in *Targum Pseudo-Jonathan* here at Gen 43.33. For a discussion of the purpose of this cup, see C. Westermann, *Genesis 37–50: A Commentary* (Minneapolis, 1986) 132.

547. Cf. Gen 43.30–34.

548. Cf. Gen 44.1–5.   549. Gen 44.9.

their sacks and the steward began by searching through Reuben's sack. When the steward did not find the cup in the sacks of the elder sons, he was saddened with grief because [he knew] the situation would not remain thus for long.[550]

(2) Then the brothers of Joseph comforted him and said, "Search, too, the sack of the youngest, then return quickly because there in the house you will find the cup of your master." But the steward, as if to do the will of these men, stuck his hand into a sack without the cup, wishing to avoid the sack that it was in. But when Benjamin bade him also to search in his sack, he thrust his hand in aimlessly and the cup came out firmly in his hand.[551]

3. The brothers did not know what to say; they found it impossible not to put the blame on Benjamin because the cup had come out from his sack, but the money that had twice come out from their own sacks did not permit them to put the blame on him. Then the brothers, confounded by the things that had befallen them, rent their garments and went back weeping to that house from which they had just departed rejoicing.[552]

(2) Joseph, with the anger of Egyptians, shouted accusations at them and said, *"What is this that you have done?* You said that you were just men. At the great meal that we prepared for you we proclaimed your righteousness among the Egyptians. But today you have become objects of scorn in the eyes of the Egyptians because you stole the cup with which I divine for all the Egyptians. *Do you not know that such a man as I can indeed divine?"* [553] Where would they have learned this except from [that occasion] when it had been filled in their presence and Joseph struck it and made them sit down one after the other?[554]

---

550. The Syriac is literally, "He would not be able to stay much longer in that place." The precise meaning is unclear, but the sense seems to be that the steward's grief was due to his knowledge of exactly where the cup was to be found and his unwillingness to discover it.

551. Cf. Gen 44.11–12.   552. Cf. Gen 44.13.
553. Gen 44.15.
554. That is, in order by age. See XXXVII.7, above, and note *ad loc.*

4. Then Judah said, *"Before God the sins of your servants have been discovered"*—not this one [of the cup], but the one for which we have been requited with these things. *"Therefore, not only he in whose sack the cup was found but we also will become slaves to our master."*[555] And Joseph said, *"Far be it from the just Egyptians to do this!*[556] These men, because of their great virtue, do not even eat bread with Hebrews lest they become unclean by them. How then can we do what is foreign to our conduct? The justice that hinders us from sinning against one who has not sinned against us compels us to be avenged on that one who has caused us offence. *The one in whose hand the cup was found shall remain and be a slave.* This will be better for him than freedom, for this later servitude which will free him from theft will be better for him than that first freedom that enslaved him to theft."[557]

Section XXXIX

1. Judah then spoke to Joseph with loud cries of lament until Joseph was overcome[558]—not to give them their brother as they hoped, but to reveal to his brothers something that they were not expecting. Joseph then commanded that every one else go out from his presence.[559] While he had shown everyone the false judgment against them, he would show no one the judgment of their guilt.

2. After every one had gone out in dismay from his presence, Joseph changed his language and his tone. In the Hebrew tongue, without a translator, he said, *"I am your brother, Joseph."*[560] But they were unable to respond for fear that, after he had made known their offences, he would kill them. Because they were still in doubt and because the Egyptians, listening outside the door, might hear him say, "I am he whom you sold as a slave," and despise them, he said to them, *"Come near to me."* When they drew near he said to them in a low voice, *"I am Joseph, whom you sold to Egypt."*[561]

---

555. Cf. Gen 44.16.
557. Cf. Gen 44.17.
559. Cf. Gen 45.1.
561. Gen 45.4.

556. Gen 44.17.
558. Cf. Gen 44.18–34.
560. Gen 45.3.

When he saw that they were gloomy and unable to look at him because of their shame, *he comforted them, "Do not be distressed that you sold me, for God sent me before you for the sake of providing for the entire earth. The famine will last for five more years and there will be no sowing or reaping for I have been tested in the seven good years that have already passed."*[562]

3. "So go up quickly to my father and tell him that God has made *me lord* not only over my brothers, as my dreams had prophesied, but even *over all of Egypt*, which they had not promised me. *Tell him of my honor in Egypt* that he might give praise on my behalf because of all that has happened to me in Egypt."[563] Then he kissed Benjamin and the two of them wept on each other's neck and Joseph turned and kissed the rest of his brothers. When they came to believe what he told them they opened their mouths and spoke with him.[564]

Section XL

1. When the things that needed to be said between them were finished, the doors of that judgment room were opened. The princes entered rejoicing and the army commanders full of gladness. This news was pleasing in the eyes of Pharaoh and his servants for they had believed that he who had become like a father to Pharaoh and ruler over the freemen and princes of Egypt was no slave but was a son of a freeman from the blessed race of the house of Abraham.[565]

2. Then [Joseph] sent them off with garments, wagons, and all sorts of valuable Egyptian goods to bring to their father.[566] He commanded them not to quarrel on the way.[567] The quarrel which he forbade them was that one say to another, "It was you who counseled us to throw him into the pit," while another contend with his brother, saying, "It was you who urged us to sell him naked and in chains to the Arabs." "As I have forgiven all of you, you forgive each other lest by all your complaining and your arguing with each

---

562. Gen 45.5–6.
563. Gen 45.9, 13.
564. Cf. Gen 45.14–15.
565. Cf. Gen 45.16.
566. Cf. Gen 45.21–23.
567. Cf. Gen 45.24.

other, your joyful trip home, because of your squabbles, turn into one of grief."

3. After the brothers departed, even though they were pleased that they had found Joseph, they were still grieving for they had no excuse [to give] to their father. They arrived and told their father the good news. When Jacob saw the wagons and gifts he was convinced that they were telling the truth. His spirit revived and he said, "As great as all these things are, that Joseph, my son, is alive is even greater than all these things."[568]

4. When they told Jacob about the honor of Joseph, about the wisdom with which he administered his affairs, and about how their last judgment was more bitter than the first, their father asked them and said, "Did you not ask Joseph how or why he went down to Egypt?" Then, when they all looked at each other and did not know what to say, Judah opened his mouth and said to his father, "We are recalling our crime today before our father." Because of the dreams of Joseph, Joseph's brothers thought, in their simplicity, that you and they would soon render him servitude. They also imagined, in their foolishness, that "it was better that he alone should be the servant than that we and our father should serve him as slaves." They did this because they took pity on you and on Benjamin and not because you loved Joseph. "You also loved Benjamin but because he did not say that we would become servants to him, all of us love him. Forgive us then for having humiliated Joseph, for it is on account of our humiliating him that he has come to this exalted state." Their father then accepted their apology and said to them, "Because of the good news about Joseph by which you have brought me joy, this offence, which caused me great suffering when I heard it, is forgiven you."

5. Jacob and his entire household packed up to go down to Egypt. Because he was afraid that Egypt's sorcery might harm his sons, *God* appeared to him and *said, "Do not be afraid to go down to Egypt."*[569] Because Jacob thought that per-

---

568. Cf. Gen 45.27–28.   569. Gen 46.3.

haps, because of the good things that would be set out for them, they would remain in Egypt and thus bring the promise to nought, [God] said to [Jacob], *"I will bring you down and I will bring you back up from there."*⁵⁷⁰ Because Jacob also feared that Joseph might die, [God] said to him, *"Joseph, your son, will set his hands on your eyes."*⁵⁷¹ After these things, Jacob rose up and, full of joy, went down with seventy persons—this included the two sons of Joseph.⁵⁷²

6. Joseph went out to meet his father with chariots and with many people. [Joseph] got down [from his horse], and bowed down to his father and they wept on each other's neck. Then Joseph commanded his brothers to say to Pharaoh, *"We and our fathers are keepers of cattle,"* so that they might dwell in Goshen and thus keep their distance from those who worship sheep and bulls.⁵⁷³

Section XLI

1. *Then Pharaoh said to Joseph, "Settle your father and your brothers in the best part of the land." And Jacob blessed Pharaoh and went out from before him.*⁵⁷⁴ Then Joseph sold the grain to the Egyptians for money and when their money had run out he sold it for cattle. In the end he bought the lands of the Egyptians so that he might provide them with food, with the exception of the land for the priests which he did not buy, because they receive an allowance that is alotted to them by Pharaoh. Joseph gave them seed in the seventh year and set it down as law that they should give one-fifth to Pharaoh.⁵⁷⁵

2. *And when the days drew near for Jacob to die, he said to Joseph, "Put your hand beneath my loins* as Abraham [said] to Eliezer when he made him swear by the covenant of circumcision."⁵⁷⁶ *Then Joseph swore to him that he would take him up and bury him with his fathers, and Jacob bowed down to him on the head of his staff.*⁵⁷⁷

---

570. Gen 46.4.
571. Gen 46.4.
572. Cf. Gen 46.5–7. For the total of seventy, cf. Gen 46.8–27.
573. Cf. Gen 46.33–34.
574. Gen 47.7, 10.
575. Cf. Gen 47.13–26.
576. Cf. Gen 24.2–3.
577. Cf. Gen 47.29–31, Peshitta.

3. When Joseph heard that his father was ill, he went and brought in his two sons that they might be blessed by Jacob before he died. *And Jacob said, "El Shaddai appeared to me in Luz while I was sleeping and a rock was set as my pillow and He blessed me and said to me, 'I will make of you nations—*that is, tribes.' *And now Ephraim and Manasseh will be mine as Reuben and Simeon are. Any more that are born to you shall be called sons of the tribe of Ephraim and Manasseh."*[578]

4. Jacob said, *"Bring your sons near to me that I may bless them."*[579] Israel crossed his hands because Manasseh was the firstborn and he put his right hand on the head of Ephraim the younger.[580] Here too the cross is clearly symbolized to depict that mystery with which Israel the firstborn departed, just as Manasseh the firstborn, and the peoples increase in the manner of Ephraim the younger.[581]

5. Then, while blessing the youths, [Jacob] said, *"Let my name and the name of my fathers be perpetuated in them,"* that is, let them be called sons of Abraham, Isaac, and Jacob.[582] Joseph was struggling to set the right hand of his father on Manasseh, but Jacob refused and said to him, "I am not depriving Manasseh of the blessing, for he will also increase, but his younger brother will increase more than he."[583] And to show that from then on the younger would take precedence over the elder, *he said, "By you shall Israel give its blessing, saying, 'May God make you as Ephraim and as Manasseh.'"*[584]

6. [Jacob] said to Joseph, *"I have given to you rather than to your brothers that which I took with my sword and with my bow,"*[585] because what had been sold to him for one hundred ewes, he had acquired by the strength of his arms.[586] While the son of

578. Cf. Gen 48.1–6.
579. Gen 48.9.
580. Gen 48.14.
581. See also *Hymns on Virginity* 20.7, 21.11.
582. Cf. Gen 48.16.
583. Cf. Gen 48.17–19.
584. Gen 48.20.
585. Gen 48.22.
586. Cf. Gen 33.19, and Josh 24.32.

Rachel was being blessed, Jacob brought back to their minds, with lamentation, the death of Rachel which had occurred by reason of her son.[587]

Section XLII
The Blessings of Jacob[588]

1. *Then Jacob called his sons and said to them, "Gather yourselves together that I may tell you what shall befall you at the end of days."*[589] Even though they were not gathered in the house they came in from their various activities outside the house and presented themselves on that day, because Joseph had come and because their father was suffering greatly. After Joseph sat down and his brothers sat around him—they were not expecting either to be blessed or cursed but to find out what would happen to them at the end—, Jacob opened his mouth and to Reuben his firstborn he said:

2. *"Reuben, you are my firstborn, my might, the first fruits of my strength,"*[590] to make known that until he took Leah he had persevered eighty-four years in virginity. *"The result of might and the result of strength,"*[591] [means] either that "you are the son of my youth and your other brothers are from the remainder of the might and strength of my youth," or "if you had been similar [to me], the greater part would have been yours because of your birthright." *"You wander about like water,"*[592] which runs out of its channel and waters another land.

(2) Because [Jacob] said that *"you wander about like water"* it is likely that Reuben had a wife but forsook her and,

---

587. Here in Gen 48.7, Jacob is recalling how Rachel died giving birth to Benjamin in Gen 35.16–21.

588. Following the Peshitta, Ephrem puts a heading on this section. For a similar heading, see *Commentary on Exodus* XV, below. Throughout these blessings, the Peshitta differs from the Hebrew text. For a study of the blessings in the targumic traditions which includes some comparison with the Peshitta, see A. Levene, "The Blessings of Jacob in Syriac Exegesis," in *SP* (Kalamazoo/Leuven, 1966) 7:524–30; and, more generally, R. Syrén, *The Blessings in the Targums: A Study on the Targumic Interpretations of Genesis 49 and Deuteronomy 33*, Acta Academiae Aboensis, Ser. A, vol. 64, no. 1 (Abo, 1986).

589. Gen 49.1. 590. Gen 49.3.
591. Gen 49.3. 592. Gen 49.4.

though not compelled by thirst, went to drink from stolen waters. *"You wander about like water, you shall not remain,"* that is, in the reckoning of the tribes. This is the reason why when Moses blessed him he said, *"Let Reuben live and not die and let him be in the reckoning of his brothers."*[593] *"You went up to your father's bed"*[594] also indicates that he went into Bilhah while she was sleeping and, therefore, she was not cursed with him. *"Truly you defiled my bed,"*[595] either by the evil act that he committed on the bed, or Jacob called that woman a bed.

3. After he finished [blessing] Reuben, Jacob turned toward Reuben's brothers and said thus, *"Simeon and Levi are brothers, weapons of wrath by their nature."*[596] *"In their secret [council]"*[597] means *"I was not aware that they were plotting to circumcise the Shechemites and slay them."* *"In their company,"*[598] that is, when they went in to slay the men. *"I will not be deprived of my honor,"*[599] for God instilled fear of them in the surrounding nations yet preserved me from disgrace. *"I was not*[600] *summoned with them to the slaughter. They slew men in their anger,"*[601] not in their justice. Because he had disgraced their sister, Shechem deserved to be put to death, but not the entire city. By their [stubborn] will *"they razed the wall,"*[602] that is, the wall [that protects] the houses of that city. *"Cursed be their anger, for it is fierce,"* against the inhabitants of Shechem *"and their wrath, for it is cruel,"*[603] in that they waited for days until they had won over and had gained the confidence of [the Shechemites], and until [the Shechemites] had been circumcised and their pain was at its greatest. Throughout those days their anger did not subside.[604]

(2) *"I will divide them in Jacob,"*[605] that is, one against the

---

593. Cf. Deut 33.6, Peshitta.
595. Gen 49.4.
597. Cf. Gen 49.6, Peshitta.
599. Cf. Gen 49.6, Peshitta.
601. Gen 49.6.
603. Gen 49.7.
594. Gen 49.4.
596. Gen 49.5.
598. Gen 49.6.
600. Read *l'* for *li*.
602. Gen 49.6, Peshitta.

604. See Ginzberg, *Legends*, 1:397–400, for the roles that Simeon and Levi played in destroying and plundering Shechem.
605. Gen 49.7.

other. For they did not possess, after the curse, the unity that they had had before the curse. They had been united to such a degree that they did not even inform their [other] brothers when they went in to be avenged for the shame committed against Dinah. *"I will divide them in Jacob,"* that is, among the descendants of Jacob, *"and I will scatter them in Israel,"*[606] that is, among the offspring of Israel.

4. They became divided from their descendants: Zimri from the tribe of Simeon and Phineas from the tribe of Levi. Because Levi had enlisted Simeon as an accomplice to kill many because of a woman, after the curse, Phineas, because of a woman, killed the son of Simeon together with that woman.[607]

(2) Although [Jacob] divided them in his mind one against the other because the former unity had been of no avail, he still scattered those two tribes among the [other] tribes. He disseminated Levi so that he might receive his inheritance from among all the tribes for, unlike his brothers, no portion had been given to him. Simeon, because his portion was the smallest, spread himself out and took as his inheritance the best part from the inheritance of all his brothers.

5. *"Judah, your brothers shall praise you,"*[608] for you restrained them from the blood of Joseph their brother. For it is on account of you that Joseph became [the head] of two tribes. If not for your counsel to let him live, all the tribes would have perished in the famine. Therefore, because you restrained them from the sin of murder and from death by famine, *"your brothers shall praise you,"* on account of these two things, for it was by your hands that they were rescued from both those things. *"Your hand shall be on the neck of your enemies."*[609] This [verse refers to] the victory that God promised to the kingdom of David which would spring up from Judah. It is that submission to which David subjugated

---

606. Gen 49.7.
607. Cf. Num 25.6–9.
608. Gen 49.8.
609. Gen 49.8.

all the nations from the [Mediterranean] Sea to the Euphrates River.

(2) *"From murder, my son, you have gone up,"*[610] [means] either "you were guiltless in the murder of Tamar and her two sons" or that he took no part in the murder of Joseph. *"He stooped down and couched"* on his property not like an old lion but *"like a lion's whelp,"*[611] that is, like a young lion who is afraid of nothing. Although *"he couched as a lion"* is to be understood as dealing with his inheritance which no one can wrest from him, it also refers to the kingdom. Despite the fact that they were tested and overcome, still no one was able to take the kingdom from them because the kingdom, with all its tribes, is protected by the Lord of the Kingdom. To make known that he was speaking about the crown that is handed down from Judah and not about the tribe, [Moses] wrote, *"The scepter shall not depart,"* that is, the king, *"nor the staff,"* that is, a prophet who announces the things to come, *"until He comes,"*[612] not David whom the kingdom raised to honor, but Jesus, the son of David, who is the Lord of the Kingdom.[613] Neither the king nor the prophet *"will depart from the house of Judah until He comes to whom the kingdom belongs."*[614]

(3) O, let them show me whether there were kings before David who descended from Judah and preserved the crown for David. Since there was no king before David, it is evident that it was by David and by the sons of David that the kingdom was handed down and preserved for the Son and Lord of David who is the Lord of the Kingdom. From [the verse] *"Judah, your brothers shall praise you"* to *"the sceptre shall not depart nor the staff"* is to be understood about Judah, about the kingdom of David and about the sons of David who are from

---

610. Gen 49.9, Peshitta.   611. Gen 49.9.
612. Gen 49.10.
613. See *Hymns on the Nativity* 1.7. See also L. Leloir, "Ephrem et l'ascendance davidique du Christ," in *SP* (Kalamazoo/Leuven, 1957) 1:389–95.
614. Gen 49.10. On this verse, see T. Jansma, "Ephraem on Genesis XLIX,10. An Inquiry into the Syriac Text Forms as Presented in His Commentary on Genesis," *PdO* 4 (1973): 247–56; and Murray, *Symbols*, 282–84.

Judah. [The verse] *"until he comes to whom it belongs,"* along with what follows, however, is to be understood, in its truest sense, about the Son of God and not about David or the sons of David, who are from Judah. Even when [Moses] said, *"He comes to whom it belongs,"* he clearly showed that all predecessors were but guardians of the post, that is, they were successors to a crown that did not belong to them.

(4) *"And for Him the nations shall wait,"*[615] that is, the church of the Gentiles.[616] *"He will bind his foal to the vine and his ass's colt to the choice vine."*[617] He calls the synagogue *"the vine,"* as David also did.[618] That *"He will bind his foal to the vine"* is because his kingdom is bound up with and handed down through the synagogue, that is, *"the scepter will not depart from Judah until He comes to whom the kingdom belongs."*

6. When our Lord came, He also bound his foal to the true vine. Just as all symbols are fulfilled by Him, He would fulfill in truth even this that was handed down to them in likeness. Either there was a vine in Jerusalem outside of the sanctuary to which He bound his foal when He entered the temple, or in that city from which the foal came it had been bound to a vine. He said, "If they say to you, 'Why are you untying that foal?' say to them, 'The master requires it.'"[619]

(2) *"He washes his garments in wine,"* that is, His flesh will be bathed in His blood, *"and His vesture in the blood of grapes,"*[620] because in His own blood He will bathe His body, which is the vesture of His divinity. *"His eyes shall be red with wine,"* for the truth of His thought is clearer than pure wine, *"and his teeth white with milk,"*[621] because the teaching of His lips is pure and beautiful.

7. *"Issachar is a strong warrior crouching along the pathways."*[622] This refers to Gideon who sent letters [with pleas] to come and destroy the Midianites and who, with three

---

615. Gen 49.10, Peshitta.
616. For the "church of the gentiles," see Murray, *Symbols*, 41–68.
617. Gen 49.11. 618. Cf. Ps 80.8, 14.
619. Luke 19.31. 620. Gen 49.11.
621. Gen 49.12. 622. Gen 49.14.

hundred men, prevailed over a great camp of thousands and tens of thousands.[623] *"He saw that his resting place was good,"* that is, the inheritance that came to him, *"and that his land was pleasant,"*[624] for it was flowing with milk and honey. Although his inheritance was no better than that of his companion tribes, his praise was greater than theirs. *"He bowed his shoulder to servitude,"* not to the nations but to God *"and he became a slave at forced labor,"*[625] that is, he became one who paid tithes from his flocks and from his produce to the sons of Levi.

8. *"Zebulun shall dwell at the shore of the sea,"*[626] that is, near the harbors of the sea, *"and in port areas,"*[627] because the commerce of all those who dwell by the sea is from the income of ships. *"And his border shall reach to Sidon,"*[628] which is also situated on the sea coast.

9. *"Dan shall judge his people,"* that is Samson, who judged Israel for twenty years, *"as one of the tribes of Israel,"*[629] that is, like one of their brothers, sons of freewomen, descended from Jacob. *"Dan shall be a serpent upon the earth."* These [serpents] are found along the surface of the ground, like those in the desert of Sinai whose heads peer out from the dust. *"And a viper on the paths."*[630] Just as those who travel about in the pathless desert tremble at serpents on the ground, and those who travel on the pathways are also terrified of vipers that hide on the paths, so were the Philistines, who travelled on paths and in the pathless desert, terrified of Samson. *"To bite the horse's heels and throw its rider backward."*[631] It was during the great famine that God brought upon the Philistines that Samson burned their crops by means of foxes, for fire was carried on their bodies like a rider on its horse.[632] Then

623. Cf. Judg 6.33–7.25.
624. Gen 49.15.
625. Gen 49.15.
626. Zebulun should precede Issachar here as in Gen 49. In XLIII.4–5, below, Ephrem follows the correct biblical order.
627. Gen 49.13, Peshitta. Literally, "along coasts of ships."
628. Gen 49.13.   629. Gen 49.16.
630. Gen 49.17.   631. Gen 49.17.
632. Cf. Judg 15.1–8.

the Philistines keeled over from lack of bread and then fell backwards from lack of nourishment.

(2) *"For your salvation I wait, O Lord."* [633] This is either that the Philistines looked for [salvation] at that time as in the days when they took captive the ark, the salvation of the Lord,[634] or it was thus spoken through the mouth of Jacob in respect to the sons of Dan or to all Israel, to show that all the saviors who rose up for them depicted the symbol of that great salvation which was about to come to all nations through Jesus, who is the true Savior.

10. *"Gad will go out with a band of robbers,"* [635] that is, those forty thousand who, girded for battle, went out before six hundred thousand who followed them with their children, their wives and their belongings.[636] *"And he shall lead the heel,"* [637] [means] he shall go out at the head, girded and confident, and his company, following him like a heel, shall be strengthened by him.

11. *"The land of Asher shall be good."* [638] As Moses said, *"Let him dip his foot in oil."* [639] It is likely that this is the land of Apamea. *"And he shall provide nourishment for kings,"* [640] with pure oil and wines of various flavors that make up his inheritance.

12. *"Naphtali is a swift messenger,"* not who brings rumors, but *"who gives favorable reports."* [641] This is Barak, who sent glad tidings to all those who escaped from before the strength and might of Sisera.[642]

13. *"Joseph is a son of growth,"* [643] for from his youth he has grown up strong. *"Rise up, O spring, O building supported,"* for he found his support in God, with great trust in God. He is also supported by his birthright, by the kingdom and by his brothers. He is also supported like arches by his two sons; one on his right and one on his left. Then *"he went up on the*

633. Gen 49.18.
635. Gen 49.19, Peshitta.
637. Gen 49.19.
639. Deut 33.24.
641. Gen 49.21, Peshitta.
643. Gen 49.22, Peshitta.

634. Cf. 1 Sam 4.11.
636. Cf. Josh 4.12–13.
638. Gen 49.20, Peshitta.
640. Gen 49.20.
642. Cf. Judg 4.4–22.

wall,"⁶⁴⁴ because he was perfected and crowned with the best things. *"Leaders of troops quarrelled with him and looked on him with malice,"*⁶⁴⁵ that is, the heads of the tribes. If "heads of divisions" were written,⁶⁴⁶ it would mean exactly the same thing, for his brothers are the sons of his division,⁶⁴⁷ and they looked on him with malice and sold him to Egypt.

(2) *"His bow returned with strength,"*⁶⁴⁸ for he became ruler and lord over them, but *"the power of his arms grew slack,"*⁶⁴⁹ because, even though the bow is strong, if there is no power in the arms the strength of the bow is of no use. So it was with Joseph. Although, like a bow, he had the authority to kill his brothers, yet he had no anger, which can be likened to power, toward his brothers. For *"the power of his arms grew slack"* from love. *"From the mighty hand of Jacob,"* that is, because of the strong God who was with Jacob, and *"because of the name of the shepherd,"*⁶⁵⁰ who would soon lead [his flock] into the barren desert to the "rock" that gave life to all Israel when they drank from it.⁶⁵¹

14. *"The God of your father will help you"* when you fight against your enemies because you refrained from taking revenge on the sons of your father, *"and God Almighty will bless you with blessings of heaven above,"*⁶⁵² that is, with abundant and continual dew and with good and delightful things which flow from there on the annual crops that they might be blessed.

(2) *"The blessing of the deep that couches beneath."*⁶⁵³ Although everything came to be from nothing, nevertheless we may say that the clouds receive [their water] from the

644. Gen 49.22, Peshitta.
645. Gen 49.23, Peshitta.
646. This is also the reading of this verse in *Targum Onkelos.*
647. That is, "coheirs."
648. Gen 49.24, Peshitta.
649. Literally, "the arms of his hands became scattered."
650. Gen 49.24, Peshitta.
651. Cf. Exod 17.6; Num 20.11; 1 Cor 10.4. See also Ginzberg, *Legends,* 3:52, 6:21.
652. Gen 49.25.
653. Gen 49.25.

deep. Just as the wisdom of God changed [the waters] to be salty lest they become stagnant when they are gathered together, so too did it make [the waters] in the clouds sweet and pleasant so that mankind, animals, herbs, and plants could drink of them. *"The blessing of heaven"* then, [refers to] rain and dew, while *"the blessing of the deep"* [refers to] rivers and springs that provide the water for his inheritance.

(3) *"The blessing of the breasts and the womb,"*[654] is the blessing of love with which a mother blesses her child when the milk of her breasts flows abundantly and that blessing of dear ones by which parents bless their loved ones with their affections. *"The blessings of your father are mighty beyond the blessings of my progenitors,"*[655] for the blessings with which I have blessed you are greater than those by which I have been blessed. For you have been blessed in faith by a father who sees, but I, in the name of another, received them in faith. As for my father, he made my brother a servant to me with the authority that he was to give to my brother on that day. Therefore my blessings are greater than those of my father, not in power but in love.

(4) *"Unto the hope of the everlasting hills,"*[656] [refers to] those blessings with which you were blessed by Isaac who was blessed on the mountain and on that high place whereon he was offered up. *"May they be on the head of Joseph,"*[657] that is, just as today he is the honor and boast of his brothers among the Egyptians, so also may he be their crown and may he rule over his brothers in his inheritance at the end of days.

15. *"Benjamin is a ravenous wolf"* who lies in wait for prey in his inheritance, *"in the morning devouring his prey,"*[658] that is, when they are delivered from the Indians, from Sennacherib, and from the house of Gog. *"And in the evening he will divide what he seizes,"*[659] for in Jerusalem he will divide his spoil peacefully with those of the house of Judah who dwell

---

654. Gen 49.25.
655. Gen 49.26, Peshitta.
656. Gen 49.26, Peshitta.
657. Gen 49.26.
658. Gen 49.27.
659. Gen 49.27.

with him, and he will bring those things we just mentioned out from the soldiers' camps.

Section XLIII

1. Now that we have spoken of the literal meaning of the blessings of Jacob, let us go back and speak of their spiritual meaning as well. We did not fittingly speak of their literal meaning nor will we write of their spiritual meaning as we ought, for we spoke too sparingly of their literal meaning and we will write of their spiritual meaning much too briefly.

2. *"Reuben, my might and the first fruits of my strength . . . you wander about like water, you shall not remain. . . ."*[660] Just as the justice of Jacob cursed his firstborn because of his evil deed, and this curse of Reuben was blotted out by Moses who was the descendant of Jacob, so too was death decreed by God against Adam when he transgressed the commandment, but the Son of God came and, with the promise of the resurrection that He promised, brought to nought the judgment that accompanied Adam out of Paradise.

3. *"Simeon and Levi are brothers, weapons of wrath."*[661] These too are figures for Satan and death. For just as Simeon and Levi, in their anger, destroyed a city and, through their greed, plundered its possessions, so also Satan, in his envy, killed the world secretly as Simeon and Levi had killed the sons of Shechem openly, and death fell suddenly upon all flesh as Simeon and Levi did on the possessions of the inhabitants of Shechem. The Gospel of our Lord raised up those whom sin had slain in secret, and the blessed promise of the Son raised up the dead upon whom the tyrant Death suddenly fell.[662]

4. *"Zebulun who dwells at the shore of the sea"*[663] is a type of the nations who dwell at the side of the prophets. And his

---

660. Gen 49.3–4.
661. Gen 49.5.
662. Ephrem devotes three hymns, *Hymns on Virginity* 17–19, to the theme of Shechem as the type of the church of the Gentiles.
663. Gen 49.13.

border, which shall reach to Sidon,[664] is just like the [nation's] border which shall reach to sin, signified by Sidon. *"What are you to me, O Tyre and Sidon?"*[665]

5. *"Issachar is a strong warrior, crouching along the pathways"*[666] of righteouness, for he hunts for life[667] the one who transgresses and repents. *"He saw that his resting place was good and that his land was pleasant,"*[668] that is, [Christ] saw that His church was good and that His dwelling was holy. *"He bowed his shoulder"*[669] to the cross and became the one who paid off the debt.

6. *"Dan shall judge his people as one of the tribes."*[670] If one from Dan judges His people, how much more will that one from Judah, to whom the kingdom belongs, judge all the nations? For our Lord became a serpent to that first serpent and a viper to Satan, just like the serpent of bronze that countered the snakes.[671] Because, however great salvation from a human being might be, it is [in fact] small, Jacob says in Spirit concerning the salvation of all, *"for your salvation, I wait, O Lord."*[672]

7. *"Gad will go out with a band of robbers,"*[673] forty thousand armed for battle. But the truth is that they are the twelve Apostles who went out with a band of robbers before all the nations to fall on the robber and wrest from him the nations who were taken by him as booty.

8. *"The land of Asher shall be good and [from it] he shall give nourishment for kings."*[674] It is the church who gives healing with the medicine of life[675]—not to kings alone but to all soldiers who accompany kings.

9. *"Naphtali is a swift messenger who gives favorable reports,"*[676]

664. Gen 49.13.
665. Joel 3.4.
666. Gen 49.14.
667. Or, "salvation." Syriac *hayyâ* is often used to translate σωτηρία in the New Testament and Patristic literature.
668. Gen 49.15.
669. Gen 49.15.
670. Gen 49.16.
671. Cf. Num 21.4–9
672. Gen 49.18.
673. Gen 49.19, Peshitta.
674. Gen 49.20, Peshitta.
675. Ephrem's favorite term for the Eucharist.
676. Gen 49.21, Peshitta.

for after our Lord taught in the territory of Zebulun and Naphtali, those who heard him went out, made it known abroad, and repeated *"the favorable reports,"* that *this is the one for whom we have been waiting.*[677]

10. *"Joseph is a son of growth."*[678] Just as Jacob depended on Joseph instead of Reuben, the firstborn, so also instead of Adam, the firstborn and rebellious one, the world had one Son of old age, in the latter days of the world, so that the whole world might stand and lean on Him as if on a pillar. *"Rise up, O spring, O building supported"* by brothers and sons. Through the power of our Lord the world is supported on the prophets and on the Apostles.[679] Joseph became a wall of plenty to his brothers in the time of famine and our Lord became the wall of knowledge to the world in the time of error.

(2) The heads of the tribes looked with malice on Joseph, and the heads of the [Jewish] people on our Lord. *"His bow returned with strength,"*[680] for the two of them held sway over their enemies and *"the power of his arms grew slack,"*[681] for they were unable to shoot arrows at their own brothers. *"From the hand of the Mighty One . . . ,"*[682] [is] because of the very name of the Son who was called by the Apostle "the Rock who walked with Israel in the desert."[683]

11. *"Benjamin is a ravenous wolf"*[684] [refers to] Paul, who was a wolf to the wolves and snatched all souls away from the evil one, and *"in the evening he will divide what he seizes,"*[685] that is, at the end of the world he will also rest with a reward greater than his labors.

677. Cf. Matt 4.13–16, citing Isa 9.1–2.
678. Gen 49.22, Peshitta.
679. The Prophets and the Apostles were inns and milestones on the path, see Beck, "Das Bild vom Weg," 1–39.
680. Gen 49.24, Peshitta.
681. Gen 49.24, Peshitta.
682. Ephrem alters the text here from "the mighty hand of Jacob," as in XLII.13, above.
683. Cf. 1 Cor 10.4.
684. Gen 49.27.
685. Gen 49.27.

Section XLIV

1. Then after he blessed his sons, Jacob died, one hundred and forty-seven years old. Joseph went up with the elders of Egypt and the entire household of his father and buried Jacob with his fathers. Then Joseph and all those with him returned to Egypt.[686]

2. The brothers of Joseph were afraid and said to him, *"Your father gave this command before his death: 'I beseech you forgive the transgression of your brothers, the sins and the evil things they have done to you.'"* Joseph wept and said, "Do not be afraid of me for although your father has died, the God of your father, on account of whom I will never strike you, is still alive. Because He turned the evil that you did to me to my good, and He placed many people in my hands, God forbid that I do any evil to those who thus became the cause of life for many. But, just as I did not kill you in Egypt, do not leave my bones in Egypt." He made them swear to this and said, "God will indeed remember you and will bring you up to the land which He swore to Abraham. Bring my bones up to there so that even if I do not inherit the land with you, I may be raised up with you from that land." *And Joseph died, one hundred and ten years old, and he was placed in a coffin in Egypt.*[687]

3. To God who, through his Son, created all creatures from nothing[688]—although they were not written down in the beginning because they were revealed to the understanding of Adam, and every generation handed down to the next [generation], just what it had learned from the previous [generation]. Because all went astray from God and all had forgotten that God was Creator, God had Moses write all this down for the Hebrew people, after He changed nature to bear witness to the creation of the elements. In the desert Moses wrote down those things that had been manifested in Adam's mind while he was in Paradise, [and they were handed down] through the ancient peoples who knew these things without their being written down,

---

686. Cf. Gen 49.33–50.14. 687. Cf. Gen 50.15–26.
688. Cf. John 1.3.

through the intermediate peoples who through the Scripture heard and believed them, and through the last peoples who added on to the books of the middle ones, and even through those who stubbornly remained in their resistance and were not convinced—and to His Christ and to His Holy Spirit be glory and honor, now and always, forever and ever. Amen. Amen.

THE END OF THE COMMENTARY ON GENESIS, THE FIRST BOOK OF TORAH.

COMMENTARY ON
EXODUS

INTRODUCTION

Ephrem entitled his *Commentary on the Book of Exodus* a *tûrgāmâ* ("interpretation"), the Syriac cognate of the Hebrew *targum*. The *Commentary* is by no means a comprehensive treatment of the Book of Exodus, nor is Ephrem's handling of the biblical text consistent throughout the work. Rather, the *Commentary* is an elucidation of selective portions of the text that Ephrem has highlighted for their theological significance.

(2) Throughout the major part of the *Commentary*, Ephrem is concerned with a straightforward explanation of the significance of the events recorded in the Book of Exodus. There is some incidental use made of the typology for which Ephrem is famous,[1] but it does not approach the more deliberate typological treatment of many of these same themes which characterizes his hymns.[2] At one point, he simply notes the typological significance of a series of items without any further development.[3] Ephrem's treatment of the Canticle of Moses (Exod 15) consists of little more than a paraphrase of the biblical text. Those sections that are concerned with the laws (Exod 20–23) are treated selectively, while a large portion of the text (Exod 26–31) is passed over with no comment at all.

(3) While we can document no direct contact between Ephrem and Jewish scholars of his day, the influence of

1. For example, the treatment of the burning bush (III.2), the staff of Moses (VII.4), the Passover lamb (XII.2), and the water at Mara (XVI.1).
2. The collection entitled *Hymns on Unleavened Bread* contains extended typological treatments of many of the Passover themes that occur in the *Commentary*, with the expressed realization of the type in the church and its ultimate fulfillment in the kingdom. See, for example, *Hymns on Unleavened Bread* 5.18–23.
3. Cf. XII.3.

midrashic and haggadic traditions abounds throughout the *Commentary*. Such literary parallels are due certainly to the early formative influence exercised by Judaism on Syriac-speaking Christianity, notably the Peshitta version of the Old Testament, which remained for some time the common Bible of Syriac-speaking Jews and Christians alike. Ephrem's approach to the biblical text is evocative of the scholarship which was underway in Jewish schools throughout Mesopotamia, and particularly in Nisibis, where Ephrem spent most of his life.[4]

(4) Although the *Commentary* ostensibly has as its focus the events narrated in Exodus,[5] the recurring theme in the first ten sections of the work is one that is common to many of Ephrem's polemical works, namely, the defense of human free will against the deterministic teachings of three of his chief theological opponents, Marcion, Mani, and Bardaisan.[6] Ephrem focuses attention on those portions of the biblical text that demonstrate his belief that the correct use of human freedom is the key to both personal and social well-being, and the prerequisite to divine blessing. Ephrem is concerned to show that Pharaoh acted as a free man, and that the plagues which befell Egypt were the direct results of Pharaoh's own obstinacy, and not the effects of anonymous forces beyond human control.[7] By disparaging the use of as-

    4. See Kronholm, *Motifs*, 25–28; and Féghali, "Influence des Targums," 71–82.
    5. A panegyric attributed to Gregory of Nyssa expresses the claim that Ephrem wrote commentaries on all the books of the Bible. See *De vita S. Patris Ephraem Syri*, 819–50; especially 829A–B. The Syrian ecclesiastical historian, Barhadbšabba, who died sometime before 650, reports, quite anachronistically, that Jacob, bishop of Nisibis, appointed Ephrem as "exegete" (in Syriac, *mpaššqānâ*) of the school in Nisibis. See Scher, "Mar Barhadbšabba ʿArbaya: cause de la fondation des écoles," 337. The Scripture commentaries of Ephrem remained the object of study in Syrian ecclesiastical schools until the works of Theodore of Mopsuestia were translated into Syriac, ibid., 382. On this point see A. de Halleux, "Saint Éphrem le Syrien," *RTL* 14 (1983): 328–55, especially 333ff.
    6. T. Bou Mansour, "La défense éphrémienne de la liberté contre les doctrines marcionite, bardesanite et manichéenne," *OCP* 50 (1984): 331–46.
    7. T. Jansma, "Ephraem on Exodus II, 5: Reflections on the Interplay of Human Free Will and Divine Providence," *OCP* 39 (1973): 5–28; idem,

INTRODUCTION 219

trology and magic, Ephrem shows the futility of Pharaoh's attempts to escape the consequences of his own irresponsible decisions. One of Ephrem's favorite ways of demonstrating his point is to draw insistent attention to the precise wording of the biblical text: "The Lord did *not* say: 'I have hardened Pharaoh's heart,' but 'Pharaoh's heart has been hardened, and he refuses to let the people go,'" (VII.1). Although Hebrews and Egyptians alike recognized that the signs which Moses worked were from God, it was Pharaoh's refusal to heed the signs that brought devastation to Egypt. Ephrem emphasizes the fact that God gave Pharaoh ample time to repent before sending the worst plague of all, the death of the firstborn of the Egyptians: "Consider how unwilling God was to strike Egypt. From the very beginning he told them to repent, but they would not" (IX.2).

(5) There is only one manuscript witness to Ephrem's *Commentary on the Book of Exodus,* Vatican Syriac Manuscript 110, which, regrettably, has been preserved only up to Chapter 32 of the biblical text. This manuscript, which dates from the sixth century, was obtained from the Monastery of Our Lady of the Syrians in Egypt. The earliest edition of the text of this manuscript which was prepared by Petrus Benedictus is not a critical edition in any sense of the phrase, and the Latin version which accompanies the Syriac text is overwhelmingly paraphrastic.[8] Moreover, although the manuscript is incomplete, the editor supplemented the missing sections[9] from a catena of the exegetical works of Ephrem and Jacob of Edessa which was prepared by Severus of Edessa.[10] As Jansma has indicated,[11] this supplemental ma-

---

"Ephraem's Commentary on Exodus: Some Remarks on the Syriac Text and the Latin Translation," *JSS* 7 (1972): 203–12.

8. Petrus Benedictus [Butrus Mubârak] and Simon Evodius Assemani, eds., *Sancti Ephraem Syri opera omnia,* 1:194–235. The Latin version of the text is the work of P. Benedictus.

9. Ibid., 226D–235.

10. The earliest witness to the catena of Severus is Vatican Syriac Manuscript 103, which is dated to the late ninth or early tenth century. See T. Jansma, "The Provenance of the Last Sections in the Roman Edition of Ephrem's Commentary on Exodus," *LM* 85.1–2 (1972): 155–69.

11. Ibid., 156ff.

terial departs from the earlier sections of Ephrem's authentic exposition in two significant areas. First, while Ephrem follows the order of the chapters and verses of Exodus when commenting on the text, the material supplied for the missing portions of the manuscript contains comments that refer back to earlier sections of the biblical narrative that have already been treated. In addition, the material used to supplement the missing chapters of the *Commentary* is predominantly typological in its treatment of the biblical text, while, as has been noted, Ephrem in his own exposition confines his comments almost exclusively to the literal sense of the text.

(6) R. M. Tonneau[12] prepared the critical Syriac edition that was used to make the present translation.

12. Tonneau, *In Genesim et Exodum.*

COMMENTARY ON EXODUS

The Commentary[1] on Exodus, the Second Book of the Law,[2] composed by Blessed Mar Ephrem

[Prologue][3]

EXODUS, the second book of the Law,[4] tells about the seventy souls who entered Egypt with Jacob,

(2) about the death of Jacob and the people of his generation, and that a new king arose who killed the infants,

(3) that Moses escaped in a basket, and became the son of Pharaoh's daughter,

(4) and that, when Moses became a man, he went out among his brothers to see if deliverance could be achieved through him,[5]

(5) and that he killed an Egyptian, and reprimanded a Hebrew who made an accusation against him, then he fled to Midian.

(6) [Moses writes] that he sat by a well and defended the women who were wrongly treated, and that he entered the house of Jethro who gave his daughter Sephora to him in marriage,

(7) and that Pharaoh died, and the children of Israel groaned[6] under their harsh servitude. They prayed and were answered.

---

1. Although Ephrem entitled his work on Exodus a *tûrgāmâ* ("translation," "paraphrase"), the Syriac cognate of the Hebrew *targum*, and his work on Genesis a *pûššāqâ* ("interpretation," "explanation"), the terms are employed synonymously in the titles of these two works.

2. The Syriac word used here is *'ûraytâ*, and derives from the same Hebrew root as "Torah."

3. The initial section of the *Commentary* is composed of a selective index of the material that is found in Exodus.

4. See note 2 above.
5. Literally "through his hand."

6. Read *wettanaḥ* for *wettnîḥ* with Jansma, "Remarks," 203–4.

(8) [And it relates] that God appeared to Moses in a bush, and about the staff that became a snake, and about his leprous hand that was cleansed,

(9) about his departure for Egypt,

(10) about the angel who appeared where he spent the night, and who wanted to kill him, and about his entering Egypt,

(11) and that Aaron went out to meet him, and that he performed signs before the elders of the people who put faith in him,

(12) and that they came before Pharaoh who refused to let them go, but he increased their affliction by withholding straw from them.

(13) [And he tells] about the staff that became a snake, and the river that turned to blood, about the frogs and the pestilence, about the gnats and insects, about the boils, and about the fire that burned in the hail, about the locust and the darkness, and about the death of their firstborn,

(14) and about the lamb they slaughtered and ate on the fourteenth [day of the month],

(15) about the hasty departure they made, armed and furnished with gold, silver, as well as the garments of the Egyptians[7] which they took,

(16) about the splitting of the sea, the crossing of the Hebrews, and the drowning of the Egyptians,

(17) and about the song Miriam sang at the sea, and that they went without water for three days.

(18) And [Moses relates] that he made the bitter water of Marah sweet with a piece of wood; and about the manna he brought down, and the quail he raised up; and about the water he made flow from a rock for them on Horeb,

(19) about Amelech who came to do battle with them,

(20) about the coming to Moses of Jethro, his father-in-law,

(21) and about the Law given to them on Mount Sinai,

---

7. Read as a nominal rather than an adjectival form with Jansma, "Remarks," 204.

about the descent of God on Mount Sinai, and about the laws and regulations He gave them there,

(22) about the ascent of Moses to bring down the tablets,

(23) about the command [to build] the tabernacle: how, and of what, it should be [constructed],

(24) and about the people who fashioned the calf because of Moses' delay on the mountain, and that he went up the mountain a second time to bring down the tablets, and to intercede for their offense,

(25) and that [Moses] petitioned God to go up with them, and about [Moses'] saying to Him: "Show me your glory that I may know you."[8] [God] showed him, and warned him about the commandments that He repeated following the worship of the calf,

(26) and about the construction of the tabernacle, and about the preparation of all its appointments, and about setting it up on the first [day] of the month, and about the cloud that overshadowed the tabernacle during the day; and when the cloud lifted, they set out.

(27) Moses wrote about all these things in the Book of Exodus. He began his account this way:

Section I

1. *Now these are the names of the children of Israel who entered Egypt with Jacob . . . seventy souls.*[9] [Moses wrote] this to show that the word that had been foretold to Abraham as a promise[10] had come to pass. Those who entered [Egypt] numbered seventy, with their old and their young. After living there for two hundred and twenty-five years, they left with six hundred thousand armed men, not including those twenty years of age and under.

2. After Joseph and those of his generation died, a new king rose to power who promulgated a new order to kill the

---

8. Cf. Exod 33.13, 18. Scripture references are from the New American Bible.

9. Exod 1.1, 5. Ephrem's method of citing Scripture is elliptical, as in the current instance, and often paraphrastic.

10. Cf. Gen 12.2.

Hebrew infants.[11] It was not without reason that he did what he did. For Satan realized that the four hundred years indicated to Abraham were completed,[12] and he desired to strangle the deliverer of the Hebrews by killing the infants. In the meantime, Pharaoh likewise realized that the people had increased, and that all of Egypt was swarming with them. He was beside himself, not only because of the immense number of Hebrews, but especially due to the agitation of those who thought they knew the future, based on the number of years that had passed, and who were also predicting the deliverance of the Hebrews.[13]

3. So Pharaoh decreed death for their infants, and imposed hard labor on their fathers in granaries that were unnecessary.[14] If the crops in Joseph's granaries were enough to sustain Egypt and Canaan and the land of the Amorites during seven years of famine, would their provisions not have been more than sufficient to sustain [Pharaoh's] own land? But the more Pharaoh became intent on the death of the children, [the more] the Hebrew children increased. And the more he tried to afflict the people, [the more] he himself became afflicted by the people. For [Moses wrote]: "The Egyptians were afflicted by the children of Israel."

4. To keep his river from becoming polluted with the corpses of infants, [Pharaoh] summoned those who give life,[15] to make them into those who give death.[16] By his authority, he wanted to make them [do] the opposite of [what] their name [implied], by proposing to turn healers

11. Cf. Exod 1.15ff.
12. Cf. Gen 15.13.
13. Jewish tradition held that Pharaoh and his own astrologers were among those who predicted a deliverer. See, S. M. Lehrman, *Midrash Rabbah* (London, 1961) 3:25. Also R. Le Déaut, *Targum du Pentateuque, SC* 245 [1] and 256 [2] (Paris, 1978) 17.
14. Not only does Ephrem agree with rabbinic literature that the granaries of Pharaoh were unnecessary, but his explanation for this is the same as that which is found in Jewish sources. Other agreements with rabbinic sources are noted in the text. See the examples cited in Féghali, "Commentaire," 92, n. 4.
15. I.e. Midwives.
16. Cf. Exod 1.15–16.

into killers. But they did not obey him. Even though he was assured that they were obeying him, they did the opposite.[17] The women whom he instructed[18] to kill the children,[19] expected to be killed in place of them. But the day they thought they would receive the crown of martyrdom, they were rescued from death by a clever statement God put in their mouth.[20] They became blessed; that is, those who thought that Pharaoh would kill their entire race became a great race because of the great number of infants to whom they gave life.

5. When Pharaoh was fooled by the women without realizing it, he decided to pollute the water with the blood of the infants, and to feed his fish with the flesh of children. But this was not in his power either, because the Hebrews had become so fertile. The rivers became filled with infants, as Pharaoh willed, but Egypt [remained] filled with [Hebrews], which was not what he willed.[21] When he saw the river rotting with children, he was elated. But when he saw Egypt swarming with them, he became despondent. His order was not rescinded, but neither had his will been attained, in accordance with his order. Infants lay heaped like locusts on the river bank, but, to his annoyance,[22] the streets of Egypt rang out with their cries.

Section II

1. Moses was born during this period of oppression for the Hebrews. When his mother saw how beautiful he was, she hid him for as long as she could.[23] She feared it would be

17. Literally, "They obeyed him in reverse." For an account of the wisdom of the midwives in Jewish tradition, see Ginzberg, *Legends*, 2:250–54.
18. Read *dapîs* with Jansma, "Remarks," 204.
19. Cf. Exod 1.17.   20. Cf. Exod 1.19.
21. Compare Ephrem's use of *ṣebyānâ* ("will") in the *Homily on Our Lord*, III:
   He submitted and bore death, according to his will,
   in order to overthrow death, which is not what it willed.
22. *Pace* Féghali: ". . . de leur agitation"; "Commentaire," 96.
23. Literally, "She hid him until she could hide him no longer." Cf. Exod 2.2–3.

discovered that they were in defiance of Pharaoh's order, that their entire family would perish, and that Moses would not survive. Consider how [the soldiers] searched until Moses could be hidden no longer. And consider how goodness protected [the Hebrews], so that six hundred thousand set out from there.

(2) Moses' mother put him in a basket, entered [her house], knelt in prayer, and with mournful tears complained to the God of Abraham about Pharaoh: "You blessed our people so they would increase, and increased they have, according to your blessing. But see, Pharaoh has schemed to deprive the land of cultivators by killing the little boys, and to eliminate and put an end to the seed which you blessed by destroying the children."[24]

2. Now Moses' sister, Miriam, remained at the river's edge to find out what would become of the youth in the basket. They had confidence in God, and in the youth's beauty, that the first one to see the basket would take the youth and let him live. Now it was an especially warm day for Pharaoh's daughter,[25] so although it was not her usual time to bathe in the river, she went out. Even though she went of her own accord because of the heat of the day, since she did not go at her usual time, she went apart from her own accord. Her freedom was led by compulsion to draw out and bring up from the river the one who would avenge in the sea the little boys who had been thrown into the river.[26]

---

24. Read *yaldê dambāṭṭel* with Jansma, "Remarks," 204.

25. Jewish legend held that the day Moses was rescued was unseasonably warm, and that Pharaoh's daughter, who suffered from leprosy, went down to the river to be relieved of her discomfort. See Ginzberg, *Legends*, 2:266.

26. In his interpretation of this passage, Ephrem is careful to preserve the free will of Pharaoh's daughter by explaining that the decision to go down to the river was her own, but the fact that she did not go at the usual time was the result of compulsion. For a full consideration of Ephrem's treatment of free will in this instance and throughout the *Commentary* (for example in X.3, X.5, and XVI.1) see Jansma, "Ephraem on Exodus II, 5." At the end of this article, Jansma proposes a reading of this line based on a scribal error which pointed the particle *man* as the preposition *men*. Féghali ("Commentaire," 98, n. 21) cites Jansma, but continues to read the line with Tonneau and Assemani, who

3. Seeing that the youth was beautiful, she supposed, as did her serving girls, that the gods of Egypt had provided a son for the sterile woman in the river. She obediently took him in order to remove her shame and increase her consolation, so that the throne of her father would be passed on to him.

(2) Miriam came along, neither sad nor happy, indifferent to both of these [emotions]. Assuming the appearance useful to her purpose, Miriam said to her: *"Shall I call one of the Hebrew women to nurse [the child] for you,*[27] one with a sincere heart and pure milk? With qualities such as these, she would be very useful to your kingdom."

(3) So she quickly ran and brought [the boy's] mother, appropriately dressed and with excellent gifts. She who[28] had been willing to give her entire house so that Moses would not be thrown into the river, was persuaded with difficulty to be the nurse of her son. And when he was given to her, she was not easily persuaded to take him. She took her son, and she did not leave the basket. She had sent him away with sadness, but welcomed him back with joy. She who had gone down to the river under cover of darkness, brought him back in broad daylight.[29] She held him in her arms out in the open as well as in the house. He who had not seen the light of day for three months[30] saw light at the river—he who had been cast into the river to be deprived of light.

4. When Moses completed the years of his education and was brought into Pharaoh's house, he gladdened his parents

---

interpret the particle *man* as the preposition *men*. The current version adopts Jansma's reading: *l-qaṭîrâ man ḥîrûtâh d-bîrâ hwât*. For the connection between liberty and grace in the behavior of Pharaoh, see X.3, X.5, and XVI.1 where *ḥîrûtâ* ("free will") and *qaṭîrâ* ("compulsion") are again contrasted. See T. Bou Mansour, "Aspects de la liberté humaine chez saint Ephrem le Syrien," *ETL* 60 (1984): 252–82, especially 255, n. 8 and 271ff.

27. Cf. Exod 2.7.
28. Read *d-kûlleh* with the relative pronoun, with Jansma, "Remarks," 204.
29. Read *nahîrâ* with Jansma, "Remarks," 207.
30. Cf. Exod 2.2.

with his beauty, but at the same time, he saddened them with his stammering.[31] Moses knew he was the son of Jochabed from his circumcision and from his name, but especially from the account he had heard from his mother and his sister.[32]

(2) As the period of four hundred years drew to a close,[33] he went out to see if deliverance could be brought about through him.[34] And because the one he killed was Pharaoh's most cruel taskmaster, who had refused to accept his repeated warnings,[35] [Moses] killed and buried in the sand the one who distressed the seed that had been blessed so that it would become as abundant as the sand. He buried him in the sand on the riverbank in front of his companions whose corpses would be strewn along the sand of the seashore.

(3) He went out again the next day and saw two men who were fighting with each other.[36] As the king's son, he had the authority to have them beaten and killed, but he did not do either of these; he justly reprimanded the one who was at fault. But rather than accept the warning, he accused the king's son of murder in the presence of many people.

5. *"Who appointed you as our ruler?"*[37] You shameless wrangler! Do you say to the king's son, *"Who appointed you as our ruler?"* [If] he has authority over those placed over you, does he not then have authority over you? Moses was troubled, because he heard the statement from someone whom he did not think was aware [of what had happened]. This man who accused him was not the one whom he had rescued from the cruel Egyptian. If [this man] had not been just, he would have received the [same] reprimand his companion did. [Moses] had not killed the Egyptian on account of him. The man he had rescued from the Egyptian was oppressed

---

31. Cf. Exod 4.10.
32. Cf. Exod 2.7–10.
33. Cf. Gen 15.13.
34. Literally, "through his hand."
35. Here and in several other places throughout the *Commentary* (e.g. II.5), Ephrem uses language that seeks to justify the killing of the Egyptian taskmaster by Moses. For parallels in Jewish targumic tradition, see Le Déaut, *Targum du Pentateuque*, 2:22; and Féghali, "Commentaire," 99, n. 24.
36. Cf. Exod 2.13.
37. Exod 2.14.

like the young girls at the well.[38] By killing the Egyptian, Moses wanted to give relief to the Hebrews who were oppressed by him. The man who had been rescued revealed [the matter] to this man out of love. But this man accused Moses out of malice.

6. When Pharaoh heard about this, an opportunity for slander presented itself to the generals and to the taskmasters whom [Moses] had reprimanded for mercilessly mistreating the Hebrews. Pharaoh became enraged, and would have soaked his hands in the blood of his son and sent the heir of his crown to Sheol. So Moses became frightened, and to prevent his true parents from enduring the torments of his adoptive parents, *"He fled to Midian, and sat by a well."*[39]

(2) When he saw some dissolute herdsmen who were forcibly trying to take the water that some young girls[40] had drawn, [Moses] being a just man, saved them from this coercion; and being a compassionate man, he drew water for the flock of the maidens. When their father asked them about their hasty return and learned of the justice and compassion of Moses, he sent after him to repay him with bread which he fed him in his house for the kindness he had extended to his daughters at the well.[41]

7. Moses was wondering where he would go, and with whom he would stay. When the priest[42] sent after him, he knew that the One who rescued him from death in the river by means of Pharaoh's daughter, and likewise let him slip through Pharaoh's hands and escape from under Pharaoh's eyes, put it in the mind of the priest to take Moses in, and make him his daughter's husband. He slipped away from

38. I.e. The daughters of Jethro. Cf. Exod 2.16ff.
39. Exod 2.15.
40. The Syriac term *šabrātā* ("young girls") is used synonymously with *ṭalyātā* ("maidens," "unmarried girls") which occurs at the end of this sentence.
41. Cf. Exod 2.18–20.
42. Ephrem refers to Jethro by the title of *kûmrâ*, a term used in the Peshitta to distinguish a pagan priest from *kahnâ*, a priest of the Mosaic Law. For alternatives to the Hebrew cognate *kôhên* in the targums see Le Déaut, *Targum du Pentateuque*, 2:24, n. 10. See also A. Catastini, "Observations on Aramaic Epigraphy," *JSS* 32/2 (1987): 273–77.

magicians, and was received by a priest. He had no fear of the priest, just as he had had no fear of the magicians. If he had helped them, he had not been harmed by them. Nonetheless, Aaron was suffering, and Miriam was mournful—those who previously had been proud to sing his praises.[43]

8. Because of Moses' beauty and integrity, and especially because of God who was with him, they convinced Moses to marry Sephora. Just as Jacob had been spared the disgrace of tending sheep because of the daughters of Laban, Moses likewise was spared the care of the flock because of Sephora and her sisters.

(2) So he married Sephora who bore him two sons. He circumcised one of them, but she did not let him circumcise the other one.[44] She was strong-willed because of her father and brothers. She may have consented to become Moses' wife, but she had not consented to become a daughter of his faith. She was a daughter of priests who was brought up on sacrificial meat, and who was accustomed to worshipping many gods. So she did not give him both of them [to circumcise], but neither did she withhold both of them. She gave one, so that the circumcision of Abraham would continue in him, but she withheld the other, through whom the uncircumcision of her father's house would be passed down.[45]

9. Moses did not follow his father or his father-in-law [regarding the names] of his sons. He named the first one after his escape and his dwelling in a strange land[46] for the sake of

43. Jansma speculates that the relative clause that closes this paragraph refers to the jealousy of Aaron and Miriam indicated in Num 12. See Jansma, "Remarks," 205.
44. Although the *Commentary* does not identify which of Moses' two sons was not circumcised, according to *Targum Pseudo-Jonathan* IV.24 it was Gershom who remained uncircumcised. See Le Déaut, *Targum du Pentateuch*, 2:39.
45. See IV.4 for the result of Moses' failure to circumcise both sons.
46. Cf. Exod 2.22 and 18.3 where the meaning of the name Gershom is explained as though it were derived from the Hebrew *ger* ("stranger") and *šam* ("there"). See also Le Déaut, *Targum du Pentateuch*, 2:26–27.

God. And he named the other one[47] after his rescue from Pharaoh.

(2) After Moses had been in Midian for forty years, *Pharaoh, the oppressor of the people, died. The Hebrews groaned*[48] *from their servitude.*[49] They recalled God's covenant with Abraham, whose time was fulfilled.[50] Thirty years in addition had passed. They prayed for this, and they were answered. God saw that the children of Israel were enslaved, and God knew their affliction, as well as the remedy he would offer them.

Section III

1. "*While Moses was tending sheep alongside Horeb, he saw an angel in the fire that burned in a bush.*"[51] Moses went to look at the bush that the fire did not consume, and as he approached, a simple vision of an angel appeared to him. As he came [closer], it was not the angel that [first] appeared to him who addressed him, but God, who later appeared to him by means of an angel in an awesome vision and said to him: "*Do not approach this spot as you would some common place. This is a holy place,*"[52] as the place where Jacob slept [was holy] on account of the ladder and the angels who were ascending and descending to guard him.[53] And this place [is holy] on account of God who dwells in the fire that burns in the bush. "*Remove your sandals*"[54] and go trample[55] the Egyptians. See, it is thirty years past the time of their picking. Up to this point, Moses proceeded without fear. But when he saw a sight that was more than his eyes [could bear], he hid his face out of fear of looking at God the way he looked at the angel.[56]

47. I.e. Eliezer. Cf. Exod 18.4.
48. See note 6 above.
49. Cf. Exod 2.23.
50. Cf. Mark 1.15.
51. Exod 3.1–2.
52. Exod 3.5.
53. Cf. Gen 28.10ff.
54. Exod 3.5.
55. The Syriac verbs ʿṣar "to trample" or "to press," and qṭap "to pick" or "to harvest" used in the following sentence are employed in reference to the processing of grapes and olives. For a parallel use of these verbs by Ephrem, see *Hymns on the Crucifixion* 5.9: "The vinedressers also picked and pressed."
56. Read the singular with Jansma, "Remarks," 207.

2. The bush which was unsuitable even as an image of dead gods[57] was able to depict within itself the mystery of the living God. Moses, this is a sign to you; as you saw God dwelling in the midst of the fire, by fire must you serve the God who dwells in the fire.

3. *And his Lord said to him: "I have indeed seen the oppression of my people in Egypt* for eighty years, *and I have come down to deliver them* through you,[58] *and to bring them into the land of the Canaanites,* the land I promised to their fathers."[59] Moses said: *"Who am I to go before Pharaoh?"*[60] Although I have a royal title, I will not be received by him. And now that I do the work of a simple shepherd, who will allow me to go before Pharaoh? And even if I were let in, what importance would he see in me to believe my words?"

4. And his Lord said to him: *"Gather the elders whose cry has ascended to me.*[61] Tell them that I am mindful of them, and that I will lead them up to the land of the Canaanites. And since you fear that they will not hear you, see, I am telling you that they will hear your voice. Enter Pharaoh's presence with the elders, and say to him: *'We shall set out on a three-days' journey to sacrifice to the Lord.'*[62] And since Pharaoh will not allow this to happen, he and his armies will set out on a three-days' journey, and will become sacrifices to animals and birds that will pounce on their drowned bodies that are heaped on[63] the seashore.

(2) "Just as I have told you that the sons of your nation will listen to you, see, I also tell you that Pharaoh will not listen to you. It will not be because of his mighty hand, or be-

---

57. Ephrem may be reflecting a popularly held Jewish belief that the bush which burned without being consumed was a thornbush, and that its thorns provided a natural deterrent against those who might think to carve its wood into images: "There were good reasons for selecting the thornbush as the vessel for a divine vision. It was 'clean,' for the heathen could not use it to make idols." See Ginzberg, *Legends,* 2:303. Other reasons for the choice of a thornbush are given in Lehrman, *Midrash Rabbah,* 3:53.

58. Literally, "through your hands." 59. Cf. Exod 3.7–8.
60. Cf. Exod 3.11. 61. Cf. Exod 3.16.
62. Cf. Exod 3.18.
63. Read simply '*al* with Jansma, "Remarks," 205.

cause of his idols that stand before him, but because of their pride that I will strike the Egyptians with all the wonders I will work among them. Then he will let you go.

(3) "But so that you may be sure that you will leave, I will show mercy to the people, and they will plunder the Egyptians.[64] By doing this, my promise to Abraham will be fulfilled. But [the Hebrews], on account of all the treasures they will seize as they are leaving, will never again be able to look at the faces of the Egyptians."[65]

Section IV

1. Since Moses knew the hardness of heart of the sons of his nation, he asked for signs that would convince them. *"They will not hear my voice, and they will say: 'The Lord has not appeared to you.'"*[66] Knowing he would ask for signs, God said to him: "In order that they may believe that it is I who have sent you, throw your staff on the ground." So he threw it down, and it became a snake. Moses shied away. By giving him this sign to convince the people, [God] also convinced him. "As you fear Pharaoh, you also fear the snake. You will overcome the army of Pharaoh with the plagues, just as you were able, by my command, to take hold of the staff when it was rigid, but which you feared when it started to slither."[67]

(2) *Then [God] said to him: "Put your hand in your bosom." So he put it in, and it became leprous. He put it in again, and it became clean.*[68] First, [God] ordered him to convince the people with the snake, and with his hand that became leprous and then clean. Then [God said to him]: "Pharaoh is no more difficult than the serpent, nor is his army, which I shall change into whatever I want, just as I changed your hand. If the Egyptians do not believe these two signs which you will work before them, and before the sons of your nation, pour water from the river onto dry land, and it will turn to blood."[69]

64. Cf. Exod 3.19–22.
65. Read *meṣrayê* with Jansma, "Remarks," 205.
66. Exod 4.1.
67. Literally, "once it was loosed."
68. Cf. Exod 4.6–7.
69. Cf. Exod 4.8–9.

2. After [God] performed for Moses the signs he requested, [Moses] also asked his Lord to loosen his tied tongue. *"I have never been an eloquent man, neither yesterday, nor the day before yesterday. And since the time that you spoke with me,* there has been no change in my stammering."[70]

(2) His Lord said to him: "You will become great by that which makes you small, so that you will become an eloquent prophet for the God who is silent. I will be with your mouth, not to loosen your tongue or improve your answers, but so that something better might result from the sound of your stammering."[71]

3. Moses returned to Midian[72] and told his father-in-law that he was going to see if he had caused his brothers in Egypt any suffering as a result of his separation from them. They certainly had not kept him [from following] the will of God which was working on their behalf from above. But because [Moses] feared the Egyptian authorities whom he had annoyed because they oppressed the people, and [because he believed] they would incite the anger of the new Pharaoh against him like the previous one, his Lord said to him: *"All the men who were seeking your life have died."*[73]

(2) So Moses gathered his wife and sons and took up his staff to go to Egypt. As he was leaving Midian, [the Lord] again commanded him to say to Pharaoh: "Thus says the Lord: *'Send my firstborn son to me that he may serve me, lest perhaps in place of my firstborn whom you withhold,* though you are unable to do so, *I should kill your firstborn,* which I am quite able to do. Before all the [other] plagues, I will strike your firstborn son, which will be the greatest of all the plagues.'"[74] God said [this] to Pharaoh by way of speech, but by way of action he showed him the plague of the snake, which was the least of all [the plagues].

4. At the place where they were spending the night, the Lord came upon Moses, and wanted to kill him,[75] because

---

70. Cf. Exod 4.10.
71. Cf. Exod 4.12.
72. Cf. Exod 4.18.
73. Exod 4.19.
74. Cf. Exod 4.22–23.
75. Cf. Exod 4.24.

he had discontinued circumcision in Midian for one of his sons who had not been circumcised. From the day [the Lord] spoke with him on Horeb, he had not been united to his wife, who was distressed; and she was under judgment because she had not put full faith in his word. [Moses] blamed her for keeping his son from being circumcised. They spent the night [preoccupied] with these thoughts. Suddenly, an angel appeared for both of these reasons, while seeming to appear only because of circumcision.

(2) [The angel] appeared to Moses in anger so that his departure [from Midian] would not be ridiculed because he had discontinued circumcision without necessity, while the Hebrews had not interrupted it in spite of the death of their children. Now whom should he have feared, God, who prescribed circumcision, or his wife,[76] who had stood in the way of circumcision?[77]

(3) When Moses' wife saw that he was about to die because she had stood in the way of circumcision, about which and on account of which he had argued with her that evening, *she took a piece of flint,* and still trembling from the vision of the angel, *circumcised her son,* letting him be spattered with his [own] blood. Then she held the angel's feet and said: *"I have a husband of blood."*[78] Do not cause suffering on the day of the celebration of circumcision." Because there was great joy on the day Abraham circumcised Isaac, she said: "I too have a husband of blood. If you do not [refrain from harm] on account of me, who circumcised my

---

76. Literally, "his rib." Cf. Gen 2.21–24.

77. By attributing the attack of the angel upon Moses to the fact that his wife Sephora had prevented the circumcision of one of their sons, Ephrem follows a tradition common to Palestinian targumic sources. See Le Déaut, *Targum du Pentateuque,* 2:38–41. For an almost identical interpretation of Moses' encounter with the angel in Aphrahat see *Demonstration* 6.3. For a full treatment of this passage see Guillaumont, "Un midrash d'Exode 4, 24–26," 89–95. In a curious version of this same story, the angel is replaced by Satan, who appears in the guise of snake, and swallows Moses, who is rescued only when his wife circumcises the uncircumcised son. See Ginzberg, *Legends,* 2:295. Also, Lehrman, *Midrash Rabbah,* 3:85.

78. Exod 4.25.

son with my own hands, or on account of Moses, refrain on account of the commandment of circumcision itself which has been observed."[79]

5. When [the angel] left, Moses took the opportunity to say to Sephora: "If you were so afraid of [the angel] who appeared to you for a single moment, how much more should I be fearful and sanctify myself for God, who is visible to me all the time, and who worked wonders through me, and who has sent me, armed with this staff, to deliver six hundred thousand?"

(2) So [Moses] returned Sephora [to Midian]; first, because of her son who had been circumcised, so the discomfort would not be too much for him on the road; and second, so that Sephora and her sons would not be entering Egypt at the very time when all of Israel would be leaving Egypt.

6. The Lord appeared to Aaron, and sent him to meet Moses, so that [by seeing] what took place in fact, just as it had been foretold to him in word, [Moses] would believe from this point on that everything else would happen in the same way. So the two of them gathered the elders and worked wonders before them, as it had been decreed. And they believed in Moses, just as the Lord had said to him.

Section V

1. They entered Pharaoh's presence together and said to him: "Thus says the Lord: 'Let my people go that they may observe a feast in my honor in the desert.'"[80] Now due to the presence of the elders of the people, and because he heard of the signs [Moses] had performed before the elders, Pharaoh did not strongly resist. Rather, he said to them: "Why, Moses and Aaron, do you keep the people from their work?"[81]

(2) As they continued speaking with him, he became enraged, and instead of asking for a sign to let the people go,

---

79. Cf. Exod 4.26.
81. Cf. Exod 5.4.

80. Exod 5.1.

he said: "Who is the Lord that I should hear his voice?" By saying "Who is the Lord?" he was asking to see, by means of signs, the one whose form was not visible to him. It was [Pharaoh] himself who brought down the plagues with the bold statement: "Who is the Lord?"[82]

(3) His harsh nature was not satisfied with what he said, so he went further, and refused [to give] the people straw, so that faced with[83] this necessity, they would not think about leaving any more.[84] So the people spread out to look for straw, which was very difficult to find since it was Nisan, the season of flowers, and not Tammuz or Ab, the season for threshing.[85] The scribes of the people complained to Pharaoh because they were being mistreated by his taskmasters. But he had no pity on them. Rather, he said to them: "You are asking to go and sacrifice to the Lord because you are lazy."[86]

2. When the scribes saw the children of Israel in such a bad state,[87] they complained to the Lord against the house of Moses, in the very presence of Moses. Moses said to the Lord: "Since I spoke to Pharaoh in your name[88] the deliver-

82. Ephrem takes up the theme which he will repeat throughout the *Commentary*, that Pharaoh was responsible for the plagues as a result of his unwillingness to repent in the face of repeated warnings. One midrashic source reads: ". . . when God warns a man once, twice, and even a third time, and he still does not repent, then does God close his heart against repentance so that He should exact vengeance from him for his sins. Thus it was with the wicked Pharaoh. Since God sent five times to him and he took no notice, God then said: 'Thou hast stiffened thy neck and hardened thy heart; well, I will add to thine uncleanness'; hence, 'For I have hardened his heart'"; Lehrman, *Midrash Rabbah*, 3:152. See note 3 on the same page. Also see the conclusion to VI of Ephrem's *Commentary*.
83. Read *b-hādê* with Jansma, "Remarks," 205.
84. Cf. Exod 5.6ff.
85. Nisan (March 15 to April 15) is the first month of the Hebrew year. Tammûz (June 15 to July 15), and Ab (July 15 to August 15) correspond to the dry summer months. For the significance of allusions to Nisan in the writings of Ephrem, see G. Rouwhorst, "L'évocation du mois de Nisan dans les hymnes sur la Résurrection d'Éphrem de Nisibe," in *OCA* 229 (Rome, 1984) 100–110.
86. Cf. Exod 5.8.
87. The Syriac simply has the adverbial form *bîšāyît* ("wickedly," "badly").
88. Cf. Exod 5.23.

ance that the people had hoped for has not come about; in fact, their oppression has increased over what it had been."

Section VI

1. *And the Lord said to Moses: "If Pharaoh asks for a sign, throw down the staff in front of him, and it will become a snake." However, Pharaoh summoned magicians who did the same thing by means of their spells,*[89] that is, they imitated [Moses], and did exactly as he had done. Now when [Scripture] says they did it by means of their spells, [it means] that what they did was not unusual, but that they employed the methods they always did. But when they thought they had beaten Moses by imitating what he did, they made a mistake that they would not [soon] forget.[90] The staff of Moses swallowed their staffs. They thought that they could change the natures [of things], but they were unable to save their staffs from the staff of Moses.

(2) The staff [of Moses] swallowed the staffs [of the magicians] so that death would not swallow the firstborn. From the staffs that were swallowed, [Pharaoh] should have learned that unless he repented, the firstborn also would be swallowed. First, [the Lord] told him to repent, but that did not happen. Then he struck [him] with [a plague] that was more severe than all the others. If they had mended their ways as a result of the earlier [plagues], they would have been spared [the plague] of the firstborn, which was more severe than all those that came before it.[91]

Section VII

1. The Lord did not say: "I have hardened [Pharaoh's] heart," but, *"Pharaoh's heart has been hardened, and he refuses to*

---

89. Exod 7.9, 11.
90. Literally, "They committed an unforgettable fault."
91. Ephrem makes it clear that the purpose of the plagues was to encourage Pharaoh to repent. When he did not, only then was Egypt struck with the tenth and most devastating plague of all. Once again, Ephrem indicates that repentance, and thus avoidance of the plagues, remained available to Pharaoh until the end. See Jansma, "Reflections," 11–13.

*let the people go,.*⁹² Again, the Lord said to Moses: *"Go to [Pharaoh], and stand on the river bank,."*⁹³ [He told him this] because [Pharaoh] went to the river early in the morning either to pour out oblations, or because he went early every day [simply] to enjoy himself. [But judging] from [Pharaoh's] reliance on the magicians, it is likely that the king of Egypt went to pour out oblations at the river of Egypt.

(2) So Moses went out and told him on behalf of his Lord to let the people go. When he refused, [Moses] struck the river that Pharaoh previously had polluted with the blood of the infants whom he had drowned in it, and the water was changed to blood. The fish that had grown fat on the corpses of little boys died. This second plague was also [intended to] be terrifying, because the fish died instead of the firstborn, and if [Pharaoh] was not convinced by the death of the fish, he would be by the death of the firstborn. *The magicians also did the same with their spells,*⁹⁴ and Moses did nothing to stop them.

2. If [the magicians] had been [acting] against Moses, he would have stopped them with the first plague, the way he stopped the plague of ulcers, and drove them off.⁹⁵ But since [the plagues] came from [Moses], and [were directed] against [the magicians'] own people, [Moses] did not stop them from striking Egypt with him,⁹⁶ because a deceitful heart which is divided against God is not at peace with itself. And so, rather than striking the oppressors of their people, or rising up so that their people would not perish, the magicians began striking their people along with Moses. So he

---

92. Exod 7.14. One of Ephrem's favorite methods of calling attention to the precise reading of the biblical passage is to point out what the passage under consideration does *not* say. Ephrem's purpose in the current instance is to preserve Pharaoh's free will so that his repeated refusals to let Israel go, as well as the plagues that followed his refusals, would be the results of his own irresponsible decisions. See note 82 above.

93. Exod 7.15.   94. Exod 7.22.
95. Cf. Exod 9.11.
96. *Pace* Féghali, "le peuple d'Egypte"; "Commentaire," 109.

did not stop them. By encouraging their ruin, they were encouraging the ruin of Egypt.

(2) Although they changed the natures [of things], which is difficult, they were careful not to change their [own] natures, which is easy. And although they turned water into blood and caused Egypt to suffer they might have turned the blood into water, to annoy Moses, but they did not do this because they could not do it. They could only do those things to which their skill[97] was accustomed.

3. After this, again he wrote not that the Lord hardened [Pharaoh's] heart,[98] but that Pharaoh's heart was hardened, and he did not hear them,[99] just as the Lord had said to Moses. And again [Scripture] says, *"Pharaoh returned and entered his house. And he gave no thought to it."*[100]

4. When Pharaoh was not convinced by this, *"Aaron again raised the staff with his hand"*[101]—the staff, a sign of the cross, that caused all the plagues when it swallowed the snakes, just as [the cross] would destroy all idols. With [the staff], [Moses] divided the sea[102] and drowned the Egyptians; that prefigured the destruction of the Canaanites.

Section VIII

1. *"Frogs came and covered the land of Egypt, but the magicians did the same with their spells."*[103] If they had loved Egypt, they would have done away with the frogs rather than add symbolic frogs to the real frogs of Moses. But neither did they have a remedy to drive away the frogs of Moses, nor could they strike back. They could only make the likeness of frogs appear in place of the frogs [of Moses]. And so, they did not

---

97. As Ephrem uses these terms, ʿabûdûtâ ("creativity") is characteristic of divine liberty which alone is able to create primary elements, while ʾûmānûtâ ("human skill") is dependent upon ʿabûdûtâ since it requires something preexistent upon which to exercise an action. See Bou Mansour, "La défense éphrémienne," 334–36.

98. See note 92 above. 99. Cf. Exod 7.22.
100. Exod 7.23. 101. Exod 8.2.
102. Read *pelgeh d-yammâ* with Jansma, "Remarks," 206.
103. Exod 8.2–3.

strike back, and they did not provide a remedy—those whose business was the making of illusions.

(2) A generation of fish died, and a generation of frogs was produced. Those who no longer were afflicted with dead fish, were afflicted with living frogs. Pharaoh asked when the frogs would be driven away. They died and were piled in heaps, so they would not think that it was an hallucination.[104] *But with this respite, Pharaoh [again] hardened his heart and would not listen to them.*[105]

2. Again *Aaron struck the dust of the earth with*[106] *his staff, and gnats descended on man and beast and on all the land.*[107] But the magicians did this also with their spells, not to increase the gnats, as in the first plague, but to drive them away. But they were unable [to do so]. When their false skill was tested and exposed as false, they confessed: *"It is the finger of God."*[108] But Pharaoh remained unconvinced by Moses or the magicians who said to him: "It is the finger of God." And [Moses] wrote not that the Lord hardened [Pharaoh's] heart, but that *Pharaoh's heart was hardened, and he did not hear them, just as the Lord had said.*[109]

3. As a result of the plague of the river, and of the frogs, and of the gnats, both the land of Goshen, where the children of Israel were living, and the land of Egypt were afflicted. But with the plague of the insects, there was a distinction made between the [two] lands. [Moses] inflicted it on the land of Egypt, but not on the land of Goshen. *So Pharaoh said to the house of Moses, "Go wherever you want in our land,* and sacrifice to your God without fear." Moses answered: "Because we sacrifice bulls and sheep, which are worshipped by you, if we were to sacrifice the gods of the Egyptians before their very eyes, they would stone us. *So we will make a three-days' journey to sacrifice to Him as He commanded us."*[110]

---

104. *Pace* Féghali, "l'esprit ne peut l'imaginer"; "Commentaire," 110. The Syriac transliterates the Greek φαντασία.
105. Exod 8.11.
106. Read *b-ḥuṭreh* with Jansma, "Remarks," 206.
107. Cf. Exod 8.13. 108. Exod 8.15.
109. See note 92 above. 110. Cf. Exod 8.21ff.

Pharaoh said: *"I will let you go, as long as you do not go far; and pray also for me."*[111] But as soon as the insects disappeared, Pharaoh broke his promise, and would not let the people go. After this, [Moses] inflicted a plague of insects on their cattle, distinguishing between the cattle of the Hebrews and the cattle of the Egyptians. *But not even as a result of this was [Pharaoh] persuaded to let the people go.*[112]

Section IX

1. Again, *Moses scattered ashes in the presence of Pharaoh, and boils spread over man and beast. The magicians were unable to stand before Moses,* because they could not cause the boils in the same way on the bodies of the Hebrews, and there was no place left on their own bodies to cause them.[113]

2. Again [the Lord] brought down pestilence on the house of Pharaoh and on his people. [The Lord] said [to Pharaoh]: *"This is why I have confirmed your contentiousness,"*[114] which means, "this is why I did not kill you with the first plague, *in order to demonstrate my power* to you through the chastisements which I myself would bring upon your land. *Tomorrow I will send severe hail. Order the cattle* that survived the pestilence *to be brought in,* so that they will not be killed by the hail."[115]

(2) Consider how unwilling God was to strike Egypt.[116] From the very beginning He told them to repent, but [Pharaoh] would not. Then [the Lord] commanded Pharaoh to bring in his cattle. If they had brought in their cattle as they were commanded, upon what would the hail

---

111. Exod 8.24.
112. Cf. Exod 9.7.
113. Cf. Exod 9.10–11.
114. Exod 9.16. *Pace* Féghali, "Voilà pourquoi je t'ai maintenu jusqu'à la fin . . ."; "Commentaire," 111. The phrase in Syriac reads: *ʾaqîmtāk b-ḥeryānā*. See XI.1 for a parallel expression.
115. Cf. Exod 9.19.
116. Ephrem's emphasis on the opportunities God gave Pharaoh to repent reflects an indebtedness to rabbinic sources. See Jansma, "Reflections," 13. Also S. Schechter, *Aspects of Rabbinic Theology,* reprint (New York, 1961) especially ch. XVIII; and G. F. Moore, *Judaism in the First Centuries of the Christian Era,* vol. 1, part 3 (Cambridge, Massachusetts, 1962) ch. 5.

have fallen? *The hail will fall*[117] so that a miracle will be witnessed as it kills the cattle of those who did not believe. *Let the animals be brought in*[118] so that [God] may keep watch over the portion of the repentant.

3. *Hail and fire fell* together; neither did the hail extinguish the fire, nor did the fire melt[119] the hail. Rather, it burst into flames in the hail as in a thicket, and turned [the hail] as red as iron in the fire, blazing in the hail, and careful of the trees. The force [of the hail] *splintered the ancient trees,*[120] but the fire in [the hail] protected the hedges, seed beds, and vineyards.[121]

4. Pharaoh said to Moses: *"This time I have sinned."*[122] And the previous times he hardened his heart, did he not sin? And even if he sinned the previous times, he did not sin the way he did this time. [The Lord] warned him to bring in the cattle, but he was not persuaded. This is why his offense was more serious in this plague than in all the [other] plagues.[123]

(2) *Moses went out, and with the raising up of his hands, the thunder stopped, and the rain fell no longer on the earth.*[124] Either it vanished from the air, or it condensed in the clouds and

117. Exod 9.19.
118. Exod 9.19.
119. Literally, "consume."
120. Cf. Exod 9.25.
121. Although the biblical text records that the hail spared nothing (Exod 9.25), Ephrem, in accord with popular Jewish belief, suggests that the destruction was not complete: "But the vegetation in the field suffered even more than man and beast, for the hail came down like an ax upon the trees and broke them. That the wheat and the spelt were not crushed was a miracle." Ginzberg, *Legends*, 2:356–57.
122. Cf. Exod 9.27.
123. See note 82 above. Ephrem refutes the determinism of three theological foes, Bardaisan, Mani, and Marcion, and traces the source of evil to the wrong use of human freedom. See Bou Mansour, "La liberté chez Saint Ephrem le Syrien," *PdO* 11 (1983): 89–156; 12 (1984/85): 3–89: "Son souci nous semble plutôt celui de rattacher le mal à la volonté humaine qui, par une décision de discernment, s'avère être capable de choisir aussi bien le mal," (XII, 13).
124. Exod 9.33.

went [back] up. It was not as light coming down as it was going back up. After this, *Pharaoh and his servants became obstinate, and would not let the people go.*[125]

Section X

1. And the Lord said to Moses: *"Go to Pharaoh,* and do not be afraid of his haughtiness, *for it is I who have hardened his heart*[126] by the patience I showed to him during the plagues [that came] through your hands. If I believed in his repentance, it was not because I was unaware of his treachery; I foretold to you that Pharaoh would not listen to you unless I performed signs which you would tell to your generations [to come].[127]

2. Moses said to Pharaoh: *"Unless you let the people go, I will send forth locusts to consume whatever you saved from the hail."*[128] Pharaoh's servants said to him: *"How long will we hold back this people to our [own] undoing? Let them go sacrifice to their Lord,*[129] otherwise we will be stricken as our land and our possessions have been. *Or are you unaware that all of Egypt has been devastated?"*[130]

(2) Pharaoh said to Moses: "You may leave with your belongings,[131] but the land of one of the kings [holds] misfortune for you."[132] Surely, if you had wanted to keep them from misfortune, you would not have made them endure misfortune in your own land. If you prevented them from

---

125. Cf. Exod 9.34–35.
126. Cf. Exod 10.1. Ephrem passes over without comment the fact that the passage explicitly states that it is the Lord who had hardened Pharaoh's heart.
127. Cf. Exod 10.2.   128. Cf. Exod 10.4–5.
129. Cf. Exod 10.7.
130. This final sentence has been left out of Tonneau's Latin version. See Tonneau, *In Genesim et Exodum, CSCO* 153.72, 119, line 18.
131. Féghali adds "et vos enfants"; "Commentaire," 113.
132. Ephrem explains Pharaoh's words by speaking of a certain king who would do the people harm. He seeks to assign the blame for this to Pharaoh himself, who kept the people subjugated. *Targum Pseudo-Jonathan* 10.10 expands the passage to indicate that, like a magician, Pharaoh was able to foresee the difficulties that the people would encounter in the desert. Cf. Le Déaut, *Targum de Pentateuque,* 2:75.

leaving out of love, you would not have added to your already heavy yoke by withholding straw from them. The people for whom this God has worked every wonder do not fear human misfortune.

3. Next, Moses sent forth locusts that devoured the grass and whatever the hail had spared. Pharaoh said: *"I have sinned against the Lord and against you. Forgive my fault."*[133] Now if he had hardened his heart, he would not have spoken these [words], because a heart that is hardened is a stranger to remorse. He prayed when he was punished, but became defiant when he was relieved. This was a free man,[134] and these two [kinds of behavior] testify to his free will.[135] [The Lord] sent forth locusts at the command of Moses, but the repentance of Pharaoh held off the locusts.

4. Then *Moses brought darkness over all of Egypt for three days* and three nights. *But the Hebrews had light*[136] to rest from their labors, and to make preparations for their departure.

5. Pharaoh said to Moses: *"Go* with your wives and children to *worship the Lord. Leave only the herds*[137] to assure us that you will return." Moses answered: "[Our] herds are too small for the great sacrifices we are going to offer to our God. This is why *you must also give us animals,* if you have any left, *so we can sacrifice some of them before the Lord.*[138] Besides, we do not know what to sacrifice to the Lord until he himself sets apart what he will choose from our flocks." *The Lord hardened the heart of Pharaoh, and he refused to let the people go.*[139] Now if [the Lord] hardened his heart, there could be no change in a heart that God hardened. But [Pharaoh] said: "I will let them go" when he was punished, and as soon as [the punishment] passed, he prevented them from going. This hardening of the heart was not from God, but from the innermost mind,[140] which submits to keeping the command-

---

133. Cf. Exod 10.16–17.
134. The Syriac reads *bar ḥîrê,* "a son of the free."
135. See note 123 above.   136. Cf. Exod 10.22–23.
137. Cf. Exod 10.24.   138. Cf. Exod 10.25.
139. Cf. Exod 10.27. See note 126 above.
140. Literally, *tarʿîtâ d-gauwâ,* "the inner mind."

ments when it is punished, but tramples [God's][141] laws as soon as [the punishment] ceases.[142]

Section XI

1. And the Lord said: *"Let each one ask his neighbor for gold and silver objects. In the middle of the night the firstborn of Egypt and the firstborn of the cattle shall die. There will be wailing throughout all of Egypt,"*[143] just as there had been wailing in all the Hebrew households when their infants were thrown into the river. *"Your servants will come down to me and say: 'Leave with this people,' and I shall leave."*[144] This plague, then, that let the people go, confirmed Pharaoh in [his] contentiousness, because by [this] time, it was not the first [plague that had occurred].[145]

Section XII

1. *This month shall stand at the head of the months of the year. And on the tenth of this month, [each] man will procure a lamb for his household, and will keep it until the fourteenth. Then he will slaughter it at sunset, and sprinkle some of its blood on the doorposts and the lintels of the house where they will eat it.*[146]

2. The lamb is a type of our Lord, who entered the womb on the tenth of Nisan.[147] From the tenth day of the seventh

---

141. Literally, "your."

142. Ephrem argues against the plain meaning of the text in order to uphold the principle of Pharaoh's free will. See note 126 above. Also Jansma, "Reflections," 10.

143. Cf. Exod 11.2, 4, 6.

144. Cf. Exod 11.8.

145. Tonneau has translated this obscure line: "Haec nempe plaga, quae dimisit populum, pharaonem perseverare fecit in contentione, eo quod prima non fuit tempore," *In Genesim et Exodum,* CSCO 153.72, 120. A possible explanation of the meaning of the line might be found among midrashic texts which record: "God revealed unto (Moses) that Pharaoh would not let Israel go free before the plague of the firstborn; hence, there was no need to tell him of this plague later"; Lehrman, *Midrash Rabbah,* 3:84. See also note 3 on the same page.

146. Exod 12.2–7.

147. In his treatment of the Passover ritual [XII.2, 3], Ephrem departs from his generally straightforward approach to the text, to draw out aspects of

month, when Zechariah received the announcement of the birth of John, until the tenth day of the first month, when Mary received the announcement of the angel, six months passed. This is why *the angel said to her: "This is the sixth month for the one who was called sterile."*[148]

3. And so, on the tenth [of Nisan] [when the lamb was confined, our Lord was conceived. And on the fourteenth, when][149] [the lamb] was slaughtered, its type was crucified. The unleavened bread, which, he said [shall be eaten] with bitter herbs, is a type of his newness. The bitter herbs are a type of those who received him and suffered. The fact that it was roasted is a type of what is baked in the fire.[150] [The command: *"You will wear] your belts around your waists, and your sandals on your feet"*[151] is a type of the new company of disciples which prepares to set out and announce the Gospels.[152] "Your staffs in your hands" [is a type of] their crosses on their shoulders. "Standing on your feet," because no one receives the living Body while seated. And "No stranger shall eat of it" because no one eats the Body who is not baptized. "No bone in him shall be broken," because although our Lord's hands and feet were pierced and his side was opened, not a bone in him was broken.

4. The firstborn of the Egyptians died in the middle of the night, and every person, in the solitude of his own house, mourned the death of his firstborn, the first of his sons. Just as the river had been filled with the firstborn of

---

its typological significance. For a fuller typological treatment of this theme, see *Hymns on Unleavened Bread*, 5.18–23, where Ephrem concludes:

The type was in Egypt/the reality in the church;
the seal of the reward/(will be) in the kingdom.

For a parallel comparison series in Aphrahat, see *Demonstration* 12.9.

148. Luke 1.36.
149. Féghali ("Commentaire," 115) has omitted the bracketed words from his version.
150. An allusion to the eucharistic bread.
151. Cf. Exod 12.11.
152. Literally, *sabrātā* "good tidings."

the Hebrew women, Egyptian tombs were filled with the firstborn of the Egyptian women.

5. Pharaoh summoned the house of Moses and said to them: *"Leave with everything you own, and invoke a blessing upon me."*[153] Moses had said concerning the servants of Pharaoh that they would ask him to leave,[154] but more than what he predicted [actually] happened: Pharaoh himself, on behalf of his servants, asked them to leave. They insisted that they go, not because [the Egyptians] had repented, but because they thought that they would all die like their firstborn.

6. Six hundred thousand men left Rameses, and made camp at Succoth. The time they spent in Egypt amounted to four hundred and thirty years.[155] This figure should not be calculated from the time Jacob entered [Egypt], but from the day God established the covenant with Abraham.[156]

Section XIII

1. The people took the spoils from the Egyptians, and *Moses [took] the bones of Joseph*,[157] and they set out well-armed. From the first day, *the Lord overshadowed them with a cloud during the day, and with a pillar of fire at night.*[158]

---

153. Cf. Exod 12.31–32.
154. Cf. Exod 11.8.
155. Cf. Exod 12.37–40.
156. Ephrem's purpose seems to be to reconcile the figure of four hundred thirty years (cf. Exod 12.40) and the figure of four hundred years (cf. Gen 15.13). The figure of four hundred years is calculated from the birth of Isaac, thirty years after Abraham's vision (cf. Gen 15). Although *Targum Neofiti* simply states: "The sojourn of the children of Israel (in Egypt) . . . lasted four hundred thirty years," *Targum Pseudo-Jonathan* expands this to read: "The time which the children of Israel spent in Egypt lasted for thirty weeks of years, which amounts to two hundred ten years; but the number was four hundred thirty since Yahweh had spoken with Abraham, since the time he spoke with him on the fifteenth of Nisan between the portions (of his sacrifice) up until the day they left Egypt"; see Ginzberg, *Legends*, 5:420. Also, Féghali, "Commentaire," 116, n. 44.
157. Cf. Exod 13.19.
158. Exod 13.21.

Section XIV

1. *But Pharaoh and his servants had a change of heart, and said: "What have we done?"*[159] After all the plagues that have come upon us, we have let the Hebrews go, after having pillaged our treasures and our clothes. Death would be preferable to us rather than to let the Hebrews mock the kingdom of the Egyptians."

2. [The Egyptians] gathered their forces and set out, confident that they could destroy the people and regain their [own] treasures in addition to the treasures of the people. So Pharaoh set out with his army against the Hebrews who had departed with their hands held high, that is, with silver and gold, garments and possessions and good health, just as God had promised Abraham.

(2) When the children of Israel saw the Egyptians, they became terrified.[160] How many Egyptians were there that six hundred thousand Hebrews should fear them? Because they had their wives and children and possessions with them, they were at a disadvantage.[161] Who would look after their families, and who would guard their possessions?

3. So Moses said to them: "As it was in Egypt, so shall it be here. *The Lord will fight on your behalf, while you shall remain undisturbed.*"[162] The Lord said to Moses: "What are you praying that I do for you?[163] I prepared what I would do for the people [even] before you prayed. Lift up your staff,"[164] which is a sign of the cross, "and strike the sea, and divide it.[165] See, I will harden the heart [of the Egyptians]," that is [to say], "I will not restrain the boldness of the Egyptians, who witness a new wonder, the dividing of the sea, but who

---

159. Exod 14.5.
160. Cf. Exod 14.10.
161. Literally, "their hands were weakened."
162. Exod 14.14.
163. Cf. Exod 14.15. Ephrem, in agreement with targumic tradition, speaks of the "prayer" of Moses rather than a "cry." See Le Déaut, *Targum du Pentateuque*, 2:114–15.
164. Exod 14.16. Read *ḥuṭrāk* with Jansma, "Remarks," 206.
165. Cf. Exod 14.16, 17.

do not take the warning.[166] For this reason, *I shall be glorified by the defeat that I will bring down on Pharaoh and his entire army. The Egyptians shall know* before they die *that I am the Lord.*" This is [why the Egyptians] said: "Let us flee before the children of Israel; the Lord has waged war on their behalf against Egypt."[167]

4. The angel took the pillar of cloud that was in front of them, and placed it between the camps of the Egyptians and the Hebrews.[168] [The cloud] overshadowed the people in the daytime, but when the angel placed it between the camps at night, it produced darkness over the Egyptians like [the darkness] which was over them for three days and three nights.[169] But for the children of Israel there was light, on account of the pillar of fire that gave light.[170]

(2) This happened to frighten the Egyptians and to encourage the Hebrews, for if [the Egyptians] had mended their ways as a result of the darkness, they would not have dared to go down to the sea. *A parching wind blew all night long to turn the sea dry*[171] for the sake of the repentance of the Egyptians, when it could have been divided with the blink of an eye.

5. The Egyptians pursued the Hebrews with no fear of the darkness that separated them from the Hebrews, and without being disturbed by the sea that was divided. During the night, through a sea that was divided, they went rushing forward to do battle with the people who were led by the column of fire. During the morning watch, the Lord ap-

---

166. Ephrem explains the biblical passage in such a way as to place responsibility for the defeat at the sea at the feet of the Egyptians, who, by failing to heed God's warning, rushed headlong to disaster. See XIV.4. See note 82 above.

167. Cf. Exod 14.17ff.

168. Cf. Exod 14.19.

169. Cf. Exod 10.21.

170. The reading of the text of Exodus is unclear on this point. Ephrem follows targumic tradition and maintains that the column of fire produced light for the Israelites. See M. Noth, *Exodus* (Philadelphia, 1962) 115. Also Le Déaut, *Targum du Pentateuque*, 2:114.

171. Exod 14.21.

peared to the Egyptians and threw them into confusion. He clogged the wheels of their chariots[172] so that they could neither pursue the people nor escape from the sea. But they did not fear the Lord who appeared to them, and they were not deterred by their wheels that were clogged. They boldly drove their chariots with full force.

6. It is written[173] that *Moses raised his hand over the sea*[174] while it was divided. Likewise, when the sea returned to its place, it is written[175] that *Moses stretched out his hand over [the sea].*[176] It seems that [from the time that the sea] was divided, until the time that all the people had passed through, the hand of Moses was actually extended, as it would be later during the battle with Amelech.[177]

7. The Lord struck the Egyptians, and not so much as one of them survived. The Hebrews saw dead Egyptians on the seashore, just as the Egyptians had seen the children of Israel heaped on the riverbank. As a result of what happened in Egypt and at the sea, *"The people believed in the Lord and in Moses, his servant."*[178]

Section XV

The Canticle of Moses[179]

1. *Moses and the children of Israel sang this canticle to the Lord.*[180] Moses led the canticle, and all the people responded after him: *Sing praise to the Lord who is clothed in majesty,* that is, the Lord who took vengeance on the horses and their riders *which he hurled into the sea.*[181] *He is powerful and praiseworthy:*[182] powerful for drowning the Egyptians, and praiseworthy for rescuing the Hebrews. Yahweh is Lord, that is, it is the Lord himself who became our rescuer, not newly craft-

---

172. Cf. Exod 14.24–25.
174. Exod 14.21.
176. Exod 14.27.
178. Cf. Exod 14.31.
173. Literally, "He wrote."
175. Literally, "He wrote."
177. Cf. Exod 17.8–16.

179. Section XV consists almost entirely of a paraphrase of the biblical passage. It is the only section of the *Commentary* which is given a title.

180. Exod 15.1.
182. Exod 15.3.
181. Exod 15.1.

ed calves. Therefore, *he is my God; I shall sing praise to him. The God of my father,* Abraham, *I shall exalt him.*[183]

(2) *The Lord is a mighty warrior.*[184] He fought for us against the Egyptians, while we remained undisturbed. *He hurled into the sea the magnificent chariots of Pharaoh,*[185] and the powerful army in which he took such pride. *His finest warriors* whom he handpicked and sent after us, *drowned in the Red Sea*; they sank to the bottom *like rocks,*[186] before their corpses became swollen. *O Lord, your right hand is adorned with power, that is, it has power to crush your enemies,*[187] the Egyptians. *You sent forth your wrath which devoured them like stubble*[188] in Egypt and in the sea. *With the breath of your mouth, the water rose up.*[189] Either with a breath from you, the water changed direction and rose up to be divided, or, at the command of your lips, the currents stood upright, as though in wineskins, until the six hundred thousand children of Israel passed through. *The depths became solid in the middle of the sea,*[190] and drowned the Egyptians. And so that we would know why they were drowned, it is written[191] that the enemy said: *"I will overtake them, and divide the spoils, and devour them . . . ,"*[192] and so on. *With your breath, the sea covered them,*[193] and their cruel thoughts perished with them.

(3) *Lord, who is like you among the gods* of renown? *Who is glorious in his sanctuary like you,*[194] that is, in your holy dwelling? You are terrifying to the Egyptians, praiseworthy to the Hebrews, working wonders in the sea and in the land of the Egyptians. *In your goodness, you led this people you rescued*[195] from Egypt with a cloud and a pillar [of fire]. *The nations heard,* that is, the Amorites heard about the river that turned to blood, and they shuddered. *Fear gripped those living in Philistia*[196] because of the death of the firstborn of the

---

183. Exod 15.2.
184. Exod 15.3.
185. Exod 15.4.
186. Exod 15.5.
187. Exod 15.6.
188. Exod 15.7.
189. Exod 15.8.
190. Exod 15.8.
191. Literally, "He wrote."
192. Exod 15.9.
193. Exod 15.10.
194. Exod 15.11.
195. Exod 15.13.
196. Exod 15.14.

Egyptians. *Fear gripped the princes of Edom and the leaders of Moab*[197] because of the sea that was divided. All those living in Canaan scattered in fear, that is, *the inhabitants of Canaan were routed*[198] when they heard that Pharaoh and his army were drowned in the sea.

(4) These nations were struck with such terror that they did not come to wage war with us, so that the people you rescued would pass over them. *You will plant them on the mountain of your inheritance,*[199] that is, the land of the Canaanites. You will establish your dwelling place in Jerusalem where you, Lord, have prepared a sanctuary. Lord, establish it with your hands, that is, so that its foundation is from you. The Lord will reign over us forever and [over] no other people. Pharaoh's chariots and horsemen went into the sea because they pursued us, and the water flowed over them and covered them.[200]

2. *The prophetess Miriam took . . .*[201] How did she become a prophetess?[202] Either, like Isaiah's wife, she had the honorary title of prophecy, although she was not a prophetess, or because she was a just woman.

3. That day the people divided themselves into two groups and sang a canticle to the one who divided the sea and drowned their pursuers on that very day. Moses led the singing for the men, and Miriam [led it] for the women: *Sing praise to the Lord who is clothed in majesty.* He is majestic because he annihilated [the Egyptians] effortlessly and easily inflicted all these plagues on them.

Section XVI

1. Once they crossed the sea, God decided to test them by depriving them of water. At Marah they complained about

---

197. Exod 15.15.
198. Exod 15.16. See also Josh 2.9–10 and 9.9ff.
199. Exod 15.17.   200. Cf. Exod 15.18ff.
201. Exod 15.20.
202. The question of the origins of Miriam's title of prophetess had been raised by Jewish sources: "Because Miriam prophesied, 'My mother is destined to give birth to a son who will save Israel'; and when the house was flooded with

[the lack of] water. God showed Moses a piece of wood. *When he threw it into the water, the water became sweet.*[203] The wood is a type of the cross which sweetened the bitterness of the nations. After changing the water, he imposed laws on them, so that just as the wood had the power to alter nature, the law might lure freedom and persuade it.[204]

2. After being tested at Marah, they came to Elim, and from Elim, to the desert of Sinai [where] the people complained about [the lack of] meat. So he gave them bread from heaven that they might gather enough food for the day, and not be concerned for tomorrow. Some [gathered too] much, out of greed, while others [gathered too] little, out of carelessness. But the identical portion yielded more to the one who had less, and less to the one who had more.[205] They had to work for the manna,[206] so idleness would not corrupt them. And so, the Sabbath was established for the slaves, the hired workers, the bull, and the ass.

---

light at the birth of Moses, her father arose and kissed her head and said: 'My daughter, thy prophecy has been fulfilled.' This is the meaning of: *And Miriam the prophetess, the sister of Aaron, took a timbrel* (Exod 15.20); 'The sister of Aaron' but not of Moses?—[She is so called] because in fact she said the prophecy when she was yet only the sister of Aaron, Moses not having been born yet." See Lehrman, *Midrash Rabbah,* 3:28. Also Le Déaut, *Targum du Pentateuque,* 2:129, n. 19.

203. Exod 15.25.

204. As Féghali indicates, two separate developments can be observed in Ephrem's treatment of the passage. The first is the common patristic understanding of the wood as a type of the cross; the second is targumic, which considers the wood as a type of the law. Féghali, "Commentaire," 121, n. 48. See Origen, *Homélies sur l'Exode, SC* 16 (Paris, 1947) 167–69. And Le Déaut, *Targum du Pentateuque,* 2:128.

205. Popular Jewish belief held that the manna fell in equal portions to every individual, regardless of the amount that was collected: "Manna, indeed, had the peculiarity of falling to every individual in the same measure; and when, after gathering, they measured it, they found that there was an omer for every man"; Ginzberg, *Legends,* 3:46.

206. Beyond the collecting of the manna itself, there is no suggestion of the work to which Ephrem may be referring. One Jewish tradition relates: "Relieved as they were of all the cares of subsistence through the gift of manna, it was plainly the duty of the Israelites to devote themselves exclusively to the study of the Torah"; Ginzberg, *Legends,* 3:50.

But they did not observe it. Some went out to gather manna, but found none.²⁰⁷

3. It is said that [the manna] was like coriander and that it tasted like honey. [This is] to indicate that the manna pleased every taste. They filled a jar with it to keep it for the generations [to come]; whatever was kept overnight became infested with maggots, but [the manna] that was in the jar for the generations [to come] did not become infested. They ate [manna] for forty years,²⁰⁸ until they reached the border of the promised land.

Section XVII

1. When they arrived at Rephidim, and there was no water, they stopped complaining and started arguing. Moses said in his prayer: *"What should I do? Before long, they will want to stone me.* If only [to prevent] my dying at their hands, give them water, so they will leave me in peace."²⁰⁹ He produced water for them at Horeb in the sight of the elders. They had said: "How is the Lord among us, when there is not even enough water for us?"²¹⁰ But he made the water flow in the sight of the elders so they would know that the Lord was truly with them.

(2) Forgetting the earlier signs, they tested [the Lord by demanding] others, while they had the continual [signs] of the cloud and the column, the manna and the quail. But because they had [these signs] for a long time, they did not think of them as signs. This is why they tested [the Lord by demanding] new signs, [to see] if [the Lord] were with them or not.

2. After these things, Amelech came to do battle with them.²¹¹ Joshua went out to meet him, while Moses went up the mountain with the staff of God in his hand. Moses held the staff only at the time of mighty works and wonders, so that you should know that it is a type of the cross, whose

207. Cf. Exod 16.27.
208. *Pace* Féghali, "quarante jours"; "Commentaire," 121.
209. Cf. Exod 17.4.   210. Cf. Exod 17.6, 7.
211. Cf. Exod 17.8ff.

power effects all wonders. Aaron and Hur, who, as they say, was the brother-in-law of Moses, went up with Moses. [As long as] he kept his hands aloft,[212] Israel had the advantage, and waged war against the boldness of the nations that threatened to wage war with the people.[213] And when [Moses] lowered [his hands], the nations gained the advantage over those who constantly complained against the Lord and Moses.

(2) With Moses' hands raised up, and with the staff lifted at his side, the sign of the cross was seen clearly in him. Joshua contended on the plain, and Moses [contended] on the mountain. When the people saw that he rested his hands, they became frightened [and started] to retreat before their enemies, but when he raised them, they were encouraged to advance against their adversaries.

3. *The Lord said to Moses: "Write this memorial in a book, because I intend to erase completely any memory of Amelech.*[214] Write, so that all nations may hear it and fear to come and wage war against you, and so that the Amelechites will repent and annul the sentence against them." Moses built an altar and called it "The Lord has tested"[215] because [the Lord] tested—through the belligerent Amelech—all nations that were weaker than he, so that if they came to wage war, they too would be destroyed as he had been. When [the Hebrews] realized that their advantage, as well as their defeat, depended on the hands of Moses, they did not seek terms of peace.[216] For he said: "Seek terms of peace with the cities before you engage them in battle."

4. *See the hand of Yahweh upon the throne,* that is, the hand of the Lord upon the throne of judgment which God established for Moses over the people. And *see the Lord's battle with Amelech from one generation to the next,*[217] that is, until he is destroyed.

---

212. Literally, "With the lifting up of the arms of Moses . . ."
213. Cf. Exod 17.11ff.   214. Exod 17.14.
215. Exod 17.15.
216. Literally, "Ask for the right hand."
217. Cf. Exod 17.16.

Section XVIII

1. *Jethro, the father-in-law of Moses, came, and Moses went out to meet him.*[218] He used to bow to him when he was in exile, and he continued to do so after all the wonders that took place through him.[219]

(2) After he bowed to his father-in-law, he told him about the wonders that had happened through him,[220] in order to make him a disciple. [Moses] had been with him for forty years without making him a disciple with his words, but when [Jethro] heard about the signs, he became a disciple, and said: *"Now I know that the Lord who did these things for you is greater than all the gods* who could not do [them] for their worshippers."[221] He said this either because of the plans that [the Egyptians] had made against them, or because [the Egyptians] murdered the infants to exterminate the people, or because, by withholding the straw, the people would become provoked with Moses, or because [the Egyptians] thought that [the people] would be destroyed in the desert, and [the Egyptians hoped to] lay hold of what was not theirs as well as what was theirs.[222]

2. *Jethro offered sacrifices to the Lord.*[223] Now either he offered [them] through Moses, or he set them aside to sacrifice in a place designated by the Lord. According to his plan, Moses established captains [of groups] of thousands and hundreds, and [groups] of fifties and tens, to judge the people, and to act on [Moses'] behalf. *After this, Jethro returned to his own land.*[224]

Section XIX

1. *In the third month, forty-five days*[225] *after their departure from Egypt, Moses went up the mountain to God who said to him: "You have seen for yourselves what I have done to the*

---

218. Cf. Exod 18.5–7.
219. Literally, "through his hand."
220. Literally, "through his hand."
221. Cf. Exod 18.9–11.   222. Cf. XIV.1, 2.
223. Cf. Exod 18.12.   224. Cf. Exod 18.27.
225. *Pace* Féghali, "quatre-cent cinquante ans"; "Commentaire," 124.

Egyptians,"²²⁶ that is, the plagues which I inflicted on them on the land and in the sea. I lifted you up, as on eagles' wings, by the cloud that guided you, and I brought you to me on this mountain. *"Now, if you hear my voice, you will be more beloved to me than all nations*, because I have chosen you alone for myself from all generations to become a kingdom of priests, and a holy nation for me."²²⁷ Accordingly, some of them [became] kings, and some [became] priests, and all of them [were] pure of the uncleanness of the nations.²²⁸

Section XX

1. [The Lord] laid down commandments for them there, saying: *"I am the Lord who visits the sins of fathers on their children, down to the third and fourth generations of those who hate me."*²²⁹ This means that in his patience, he tolerates the wicked man, his son, and his grandson. But if they do not repent, he will punish the first [one born] of the fourth generation who imitates the wickedness of his fathers. *"But I will do justice down to the thousandth generation* [to him] *that loves and keeps my commandments,* as I have done for you and your people because your fathers are of the house of Abraham and Isaac."²³⁰

2. All the commandments he laid down for them depend on this saying: Do not do to your neighbor what is hateful to you. *"Do not kill,"* so that no one else will kill you. *"Do not covet your neighbor's wife,"* so that you will not be punished through your wife for the trap which you set for someone else's wife. *"Do not steal what is not yours,"* so that others will not steal what is yours. *"Do not bear false witness against your neighbor,"* so that no one else will witness falsely against you. *"Do not covet anything of your neighbor's,"* so that no one will covet anything in your house.²³¹

---

226. Exod 19.4.   227. Cf. Exod 19.6.
228. The fact that Ephrem knew neither 1 Pet 2.9 nor Rev 5.10 may account for the fact that he failed to apply this classic text from Exodus to the Church.
229. Cf. Exod 20.5.   230. Cf. Exod 20.6.
231. Cf. Exod 20.13ff.

COMMENTARY ON EXODUS   259

3. Consider how well our Lord spoke when he said: *"The Law depends on these two commandments,"*[232] this is, the natural precepts that are found in the Law and the Prophets, apart from those laws which were formulated for particular circumstances, [for example]: *"You shall build an earthen altar; you shall apply no iron tool to the stones, so that you do not defile it."*[233] *"See, I have spoken to you from heaven. You shall not make gods of gold and of every other sort with me. You shall not ascend to my altar by way of stairs, and no carved stone shall be found there at all,"*[234] lest, while working on the stones of the altar, they should fashion for themselves a god for that altar.

Sections XXI–XXII

1. On this day, he laid down for them the precepts of the laws between a man and his neighbor. *"When a man sells his daughter as a serving girl, and she displeases her master,"* who then does not receive her as he had promised her when he first desired her, *"he may not sell her to foreigners,"*[235] since this would be breaking faith with her after having been satisfied with her.

2. *"Whoever beats a man to death shall be put to death. But if he did not hunt down [his victim], but God handed him over into his hand,"* that is, if the day of his death has arrived, and this man, without willing it, has served the will of God, *"I will make for this man a place to which he may flee."*[236] The man who has died, and whose killer had no intention of killing him,[237] has not died apart from the will of God, for it is He who placed the killer face-to-face with the one who was killed lest the outcome determined by the will of God be deviated from, with the result that [God] leave the deceased among the living.

3. *"When two men who are fighting strike a pregnant woman, but cause her no injury,"* that is, if the foetus has not matured and its body is not fully formed, [the one who strikes her]

232. Matt 22.40.
234. Cf. Exod 20.26.
236. Exod 21.12ff.
237. Literally, "of doing this."
233. Cf. Exod 20.25.
235. Cf. Exod 21.7–8.

shall pay dearly. But if [the foetus] has matured, *"he must render a life for a life."*[238]

Section XXIII

1. *"Do not sacrifice the blood of a victim with leavened bread."*[239] [This might happen] either because *"there should not be found any leavened bread"*[240] among them when slaughtering the lamb, or so they would not mix sacrifices, and thereby offer up the blood of one sacrifice with that of another which had been slain and placed on the altar. *"The fat of the feast shall not be kept until morning"*;[241] the fire of the altar shall consume it the same day. The care which you give to the fat is an indication of your care for a better sacrifice.

2. *"Do not boil a kid in its mother's milk"*;[242] that is, *"it shall stay with its mother for seven days, and on the eighth day you shall give it to me."*[243]

3. *"See, I am sending my angel before you. Pay attention to him, for my name is upon him."*[244] This means that he occupied the place of God by virtue of the divine name that He placed upon him.

Section XXIV

1. *Moses built an altar . . . and sent young Israelites,*[245] that is, the sons of Aaron, to prepare bulls for the holocausts. They had not yet been anointed to serve as priests. *Then he read the book of the covenant before them, and they said: "We will do everything the Lord has said." Then he sprinkled some of the blood on the people, and said: "This is the blood of the covenant which you have ratified, so that we should hear and do everything the Lord has said."*[246] With this blood of the covenant, a type of the Gospel is depicted, since, by the death of Christ, [the covenant] is given to all nations.[247]

---

238. Exod 21.22–23.
240. Exod 12.19.
242. Exod 23.19.
244. Exod 23.20–21.
246. Cf. Exod 24.4–8.
239. Exod 23.18.
241. Cf. Exod 23.18.
243. Exod 22.28.
245. Cf. Exod 24.4–5.

247. It is curious, though typical of Ephrem and other early Syriac authors,

2. *The house of Moses and the seventy elders went up [the mountain] to see God. Under their feet [there appeared to be] sapphire bricks [that were] as clear as the color of the sky.*[248] The bricks reminded them of their slavery in Egypt, and the sapphire recalled the sea which was divided for them, and whose color was as clear as the sky. He said: "You shall not use the lewd colors of adulterous women." God did not impose His hand on the elders to protect them. . . .[249] He brought them up [the mountain] for the vision, not for the gift of prophecy which would be given to them later.

3. He gave them tablets written by the finger of God, so that the commandments of God would be precious in their eyes because God had written them. *Moses and Joshua went up the mountain. And the Lord called to Moses on the seventh day from within the cloud,* and the entire house of Israel saw the glory of the Lord.[250]

Sections XXV–XXXI

1. During these same days, [God] gave [Moses] commandments concerning the building of the tabernacle: of what it should be made, and how; and the vessels they should make for the sanctuary; and [the commandments] concerning the holy oil, the incense, and the priestly sacrifice. By saying [to him]: *"You shall make everything according to the model of the tabernacle that I will show you,"*[251] he first called it a model and a temporal tabernacle,[252] to indicate that it was transitory and that it would be replaced by the church, the perfect prototype which lasts forever, and so that they would esteem it[253] because of its likeness to the heavenly tabernacle.

---

that the blood of the Sinai covenant is not viewed as a type of the Eucharist as one might expect. On this point see Murray, *Symbols*, 54.

248. Cf. Exod 24.9–10.
249. Exod 24.11. A short lacuna occurs in the Syriac text at this point.
250. Cf. Exod 24.13–16.   251. Exod 25.9.
252. On the Peshitta's interpretation of the Hebrew ʾōhel mōʿed ("tent of meeting") as *maškan zabnâ* ("temporary tabernacle"), see Murray, *Symbols*, 222.
253. Literally, "so that it would be precious in their eyes."

2. And He also said: *"I will meet to speak with you above the propitiatory."*[254] [This means that] the voice of God would come from between the cherubim to the priest who would enter once a year.

Section XXXII

1. When the people saw that Moses delayed coming down from the mountain, they made Aaron fashion gods to lead them, "because [they said] *we do not know what has become of this Moses who brought us out of Egypt."*[255] But did he not go up the mountain in your presence? And did he not enter the cloud before your very eyes? Go up the mountain, and if you do not find him or Joshua, do whatever seems best to you. But if you have the manna and the quail, and the column and the cloud, how then is Moses himself not there, since everything you have, you have through him?[256]

2. While Aaron was arguing with them, he realized that they wanted to stone him as they had done to Hur. It was to Hur that Moses ordered the elders to render their judgments when he went up the mountain. But when Moses came down, there is no mention of his charge. This is why it is said that they killed [Hur] during their revolt against Aaron over the golden calf, because he rebuked them, saying: "Do not make a substitute for God." And so, lest Aaron also die and they be liable for a blood feud for his murder at their hands, and lest they make many calves for themselves instead of just one, and lest they return to Egypt,[257] [Aaron] sent craftsmen to collect their wives' earrings, so they would prevent their husbands from forging calves, either to protect their earrings, or because of their love of God.[258]

---

254. Cf. Exod 25.22.
255. Cf. Exod 32.1.
256. Literally, "through his hands."
257. Féghali adds "et à ses dieux"; "Commentaire," 129.
258. Ephrem's intention seems to be to justify Aaron's complicity in making the golden calf. "Aaron had no fear for his life, but he thought: 'If Israel were to commit so terrible a sin as to slay their priest and prophet, God would never forgive them'"; Ginzberg, *Legends,* 3:121ff.

3. It is written: *All the people removed the gold earrings that were in their ears, and brought them to Aaron.*[259] As these earrings had been given to them with love when they received them from the Egyptians, so now, the calf had become so beloved by them that they gave their earrings to make [it].

4. The craftsmen took the gold and designed a model. Then they made a molten calf and said: *"This is your God who brought you out of the land of Egypt."*[260] They denied God all the wonders he worked for them in the sea and on the land, in order to attribute to the calf which they loved things it never did. Regarding the fact that it says: *Aaron was afraid and built an altar before them,*[261] it seems that, when they made them[262] exercise the priesthood before the calf, they killed Hur.

5. In order to delay them until Moses came down the mountain, Aaron said to them: *"Tomorrow [shall be] a feast of the Lord."* So they got up early and offered sacrifices, and ate manna, and drank the water that Moses made flow. *They rose up early to revel frantically before the calf,*[263] under the [very] cloud that protected them.

6. *And the Lord said,* that is, the true God said to the god of his people: *"Your people have become depraved; they have made a calf."*[264] And [the people] said: *"This is your god who brought you out of the land of Egypt."*[265] By revealing this, [God] prepared [Moses] for the prayer he would say. He said further:

---

259. Cf. Exod 32.3. 260. Exod 32.4.
261. Cf. Exod 32.5.

262. The precise sense of the Syriac is somewhat obscure. Tonneau [*In Genesim et Exodum, CSCO* 153.72, 132] translates "videtur, ab eis coacto Aaron fungi sacerdotio coram vitulo, Hur occisum esse." Jansma ["Remarks," 212] has suggested the emendation: "while they (the Israelites) compelled them (Aaron and Hur). . . ." Finally, Féghali's version ["Commentaire," 129] approaches a paraphrase: "Il semble que, quand ils forcèrent (les prêtres) à exercer leur fonction sacerdotale devant le veau, ils tuèrent Hour." The root of the ambiguity may stem from a scribal error that inadvertently substituted the masculine plural pronoun *l-hûn* for the proper name *l-harûn*. Based on this reconstruction, the sentence might more plausibly read: "When they made Aaron exercise the priesthood before the calf, they killed Hur."

263. Cf. Exod 32.5–6. 264. Cf. Exod 32.7.
265. Cf. Exod 32.8.

"*Let me put an end to them,*"²⁶⁶ instead of saying to him: "Prevent me from putting an end to them." If He had wanted to do harm to the people, He would not have revealed their ruin to the one who breached their gaps.²⁶⁷ Therefore, by revealing this to [Moses], it is clear that He was not going to do the people harm; He was prepared to forgive. So He invited Moses to pray, for a great fault could not be forgiven without them incurring a great penalty. He revealed to Moses that He was going to destroy them, so that, when Moses interceded and they were forgiven, the pardon would be magnified in their eyes and the intercessor would be loved with [all] their minds.

7. Through the intercession of Moses and the memory of their fathers, [Moses] appeased the Lord on the mountain. He turned to go down with Joshua, [carrying] the two tablets in his hands. Joshua said to Moses: "*There is the sound of battle in the camp.*"²⁶⁸ If Joshua had been in the camp, he would not have said this, because he would have known about the statue of the calf. And if he had been with Moses on the mountain, he would not have said this, because he would have heard God say to Moses that the people had become depraved. But he was not with Moses, and he was not with the people; he was between Moses and the people. He stayed with his master for seven days, and when the Lord called Moses, [Joshua] remained alone, without his master.

8. When Moses saw the calf and [heard] the cymbals, he broke the tablets at the foot of the mountain which he brought down from the mountain.²⁶⁹ Of what use were the commandments to a people who had replaced the One who laid down the law with a calf? Moses did not know . . . ²⁷⁰ *He had the calf ground into powder, and put it into water which he made the people drink.*²⁷¹ Those who had caused the calf to be

---

266. Cf. Exod 32.10.
267. See *Hymns on Nisibis* 13.17, where Ephrem speaks of the prayer of the bishop as breaching the defenses of the city against the enemy.
268. Exod 32.17.   269. Exod 32.19.
270. A short lacuna in the Syriac occurs here.
271. Cf. Exod 32.20.

made were made to drink the dust of the calf. Although all the people gave earrings, some gave out of fear, like Aaron, who built that altar because he was afraid. Only those who originated [the idea] in their minds, and then encouraged the others, were made to drink the dust. [Moses] said to Aaron: *"What has this people done to you that you should lead them into so serious a sin?"*[272] He did not [say]: "You led them into sin . . . ."[273]

(2) *Moses stood at the entrance of the camp, and said: "Whoever is for the Lord, let him come to me."* The sons of Levi gathered [around him]. He said to them: "Thus says the Lord: '*Let every man put his sword on his hip.*'"[274] The Lord did not say to him . . .[275] before he relented. When [the Lord] was convinced by him, [Moses] said: *"The Lord relented from the punishment He said He would inflict on the people."*[276] At the top [of the mountain] stood the intercessor, and at the bottom of the mountain, the avenger. Faced with justice . . . mercy. And in the camp [stood] one who was anxious to discipline . . . the command of God . . .

   272. Exod 32.21.
   273. Four lines of the manuscript are illegible.
   274. Exod 32.25–27.
   275. See note 92, above. A series of lacunae, which are indicated in the version by ellipses, interrupt the final paragraph.
   276. Cf. Exod 32.14.

THE HOMILY ON OUR LORD

INTRODUCTION

As the only surviving example of a prose *mîmrâ* by Ephrem, *The Homily on Our Lord* preserves rare evidence of Ephrem's ability to achieve rhetorical elegance in a non-poetic form of writing.[1] The *Homily* is replete with elaborate stylistic devices that demonstrate a highly developed technical skill. This carefully crafted prose style, sometimes called "artistic prose," is also found among Ephrem's contemporaries in the Greek-speaking world, notably the Cappadocian Fathers.[2] Syria stood at the crossroads of the ancient world where Semitic, Hellenistic, and Mesopotamian cultures freely intermingled. The existence of similar rhetorical styles in Syriac and Greek is a reminder of the fact that many areas of Syria were bilingual, and this encouraged the development of similar literary styles in both languages.[3]

(2) *The Homily on Our Lord* is divided into fifty-nine sections of unequal length, and contains many of the great Christological and Trinitarian teachings that Ephrem elaborated in his hymns. Although Ephrem devotes much of the *Homily* to the universal Christian themes of the person of Christ, the incarnation, and the mystery of redemption (Sections I–XIII), he develops these themes in the evocative and highly nuanced theological idioms of native Syriac-speaking Christianity. The initial phase of the *Homily* culminates in the expression of one of the richest themes in early

---

1. For a convenient introduction to Ephrem's poetic form see Brock, *Hymns on Paradise*, 33–39. For an analysis of the construction of the doctrinal hymns see idem, "The Poetic Artistry of St. Ephrem," 21–28. Also, idem, "Ephrem's Letter to Publius," 261–305.

2. See Murray, "The Characteristics of the Earliest Christianity," 3–14, especially 9–14; idem, "Some Rhetorical Patterns in Early Syriac Literature," 109–31.

3. See Brock, "Ephrem's Letter to Publius," 266.

Syriac-speaking Christianity, the cosmic drama of Christ's descent to Sheol, his freeing of Adam and all those who were imprisoned with him, and the ultimate victory over death. This is all by way of preparation for the central focus of the *Homily* (Sections XIV–XXIV), the explanation and interpretation of Christ's encounter with the sinful woman in the house of Simon the Pharisee which is recorded in Luke 17. With penetrating insight into the biblical narrative, Ephrem contrasts the suspicion and doubt of Simon with the faith and solicitude of the sinful woman whose actions are an acknowledgement of Christ as Son of God. Ephrem combines his detailed knowledge of Scripture with his literal reading of the text to show that mildness always accompanied Christ's speech, even when there seemed to be a violent result, as in the case of the blinding of Paul (Sections XXV–XXXIII).[4] Ephrem explains that it was altogether appropriate for Christ to combine speech that was mild to Paul's ears with an appearance that was overwhelming to his eyes since only this combination could have had the desired impact on Paul. Sections XXXIV and XXXV of the *Homily* initiate a digression on the divine and human natures in Christ which reveals a dogmatic preoccupation uncharacteristic of the authentic Ephrem; in all likelihood, these sections of the *Homily* represent later additions to the text. Ephrem continues with the theme of the Pharisee's inability to understand the true meaning of the events taking place in his house (Sections XLI–XLIX), and then goes on to link Simeon the priest and Simon Peter the Apostle (Sections L–LVIII), both of whom share the same Syriac name with Simon the Pharisee, Šemʿûn. Ephrem's purpose is to show how Old Testament prophecy and priesthood came to be passed on to Christ, who fulfilled prophecy

---

4. Ephrem's impressive knowledge of Scripture is also evident in his mention of the fact that although Old Testament Prophets were able to cure diseases such as leprosy, there is no recorded instance of a Prophet restoring the use of the senses to a disabled person (XII). Elsewhere, Ephrem's familiarity with Scripture allows him to mention almost off-handedly that Christ pronounced precisely "ten woes" against those who crucified Him (XXVI).

and passed the priesthood on to Simon Peter and the other Apostles.

(3) Throughout the *Homily* Ephrem draws from the rich repertoire of titles of Christ which represents a unique legacy of Syriac-speaking Christianity.[5] While the New Testament inspiration of many of these titles is obvious, for example, "Shepherd," "Fisherman," and "Carpenter," others such as "Physician," "Medicine of Life," "Master Builder," and "Treasurer" depend on Sumerian, Akkadian, and Persian antecedents.

(4) Translations of the works of Ephrem can never adequately represent the full range of his literary artistry or his alertness to the subtleties of the sounds and rhythms of his native Syriac.[6] Ephrem, who is known from his hymns as a master of parallelism and antithesis, often uses these same devices in the *Homily* to summarize and to punctuate the point which he has been developing. At the end of a section in which he links the eternal power of the Creator with the cure of the deaf-mute recorded in Mark 7.32–37, he concludes: "The one who let Adam speak all at once, without instruction, let deaf-mutes, whose tongues are taught only with difficulty, speak with ease," (X). When the resurrection of Christ was denied, and with it, his power to create and give life, Ephrem shows with subtle irony that the power of Christ was alive in His disciples: "The disciples, who were thought to have stolen a lifeless corpse, were found to be giving life to other corpses!" (XIII).

(5) The *Homily* refutes the severely ascetical image of Ephrem which is found in his Syriac *Vita* and in many monastic-inspired works that were falsely attributed to him.[7] This ascetical influence which is marked by a decidedly negative attitude toward women and a tone of rigorous moraliz-

---

5. See the discussion in Murray, *Symbols*, 159–204.
6. For some examples of Ephrem's rhythmic prose style in transliteration see the General Introduction.
7. For a general orientation to the development of the Syriac *Vita* of Ephrem, see Outtier, "Saint Ephrem d'après ses biographies et ses oeuvres," 11–33.

ing is countered by the *Homily's* emphasis on the fervent faith of the sinful woman in contrast to the spiritual blindness of Simon the Pharisee. The *Homily* reflects the mildness and moderation which represent Ephrem's authentic spirit:

> Our Lord gave his assistance through persuasion rather than through admonition. Gentle showers soften the earth and thoroughly penetrate it, but a beating rain hardens and compresses the surface of the earth so that (the rain) will not be absorbed (XXII).

Like the parables, the Lord's gentleness and humility were intended to serve as timeless examples: "Our Lord spoke humbly . . . so that the leaders of his church would learn to speak humbly," (XXVI).

(6) The complete text of the *Homily* is preserved in only one manuscript, British Library Manuscript 14570, ff. 22–52 (hereafter, MS. A), which was published with a Latin translation by Thomas J. Lamy.[8] A quite literal English translation of the text of the *Homily* contained in this manuscript was published by A. E. Johnston.[9] In 1966, Dom Edmund Beck prepared the critical edition of the *Homily* based on the above-mentioned manuscript and a second mansucript, British Library Manuscript 14656 (hereafter, MS. B), which contains only a portion of the *Homily*.[10]

8. Lamy, *Sancti Ephraemi Syri hymni et sermones* 1:147–247, and 2:XXI–XXIII.

9. J. Gwynn, ed., *The Nicene and Post Nicene Fathers* (Oxford, 1898) 13.2:305–30.

10. E. Beck, ed., *Des heiligen Ephraem des Syrers Sermo de Domino Nostro*, CSCO 270/71 (Louvain, 1966).

THE HOMILY ON OUR LORD

The Homily of Mar Ephrem on Our Lord[1]

Section I

OODNESS ENCOUNTERED slandering mouths and made them praising harps; this is why all mouths should give praise to the one who removed slanderous speech from them.[2] Praise to you who set out from one haven and resided in another, to come and make us a haven for the One who sent you.[3]

(2) The Only-Begotten[4] journeyed from the God-

1. The *Homily* opens with four lines of approximate isocola that have been carefully crafted for rhythm and sound. Similar patterns are found throughout the composition. See Brock, "Ephrem's Letter to Publius," 261–65.

2. Ephrem uses the Syriac *gdap* ("slander," "blaspheme") and its derivatives in his treatment of the theme that will occupy the major part of the *Homily*, the encounter of Jesus with the sinful woman in the home of Simon the Pharisee (Luke 7.36–50). From Ephrem's perspective, Simon becomes a metaphor for the chronic unbelief of Israel. As Simon failed to discover the truth of who Jesus was, Israel consistently failed to grasp the meaning of the signs with which God surrounded it. See Sections XXIII and XLVII where "blasphemy" is turned into "praise." The following table locates the primary passages where the term occurs in the *Homily*. The references are to Beck's critical edition:

Section	Page	Line	Section	Page	Line
I	1	1	XXIII	21	2
I	1	3	XXX	28	11
XXI	17	17	XLII	38	15

3. Literally, "him." Cf. John 14.23.

4. In Syriac *îḥîdāyā*. As perhaps the most written about technical term in Syriac-speaking Christian tradition, *îḥîdāyā* has generated a vast body of scholarly literature. In addition to its use in Syriac versions of the New Testament to mean "Only-Begotten," it is also common in Syriac ascetical literature where it designates a hermit, and eventually, even a monk. Some scholars have speculated that the term *îḥîdāyā* may underlie the Greek μοναχός. See Beck, "Asketen-

head[5] and resided in a virgin, so that through physical birth the Only-Begotten would become a brother to many.[6] And he journeyed from Sheol and resided in the kingdom, to tread a path from Sheol, which cheats everyone, to the kingdom, which rewards everyone.[7] For our Lord gave His resurrection as a guarantee to mortals that He would lead them out of Sheol, which takes the departed without discrimination, to the kingdom, which welcomes guests with discrimination, so that we might journey from where everyone's bodies are treated the same, to where everyone's efforts are treated with discrimination.[8]

(3) It is He who went down to Sheol and came up from

---

tum und Mönchtum bei Ephraem," 341–63; idem, "Ein Beitrag zur Terminologie des ältesten syrischen Mönchtums," 254–67; also E. A. Judge, "The Earliest Use of Monachos for 'Monk' (P. Coll. Youtie 77) and the Origins of Monasticism," *JAC* 20 (1977): 72–89; and Brock, *Hymns on Paradise*, 25–33.

5. In Syriac *îtûtâ*, literally "Being." This noun and its derivatives are of paramount importance to Ephrem, especially in his polemical works. The root *ît* is cognate to the Greek ὁ ὤν and the Hebrew *YHWH* (cf. Exod 3.14). In several hymns, Ephrem uses *îtûtâ* as an epithet for the Father: "Blessed is he, O Lord, who knows that you are in the bosom of *îtûtâ*" (cf. *Hymns on Faith* 3.13; also John 1.18). The term likewise occurs in the earliest eucharistic *anaphorae* to identify the Father. See, for example, W. Macomber, "The Ancient Form of the Anaphora of the Apostles," in *East of Byzantium*, 85, where Christ is spoken of as *bukrâ d-îtûtâ*, ("the firstborn of Being"). Finally, by employing *îtûtâ* in this position in the sentence, Ephrem is able to parallel the following phrase *ba-btûltâ* ("in a virgin"). See Beck, *Die Theologie*, 5–13; also Bethune-Baker, *Nestorius and His Teaching*, 212–17.

6. Cf. Rom 8.29; also *Hymns on Faith* 62.10.

7. For imagery similar to that in this paragraph, see *Hymns on Paradise* 2.2, and Brock, "Ephrem's Letter to Publius," 13. Murray has shown that the eschatological sense of *malkûtâ* ("kingdom") persisted among early Syriac-speaking writers. See Murray, *Symbols*, 239–46.

8. This sentence previews the *Homily*'s lengthy treatment of Simon the Pharisee and the sinful woman (Luke 7.36–50). Simon, who had not welcomed Jesus appropriately, is here paralleled to Sheol, which sentences the departed indiscriminately. The sinful woman who attended to Jesus evokes the kingdom, where guests are welcomed as they deserve. Significantly, the verb *mšawyâ* which is used in the *Homily* in its sense of "treated the same" (I) is the same verb that appears in the Peshitta's version of this pericope where it is used in its sense of "to dry," in the phrase "dry . . . his feet with her hair" (cf. Luke 7.38).

that (place) which corrupts its lodgers, in order to bring us to that (place) which nurses its inhabitants with its blessings. Its inhabitants are those who have crowned and festooned unfading dwellings for themselves[9] in that world with what they possess of the fading buds and blossoms of this world.[10]

(4) The Firstborn, who was begotten according to His nature, underwent yet another birth outside His nature, so that we too would understand that after our natural birth, we must undergo another (birth) outside our nature.[11] As a spiritual being, He was unable to become physical until the time of physical birth. And so too physical beings, unless they undergo another birth, cannot become spiritual. The Son, whose birth is beyond investigation,[12] underwent another birth which can be investigated.[13] So, by the one we learn that His majesty is limitless, and by the other we realize that His goodness is boundless. For His majesty increases without bounds, whose first birth cannot be imagined by any mind; and His goodness overflows without limit, whose other birth is proclaimed by every mouth.

---

9. Cf. Neh 8.15 and John 14.2.
10. Ephrem expressed the identical image in poetry:

> I also saw there the dwellings of the righteous,
> scented with ointment, fragrant with perfumes;
> they are festooned with flowers,
> crowned with blossoms.
> A person's dwelling is in proportion to his deeds:
> one is humble in its decor,
> another astounds with its beauty.
> The colors of one are fading;
> another is brilliant in its glory.
> *Hymns on Paradise* 5.6.

11. "According to nature" and "outside of nature" are similarly distinguished in Aphrahat, *Demonstration* 6.10.

12. Ephrem is here referring to the generation of the Son from the Father, which is beyond human understanding. See the following note.

13. The Syriac term '*uqqābâ*, variously translated "analyze," "investigate," "pry into," is one of several terms that Ephrem uses in a negative sense to characterize inappropriate theological speculation. See Murray, "The Theory of Symbolism," 1–20. Section three of this article outlines Ephrem's polemic against rationalism.

Section II

It is He who was begotten of Divinity,[14]
according to His nature,
and of humanity,
which was not according to His nature,
and of baptism,
which was not His habit;
So that we might be begotten of humanity,
according to our nature,
and of divinity,
which is not according to our nature,
and of the Spirit,
which is not our habit.[15]

(2) And so the one who was begotten of Divinity underwent a second birth in order to bring us to birth again.[16]

(3) His birth from the Father is not to be investigated; rather, it is to be believed.[17] And His birth from a woman is not offensive; it is noble![18] His death on a cross is evidence of His birth from a woman, for whoever dies was also born.

    14. Here Ephrem uses *'alāhûtâ* ("divinity," "Godhead") as an abstraction for the Father. The term is used in the *Homily* in reference to the Son as well.

    15. Here and in several hymns, Ephrem indicates that it is as a result of the incarnation and the working of the Spirit in baptism and in the other sacraments that human divinization is possible. See *Hymns on Virginity* 46; *Hymns on Faith* 10 and 18.

    16. The carefully structured prose that opens this section of the *Homily* indicates something of Ephrem's masterful handling of parallelism and antithesis. The lines are arranged in chiastic units.

    17. See *Hymns on Faith* 51.3.

    18. In his polemic against dualism that denigrated the physical body, Ephrem insistently draws attention to the physical body of Jesus (see also Sections X and XIII) and argues that neither the body nor any part of the created order is to be despised. For example, the following words attributed to Mary:

> The Son of the Most High came and dwelt in me,
> and I became His mother. As I gave birth to Him,
> His second birth, He too gave birth to me
> a second time. He put on His mother's robe,
> His body, and I put on His glory."
>   *Hymns on Virginity* 16.11.

See also *Hymns against Heresies* 47. 2 and *Hymns on Faith* 19. 2–3.

(4) The announcement of Gabriel declares His generation[19] from His Father: *"The power of the Most High will overshadow you."*[20] Now, since it is the power of the Most High, it is certain that He is not the offspring of a mortal. So His conception in the womb is related to His death on a cross, and His first birth is related to the angel's explanation. For whoever denies His birth will be refuted by His cross. And whoever supposes His origin was from Mary will be corrected, since His divinity is prior to all else. For whoever thinks that His origins were physical falls into error by reason of (the Scripture): *Who shall declare his generation?*[21]

(5) The Father begot Him, and through Him He made all creation.[22] Flesh begot Him, and in His flesh He put passions to death.[23] Baptism begot Him, that through Him it might make (our) stains white. Sheol begot Him to have her treasuries despoiled by Him.

(6) In the way[24] of those who are born, He came to us from His Father. And in the way of those who die, He set out to go to His Father, so that, by the fact that He came by birth, His coming would be seen; and by the fact that He returned by resurrection, His going would be affirmed.

Section III

Our Lord was trampled by death, and turned to tread a path beyond death. He is the one who submitted and en-

19. Here Ephrem employs the factive form *mawledâ*, rather than the simple form *yaldâ* that he has used up to this point.
20. Luke 1.35. On the Jewish Aramaic background of the Syriac verb *aggen* ("overshadow," "cover over") see S. P. Brock, "Passover, Annunciation and Epiclesis: Some Remarks on the Term AGGEN in the Syriac Versions of Luke 1:35," *NT* 24 (1982): 222–33.
21. Isa 53.8. The limit of human knowledge is a constant preoccupation of Ephrem, especially as it relates to his struggle against Arianism. See Beck, *Die Theologie*, 23–34, 62–80; and Brock, *The Luminous Eye*, 12–15.
22. Literally, "through him he created creatures." See John 1.3; Col 1.16; 1 Cor 8.6; Heb 1.2.
23. Cf. 1 Pet 2.24.
24. E. Beck has written extensively on the importance of the term *'ûrḥâ* ("way") in Ephrem. See Beck, "Das Bild vom Weg," 1–39; also Murray, *Symbols*, 246–49.

dured death, as it willed, in order to overthrow death, contrary to (death's) will. Our Lord carried his cross[25] and set forth as death willed. But on the cross He called out and brought the dead out of Sheol, contrary to death's will. With the very weapon[26] that death had used to kill Him, He gained the victory over death.[27] Divinity[28] disguised itself in humanity and approached (death), which killed, then was killed: death killed natural life, but supernatural Life killed death.

(2) Since death was unable to devour Him without a body, or Sheol to swallow Him without flesh, He came to a virgin to provide Himself with a means to Sheol. They had brought Him a donkey to ride when He entered Jerusalem[29] to announce her destruction and the expulsion of her children.[30] And with a body from a virgin He entered Sheol, broke into its vaults, and carried off its treasures. Then He came to Eve, *mother of all the living*.[31] She is the vine[32] whose fence death broke down with her own hands[33] in order to sample her fruit. And Eve, who had been *mother of all the living*, became a fountain of death for all the living. But Mary, the new shoot, sprouted from Eve, the old vine, and new life dwelt in her.[34] When death came confidently, as usual, to feed on mortal fruit, life, the killer of death, was lying in wait, so that when death swallowed (life) with

---

25. Cf. John 19.17.
26. For Ephrem's use of a similar image see *Hymns on Faith* 24.1.
27. Cf. Matt 27.50–52.
28. In Syriac *'alāhûtâ*, here used as an abstraction for the Son. See note 14 above.
29. Cf. Matt 21.1–11; Mark 11.1ff.; Luke 19.29ff.; John 12.12ff.
30. Cf. Matt 23.37–25.46.
31. Gen 3.20.
32. Vine imagery is common among early Syriac-speaking authors, particularly in the context of the incarnation where Mary is spoken of as "the vine" who bears Christ "the grape." However, the image is rarely used so explicitly of Eve. See R. Murray, "The Vineyard, the Grape and the Tree of Life," in *Symbols*, ch. 3.
33. The image is common in the hymns, for example: ". . . the vineyard itself made a breach in its fence for the tramplers" (*Hymns on Nisibis* 43.3).
34. Cf. Murray, "Mary the Second Eve," 372–84.

no apprehension, it would vomit it out, and many others with it.

(3) So the Medicine of Life[35] flew down from above and joined Himself to that mortal fruit, the body. And when death came as usual to feed, life swallowed death instead. This is the food that hungered to eat the one who eats it. Therefore, death vomited up the many lives which it had greedily swallowed because of a single fruit which it had ravenously swallowed. The hunger that drove it after one was the undoing of the voraciousness that had driven it after many. Death succeeded in eating the one (fruit), but it quickly vomited out the many. As the one (fruit) was dying on the cross, many of the buried came forth from Sheol at (the sound of) His voice.[36]

(4) This is the fruit that escaped death, which had swallowed it, and brought the living out of Sheol, after whom it had been sent. Sheol stored up all that it had devoured. But because of one thing which it could not eat, it gave back everything inside which it had eaten. When a person's stomach is upset, he vomits out what agrees with him as well as what disagrees with him. Death's stomach became upset, so when it vomited out the Medicine of Life which had soured it, it vomited out with Him the living as well, whom it had been pleased to swallow.

---

35. "Medicine of Life" (*samm ḥayyê*) is a particularly rich Syriac title for Christ. For the background of the phrase in ancient Mesopotamian religion see Widengren, *Mesopotamian Elements in Manichaeism*, 129–38. A comprehensive treatment of the title in a sacramental setting may be found in P. Yousif, *L'Eucharistie chez Saint Ephrem de Nisibe*, OCA, no. 224 (Rome, 1984) 317ff.

36. Cf. Matt 27.52–53. Ephrem's use of "the buried" conforms more closely to the Diatessaronic reading "dead men" than to the canonical reading "bodies of the saints." On this point see W. Petersen, *The Diatessaron and Ephrem Syrus as Sources of Romanos the Melodist*, CSCO 475.74 (Louvain, 1985) 96–99. But see *Hymns on Unleavened Bread* 3.14.

Section IV

This is the Son of the skillful carpenter[37] who set up His cross over all-consuming Sheol and conducted humanity over to the place of life.[38] Since humanity fell into Sheol because of a tree,[39] it passed over to the place of life upon a tree.[40] And so, on the tree where bitterness was tasted, sweetness has been tasted, so that we might learn who it is who has no rival among his creatures. Praise to you who suspended your[41] cross over death so that souls could pass over on it from the place of the dead to the place of life.[42]

Section V

The nations confess you because your word became a mirror[43] before them in which they might see hidden death devouring their lives. Idols are ornamented by those who craft them, but they disfigure their crafters with their ornamentation. (The mirror) brought (the nations) directly to your cross where physical beauty is disfigured, but spiritual beauty is resplendent. The one who was God pursued the nations who were pursuing gods that were not gods at all. And (using) words like bridles,[44] he turned them away from many gods (and brought them) to one.

---

37. Christ is also identified as "Carpenter" and "Son of the Carpenter" in *Hymns on Faith* 17.11.

38. See *Hymns on Faith* 6.17. On Ephrem's use of the image of the chasm in Luke 16.26 see Brock, "Ephrem's Letter to Publius," 275.

39. Cf. Gen 3.3.

40. The cross as the "Tree of Life" and source of the sacraments is a popular image among Syriac-speaking authors. See Murray, *Symbols,* 320–24.

41. Literally, "his."

42. For the image of the cross as a bridge see *Hymns on Virginity* 8.1; and *Hymns on the Church* 49.8.

43. The mirror (cf. Section XXI) is an image of great importance for Ephrem. See, for example, Brock, "Ephrem's Letter to Publius," § 10, where Ephrem's entire meditation is "seen" in a mirror; also, Beck, "Das Bild vom Spiegel," 5–24. Cf. 2 Cor 3.18.

44. Imagery of the bridle is commonly employed by Ephrem in connection with discussions of free will in order to indicate the limited nature of human knowledge: "Our ignorance is a bridle to our knowledge. And from these in-

(2) This is the mighty one whose proclamation (of the Gospel) became a bridle in the jaws of the nations,[45] turning them away from idols to the one who sent Him. Dead idols with closed mouths fed on the life of their worshippers. For this reason, you mixed your blood, which repelled death and terrified it, in the bodies of your worshippers, so that the mouths of those who consume them would be repelled by their life.[46]

(3) You even repelled death from Israel who killed you, and who is marked with your blood, because idolatry tasted your blood on (Israel). That is, paganism learned to avoid (Israel) because of your blood, even though (Israel) never learned to avoid paganism.[47]

Section VI

Israel crucified our Lord on the charge: "He turns us away from the one God."[48] But they continually turned away from the one God through their many idols. So, believing that they had crucified the one who was turning them away from the one God, they discover that it is precisely because of Him that they turned away from all the idols to the one God. Since they did not learn on their own that He is God, they should have learned by His prodding that He is God. For the good that befell them through His hand indicts

---

stances it does not follow that the All-knowing One wished to make us ignorant, but He placed our knowledge under a helpful guardian," *Letter to Hypatius*, in *S. Ephraemi Syri, Rabulae episcopi Edesseni, Balaei aliorumque, Opera Selecta*, ed. J. J. Overbeck (Oxford, 1865) 42, 12–16. See its use again in Section XL. For the possible biblical inspiration behind Ephrem's use of bridle imagery, see Ps 32.9, Prov 26.3, and Isa 30.28.

45. Cf. Isa 30.28.

46. Ephrem links physical contact with the historical/eucharistic body of Jesus to the ability to escape from eternal death. For a rare expression of this relationship outside of Syriac-speaking tradition, see Irenaeus, *Against Heresies* IV.18.5.

47. The theme of Israel's turning away from God recurs throughout the *Homily* (cf. Sections VI, XVIII, and XIX). Ephrem will use the example of Simon the Pharisee, a "son of Israel" (Sections XLII, XLIII, XLIV), as evidence that idolatry (*ptakrûtâ*) and paganism (*ḥanpûtâ*) are endemic to Israel.

48. Cf. John 19.7.

them of the evil that their hands did. And so, even if the tongues[49] of the ungrateful denied Him, the advantage they gained (through Him) proves them wrong.

(2) Goodness weighed them down more than they could stand, in order to make them aware that, while bearing your blessings, they were denying your existence. (Your goodness) even took pity on them because they had made their lives into a pasture for dead idols: a single calf which they fashioned in the wilderness fed on their lives, as though on grass in the wilderness. When the idolatry that they had hid away in their hearts and brought out of Egypt came out in the open, it openly killed those in whom it secretly had dwelt. It was like fire hidden in wood; when it emerges[50] from the wood, it consumes it.[51] Moses pulverized the calf and made them drink it in the waters of testing,[52] so that all who had lived to worship the calf would die by drinking it. The sons of Levi, who rallied to Moses with drawn swords, attacked them.[53] But the sons of Levi did not know whom they should kill, because those who had worshipped mixed with those who had not worshipped. But the One for whom distinctions are easy to make separated those who committed idolatry from those who had not, so that the innocent would be grateful that their innocence had not escaped the notice of the just one, and the guilty would be brought to justice because their crime had not escaped the Judge.

(3) The sons of Levi became avengers in the open: (Moses) placed a mark on the offenders to make it easy for the avengers to avenge. The drink of the calf entered those in whom the love of the calf had dwelt and left a clear mark on them,[54] so that the drawn sword could cut them down. (Moses) gave the waters of testing to the synagogue that had fornicated with the calf, so that the mark of the adulteresses

---

49. Literally, "tongue."   50. Literally, "is born."
51. The image is of fire potentially existing in wood. Cf. *Hymns on Virginity* 3.7 and *Hymns on Faith* 65.8.
52. Cf. Exod 32.20.   53. Cf. Exod 32.26–28.
54. Cf. Tonneau, ed., *In Genesim et Exodum*, 20–31. The Syriac verb *nfaḥ* used in Num 5.19 suggests that the sign was a swelling of the bodies of those who had worshipped the calf.

would appear on it.⁵⁵ This is where the law comes from concerning women drinking the waters of testing,⁵⁶ so that, in the mark which appeared on the adulteresses, the synagogue would recall its fornication with the calf, and with fear be on guard against another (fornication), and with regret remember the first one. So when they pass judgment on their women who stray from them, they are passing judgment on themselves for straying from their God.

Section VII

Glory to you who, by your cross, removed the paganism over which both uncircumcised and circumcised stumbled! Thanksgiving to you, Medicine of Life⁵⁷ for all, who plunged down after life for all, and returned it to the Lord of all! The lost who have been found bless you, for by finding the lost, you made the ever-present angels rejoice,⁵⁸ who were not lost. The uncircumcised give you thanks because you broke down the intervening hostility with your peace.⁵⁹ In your own flesh you received the external sign of circumcision, according to which the uncircumcised who were yours were not considered to be yours. Then you conferred your sign, circumcision of the heart,⁶⁰ by which the circumcised were recognized as not being yours. For you came to your own, but your own did not accept you.⁶¹ And it is by this fact that they are recognized as not being yours. But those to whom you did not come in your love cry out after you⁶² to fill them with the crumbs which fall from the children's table.⁶³

55. The same idea is found in the hymns:

> Holy (Moses) took the synagogue up Mount Sinai;
> he made her body bright with white clothes, but her heart was dark.
> She committed adultery with the calf, and despised the Most High.
> He broke the tablets, the book of the covenant.
> *Hymns on Faith* 14.6.

56. Cf. Num 5.16–28.
58. Cf. Luke 15.10.
60. Cf. Rom 2.29.
62. Cf. Matt 15.22.
57. See note 35 above.
59. Cf. Eph 2.14.
61. Cf. John 1.11.
63. Cf. Matt 15.27.

Section VIII

God[64] was sent by the Divinity[65] to come and shatter the images which were not gods. Once He removed the title[66] of "god" which dressed them up, their defects became apparent. And their defects are these: *They have eyes but do not see, and ears but do not hear.*[67] Your proclamation convinced their worshippers to exchange their many gods for one. By taking away the title of divinity from idols, the worship that had been attached to the title was likewise withdrawn. Worship accompanies the divine title, so worship returned to Him from all nations. In the end, that praiseworthy title will fully return to its Lord. This is why in the end worship will also fully return to its Lord, so that it will come about that *everything is subject to him; then he will subject himself to the one who made everything subject to him.*[68] So the title, rising from one level to another, will be joined to its source. When all creatures are joined in love to the Son by whom they were created, and the Son is joined in the love of the Father from whom He was begotten, then, at last, all Creation will confess the Son through whom it has received all blessings. And in Him and with Him, it shall also confess His Father who distributes all riches to us from His treasury.[69]

Section IX

Glory to you who clothed yourself with the body[70] of mortal Adam, and made it a fountain of life for all mortals! You are the Living One whose killers became the sowers of your

---

64. In Syriac *'alāhâ* ("God"), i.e., the Son.
65. In Syriac *'alāhûtâ* ("divinity") is used here as an abstraction for the Father. See note 14 above.
66. Literally, "name."
67. Ps 115.5, 6.
68. 1 Cor 15.27–28.
69. 1 Cor 15.27–28.
70. The phrase *lbeš pagrâ* ("clothed himself with a body") is the favorite metaphor of Syriac-speaking authors to describe the incarnation. Ephrem employs it in its various forms throughout the *Homily*. See Brock, "Clothing Metaphors," 15ff.; and Murray, *Symbols,* 69–94 and 310–12; also Bou Mansour, *La penseé,* 235–38.

life: like a grain of wheat, they sowed it in the depths, so that it would sprout and raise up many with it.[71]

(2) Come, let us make our love a great, common censer. Let us offer up our songs and prayers[72] like incense to the One who made His cross a censer to the Divinity,[73] and offered His blood on behalf of us all.

(3) The Most High bent low to earth-dwellers and distributed His treasures to them. And although the needy approached His humanity, they received the gift from His divinity. Thus, He made the body He put on (to be) the treasurer[74] of His wealth. My Lord, bring it forth from your vaults, and distribute it to the needy, the members of your family.[75]

Section X

Glory to the One who took from us in order to give to us,[76] so that we should all the more abundantly receive what is His by means of what is ours. Through an intermediary, humanity was able to receive life from its helper, just as, in the beginning, it had been through an intermediary that it had received death from its killer. You fashioned a body for yourself to be a servant,[77] so that through it you might give your love to all who love you. And because you put on a visible body,[78] the hidden designs of those who killed (you) and those who buried (you) became visible in you. For your killers killed you and were killed by you because of your body. And those who buried you were raised up by you because of your body; their love buried you, but their faith was raised up with you.

(2) That unreachable power came down and put on

---

71. Cf. 1 Cor 15.36. 72. Cf. *Hymns on Virginity* 31.5.

73. In Syriac *'alāhûtâ*. Used as an abstraction for the Father. See note 14.

74. In Syriac *gîzabrâ* is a common title of Christ (cf. Sections LIV and LV), which occurs throughout early Syriac literature. For the pre-Christian background of the term, see, Murray, *Symbols*, 193–95.

75. Literally, "the sons of his lineage."

76. Cf. Irenaeus, *Against Heresies* XXXII.9.

77. Cf. Phil 2.6, 7. 78. See note 70 above.

limbs that could be touched so that the needy could approach Him and, embracing His humanity, become aware of His divinity. By means of the fingers of (Jesus') body, the deaf-mute sensed that He came near his ears and touched his tongue. So, by means of fingers that could be touched, the deaf-mute touched his untouchable divinity at the moment the restraint on his tongue was loosed and the impenetrable canals of his ears were opened.[79] For the Architect of the flesh, the Crafter of the body, came to him. And with His gentle voice He made painless openings in deaf ears. And a closed mouth, incapable of producing speech, produced praise for the one who made its impotence fertile with a birth of words.[80] So the One who let Adam speak all at once, without instruction, let deaf-mutes, whose tongues are taught only with difficulty, speak with ease.

Section XI

See, yet another question arises: what languages[81] did our Lord permit deaf-mutes to speak, who came to Him from all languages? And if this is easy to know, let us turn to what is more important than this, namely, to know that it was through the Son that the first person was made. By the fact that it was through (the Son) that speech was given to the mute children of Adam, we should also know that it was through (the Son) that speech was given to Adam, their first father. Here likewise, deficient nature was filled up by our Lord. The One in whom the fullness of nature exists certainly is able to fill up the deficiencies of nature. And there is no greater deficiency than when a person is born without

---

79. Cf. Mark 7.32, 33.
80. The signs that Christ worked are spoken of by Ephrem as "inspiring praise" (see the opening line of the *Homily*). He also expressed this in poetic form:

> The wine in the jars (John 2.1ff.) is similar to and related to
> this eloquent wine that gives birth to praise,
> As that wine also gave birth to praise
> from (its) drinkers who witnessed the wonder.
> *Hymns on Faith* 14.2.

81. Literally, "tongues."

speech. If it is by reason of speech that we surpass all creatures,[82] then its deficiency is the greatest of all deficiencies. Certainly, all fullness exists in the one through whom all deficiency is filled. Since it is through Him that all parts of the body receive fullness in the womb secretly, their deficiency was filled by Him openly, so that we would learn that the entire body was formed by Him in the beginning.

(2) He spat on His fingers and put them in the deaf-mute's ears.[83] *And he made mud with his saliva, and applied it to the blind man's eyes,*[84] so we would know that, just as there was a deficiency in the pupils of that blind man from his mother's womb,[85] so too, there was a deficiency in the ears of this deaf man. So, with yeast[86] from the body of the one who completes, the deficiency of our creation was filled up. It would not have been appropriate for our Lord to sever a part of His body to fill up the deficiency of other bodies. He filled up the deficiency of the deficient with something He was able to separate from Himself. Just as mortals consume Him by means of something edible, in the same way He filled up deficiency and gave life to mortality. So we should learn that the deficiency of the deficient was filled up from a body in which fullness resided. And life was given to mortals from a body in which life resided.

Section XII

The prophets worked all (sorts of) signs, but nowhere (is it recorded that) they filled up a deficiency in the parts of the body. Physical deficiency waited to be filled up by our

82. Cf. *Hymns on Faith* 2.251 and *Prose Refutations* 1.113.5.
83. Cf. Mark 7.33.
84. John 9.6.
85. John 9.1–3, 19–20.
86. By referring to Christ's saliva as "yeast," Ephrem demonstrates his ability to let certain images overlap to achieve a kind of *communicatio idiomatum,* or exchange of attributes. This allows him the creative flexibility to speak of the eucharist as though it were the historical body of Jesus, and to speak of the historical body of Jesus as though it were the eucharist. In this complex typological parallel, Ephrem merges the all-healing capacity of Christ's body, even his saliva, with yeast, which for Ephrem constituted an intrinsic element in the eucharistic bread. Cf. 1 Cor 5.6.

Lord, so that souls would realize that every deficiency is filled up by Him. The discerning should realize that the one who fills up the deficiencies of creatures is the Master Craftsman of the Creator. When our Lord was on earth He let deaf-mutes hear and speak languages they had never learned, so that once He was raised up, they would know that He would let His disciples speak in every language.[87]

Section XIII

The crucifiers assumed that our Lord had died, and that His signs had died with Him. But His signs were seen living through His disciples, so that the killers would recognize that the Lord of the signs was alive. First, the accusations of His killers that His disciples had stolen His corpse caused a tumult.[88] Then later, His signs (performed) by His disciples caused a tumult. The disciples, who were thought to have stolen a lifeless corpse, were found to be giving life to other corpses![89] But the unbelievers were quick to say that His disciples had stolen His body, so that (the unbelievers) would be caught in the humiliation which was about to be revealed. And the disciples, who (they claimed) stole a dead body from living guards, were found to be banishing death in the name of the One who was stolen, so that death would not steal the life of the living.

(2) Now our Lord permitted the deaf to hear up to the time he was crucified, so that once He was crucified, all ears would hear and believe in His resurrection. His truth first came to our hearing by the mouths[90] of deaf-mutes which were opened, so that (our hearing) would not be in doubt about the proclamation of the account (of His resurrection). Our Savior armed Himself in every way so as to rescue us in every way from our captor. For it was not simply a body that our Lord put on; He likewise arrayed Himself with limbs[91] and clothes, so that by reason of His limbs and clothes, the afflicted would be encouraged to approach the

---

87. Cf. 1 Cor 13.1ff. and Acts 2.4; also *Hymns on Unleavened Bread* 13.7.
88. Matt 28.13.   89. E.g. Acts 9.36–43, 20.9–12.
90. Literally, "speech."   91. Or "physical organs."

Treasury of Healing, and so that those who were encouraged by His tenderness would approach His body, while those who were apprehensive for fear of Him would approach His clothing. One woman's fear allowed her to come only as close as the hem on His cloak,[92] while another woman's love drew her eagerly to His body.[93] Those who had not been healed by His words were disgraced by a woman who received healing from His clothes. And the man who had not wanted to kiss His lips was humiliated by a woman who kissed His feet.[94]

Section XIV

Our Lord worked wonders with common things so that we would know of what those who scorn wonders are deprived. For, if such healing as this was snatched from His hem in secret, He was most certainly capable of the healing that His word worked in public. And if impure lips became holy by kissing His feet,[95] how much holier would pure lips become by kissing His mouth. With her kisses the sinful woman received the favor of blessed feet that had labored to bring her the forgiveness of sins. She was graciously comforting the feet of her Physician[96] with oil, who had graciously brought the treasury of healing to her suffering. The One who fills the hungry was not invited on account of His stomach; the One who justifies sinners invited Himself on account of the sinful woman's repentance.

Section XV

Our Lord was not hungry for the Pharisee's refreshments; He hungered for the tears of the sinful woman. Once He had been filled and refreshed by the tears He hun-

92. Cf. Matt 9.20; Luke 8.44.
93. Cf. Luke 7.47.
94. Cf. Luke 7.45.   95. Cf. Luke 7.38.
96. In Syriac *'āsyâ* ("Physician") is a favorite Syriac title for Christ, and one that Ephrem employs frequently in his *Commentary on the Diatessaron*. In *Hymns on Nisibis* 34, Ephrem expands the application of the term to include Old Testament "physicians" who ministered to an ailing world before the coming of the "Medicine of Life." See note 35 above.

gered for, He then chastised the one who had invited Him for food that perishes,[97] in order to show that He had been invited not to nourish the body but to assist the mind.[98] Nor was it as the Pharisee supposed, that our Lord mixed with eaters and drinkers for enjoyment,[99] but rather to mix[100] His teaching in the food of mortals as the Medicine of Life.[101] For just as the evil one had given his bitter counsel to the house of Adam under the guise of food, the Good One gave His living counsel to the house of Adam under the guise of food.[102]

(2) This is the Fisherman[103] who came down to catch the lives of the lost.[104] He observed publicans and prostitutes running off to debauchery and drunkenness, so He hurriedly spread His nets where they gathered, to snatch them from the food that sustains the body, (to bring them) to fasting that sustains spirits.

Section XVI

Now, the Pharisee had made elaborate preparations for our Lord at his banquet, while the sinful woman did simple things for Him there. For all his elaborate fare, the Pharisee only let our Lord taste the feebleness of his love. But with her tears, the sinful woman let our Lord taste her abundant love. The one who had invited Him to a grand banquet was chastised because of his feeble love, while (the sinful

---

97. Cf. Luke 7.44–47; John 6.27.
98. In Syriac, *re'yānā* "mind," but often used for "soul."
99. Cf. Luke 7.37.
100. The image is that of a physician using mortar and pestle to combine (in Syriac, *mzag*) remedies. The same Syriac root is used to express the union or "mixing" of the divine and human natures in Christ. See note 195 below.
101. See note 35 above.
102. Here Ephrem explicitly relates the title "Medicine of Life" to its eucharistic context.
103. The title "Fisherman" (in Syriac, *sayyādā*), with its obvious New Testament links, is applied to Christ, the Apostles, and the bishops by Ephrem and other Syriac-speaking authors. See Murray, *Symbols*, 176–78.
104. Cf. Mark 1.17.

woman) blotted out the great bond[105] of her debt with her meager[106] tears.

(2) Simon the Pharisee had welcomed our Lord as a prophet on account of the signs (he had performed), not because of faith. For he was a son of Israel,[107] who, when signs approached, likewise approached the Lord of the signs.[108] But when signs ceased, there he stood, naked and without faith. This man also thought our Lord was a prophet when he saw signs accompany Him. But when our Lord stopped (performing) signs, (the Pharisee) was overcome with the doubt of his countrymen: *"If this man were a prophet, he would know that this woman is a sinner."*[109] But our Lord, for whom anything is always simple, even then did not stop performing signs. For He observed that the blind mind of the Pharisee slipped away from Him as soon as he set aside signs for a while. He mistakenly said: *"If this man were a prophet, he would know. . . ."* With this thought, the Pharisee doubted that our Lord was a prophet. And with this same thought, he learned that He is Lord of the Prophets. Our Lord brought him help from the very source of his error.[110]

Section XVII

Our Lord told (the Pharisee) the parable of the two debtors, and He let him be the judge, to catch someone who did not have truth in his heart with his own tongue. *"One owed five hundred denarii . . . ,"*[111] by which our Lord indicated to the Pharisee the enormity of the sinful woman's debts. So the man who had thought that our Lord did not know that she was a sinner, found himself hearing from (our Lord) how great was the debt of her sins. The Pharisee, who had supposed that our Lord did not know who the sinful woman

---

105. Cf. Col 2.14. 106. Literally, "small."
107. For Ephrem, Simon the Pharisee's unbelief represents the persistent unbelief of Israel: "The Pharisee was overcome with the doubt of his countrymen," Section XVI. See also Sections XLII, XLIII, and XLIV.
108. Cf. Matt 12.38ff. 109. Luke 7.39.
110. Literally, "at the place error had entered him."
111. Luke 7.41.

was, or her reputation, found himself the one who did not know who our Lord was, or His reputation. The one who had not even realized his mistake was admonished by his mistake. His mistake prevented him from knowing how mistaken he was, so he received a reminder from the one who came to remind the mistaken.

(2) The Pharisee witnessed wondrous signs at the hand of our Lord, just as Israel had at the hand of Moses.[112] But because there was no faith in him, faith on which to secure the wonders he saw, a feeble excuse scattered them: *"If this man were a prophet, he would know that this woman is a sinner."*[113] He put aside the amazing things he had seen and blindness overcame him on account of a slight provocation, for he was a son of Israel.

(3) Bitter signs had accompanied (Israel) as far as the (Red) Sea so that they would fear (God). And blessed wonders surrounded (Israel) in the desert waste so that they would be reconciled (to him). But for want of faith (Israel) rejected (the signs) with the feeble excuse: *"As for the man Moses who brought us out, we do not know what has become of him."*[114] They no longer considered the triumphs that had accompanied them; they only saw that Moses was not near. And so, with this as a convenient excuse, they could draw near to the paganism of Egypt. Therefore, Moses was not seen by them for a while, so that the calf could be seen with them, (and) so that they could worship openly what they had been worshipping secretly in their hearts.

Section XVIII

When their paganism came out of hiding and into the open, Moses also came out of hiding and into the open to deliver openly the penalty to those whose paganism had become unrestrained beneath the holy cloud that overshad-

---

112. In the following several sections Ephrem explores the parallels between Israel's unbelief in Moses and Simon the Pharisee's unbelief in Jesus. Cf. *Hymns on Faith* 3.317–18; and Murray, *Symbols,* 52–55.
113. Luke 7.39.
114. Exod 32.1.

owed them.[115] God deprived the flock of its shepherd for forty days, so that it would show that it trusted securely in the calf as the god that had pastured it with every delight. It made as its shepherd a calf which could not even graze! Moses, who inspired fear in them, was taken away from them, so that idolatry, which fear of Moses had quieted in their hearts,[116] would cry out from their mouths.[117] And they did cry out: *"Make gods for us to lead us."*[118]

Section XIX

When Moses came down, he realized from the tambourines and cymbals that their paganism was raging in the vast desert. He immediately restrained their madness by means of the Levites and (their) drawn swords. And here too our Lord concealed His knowledge a while when that sinful woman approached Him, so that the obstinate thinking of the Pharisee could take shape, like the rebellious calf his fathers had shaped. When the Pharisee realized his mistake,[119] the Lord's knowledge shone upon it and dispelled it: *"I entered your house, and you offered me no water for my feet. But this (woman) has moistened them with her tears. Because of this, her many sins are forgiven her."*[120] Now when the Pharisee heard our Lord refer to her sins as "many sins" he felt completely ashamed because he had been so completely mistaken in thinking that our Lord did not truly know that she was a sinner. From the beginning, our Lord appeared as though He did not know that she was a sinner. He permitted the man who saw His signs to show the doubt in his mind, so that it would become clear that his mind was bound to the unbelief of his fathers.

(2) The Physician[121] who brought a hidden disease out into the open did not help the disease along, He killed it. So long as a disease remains hidden, it afflicts the parts of the body. But once it is discovered, it is destroyed by means of

---

115. Cf. Exod 13.21.
116. Literally, "heart."
117. Literally, "mouth."
118. Exod 32.1.
119. Literally, "when the error of the Pharisee gathered in him."
120. Luke 7.44, 47.
121. See note 96.

medicines. And so, while the Pharisee witnessed great things, he fell into doubt over small things. When our Lord realized that smallness made great deeds small in the (Pharisee's) mind, He immediately let him know not only that she was a sinner, but also that she had sinned greatly,[122] so that the man who had not put faith in wonders would be put to shame by small things.

Section XX

God gave Israel the opportunity to display its paganism in the vast desert in order to chastise Israel with sharpened swords so that its paganism would not spread among the nations. Our Lord permitted the Pharisee to think wrong thoughts so that He could quite rightly chastise him for his arrogance.

(2) The Pharisee thought wrongly about things the sinful woman had quite rightly done. But then our Lord rightly corrected him about the right things he had wrongly failed to do: *"I entered your house, and you gave me no water for my feet"*—the failure of an obligation. *"But she has moistened them with her tears"*[123]—the fulfillment of an obligation. *"You did not anoint me with oil"*—an indication of carelessness. *"But this (woman) anointed my feet with scented oil"*[124]—a sign of solicitude. *"You did not kiss me"*—evidence of hostility. *"But this woman has not stopped kissing my feet"*[125]—a token of love.

(3) Our Lord believed and indicated that the Pharisee owed Him all these things, and that he had withheld them from our Lord. But the sinful woman entered and performed everything that (the Pharisee) had failed (to do). Because she paid the debts of a man who failed to pay them,[126] the Just One forgave her her own debt, her sins.

---

122. Literally, "the abundance of her sins."
123. Luke 7.44.   124. Luke 7.46.
125. Luke 7.45.
126. Literally, "because she paid the debts of the unjust one. . . ." "Oil (in Syriac, *mešḥâ*) in its love, like Christ (*mšiḥâ*) pays debts that are not its own," *Hymns on Virginity* 7.12. Cf. Col 2.14.

Section XXI

While the Pharisee doubted that our Lord was a prophet, he was unwittingly pledging himself to the truth (by thinking): *"For if this man were a prophet, he would know that this woman is a sinner."*[127] Therefore, if it should be found that our Lord knows that she is a sinner, then, Pharisee,[128] by your own reasoning He is a prophet. And so our Lord did not hesitate to indicate not only that she was a sinner, but also that she had sinned very much, so that the testimony of his own mouth would trap the accuser.[129] (The Pharisee) was one of those who had said: *"Who can forgive sins but God alone?"*[130] Our Lord took the testimony from them, that whoever would be able to forgive sin is God. From this point on, the struggle was this: for our Lord to show them whether or not He was able to forgive sin. And so He quickly healed the parts (of the body) that were visible, to confirm that He had forgiven the sins which were not visible.

(2) Our Lord put a statement before them that was intended to trap the one who spoke it. When they sought to trap Him as they intended, they were trapped by Him as He intended.[131] (He said): *"Do not fear, my son; your sins are forgiven you."*[132] Anxious to trap Him on (the charge of) blasphemy, they unwittingly pledged themselves to His truth (by saying): *"Who can forgive sins but God alone?"*[133] So our Lord corrected them: "If I show that I am able to forgive sins, even though you do not believe I am God, stand by your statement to the effect that 'God forgives sins.'" So, to let them know that He forgives sins, our Lord forgave his sin

---

127. A short form of Luke 7.39 as in Section XVII.
128. Ephrem frequently employs the literary device of direct address to add a sense of immediacy and to heighten the drama of the passage. Here, as in Section XLIV, he speaks directly to Simon. See the last paragraph of Section XXVI where Ephrem addresses Paul.
129. Literally, ". . . so that the testimony of his own mouth would prove the liar wrong."
130. Luke 5.21.
131. For a parallel construction see the opening paragraph of Section III.
132. Matt 9.2. Cf. Luke 5.20. 133. Luke 5.21.

that was hidden, and made him carry his stretcher in the open,[134] so that by carrying a stretcher, which had (previously) carried the one who was carrying it, they might be convinced that deadly sin had been put to death.

(3) This is amazing: while our Lord was calling Himself Son of Man, His enemies had unwittingly made Him God, the forgiver of sins! Thinking they had trapped Him with their strategy, it was He who had confused them with their own strategy. And by confusing them with their own strategy, He made them testify to His truth. Their evil thinking was their bitter bondage, and to make sure that they would not escape their bondage, our Lord strengthened it for them by strengthening (the paralytic and saying): *"Get up; take your stretcher and go home."*[135] It would be impossible for them to retract their testimony that He is God, because He had (in fact) forgiven sins. Nor could it be proved that He had not forgiven sins, because He had (in fact) restored limbs. So our Lord linked hidden testimony to visible testimony, so that the infidels would choke on their own testimony. And this is how our Lord turned their own argument against them, because they did battle against the Good One, who battled against their sickness with His cure.

(4) What Simon the Pharisee thought, and what his associates, the scribes, thought, they thought secretly in their hearts. But our Lord brought it out in the open. Right be-

---

134. Ephrem commonly contrasts *kasyâ* ("hidden," "concealed") and *galyâ* ("revealed," "open") to distinguish the divine nature in Christ, which is beyond human understanding, and His human nature, which has become accessible by the goodness of God. See *Hymns on the Nativity* 16.5. Section I of the *Homily* expresses the same thought in slightly different terms: "The Son, whose birth (from the Father) is beyond investigation, underwent another birth, which can be investigated." In the present instance, and frequently throughout the *Homily*, the terms distinguish between the activity of God on a supernatural level from what is perceived on a purely human level. This distinction is repeated in various ways in the paragraphs that follow: "hidden testimony"/"visible testimony," "secretly in their hearts"/"brought it out in the open," "his visible signs"/"their hidden thoughts," "hidden thinking"/"hidden divinity." See Brock, *The Luminous Eye*, 14–15.

135. Luke 5.24.

fore them, our Lord depicted their hidden thoughts, so that they would realize that His knowledge is a mirror disclosing hidden thoughts. And since they failed to recognize Him in His visible signs, they might recognize Him as He depicted their hidden thoughts. Then their hearts would know that He is God, by the fact that He had searched them out.[136] And once they realized that they were unable to conceal their thoughts from Him, they would stop thinking evil of Him. They thought evil in their hearts, but He exposed it openly (by asking): *"Why are you thinking evil in your hearts?"*[137] Thus by the fact that our Lord saw their hidden thinking, they would see His hidden divinity. The fact that the erring were speaking ill of His divinity made them recognize His divinity.

(5) They spoke ill of our Lord because of His body and thought that He was not God. They threw Him down, yet it was because of His body—the body that they experienced as passing among them—that they recognized that He is God.[138] By throwing Him down, they showed that God on high could not be born with a body here below. But by his quick movement upward, He taught them this: indeed, the body which was thrown down was not His (only) nature, for it rose quickly upward rather than descend. So, by means of a body that moved quickly upward through the air from below, they came to know the God who came down to the depths from on high in His goodness.

---

136. Cf. Ps 139.1.
137. Matt 9.4.
138. Cf. Luke 4.30. Here, as well as in several hymns, Ephrem indicates a different ending to Luke 4.28–30 that records the rejection of Jesus at Nazareth. The Diatessaron apparently presented a conclusion to this episode in which Jesus was actually thrown over the edge of the hill, but escaped death by "flying through the air." Cf. *Hymns on Unleavened Bread* 16.10–13; *Hymns on Nisibis* 43.22. For evidence of a similar reading of the pericope in Aphrahat, see *Demonstration* 2.7. For a discussion of the passages in Ephrem in which this occurs, and possible origins of the Diatessaronic reading, see T. Baarda, "'The Flying Jesus': Luke 4:29–30 in the Syriac Diatessaron," *VC* 40 (1986): 331–41.

Section XXII

Now why did our Lord offer that Pharisee a persuasive parable rather than a stiff reprimand? He offered that crafty fellow a parable to lure him, without his even being aware, to straighten out his crooked ways. A ray of sun effortlessly melts away water that has been frozen by a blast of bitter wind. So our Lord did not confront him provokingly, thus denying one who was obstinate the opportunity of being obstinate again. Rather, He tamed him, then He introduced him to the yoke, so that, once yoked, (our Lord) might plow with the obstinate man the way He intended. Because Simon had been so presumptuous in his thinking, our Lord approached him meekly, so that (Simon's) teacher would cause him no offense.[139]

(2) If the Pharisee had the Pharisees' pride, how was our Lord to grant him humility, so long as the treasury of humility was not within his reach?[140] But since our Lord taught humility to everyone, He showed how his treasury was free of the symptoms of pride. This happened on our account, to teach us that the pride that intrudes upon treasures dissipates all of them with its own bragging. This is why *"you should not let your left hand know what your right hand is doing."*[141]

(3) So our Lord did not admonish him roughly, because His coming was (one of) goodness. Yet He did not refrain from admonishing him, because His next coming would be (one of) retribution. He terrified them by coming in humility, because *it is a terrible thing to fall into his hands*[142] when He comes with flaming fire. Our Lord gave most of His assistance with persuasion rather than with admonition. Gentle showers soften the earth and thoroughly penetrate it, but a beating rain hardens and compresses the surface of the earth so that it will not be absorbed. *A harsh statement evokes anger*[143] and with (a harsh statement) comes injury. Whenev-

---

139. Literally, "so he would not have an offender as a teacher."
140. Literally, "under his hand."
141. Matt 6.3.
142. Heb 10.31.
143. Prov 15.1.

er a harsh word opens a door, anger enters in, and on the heels of anger, injury.

Section XXIII

Since all assistance accompanies humble speech, He who came to give assistance used (humble speech). Consider the power of humble speech: it suppresses fierce rage and it calms the waves of a tempestuous mind. Listen to what that Pharisee was thinking: *"If this man were a prophet, he would know. . . ."*[144] Mockery as well as slander is detected here. Listen to what our Lord devised in the face of this: *"Simon, I have something to say to you."*[145] Love and admonition are detected here. This is the loving speech friends use with friends; when an enemy rebukes an enemy, he does not speak to him like this! The ferocity of their rage does not permit enemies to speak reasonably to each other.

(2) It was He who interceded for His crucifiers,[146] so that we would know that raging fury did not rule Him. The torture of His crucifiers was to come, to show that He was governed by discretion and not by rage.

Section XXIV

And so, at the very outset of His parable, our Lord offered an expression of conciliation to reconcile a Pharisee whose mind had grown doubtful and divided.

(2) This is the Physician[147] who prepared cures[148] for (our) adversities. Our Lord devised a statement that was like an arrow. At its tip He put conciliation and anointed it with love to soothe the parts (of the) body. He no sooner shot it at the one who was filled with conflict, than conflict turned to harmony. Directly following the humble statement of our Lord who said: *"Simon, I have something to say to you,"*[149] he who had secretly detracted responded: *"Speak, my Lord."*[150] A sweet utterance penetrated a bitter mind and brought forth

144. Luke 7.39.
146. Cf. Luke 23.34.
148. Literally, "helps."
150. Luke 7.40.
145. Luke 7.40.
147. See note 96 above.
149. Luke 7.40.

fragrant fruit. He who had been a secret detractor before the utterance gave public praise after the utterance.[151] With a sweet tongue, humility subdues even its enemies to do it honor. For it is not among its friends that humility puts its power to the test, but among those who hate it that it displays its trophies.

Section XXV

The King of heaven armed Himself with the weapon of humility and conquered an obstinate man, eliciting a good response from him as proof! Of this weapon Paul says: *With it we lay low the pride which rears itself against the knowledge of God.*[152] Paul based this on his own experience. For just as he had battled proudly but was humbly defeated, so is every pride defeated that rears itself against this humility. The Saul who had set out with harsh words to subdue the disciples was subdued by the Lord of those disciples with a humble word. The One for whom everything is possible forsook everything and appeared and spoke to him in humility alone, to teach us that nothing is better suited to harsh minds than a humble tongue.

(2) Paul heard neither rebukes nor threats, but faint words unable to avenge even themselves: *"Saul, Saul, why do you persecute me?"*[153] Words considered incapable of avenging even themselves were found to be avenging and snatching him from the Jews as a worthy instrument. He who had been filled with the bitter will of the Jews became filled with the sweet message of the cross. When he was filled with the bitterness of the crucifiers, he troubled the churches with his bitterness. But once he became filled with the sweetness of the cross, he embittered the synagogues of the crucifiers.

(3) And so with humble words our Lord opposed the one who laid siege to his churches with oppressive chains. Saul, who subdued the disciples with bitter chains, was subdued with pleasant persuasion, so that he would not subdue the disciples again. He was subdued by the cross, silencer of evil

---

151. See the opening sentence of Section I for the source of this imagery.
152. 2 Cor 10.4–5.   153. Acts 9.4.

voices; none who are nailed to it can do harm or strike a blow. When Paul stopped imprisoning the disciples, he was subdued by the bonds of the deniers.[154] Once subdued in bonds, he loosed the chains of idolatry by his fetters.

Section XXVI [155]

"Saul, Saul, why do you persecute me?"[156] The One who conquered persecutors (here) below, and reigns over angels (in heaven) above, spoke from above in a humble voice. The One who on earth pronounced ten woes[157] against His crucifiers, above pronounced not a single woe against Saul, His persecutor. Our Lord pronounced woes against His crucifiers to teach His disciples not to flatter their killers. Our Lord spoke humbly from above so that the leaders of His church would speak humbly.[158]

(2) Now, if someone should ask: "How did our Lord speak humbly with Paul if Paul's eyes were seriously injured?" they should realize that this impairment did not (result) from our compassionate Lord, who spoke humbly there. Rather, (it was the result) of the intense light that shone intensely here. This light was not a punishment that befell Paul on account of the things he had done. It injured him with the intensity of its rays, as he himself said: *"When I arose, I could see nothing because of the brilliance of the light."*[159] If it was a brilliant light, Paul, how did a brilliant light become for you a blinding light? It was a light that shone according to its nature above (in heaven). It was not in its nature to shine below (on earth). So long as it shone above, it was pleasing. But as soon as it shed forth its rays below, it be-

---

154. I.e. The Jews, who denied that Jesus was God.

155. Section XXVI marks the beginning of a lengthy digression in which Ephrem considers the physical result of a human encounter with divinity. He cites examples of divine epiphanies to Paul, Moses, and Daniel.

156. Acts 9.4.

157. Cf. Matt 18.7, 23.13, 14, 15, 16, 23, 25, 27, 29, 26.24. See also *Hymns on the Nativity* 25.10; and *Hymns on the Church* 27.3.

158. This statement is remarkable for its directness. Ephrem generally prefers more allusive language.

159. Acts 22.6, 11; cf. Acts 9.8, 26.13.

came blinding. The light was both harsh and pleasing: harsh and intense to physical eyes, but agreeable and pleasing to (eyes) of fire and spirit.[160]

Section XXVII

"*I saw a light from heaven more brilliant than the sun, and its light shone upon me.*"[161] Thus immeasurably intense rays streamed forth and flowed over weak eyes, for which rays of light in moderation are comforting. Even the sun in moderation helps the eyes, but immoderate and unrestrained, it is harmful to the eyes. Yet it does not harm the eyes like some avenger, out of anger. In fact, it is the friend of the eyes, and beloved of (its) pupils. This is amazing: with gentle rays, it is friend and helper of the eyes, but with intense rays, it is the harmful enemy of (its) pupils.

(2) Now if the sun here below, of the same nature as our eyes here below, can do harm to them with its intensity, not with its anger, and with its brilliance, not with its rage, how much more can a light from above, of the same nature as the things from above, do harm with its intensity to one who is below, who is not of its nature and who looks at it suddenly?

(3) Now if this sun to which Paul was accustomed could cause injury from its intensity when he looked at it in an uncustomary way, how much more harmful would the brilliance of that light be for one whose eyes had never been accustomed to it. Daniel also "melted and flowed away from every side" in the presence of the glory of the angel whose intense brightness suddenly shone upon him.[162] It was not because of the angel's fury that human frailty melted away, just as it is not because of any fury or hostility in fire that makes wax melt before it, but rather because of the frailty of wax that it is unable to remain firm and withstand the fire.

---

160. In Syriac-speaking Christianity, heavenly beings are metaphorically spoken of as "creatures of fire and spirit," and are contrasted with the purely "physical" eyes of mortals. See Brock, *Holy Spirit in the Syrian Baptismal Tradition*, 11–14; and idem, *The Luminous Eye*, 24.

161. Acts 26.13; cf. Acts 22.6, 9.13.   162. Cf. Dan 10.8.

And so, when the two approach each other, the force of the fire prevails of itself, and the wax deteriorates even beyond its original frailty.

Section XXVIII

The majesty of the angel was seen in itself. The frailty of the flesh in itself did not endure: *"I became utterly powerless."*[163] Even when men view their fellow men, they wither in their presence. And this is not because of any shining splendor of theirs that they tremble, but because of their severe will. Servants become alarmed at their masters' fury, and the convicted tremble for fear of their judges.

(2) These things did not happen to Daniel because of the angel's threat or displeasure, but because of (the angel's) awesome nature and intense brightness. The angel did not come to him threateningly. If he had come threateningly, how did a mouth filled with threats become filled with a greeting of peace? *"Peace to you, desirable man."*[164] The mouth that was a thundering fountain—*"the sound of his words was like the sound of many armies"*[165]—this same mouth became a fountain that inspired peace. And when it reached those terrified ears that thirsted for an encouraging greeting of peace, a draft of its peace broke loose and flowed forth. And ears that had been terrified by the initial sound were encouraged by the greeting that followed, (for Daniel said:) *"Let my Lord speak, for I have been strengthened."*[166]

(3) So as not to bring him the message with an appearance that would strike terror in the heart, the majesty (of the angel) first greeted the weakness (of the man), and with the encouraging greeting that the majesty (of the angel) gave, the weakness (of the man) that had been aggravated dismissed the fearful conclusion (it had drawn).

---

163. Dan 10.8. Literally, "My insides were turned to destruction." This reading, which agrees with the Peshitta, is followed consistently throughout the text.

164. Dan 10.11.   165. Dan 10.6.

166. Dan 10.20.

Section XXIX

What then shall we say concerning the Lord of the angel who said to Moses: *"No man sees me and lives"*?[167] Is it because of the fury of His wrath that whoever sees Him dies? Or is it because of the splendor of His essence?[168] Eyes that have been fashioned and created cannot look at that essence,[169] which is neither fashioned nor created. For if it is because of wrath that no one lives who sees Him, He (must have) let Moses see Him out of His great love.

(2) And so, the Self-Existent[170] One is deadly to those who see Him,[171] not because of His severe wrath, but because of His intense brightness. This is why the one who let Moses see His glory in His great love, likewise in His great love prevented (Moses) from seeing His glory. This is not because the glory of His majesty was in any way diminished, but because frail eyes would not have been able to endure the overwhelming flood of its brilliance. This is why God, who out of love intended that the gaze of Moses be directed to the fair radiance of (His) glory, likewise out of love did not intend that the gaze of Moses be overwhelmed by the mighty rays of (His) majesty.[172]

(3) This is why Moses saw without seeing: he saw in order to be uplifted, but he did not see so that he would not be harmed. By the fact that he saw, his frailty was uplifted, and by the fact that he did not see, his weakness was not overwhelmed. In the same way, our eyes look at the sun but do not see it. They are aided by what they see, but by what they do not see, they are not harmed. The eye sees so as to be of use; it is not bold, in order to avoid being damaged. And so, out of love, God kept Moses from seeing the glory that was too harsh for his eyes.

(4) In the same way Moses, out of love, kept his fellow

---

167. Exod 33.20.
168. In Syriac, *îtûteh*. See note 5 above.
169. Exod 33.20.
170. In Syriac, *îyâ*, a form derived from *îtûtâ*. See note 5 above.
171. Literally, "see his sight."   172. Cf. Exod 33.17–23.

countrymen from seeing the splendor that was too intense for their eyes. He learned from the One who overshadowed and spread out His hand,[173] hiding the radiance of His glory from him so it would not harm him, that (Moses) should also spread out a veil and hide (his) intense brilliance from the frail so that it would not harm them. When Moses realized that children of flesh like himself were unable to look at the borrowed glory on his face,[174] he was overwhelmed that he had dared to look at the glory of that essence[175] in whose flood heavenly and earthly creatures submerge and emerge, neither fathoming its depths, nor reaching its shores, nor finding its boundary or limit.

Section XXX

Now if someone should say: "Would it not have been easy for God to allow Moses to look upon His glory without being harmed, or to allow Paul to see the light without being injured?" Whoever says these things should know that, while it would be easy for the sovereign rule of God to alter the natures (of things), it would be contrary to the provident nature of God that the course (of nature) should be interrupted. Just as it would be easy for the arm of the craftsman to destroy what he has made, it would be contrary to the judgment of the craftsman to damage his masterpieces.[176] If someone wants to say concerning this, based on what seems right to him: "God should have done this," (that person) should know that this is what he should do: he should not say this about God! The first requirement of all is this: man does not teach God what He should do. It is not man who should be God's teacher. It is the greatest insult that we should become masters of the one by whose exquisite creation these created mouths of ours are able to speak. It is an unpardonable offense that an audacious mouth should teach God, who in His goodness taught it how to speak, what (God) should do.

173. Exod 33.22.
174. Exod 34.33.
175. In Syriac, *îtûtâ*. See note 5 above.
176. Literally, "finely crafted objects."

(2) If someone should say: "God should have done this," then I too will say, since I have a mouth and a tongue: "God should have denied humanity[177] the freedom[178] that it uses to find fault with the One who is faultless." But I would not dare say: "He should have denied (freedom)," lest I too become a teacher of the One who is not taught. After all, the Just One would have found fault with Himself if He had withheld freedom from humanity, and out of jealousy had denied a feeble creature the gift that made it great.[179] This is why in His goodness He gave (freedom) without hesitation, so that He could not justly find fault with Himself, even though slanderers, using His gift of freedom, unfairly find fault with Him.

Section XXXI

Why did the eyes of Moses radiate with the glory he saw, (while the eyes) of Paul, rather than radiating, were utterly blinded by that light? We should know that the eyes of Moses were not stronger than Paul's; they shared the same relationship to flesh and blood. Another power graciously sustained the eyes of Moses, but no power lovingly reinforced (the eyes) of Paul beyond their natural power. Was it withheld from them in anger? If we say that their natural power was taken from them, and this is why they were overwhelmed and overcome by the intense light, or, on the other hand, (if we say) that, had their natural power re-

---

177. Literally, "a man."

178. *ḥîrûtâ* ("liberty," "free will") is a central theme in the writings of Ephrem. Faced with deterministic doctrines that attempted to limit divine freedom, Ephrem stresses the transcendence of the Divine Being (in Syriac, *îtyâ*) and the chasm that separates God from the created order. Human freedom is nothing less than a participation in divine freedom (cf. *Hymns on the Church* 22.3), and the way in which human beings most resemble the Creator (*Hymns on Paradise* 12.18). It is through the proper use of freedom that humanity realizes its potential and fulfills the divine will (*Hymns on the Church* 3.9). The ultimate abuse of human freedom consists in questioning the freedom with which God chose to create and to save. See Beck, *Ephräms Polemik gegen Mani und die Manichäer;* and T. Bou Mansour, "La liberté chez saint Ephrem le Syrien," *PdO* 11 (1983): 89–156, 12 (1984/85): 3–89.

179. *Hymns on Paradise* 12.18; *Hymns on the Church* 22.3.

mained, they would have been able to endure that light that was not of their nature, we should realize this: whenever anything is revealed to us that is greater than and beyond our nature, the strength of our nature is unable to endure in its presence. But if another power beyond our nature reinforces us, we are able to endure the presence of something extraordinary which we do not experience in nature because of what we receive above and beyond nature.

Section XXXII

Consider that while the power of our ears and eyes exists in us by nature and is found in us by nature, not even our sight and hearing can withstand intense thunder and lightning—first, because they occur with such power, and second, because their intensity suddenly surprises and stuns our weakness. This is precisely what happened to Paul: that light with all its intensity suddenly struck his weak eyes and injured them, but the majesty of the voice diminished its strength, passed through his ears, and opened them. The contentiousness of the Jews had sealed up (his ears) like wax. But the voice did not harm his ears the way the light harmed his eyes. Why? So that he would hear, but not see. This is why the doors of hearing were opened with their key, the voice. But the doors of sight were closed shut by light, which opens them.

(2) Why was it necessary (for the ears) to hear? Because through speech, our Lord was able to show that He was persecuted by Saul, but He was not able to show through sight that He was persecuted. There was no way to show the Son of David fleeing and Saul chasing after him. This in fact happened with the first Saul and the first David.[180] Both the one who was persecuting and the one who was persecuted saw and were seen one by the other. But here,[181] only the ear was able to hear of the persecution of the Son of David. The eye was unable to see His persecution. The one who had been persecuted in person while He was below was being

180. Cf. 1 Sam 23, 24.
181. I.e. In our Lord's case.

persecuted through others now that He was above. This is why (Saul's) ears were opened but his pupils were closed shut. He who was unable to show Saul through sight that He was being persecuted, showed him by word that He was being persecuted when He cried out saying: *"Saul, Saul, why do you persecute me?"*[182] So the eyes were kept closed because of their inability to see His persecution. But the ears were opened because they were able to hear of His persecution.

(3) Even though the eyes of Moses were physical, like those of Paul, his interior eyes were Christian. For *"Moses wrote concerning me . . . ."*[183] In the case of Paul, his exterior eyes were as open as those within were closed. The exterior eyes of Moses radiated because his interior eyes saw clearly. Paul's exterior eyes were kept closed, so that by the closing of his exterior eyes those within would be opened. He who had been unable to perceive our Lord through His signs with exterior eyes, perceived Him with interior eyes once his physical (eyes) were closed. And because he took an example from his own experience, he wrote to those whose bodily eyes saw clearly: *"May he enlighten the eyes of your hearts."*[184] So, visible signs in no way helped the exterior eyes of the Jews; faith of the heart opened the eyes of the hearts of the nations.

(4) If Moses simply had come down from the mountain without his face radiating, and had said, "I saw the radiance of God there," the infidel fathers would not have believed him. And likewise with Paul: the crucifying sons would not have put faith in him if his eyes had not been injured, and he had said, "I heard the voice of Christ." This is why, as though out of love, (God) set a desirable mark of radiance on Moses in order to convince them that (Moses) had seen the waves of divine radiance. But on Saul, as on a persecutor, He set the infamous mark of blindness so that the liars would believe that he had heard the words of Christ. And so

182. Acts 9.4.
183. John 5.46.
184. Eph 1.18.

that those (fathers) would not speak against Moses, nor these (sons) doubt Paul, God placed (miraculous) signs on the bodies of the blind and sent them out among those who had strayed, (among) those who wore signs on the fringes of their garments.[185] They did not remember the signs on their garments, and they strayed even farther with the bodily signs. For neither the fathers who saw the radiance of Moses obeyed Moses, nor did the sons who saw the blindness of Paul put faith in Paul. Three times in the desert they threatened to stone the house of Moses like dogs. For they said: *The entire assembly shouted to stone them.*[186] And three times, in the middle of civilization,[187] they beat Paul with rods like a dog (as he said): *"Three times I was beaten with rods."*[188]

(5) These are lions who, for the love of their Lord, were beaten like dogs. They were torn apart by flocks of sheep. The flocks stoned the shepherds who protected them, so that treacherous wolves could rule them.[189]

Section XXXIII

Now the crucifiers who plied the soldiers with bribes[190] might possibly allege of Paul: "The disciples bribed him; this is why he agrees with the disciples." Those who quickly offered a bribe, intending that our Lord's resurrection would not be proclaimed, were using the excuse of a bribe to make false accusations, so that Paul's vision would not be believed. This is why the voice confused him, and the light blinded him, so that his confusion might pacify his temper, and his blindness might confound his detractors.

(2) The voice confused his hearing because it spoke gently: *"Saul, why do you persecute me?"*[191] And the light blinded his sight so that when the detractors alleged that he had accepted a bribe, and (said) this was why he had been persuaded to lie, his blindness (that resulted from) the light

---

185. Cf. Matt 23.5.
186. Num 14.10; cf. Exod 17.4.
187. In Syriac, *šaynâ* ("the sown"). Ephrem contrasts it with *ḥûrbâ* ("the desert").
188. Cf. 2 Cor 11.25.
189. Cf. Matt 10.16–23.
190. Matt 28.12.
191. Acts 9.4.

would refute them. It was because of that (light) that he was persuaded to speak the truth. Those who thought that his hands had taken a bribe, and that was why his lips had lied, should know that his eyes gave (up) their light, and that was why his lips proclaimed the truth.

Section XXXIV[192]

Furthermore, this is why the humble voice accompanied the intense light, so that, from the combination of the humble and the sublime, our Lord might produce help for the persecutor, just as all His assistance is produced from a combination of the small and the great. For the humility of our Lord prevailed from the womb to the tomb. Observe how majesty accompanies and escorts His weakness, and the sublime His humility. For just as His humanity[193] was observed in a multiplicity of ways, His divinity was revealed through glorious signs, so that it would be known that the One who existed among them was not one, but two. His nature is not simply humble, nor is it simply sublime; rather they are two natures, lofty and humble, one mixed[194] in the other. For this reason, both these natures display their properties, so that by the properties of both of them, humanity would become aware of both of them so that it would not be concluded that He is simply one, who in fact is two through a mixing,[195] but that it would be understood that He is two on account of a mingling,[196] who is one with respect to

192. Sections XXXIV and XXXV take up analytical and dogmatic concerns that reflect less Ephrem's authentic writings than Christological developments in the fifth century. These sections of the *Homily* have been judged by Beck to be later insertions into the text. Cf. Beck, *Sermo de Domino nostro, CSCO* 271, i.

193. Based on the contextual sense required here, Beck has corrected the Syriac that has: "his majesty."

194. In Syriac, *ḥlaṭ*.

195. In Syriac, *mûzāgâ*. Ephrem and other early Syriac-speaking authors use the verb *mzag* ("mix," "fuse") and its derivatives to express the union of the divine and human in Christ, as well as the union of the divine persons. See Beck, *Die Theologie*, 38. For the use of *mzag* in a sacramental context see R. Murray, "A Hymn of St. Ephrem to Christ on the Incarnation, the Holy Spirit and the Sacraments (=Hymns on Faith, 10)," *ECR* 3 (1970): 142–50.

196. In Syriac, *ḥûlṭānâ*.

essence.[197] These are the things our Lord taught by His humility and His majesty to Paul on the road to Damascus.

Section XXXV

Our Lord appeared to Paul humbly, because humility accompanied His majesty, so that it would be known with regard to His majesty who it was who spoke humbly. Just as the disciples here below proclaimed our Lord in humility and in exaltedness, in humility by virtue of the persecution (they suffered), and in exaltedness by virtue of the signs (they worked), our Lord likewise proclaimed Himself in humility and in exaltedness in Paul's presence, by the exalted intensity of that light that radiated and by the humility of that humble voice that said: *"Saul, why do you persecute me?"*[198] (This happened) so that the proclamation of (the Lord) by His disciples before multitudes would be like His proclamation of Himself. Just as it would not have been known there that He was humble had He not spoken humbly, in the same way, if He had not appeared there with a bright light, it would not have been known that He was exalted.

Section XXXVI

If you should ask: "Why was it necessary to speak humbly, since He could have convinced him by the majesty of the light?" you should know, inquirer, that this is the answer you will be given: He spoke humbly because it was necessary that He speak humbly. And this is also why He spoke humbly: because the All-Wise did nothing there that was not appropriate. He who gave the skill to craftsmen to use the appropriate tool for whatever they undertake, does He Himself not know what He has granted others to know? This is why everything in which divinity either has engaged or engages, (that is) the very thing in which it engages at a given time, serves the purpose at that time, even if divinity's finest works seem just the opposite to the blind. But, so that we do not stifle a wise inquirer with repressive words, one who desires

---

197. In Syriac, *ûûtâ*. See note 5 above.
198. Acts 9.4.

to grow with honest conviction like a seed (grows) in the rain, know, inquirer, that since Saul was the persecutor, our Lord sought to make him the persecuted rather than the persecutor.

(2) This was why he was quick to cry out wisely: *"Saul, why do you persecute me?"*[199] so that when the one being made a disciple heard the one who was making him a disciple cry out: *"Why do you persecute me?"* Saul would know that the Master who was making him a disciple was a persecuted Master, and he would quickly lay aside the persecution of his former masters and put on the persecution of the persecuted Master. Any master who intends to teach a person something teaches either by deeds or by words. If he does not teach by words or deeds, a person could not be instructed in his craft. And so, although it was with deeds that our Lord taught Paul humility, He taught him with words about that persecution of which He was unable to teach him with deeds.[200] Before He was crucified, when He taught the persecution that is humility, our Lord taught His disciples by deed.[201] After He completed (His) persecution by the crucifixion, as He said, *"Everything is finished,"*[202] He could not go back again and foolishly begin something that once and for all had been finished wisely. Or do you want to repeat the crucifixion and humiliation of God's Son?

Section XXXVII

Now, although our Lord in His goodness had previously humbled the greatness of His divinity, in His justice He did not want to humble again the feebleness of His humanity that had been magnified. But since He had to teach perse-

---

199. Acts 9.4.

200. Here, as in Sections XXXVII and XL, Ephrem considers the question of how Christ, who is in heaven, can be persecuted on earth. It is noteworthy that he never concludes that this persecution continues in Christ's Mystical Body. See Murray, *Symbols*, 86.

201. If Ephrem has John 13 in mind, the phrase might be translated more freely: ". . . our Lord taught His disciples by serving them."

202. John 19.30.

cution to the persecuting disciple, and since it was not possible for the Master to descend to be persecuted over again, He taught him with his voice what He could not teach him with a deed: *"Saul, why do you persecute me?"*[203] the interpretation of which is: "Saul, why are you not being persecuted for me?"

(2) The strength of that intense light which shone upon Saul persuaded him not to assume that our Lord was being persecuted on account of his weakness. If Saul's eyes were unable to endure the rays of that light, how would Saul's hands be able to bind and tie the disciples of the Lord of the light? But his hands tied the disciples so that, by their bonds, he might learn their strength. His eyes were unable to endure the rays so that he might learn his weakness by their strength. If the intensity of that light had not shone upon him, and our Lord had said to Saul: *"Saul, why do you persecute me?"* given the arrogant pride that Paul possessed at that time, he might have said to Him: "This is why I persecute you, because you said, 'Why do you persecute me?' Who would not persecute you when powerlessly you provoke your persecutor with these feeble words?"

(3) But the humility of our Lord was heard in that voice, and the intensity of the light shone in the rays, so that Paul was unable to ignore the humility of the voice because of the radiance of the light.

Section XXXVIII

His ears became disciples to the voice that they heard, because his eyes could not endure the rays that they saw. Now this is amazing: the appearance of the light stunned his eyes and injured them, while the voice of the Lord of the light penetrated his ears without injuring them. Which should be stronger: the light, or the Lord of the light? If the light that His hand fashioned is this mighty, then how mighty must be the One in whose hand it was fashioned? If the Lord of the light is mighty, as He surely is, how did the voice penetrate

---

203. Acts 9.4.

the hearing without injuring it as the light injured his sight? Now listen to the amazing wonder that our Lord did in His goodness to bring assistance. Our Lord did not want to humble the light that He possessed, so the Lord of the light humbled Himself. Just as the Lord of the light is mightier than the light itself, mightier yet is the glory of the Lord of the light who humbled Himself rather than humble the light.

Section XXXIX

As it also is written: *An angel appeared to him to strengthen him during the night as he prayed.*[204] Now all the mouths of heavenly and earthly creatures are too feeble to give thanks to Him by whose hand the angels were created, who, for the sake of sinners, was strengthened by that angel that was created by His own hand. Just as that angel then was glorious and radiant while the Lord of the angel, in order to raise up fallen Adam, was weak and submissive, so here too, the light shone with intense brightness while the Lord of the light, in order to aid one persecutor, spoke in weak and submissive words.

Section XL

This is why that light, whose intensity was not decreased, penetrated the pupils (of his eyes) with its intense brightness and injured them, while the humble voice of the Lord of the light, who humbled his aid, penetrated needy ears and aided them. But so that the aid of that voice that was humbled could not be accused of deceit, the strength of that light was not humbled, so that by the light which was not humbled, the aid of that voice that was humbled would be believed. Now this is amazing. Until our Lord humbled His voice, Paul did not humble his actions. Although our Lord was in splendor with His Father before He came down to put on a body, people did not learn of His humility from His splendor. But when He humbled Himself and came down from His splendor, then in His humiliation His humility

204. Luke 22.43.

took root among people. When He was raised and ascended, again He was in glory at the right (hand) of His Father. But Paul did not learn his humility from this splendor. This is why the One who was exalted and sat at the right (hand) of His Father forsook glorious and exalted sounds, and in feeble, humble tones, like someone oppressed and wronged, cried out and said: *"Saul, Saul, why do you persecute me?"*[205] Then humble whispers overcame harsh bridles, for with humble whispers as bridles, the One who was persecuted led His persecutor from the wide road of persecutors to the narrow road of the persecuted. When all the signs that took place in the name of our Lord failed to convince Paul who was hurrying down the road to Damascus with arrogant haste, our Lord rushed to refute him humbly. Then with the sounds of humility He put an end to the rough haste of his arrogance.

Section XLI

The one who used humble words with Paul, His persecutor, used the same humble words with the Pharisee. Humility is so powerful that even the all-conquering God did not conquer without it. Humility was even able to bear the burden of a stiff-necked nation in the desert. Moses, the humblest of men, was given charge of the nation that was the most stubborn of all men. God, who needed nothing to save His people, later found Himself in need of the humility of Moses just to abide the grumbling and complaining of (His) critics. Only humility could tolerate the perversity of a nation that dismissed signs in Egypt as well as wonders in the desert. Whenever pride caused divisions in the nation, the prayer of humility[206] healed their divisions. Now, if the humility of a tongue-tied[207] man endured six hundred thousand,[208] how much more does His humility endure, who granted speech to the tongue-tied! For the humility of Moses is a (mere) shadow of the humility of our Lord.

205. Acts 9.4.
206. Literally, "humility through its prayer."
207. Cf. Exod 4.11.
208. Cf. Exod 12.37.

Section XLII

Our Lord realized that Simon the Pharisee was unconvinced by the wondrous signs he saw, so He came to him to convince him with humble tones. And the one whom mighty wonders failed to subdue submitted to humble words. Now, what were these wonders the Pharisee saw? He saw the dead live, lepers cleansed, and sight returned to the blind.[209] These are the signs that prompted the Pharisee to invite our Lord as a prophet. But he who invited Him as a prophet then insulted Him as someone who was ignorant, (for he said:) *"If this man were a prophet, he would know that this woman who approaches him is a sinner."*[210] Now let us insult the Pharisee and say: "If *he* were discerning,[211] he would have learned from the sinful woman who approached him that our Lord is not a prophet, but Lord of the Prophets!" The tears of the sinful woman were testimony that they were not appealing to a prophet, but to one who, as God, was angered by her sins. Because prophets were unable to give sinners life, the Lord of the Prophets Himself descended to heal those who engaged in all kinds of evil. What physician prevents the stricken from coming to him, you blind Pharisee who slandered our Physician?[212] Why did the stricken woman, whose wounds were healed by her tears, approach Him? He who descended to be a fountain[213] of healing among the sick announced: *"Whoever is thirsty, let him come and drink."*[214] When this man's fellow Pharisees took exception to the healing of sinners, the Physician explained this about His art, that the door was open to the sick, not to the healthy: *"The healthy have no need of a physician,* but those who have engaged in all kinds of evil."[215]

---

209. Matt 11.5; Luke 7.22; cf. Isa 29.18–19, 35.5–6, 61.1.
210. A free rendering of Luke 7.39.
211. Ephrem plays on the words *parāšā* "discerning" and *prīšā* "Pharisee."
212. See note 96 above.
213. MS. B, which left off at Section XXV, takes up again at this point.
214. John 7.37.
215. Cf. Matt 9.12; Mark 2.17; Luke 5.31–32.

(2) Healing the sick is a physician's glory. But to increase the disgrace of the Pharisee, who had disparaged the glory of our Physician, our Lord who worked signs in the streets, worked even greater signs once He entered the Pharisee's house than those that He had worked outside. In the streets, He had healed sick bodies, but inside, He healed stricken souls. Outside, He had given life to the death of Lazarus; inside, He gave life to the death of the sinful woman. He restored the living soul to a dead body that it had left, and He drove off the deadly sin from a sinful woman in whom it had dwelt. But that blind (Pharisee), for whom wonders were not enough, discredited the common things he saw because of the wondrous things he failed to see.

(3) He was a son of Israel who attributed weakness to his God, rather than to himself, (for they had said): *"If he struck a rock, and water poured out, is he not also able to give us bread?"*[216] When our Lord realized how wondrous things had eluded (the Pharisee's) feebleness, and with them common things as well, He quickly came up with a simple statement suited to an infant growing up on milk but incapable of solid food.[217]

Section XLIII

Pharisee, by whatever it is you know that our Lord is not a prophet, we know[218] that you do not know the Prophets. By stating: *"If this man were a prophet, he would know..."*[219] you indicated that whoever is a prophet knows everything. But note, there were things that were hidden from the Prophets. How, then, do you attribute the disclosure of all hidden things to the Prophets?[220]

216. Ps 78.20, Peshitta.
217. Heb 5.12; cf. 1 Cor 3.1–2.
218. Literally, "it is known."
219. Luke 7.39.
220. The section that follows incorporates several shifts in address. Although this is not uncommon in Syriac, the modern reader may find it distracting.

(2) This foolish teacher who scrutinizes the writings of the Prophets does not even know the (correct) interpretation[221] of their writings. It is not simply that this Pharisee failed to see our Lord's majesty; he did not see the weakness of the Prophets, either. Our all-knowing Lord allowed that sinful woman to enter and receive His greeting, but Elisha, who was ignorant, said to the Shunammite woman: *"Greetings to you and your child."*[222] So the man who thought he knew that our Lord was not a prophet is known as being someone who does not know the Prophets. Evil that is hidden in a mind that cannot restrain it, the evil that is in a clever one, always knows how to find an excuse for opening a door. As soon as the excuse that shelters the liar is discovered, he knows he will find yet another (excuse) to turn to his use.[223]

(3) Observe this son of Israel, whose fraudulence is like that of Israel, for paganism was hidden away in the mind of that nation.[224] This is why Moses was taken away from them, so that the evil within them would show itself. But in order neither to dishonor themselves nor to let it be known that they were asking for idols, they looked for Moses first, then for the idols. (They said:) *"We do not know what has become of this Moses."*[225] If God, who cannot die, brought you out of Egypt, why are you asking about a man who someday will die? Or perhaps Moses assured you: "I am your god, because your God is going to destroy the other god you petitioned"?

(4) Now they certainly did not want Moses to be their god, because Moses could hear and see and find fault. They were looking for a god who did not hear or see or find fault. And since Moses would die someday, what good would he be? For your God lives and has revealed Himself to you in

---

221. Literally, "readings."
222. 2 Kings 4.26, Peshitta. Elisha indicates by his greeting that he is ignorant of the child's death.
223. This thought is expressed again in the concluding sentence of Section XLIII.
224. The identical argument was presented in Section XIX.
225. Exod 32.1, Peshitta.

living testimony: that bright cloud above them sheltered them, the pillar of fire gave light to them by night, water flowed from the rock, and they drank from its streams. Everyday they enjoyed the taste of the manna, whose report we have heard. In what way was Moses removed from you, when behold, the signs of Moses were all around you? What advantage is the person of Moses to you when you have a provider such as this: your clothes do not wear out,[226] you are refreshed by soft breezes, heat and cold do not trouble you, you are free of battles and far from the fear of the Egyptians! So what did Israel lack that it should be searching for Moses? Blatant[227] paganism was all that it lacked. (Israel) was not searching for Moses; Moses was merely the excuse to go after the calf. And so we have briefly demonstrated that when the mind is intent on a certain thing, but it meets with some contradiction, it forcibly manipulates it to open the door to whatever it wants.

Section XLIV

And you, Pharisee, so thirsty for blasphemy, how did our Lord not seem to you to be a prophet? See, all the marks of the Lord of the Prophets could be observed in Him. Streaming tears immediately announced that they were being shed as in the presence of God. Plaintive kisses testified that they were coaxing the master of the debt to tear up the bill. The precious oil of the sinful woman proclaimed that it was a "bribe" for her repentance. These were the medications the sinful woman offered her Physician,[228] so that He could whiten the stains of her sin with her tears, and heal her wounds with her kisses, and make her bad name as sweet as the fragrance of her oil. This is the Physician who heals a person with the medicine that that person brings to Him!

(2) These were the wonders that were visible on that occasion. But instead of these, the Pharisee saw (only) blasphemy. What was there to conclude from the weeping of the

---

226. Deut 8.4; 29.4.
228. See note 96 above.
227. Literally, "open."

sinful woman, except that here is the One who justifies sinners? Decide in your own mind, foolish teacher. Why was this woman weeping so bitterly at a festive banquet, so that, while the guests were enjoying the food, she should be tearfully grieving? As a sinner, she was accustomed to engage in lewd behavior. If, on this occasion, she found her way back to innocence from sinful lewdness, then recognize, you who say, *"If he were a prophet,"*[229] that here is the One who makes the lewd respectable. From the fact that you know she is a sinner and that you now observe her repentant, ask yourself: "What changed her?" You[230] should have fallen down and worshipped the Silent One who made sinners pure with His silence, when the Prophets were unable to make them pure with their mighty voices.

(3) Something amazing and wonderful was witnessed in that Pharisee's house: a sinful woman sitting and weeping, without saying why she was weeping. Nor did the One at whose feet she sat ask: "Why are you weeping?" The sinful woman had no need to ask our Lord anything with her lips, because she believed that, as God, He knew the requests that were concealed in her tears. Nor did our Lord ask her: "What have you done?" because He knew that she was paying for shameful deeds with innocent kisses. And so, because she believed that He knew hidden things, she offered Him the prayers in her heart. The One who knows hidden things has no need of outward lips. If the sinful woman did not prevail upon our Lord with (the words of) her lips, (it was) because she knew He was God; and our Lord, being God, could see her thoughts. This is why she did not ask Him anything.

(4) You obstinate Pharisee, from the silence of the two of them, do you not discern the bearing of the two of them? She was asking Him in her heart, as God, and as God, He silently fathomed her thoughts.

(5) But the Pharisee could neither see nor understand

---

229. A gap begins in MS. A at this point. The text is supplied from MS. B for the length of the lacuna.

230. Literally, "he."

these things. Because he was a son of Israel, although he looked, he did not see. And when he heard, he failed to understand. When our Lord realized that the Pharisee was thinking evil of Him, He treated him kindly, not harshly. Sweetness came down from above to moderate our bitter propensity for evil. And so our Lord taught that Pharisee from his own experience:[231] "As I recognized the evil in your heart but dealt with you kindly, so I lovingly received this woman although I recognized her evil deeds."

Section XLV

Let us hear how patience pursued a hasty conclusion, and drew it from haste to discernment.

(2) *"A creditor had two debtors. One owed him five hundred dinars, the other, fifty dinars."*[232] Hearer, do not be wearied by the length of the parable's recitation, and act counter to the one who showed patience in the parable, for the sake of assistance. *"Finally, since neither of them was able to repay him, (the creditor) exonerated both of them. To which, do you suppose, was he more kind?"*

(3) *Simon answered, "I suppose to the one who had been forgiven more."*

(4) *Our Lord said to him, "You are correct."*

(5) Our Lord, in His justice, congratulated the perverse man for his correct judgment, who, in his wickedness, had condemned the Good One for the compassion He had shown.

(6) Many things are concealed in this parable; it is a treasury filled with much assistance.

(7) What[233] need did our Lord have for the Pharisee to decide about the two debtors, except to show majesty itself in pursuit of feebleness? A feeble thing does not follow after majesty. Our Lord, who knows hidden things, patiently questioned Simon, in order to shame the ignorant, who are quick to condemn but not to ask. "If I did not exonerate until I heard your opinion, why did you rush to condemn

---

231. Literally, "from and of himself."   232. Luke 7.41ff.
233. MS. A resumes.

the sinful woman before hearing her story from me?" This happened to teach us to be prompt to investigate, but slow to pass judgment.

(8) If the Pharisee had been patient, our Lord's forgiveness of the sinful woman would have taught him everything. Patience has a habit of granting everything to those who possess it.

Section XLVI

Again, by forgiving the two debtors, our Lord let the one experience forgiveness who stood in need of forgiveness, but in whose eyes the forgiveness of debts was abhorrent. While the Pharisee's own debts needed forgiving, forgiveness of the sinful woman's debts was abominable in his eyes. If forgiveness of debts had been on the Pharisee's mind, that sinful woman who came to God, not to priests, to forgive her debts, would not have appeared (so) disgraceful in his eyes. Priests were unable to forgive sins such as these, but because of the wonders our Lord worked, the sinful woman had faith that He could likewise forgive sin. She also knew that whoever could heal the parts of the body could whiten the stains of the soul as well. But the Pharisee, despite the fact that he was a teacher, did not realize this. The foolish teachers of Israel were used to being disgraced by the despised and rejected. They were disgraced by that blind man, to whom they said: *"We know that this man is a sinner."*[234] He said to them: "How did He open my eyes? After all, does God not hear the cry of sinners?"[235]

(2) These were the blind teachers who became the leaders of others, but whose own crooked path was set straight by a blind man.[236]

Section XLVII

Listen to the amazing thing our Lord did. Because the Pharisee had thought that our Lord did not know that the

---

234. John 9.24.
235. Cf. John 9.30.
236. Cf. John 9.39–41.

woman who approached Him was a sinner, our Lord made the Pharisee's own lips like harp strings, and played her sins on his lips without the Pharisee even realizing it.[237] And the one who had shown his disapproval as though he knew, found himself a harp on which someone else played what He knew. Our Lord compared the debts of the sinful woman to the five hundred dinars, and related them within the Pharisee's hearing in the parable that he heard. Then (the Lord) drew them out of his mouth with the judgment he rendered, without Simon realizing as he judged, that the five hundred dinars represented the sinful woman's debts. This same Pharisee who thought that our Lord did not know her sins, was found to be the one who did not know them when he heard her debts in the parable and voiced his opinion about them. But once it was finally interpreted for him by our Lord, then the Pharisee realized that his ears and lips had become like strings on which our Lord played the praises of his knowledge. This Pharisee was an associate of those scribes against whom our Lord passed judgment with their own mouths:[238] *"What will the owner of the vineyard do to those workers?"*[239] They said to Him, against themselves: *"He will utterly destroy them, and will lease the vineyard to workers who will bring him fruit at (harvest) time."* This is the divinity[240] for whom everything is easy: with the same mouths that slandered Him, He passed judgment against those very mouths.

Section XLVIII

Glory to the Hidden One who put on visibility so that sinners could approach Him.[241] Our Lord did not keep the sinful woman away, as the Pharisee thought (that He should). The sole reason He descended from the heights, which no

---

237. See the opening sentence of the *Homily* for the image of the harp.
238. Literally, "mouth."
239. Matt 21.40; cf. Mark 12.9; Luke 20.15.
240. In Syriac, *'alāhūtâ*, here applied to Christ. See note 14 above.
241. The juxtaposing of *kasyâ* ("hidden") with *lbeš galyūtâ* ("put on visibility") is classic Ephremic language for the incarnation. See notes 70 and 134 above.

one could reach, was so that short publicans like Zacchaeus could reach Him.[242] He who cannot be contained clothed Himself[243] in a natural body so that all lips might kiss his feet as the sinful woman (had done). The blessed ember[244] hid Himself in a garment of flesh that touched all unclean lips and made them holy. His feet invited tears, whose stomach, it was thought, had been invited to a banquet.

(2) This is the good Physician[245] who set out to go to the sinful woman who sought Him out in her soul.[246] She anointed the feet of our Lord, who had not trampled over her, she whom all had trampled over like dust. The Pharisees trampled over her. They justified themselves but ridiculed everyone (else). But the Merciful One, whose pure body made her impurity holy, showed her compassion.

Section XLIX

Mary anointed the head[247] of our Lord's body, as a symbol of the "better part" she had chosen.[248] The oil was a prophecy of what her mind had chosen.[249] While Martha was occupied with serving, Mary hungered to be satisfied with spiritual things from the one who also satisfies bodily needs for us. So Mary refreshed Him with precious oil, just as He had refreshed her with His most excellent teaching. With her oil, Mary indicated a symbol of the death of Him who put to death her carnal desire with His teaching.[250] With the investment of her tears, the sinful woman confidently gained the

---

242. The allusion is to Luke 19.2–10. 243. See note 70 above.
244. "Blessed Ember" is a Syriac title of Christ, used particularly in a eucharistic context in allusion to Isa 6.6. See Brock, *The Luminous Eye*, 81–82.
245. See note 96 above. 246. Literally, "mind."
247. Ephrem identifies Mary (and Martha) who anoints the feet of Jesus (John 12.3), with the woman mentioned in Matt 26.7 (Mark 14.3) who anointed the head of Jesus. On the fusing of Mary the mother of Jesus with Mary Magdalene see S. Brock, "Mary and the Gardener," *PdO* 11 (1983): 223–34; and Murray, *Symbols*, 146–48 and 329–35.
248. Cf. Luke 10.42.
249. Ephrem is here playing on the relationship between *mešḥâ* ("oil," "ointment") and *mšiḥâ* ("anointed," "Christ").
250. Cf. Matt 26.12; Mark 14.8: "She has contributed toward my burial preparation."

forgiveness of debts at His feet, while the woman with a flow of blood received healing from the hem of His garment.[251] Mary openly received the title "blessed" from His mouth in payment for the work of her hands at His head. She poured precious oil on His head and received a wonderful promise from His mouth.

(2) This is the oil that was planted on high but that put forth its fruit here below.[252] (Mary) planted at His head, and reaped fruit from His lips: *"She will have renown and this memorial everywhere my good news is proclaimed."*[253] What she received from Him was allowed to pass down to all generations, nor can it be kept from all generations. As the oil she poured on His head before all the guests gave off its fragrance and pleased Him, so too the good name He gave her spreads out to all generations and honors her. And just as all the banquet guests were aware of her oil, so too all who enter this world should be aware of her deed. This is the investment whose interest accrues throughout all generations.

Section L

When Simeon the priest took Him into his arms to present Him before God,[254] he saw and understood that (Simeon) was not presenting (Jesus), but that it was (Simeon) who was being presented by (Jesus). The Son was not presented to His Father by a servant; the servant was presented to his Lord by the Son. The One through whom every offering is presented cannot Himself be presented by another. An offering does not present the one who offers it; rather, offerings are presented by those who offer them. Conse-

---

251. Matt 9.20ff; Mark 5.27–29; Luke 8.44.

252. Ephrem merges the image of the oil (in Syriac, *mešḥâ*) that was poured on the head of Christ (in Syriac, *mšiḥâ*), with Christ himself, who was "begotten of divinity" and "underwent a second birth" (cf. Section II). Oil occupies a place of considerable importance in Syrian baptismal rites (see Brock, *The Holy Spirit in the Syrian Baptismal Tradition*, 37–40), and functions as a type of the gifts that Jesus gave, as well as the repository of divine gifts in the sacramental life of the church; see *Hymns on Virginity* 7.1–15). For the possible inspiration of this sentence see Ps 85.12–13.

253. Matt 26.13.   254. Luke 2.28.

quently, the receiver of offerings allowed Himself to be presented by someone else, so that, while presenting Him, those who presented Him might present themselves through Him. Just as He gave His body to be eaten, so that once eaten, it would give life to those who eat it, in the same way He allowed Himself to be presented, so that the hands of those who presented Him might be sanctified by His touch.

(2) So even though the arms of Simeon seemed to be presenting the Son, the words of Simeon testified that it was he who was being presented by the Son. Therefore, there can be no question for us about what happened; what was said puts an end to questioning: *"Now, therefore, you dismiss your servant in peace."*[255] Whoever is dismissed in peace to go to God is presented to God as an offering. And to make it known by whom he was being presented, he said: *"For my eyes have seen your compassion."*[256] Now, if goodness had not been at work in him, why would he be giving thanks? He was quite properly giving thanks because he had been (found) worthy to receive into his arms the one whom angels and prophets had eagerly longed to see: *"For my eyes have seen your compassion."*[257] Let us understand clearly: is compassion compassionate toward another, or is it shown compassion by another? If compassion is all-compassionate, then Simeon properly called our Lord "compassion," who showed him compassion by releasing him from a world filled with deceptions to go to an Eden filled with delights. It was the priest who said and attested that he was being presented like an offering that was being taken from this passing world to be deposited in safekeeping. Whenever a person finds what has been lost, he has the responsibility of safeguarding it. There was no possibility of our Lord becoming lost; those who had been lost were found by Him! So the servant, who had been very careful not to become lost, was presented by the Son, who could not be lost. *"For my eyes have seen your compassion."*[258] It is clear that Simeon carried compassion in the

255. Luke 2.29.
257. Luke 2.30.
256. Luke 2.30.
258. Luke 2.30.

baby he carried. He invisibly received peace from the child he visibly held in his arms. (That child) was glorious even when a feeble, little man carried him, and the one who carried Him became exalted by Him.

Section LI

Because Simeon was able to carry in his weak arms the very majesty that created things cannot endure, he knew that his weakness was strengthened by the power he carried.[259] At the same time Simeon, with all creatures, was invisibly being lifted up by the all-prevailing power of the Son Himself. This is amazing, that while a weak man was visibly carrying the power that gave him strength, that power was invisibly carrying the one who carried it. Majesty made itself small so that those who held it could endure it. As majesty bent itself down to our smallness, so should our love lift itself above every desire in order to meet majesty.

Section LII

And the boat that carried our Lord—it was (our Lord) who carried it when He stopped the wind that threatened to sink it (when He said): *"Be silent, be still."*[260] Although He was on the sea, His arm was able to reach the source of the wind and stop it. The boat carried His humanity, but the power of His divinity carried the boat and everyone in it. To show that not even His humanity required a boat, in place of the boards that the carpenter assembled and nailed, the Architect of Creation made the waters firm, assembling and subduing them under His feet. Our Lord strengthened the hand of Simeon the priest in the temple so that he could carry the power that carries all, just as it was He who strengthened the feet of Simon the Apostle so that they could support themselves on the water.[261] And so, the name[262] that carried the Firstborn in the temple, the First-

---

259. Cf. Section XXVIII. 260. Mark 4.39.
261. Cf. Matt 14.28–33.
262. I.e. *šemʿûn*, the Syriac for Simon the Pharisee, Simeon the priest and Simon the Apostle.

born later carried on the sea to show that, if He could carry him over a threatening sea, He did not need to be carried by him on dry land. Our Lord visibly carried him on the sea to teach us that He was also invisibly carrying him on dry land.

Section LIII

The Son came to the servant not to be presented by the servant, but so that, through the Son, the servant might present to his Lord the priesthood and prophecy that had been entrusted to his keeping.[263] Prophecy and priesthood, which had been given through Moses, were both passed down, and came to rest on Simeon. He was a pure vessel who consecrated himself, so that, like Moses, he too could contain them both. These were feeble vessels that accommodated great gifts, gifts that one might contain because of their goodness, but that many cannot accept, because of their greatness. Simeon presented our Lord, and in Him he presented the two gifts he had so that what had been given to Moses in the desert was passed on by Simeon in the temple. Because our Lord is the vessel in which all fullness dwells,[264] when Simeon presented Him to God, he poured out both of these

---

263. Ephrem views the presentation in the temple as the occasion upon which Jesus received the gifts of prophecy and priesthood from the priest Simeon, even though, in the *Commentary on the Diatessaron*, he traces the priestly line to Jesus through John the Baptist, who received it from his father, Zechariah. See Leloir, ed., *Saint Ephrem. Commentaire de l'évangile concordant*, 47–48. In either case, it is the understanding of the Syriac-speaking authors that Jesus received the Aaronic priesthood, perfected it, and transmitted it to the church. See Aphrahat, *Demonstration* 6.289.22. In at least one instance, in an apparent reference to Heb 5.6ff., Ephrem traces the priesthood that Jesus receives to Melchizedek:

> His divinity is from God,
> and His humanity is from mortals,
> His priesthood is from Melchizedek,
> His kingship is from the house of David.
> Blessed is His combining (of them)."
> *Hymns on the Resurrection* 1.12.

264. Col 2.9.

upon Him: the priesthood from his hands, and prophecy from his lips. The priesthood had always been on Simeon's hands, because of (ritual) purifications. Prophecy, in fact, dwelt on his lips because of revelations. When both of these saw the Lord of both of these, both of them were combined and were poured into the vessel that could accommodate them both, in order to contain priesthood, kingship, and prophecy.

(2) That infant who was wrapped in swaddling clothes[265] by virtue of His goodness was dressed in priesthood and prophecy by virtue of His majesty. Simeon dressed Him in these, and gave Him to the one who had dressed Him in swaddling clothes. As he returned Him to His mother, he returned the priesthood with Him. And when he prophesied to her about Him: *"This child is destined for the downfall and rising . . ."*[266] he gave her prophecy with Him as well.

Section LIV

So Mary took her firstborn and left. Although He was visibly wrapped in swaddling clothes, He was invisibly clothed with prophecy and priesthood.[267] Thus, what Moses had been given was received from Simeon, and it remained and continued with the Lord of these two (gifts). The former steward and the final treasurer handed over the keys of priesthood and prophecy to the One in authority over the treasury of both of these.[268] This is why His Father gave Him *the Spirit without measure,*[269] because all measures of the Spirit are under His hand. And to indicate that He received the keys from the former stewards, our Lord said to Simon: *"I will give you the keys of the gates."*[270] Now how could He give them to someone unless He had received them from someone else? So the keys He had received from Simeon the

---

265. Luke 2.12.   266. Luke 2.34.
267. See notes 70 and 241 above.
268. Ephrem introduces the image of the keys (Matt 16.19) as symbols of the passing of authority to Christ. Ephrem refers to Christ as both "steward" and "treasurer." See note 74 above.
269. John 3.34.   270. Matt 16.19.

priest, he gave to another Simeon,[271] the Apostle. So even though the (Jewish) nation did not listen to the first Simeon, the (Gentile) nations would listen to the other Simeon.[272]

Section LV

Because John also was the treasurer of baptism, the Lord of stewardship came to him to take the keys of the house of forgiveness[273] from him. John had been whitening the stains of debt with common water, so that bodies would be fit for the robe of the Spirit imparted by our Lord. Therefore, since the Spirit was with the Son, he came to receive baptism from John to mix[274] the Spirit, which cannot be seen, with water, which can be seen, so that those whose bodies feel the wetness of the water should be aware of the gift of the Spirit in their souls, and that as the outside of the body becomes aware of water flowing over it, the inside of the soul should become aware of the Spirit flowing over it. So when our Lord plunged down into baptism, He clothed Himself with baptism[275] and drew it out with Him, just as He had put on prophecy and priesthood when He was presented in the temple, and He left bearing the purity of the

271. See note 262 above.
272. Ephrem engages in simultaneous wordplays on *šemʿûn* ("Simeon"/ "Simon"), *šmaʿ*, ("hear"/"obey"), and *ʿammâ/ʿammê*, ("nation"/"nations"). For an example of similar verbal dexterity, see *Hymns on Virginity* 36.6, as noted by McVey, trans., *Ephrem the Syrian Hymns*, 422, n. 583.
273. In Syriac, *bêt ḥussāyâ*. The term *ḥussāyâ* has a long and rich history in Syriac. It was used by the translators of the Peshitta to render the Hebrew *kapporeth*, or "mercy seat" (Exod 25.17–19), the gold lid of the ark of the covenant where God was invisibly present on the Day of Atonement to accept the repentance of the people. In liturgical usage, it carries with it the sense of "absolution," "pardon," and even "exorcism." Finally, Syriac-speaking tradition uses the term as a title for Christ who became the forgiveness of sins and the locus of reconciliation with the Father. See R. Payne Smith, *Thesaurus Syriacus* (Oxford, 1879) 1:1222–23; also J. P. Amar, "The Syriac *Hussaya:* A Consideration of Narrative Techniques," *Diakonia* 22.3 (1988–89): 153–68.
274. In Syriac, *mzag*. See notes 100 and 195 above.
275. In Syriac, *lbeš maʿmûdūtâ*. See notes 70 and 241 above. Ephrem now speaks of Christ as "putting on baptism" as another necessary passage in His pursuit of fallen humanity. For the full progression of this movement, see *Hymns on the Church* 36.3–6 in Brock, *The Luminous Eye*, 70–74.

priesthood on His pure limbs and the words of prophecy in His innocent ears. When Simeon consecrated the body of the infant who consecrates all, that body took the priesthood with its consecration. Likewise, when Simeon prophesied over Him, prophecy hastened to the child's ear. If John leaped for joy in the womb[276] at the words of the Lord's mother, how much more should our Lord hear (Simeon's words) in the temple? For behold, it was because of Him that John was able to hear in the womb.

Section LVI

Every one of the gifts that had been laid aside for the Son, He picked from its[277] proper tree. He took baptism from the Jordan, even though John baptized again after Him. He took priesthood from the temple, even though the high priest Annas exercised it. And He also took prophecy, which had been handed down by the righteous, even though Caiaphas used it once to weave our Lord a crown.[278] And He took kingship from the house of David, even though Herod[279] kept the position and functioned in it.

Section LVII

This is the One who flew down from the heights, and when all those gifts He had given to the ancients saw Him, they came flying from everywhere and settled on the one who gave them. They assembled from everywhere and came to be grafted on their natural tree. For they had been grafted on bitter trees, that is, among wicked kings and priests. This is why they quickly came to their sweet root.

(2) This is the Divinity[280] who came down like rennet within the nation of Israel so that its parts would be gathered to Him. When He took from them what was His own, He left what was not His own. For the sake of what was His own, He even endured what was not His own. He endured

---

276. Luke 1.41.
277. Literally, "their."
278. Cf. John 11.50, 18.13–14, 19.2. 279. MS. B leaves off here.
280. In Syriac, 'alāhûtâ, here used in the context of the incarnation. See note 14 above.

Israel's idolatry for the sake of the priesthood. He endured (Israel's) soothsaying for the sake of prophecy. And he endured Israel's wicked authority for the sake of His holy crown.

Section LVIII

When our Lord took His priesthood from them, He consecrated all nations with it. When he took His prophecy, He revealed His promises to all generations with it. And when He wove His crown, He also tied up the mighty one who captures everyone,[281] and He divided his spoils. These gifts were absent from the fig tree[282] which, lacking fruit, lacked great deeds like these. This is why the one without fruit was cut down, so that these gifts might go forth and its fruits increase among all nations.

Section LIX

All these havens He passed through to come and make our bodies havens for His dwelling. Therefore let each of us become His dwelling! *"Whoever loves me, we will come to him, and make our haven with him"*[283] (says) the Godhead,[284] whom, without a single creature being lost to Him, a small, humble mind[285] can accommodate.

THE END OF THE HOMILY ON OUR LORD.

---

281. A return to the imagery in Section I.
282. Matt 2.19ff. Ephrem applies the image of the barren fig tree to Israel.
283. John 14.23.
284. In Syriac, *'alahûtâ*, here used in reference to Christ. See note 14 above.
285. Or "soul."

LETTER TO PUBLIUS

INTRODUCTION

The *Letter to Publius* was relatively unknown until 1901, when the great British scholar F. C. Burkitt, in his study of Ephrem's Gospel quotations, remarked that it was "surprising that no one has ever thought it worth while to edit."[1] Despite Burkitt's urging, no one undertook the task for over seventy years until Sebastian Brock edited the *Letter* with an accompanying English translation and commentary in 1976.[2] The *Letter* survives in a single manuscript, Brit. Lib. Add. 7190, ff. 188^r–193^r,[3] which W. Wright dates to the twelfth century.[4] The manuscript contains numerous extracts, from both Greek and Syriac writers, on various ascetical topics. It is from Brock's edition that the present translation was made.[5]

(2) Nothing is known of this Publius to whom the letter is ostensibly written. From section 17, we know that he was a baptized Christian, as Ephrem refers to the "imprint" he had received. Theodoret writes in his *History of the Monks of Syria* of a Publius who forsook his royal lineage and went off to live a solitary life in a hut not far from Zeugma in Euphratensis during the time of Valens (364–78).[6] The dates

---

1. F. C. Burkitt, *S. Ephraim's Quotations from the Gospels*, Texts and Studies (Cambridge, 1905) 7.2:70.

2. Brock, "Ephrem's Letter to Publius," 261–305. As will be evident, the present translation and commentary owe much to this edition. See also idem, "An Unpublished Letter of St. Ephrem," *PdO* 4 (1973): 317–23.

3. V. Rosen-J. Forshall, *Catalogus Codicum Orientalium qui in Museo Britannico asservantur,* part 1 (London, 1838) 80, n. 48.

4. W. Wright, *Catalogue of Syriac Manuscripts in the British Museum* (London, 1871) 1206.

5. The present translator would like to take this opportunity to thank Dr. Brock for passing on several suggested emended readings to a manuscript that is very difficult to read.

6. P. Canivet and A. Leroy-Molinghen, eds., *Théodoret de Cyr, Histoire des*

of Publius' solitary life thus correspond to Ephrem's final years in Edessa. It is also tempting to explain Ephrem's use of the imagery of royalty in terms of Publius' former life. The connection, however, is much too tenuous and nothing of certainty can be stated here.

(3) The literary format is that of a letter. Although there are not a few letters attributed to Ephrem, the *Letter to Publius* is one of the very few that are likely to be authentic.[7] The *Letter to the Mountaineers*,[8] the *Letter to the Men of Homs*[9] and the letter of Ephrem to the Catholicos Papa[10] are all spurious.[11]

(4) The *Letter to Publius* is essentially a meditative vision on the last judgment. Ephrem opens immediately with the imagery of the Gospel as a mirror. In this mirror, a favorite image of Ephrem,[12] the righteous are able to envision themselves in Paradise while the wicked and impious can only see the utter destitution and endless agony of Gehenna. This of course leads Ephrem to consider the sheep and the goats as

---

moines de Syrie 1:328–44. English translation in Price, trans., *A History of the Monks of Syria*, 58–62.

7. On the basis of the biblical text, Burkitt concluded that the letter was genuine, *S. Ephraim's Quotations from the Gospels*, 70. In his edition, Brock saw "nothing in its contents which militates against such a conclusion: the artistically balanced prose style, the imagery (in particular that of the mirror), the phraseology and the thought are all in favour of the attribution given in the manuscript." Brock, "Ephrem's Letter to Publius," 261.

8. See Beck, ed., *Sermones IV*, 28–43, and his comments in the accompanying translation volume, viii–xi. The contrary arguments of A. Vööbus, *A Letter of Ephrem to the Mountaineers: A Literary-Critical Contribution to Syriac Literature*, Contributions of the Baltic University, no. 25 (Pinneberg, 1947), can no longer be maintained.

9. This letter is still unedited; an extract is found in Brit. Lib. Add. 17193, fol. 10ᵛ–11ᵛ.

10. The apocryphal letter from Ephrem to the Catholicos Papa exists in an unedited Vatican manuscript. See P. Cersoy, "Les manuscrits orientaux de Mgr. David au Musée Borgia de Rome," *Zeitschrift für Assyrologie* 9 (1894): 370, no. 19 (f).

11. The only other letter that is certainly authentic is the *Letter to Hypatius*. See E. Beck, "Ephräms Brief an Hypatios übersetzt und erklärt," *OC* 58 (1974): 76–120.

12. See Beck, "Das Bild vom Spiegel," 1–24.

well as the parable of Lazarus and the rich man on which he dwells at some length.

(5) As Brock has already pointed out, this text is most remarkable for Ephrem's views on the nature of Gehenna. Ephrem insists that the traditional language and imagery about the last judgment are metaphorical; it is rather the individual's conscience, here reflected in the mirror, that serves as the real judge before Christ.[13] In many ways this notion is consistent with Ephrem's ideas on free will[14] and also anticipates the ideas found in the *Commedia* of Dante.

13. See, however, the very realistic vision given in *Sermones* II.2:137–76. Beck, however, questions the authenticity of this hymn. Ironically, Ibas was accused at the second Council of Ephesus of denying the literal reality of Gehenna.

14. See Bou Mansour, "Aspects de la liberté humaine chez saint Ephrem le Syrien"; and idem, "La liberté chez saint Ephrem le Syrien."

LETTER TO PUBLIUS

From the Letter to Publius

YOU WOULD do well not to let fall from your hands the polished mirror of the holy Gospel of your Lord,[1] which reproduces the image of everyone who gazes at it and the likeness of everyone who peers into it. While it keeps its own natural quality, undergoes no change, is devoid of any spots, and is free of any soiling, it changes its appearance before colors although it itself is not changed.[2]

> Before white things it becomes [white] like them.
> Before black things, it becomes dark like them.
> Before red things [it becomes] red like them.
> Before beautiful things, it becomes beautiful like them[3] and before ugly things, it becomes hideous like them.[4]

It paints every detail on itself. It rebukes[5] the ugly ones for their defects so that they might heal themselves and remove the foulness from their faces. It exhorts the beautiful to be watchful over their beauty and even to increase their natural

---

1. For the Gospel as a polished or smooth mirror, see *Hymns on Faith* 2.1, 12.19, 40.1, 67.8; and *Hymns on Virginity* 31.12. See also Beck, "Das Bild vom Spiegel," 5–24; idem, "Zur Terminologie von Ephraems Bildtheologie," in *Typus, Symbol, Allegorie bei den östlichen Vätern und ihren Parallelen im Mittelalter*, 239–77.

2. This same image is also found in *Hymns against Heresies* 32.7, 16.

3. See also *Hymns on Fasting* 9.1.

4. This is a common image in Ephrem for moral depravity. See *Hymns on Virginity* 11.1, 31.12; *Hymns against Heresies* 32.11. In *Hymns against Heresies* 32.3, Ephrem says the mirror becomes "perfect before the perfect and sickly before the sickly." See also below, 19.

5. The mirror also rebukes in *Hymns on Virginity* 11.1, 31.12; *Hymns on Faith* 18.12; *Hymns against Heresies* 55.7; and *Hymns on Nisibis* 16.4.

beauty with whatever ornaments they wish, lest they become sullied with dirt.

> Although it is silent, it speaks.
> Although it is mute, it cries out.
> Although it is reckoned as dead, it makes proclamation.
> Although it is still, it dances.
> Although it has no belly, its womb is of great expanse.[6]

And there in those hidden inner chambers every limb is painted and every body is framed in a bare fraction of a second. Within it they are created with undetectable quickness.

2. For this mirror is a foreshadowing of the holy tidings of the outer Gospel,[7] within which is depicted the beauty of the beautiful ones who gaze at it.[8] Also within it the blemishes of the ugly ones who are despised are put to shame. And just as this natural mirror is a foreshadowing of the Gospel, so also is the Gospel a foreshadowing of that heavenly unfading beauty by which all the sins of Creation are reproved and by which reward is given to all those who have preserved their beauty from being defiled with filth. To everyone who peers into this mirror, his sins are visible in it. And everyone who takes careful notice will see in it that portion which is reserved for him, whether good or evil.

> There the kingdom of heaven is depicted and can be seen by those who have a pure eye.[9]
> There the exalted ranks of the good ones can be seen.
> There the high ranks of the middle ones can be discerned.
> There the lowly ranks of the evil ones are delineated.[10]

---

6. Similar imagery is found in *Hymns on Faith* 81.6; for the womb of the mirror, see also *Hymns against Heresies* 32.4.

7. See Beck, "Das Bild vom Spiegel."

8. See *Hymns on Fasting* 9.1.

9. See *Hymns on Faith* 67.8, for the necessity of a pure eye. See also Brock, *The Luminous Eye*, 52–60. The image is clearly based on Matt 5.29.

10. Ephrem divides Paradise into three similar levels, *Hymns on Paradise* 2.10. See also Sed, "Les hymnes sur le paradis de saint Ephrem," especially, 463–67.

> There the beautiful places, which have been prepared for those
> worthy of them, are evident.[11]
> There Paradise can be seen rejoicing in its flowers.[12]

3. In this mirror, Gehenna in flames can be seen by those who deserve to dwell there.[13] In Paradise there are joyous promises for the good as they wait for [the day] when they will receive their masters with uncovered faces. But in Gehenna, the promises for the wicked will be grievous at the time when they see their masters abased in stature.

> There the *outer darkness* can be seen clearly and from within it
> can be heard the sound of wailing and *weeping,* of groans,
> *and of gnashing of teeth.*[14]
> There in their bonds people wail as they are tortured, and it be-
> comes more intense according to their wickedness so that
> they are punished with all justice.

4. There that *rich man,*[15] who used to wear different clothes every
> day and used to take delight in his luxuries, wails from
> anguish inside Sheol.
> There the groaning cry of the rich man can be heard crying
> out to Abraham, the father of the just, *"Send Lazarus,* your
> son, *to moisten my tongue for I am afflicted,*[16] for my sins are
> burning me up and my evil deeds *like coals of a broom tree*[17]
> are roasting me."

And there was sent from the mouth of the Just One[18] to that evildoer a direct reply, like a swift messenger with swift wings flying over that *dreadful chasm*[19] that has been set as a boundary between the good and the evil. And that letter of jus-

11. Cf. John 14. 2–3.
12. See *Hymns on Paradise* 10, *passim.*
13. See *Homily on Our Lord,* 5, above.
14. Cf. Matt 8.12, 22.13, 25.30.
15. Or, Dives, see Luke 16.19–31. Ephrem often alludes to this parable. See *Hymns on Paradise* 1.12, 7.27; *Hymns on Nisibis* 10.7; and *Sermones* I:3.159ff. See also 14, below.
16. Luke 16.24.
17. Ps 120.4. For this translation, see M. Dahood, *Psalms III*, Anchor Bible 17A (New York, 1970) 197.
18. Read *"dək'inâ"* for *"k'inâ."* The manuscript reads, literally, "the just mouth."
19. Luke 16.26.

tice, which was written by the mouth of the Just One, was carried forthwith and sent to the deaf ear of that one who had never opened the gate of his ear for any holy voice to enter. And in that letter, which it carried like a speedy messenger, were drawn those gentle sounds of just judgment: *"My son, remember that you received your precious and luxurious things while you were alive whereas at that time Lazarus* received his evils and *his afflictions.* And now he is unable to come to help you *in your torments* because you did not help him when he was in anguish from his diseases. For this reason you are seeking his aid just as he once sought your aid. But you refused. Now he is unable to come because that *great chasm,* which cannot be crossed, *is between us. No one* from you *can come to us, nor can any from us come to you."*[20]

5. Fix the eye of your mind and gaze on this mirror of which I spoke to you above.

Notice[21] *the twelve thrones* that are fashioned on it *for judgment.*[22]
Notice how the tribes stand there trembling and how the many nations stand there quaking.[23]
Notice how their bodies shake and their knees knock.
Notice how their hearts palpitate and how their minds pine.
Notice how their faces are downcast and how their shame is thick upon them like darkness.
Notice how their souls languish[24] and how their spirits flicker.
Notice how their tears overflow and soak the dust beneath them.
Notice how their complexions are changing to green. One takes on that color and hands it on to his companion.
Notice their faces, which used to be joyful, have been transformed to look like *soot from a cauldron.*[25]
Hear their many groans and their wailing moans.
Hear their sighs of grief and their churning innards.

20. Cf. Luke 16.25–26.
21. Similar anaphoras starting with "Notice" occur in *Hymns on Faith* 53; *Sermons on Faith* 6.233ff.; and *Sermones* I:5.568ff.
22. Cf. Matt 19.28 [=Luke 22.30].
23. The tribes are the Jews and the nations are the Gentiles. See also below, 7.
24. The root of this word, *psd*, is not found in any of the lexica. I follow here the suggested translation of Brock, "Ephrem's Letter to Publius," 296.
25. Cf. Joel 2.6; Nah 2.10 (11 in Peshitta).

Notice their deeds:
> those that were in secret have now become manifest;
> those that were done in darkness now shine forth like the sun;[26]
> those that they had committed in secret now make their complaint with loud voice.

Notice how everyone stands, his deeds before him justly accusing him in the presence of his judge.

Notice how their evil thoughts have now taken on shape and stand before their masters to accuse them.[27]

Notice their slanderous whisperings crying out in a loud voice, and how the snares once hidden are now revealed before them.

A little further . . .[28]

6. Notice that Judge of righteousness[29] as he sits,

> *the Word* of His father,[30]
> *the wisdom* of His nature,[31]
> the arm of His glory,
> the right hand of His mercy,
> the ray of His light,[32]
> the manifestation of His rest,
> that one who is equal in essence[33] with the one who begot Him,
> that one whose nature is commensurate with the nature from which He sprang forth,
> that one who is at once near and far from Him,[34]

---

26. Cf. Mark 4.22; Matt 10.26; Luke 8.17, 12.2. The same image occurs in *Sermones* I:5.326.

27. A similar image is found in *Hymns on the Church* 17.6, and in the appendix to the same collection, on p. 139.

28. Here is the division between the two fragments in the manuscript. We have numbered the paragraphs consecutively following Brock's "Ephrem's Letter to Publius."

29. Cf. Ps 9.8, 96.10–13, 98.9, et al.; 2 Tim 4.8. For Syriac love of titles, see Murray, *Symbols*, 159–204, 354–63.

30. Cf. John 1.1.

31. 1 Cor 1.24, 30.

32. See *Hymns on Faith* 71.20; and E. Beck, *Ephräms Trinitätslehre im Bild von Sonne/Feuer, Licht und Wärme*, *CSCO* 425 (Louvain, 1981).

33. In Syriac, šāweh b'îtûtâ. See Beck, *Die Theologie*, 5–13.

34. For Christ being both "near" and "far" from the Father, an Ephremic metaphor for "divine" and "human," see *Hymns on Virginity* 36.9; *Sermons on Faith* 2.711; and *Hymns on Nisibis*, 21.13, 50.6.

that one who is at once joined with Him and separated from Him,[35]
in His presence and not at a distance,[36]
at His right hand and not far away,[37]
who shares the same dwelling but not as a foreigner,[38]
the gate of life,[39]
the way of truth,[40]
the propitiatory *lamb*,[41]
the pure *sacrifice*,[42]
the *priest* who remits debts,[43]
the sprinkling that purifies,[44]
the one who created [all] that was made,[45]
the one who formed and the one who established,
the one who fashioned creatures,
the one who gives senses to the dust,
who clothes the earth with perception,[46]
who gives movement to all flesh,
who separates the places of every species,
who differentiates faces without number,
who renews the minds of all races,[47]
who sows all wisdom everywhere,
who *stretches out the heavens*,[48]
who adorned them with lights,[49]

35. See also *Hymns on Faith* 32.16, 40.2; *Sermons on Faith* 1.156, 2.593.
36. Cf. John 1.1.
37. Cf. Matt 26.64; Acts 2.33, 7.55, 56.
38. This is perhaps an anti-Marcionite phrase here. See also *Hymns on the Nativity*, 17.17.
39. Or "salvation." Cf. John 10.9.
40. Cf. John 14.6.
41. Cf. John 1.29, 36. This same progression of "gate . . . way . . . lamb" occurs also in *Hymns on Faith* 57.3. For the propitiatory lamb, see *Hymns on Faith* 62.3, and *Hymns on the Nativity* 3.15.
42. Cf. Eph 5.2.
43. Cf. Heb 2.17; see *Hymns on Paradise*, 4.3.
44. Lev 14.7, 17 et al. Cf. Num 8.7. The same expression is found in *Hymns on Virginity*, 31.4.
45. See John 1.3; Col 1.16; Heb 1.2.
46. Cf. Gen 2.7, and *Hymns on Faith* 50.5.
47. Cf. Rom 12.2.
48. Cf. Ps 104.2; Isa 40.22, 42.5, 44.24; Zech 12.1.
49. Cf. Gen 1.16–17.

who *gave names to them all*,[50]
who *spread out the earth on a foundation*[51] that cannot be touched,
who is the architect of the mountains,[52]
who built the high places,
who commands the grasses,
who causes trees to spring forth,
who causes woodplants to give seed,[53]
who causes fruit to grow,
who distinguishes tastes,
who gives color to blossoms and shape to all flowers,
who *measures heaven with His span*, with that power that can not be measured,
who meted out in the palm of His hand the dust of the earth in that right hand which cannot be meted out,
who weighed the mountains on scales with a knowledge that cannot be comprehended,
and the hills on a balance[54] with an unerring understanding

by which the *gathering places of the seas*[55] that envelop all Creation and the depths of the sea that cannot be grasped by us are considered to be even *less than a drop* there before Him.[56]

    7. God from God,[57]
       the second light of Being,[58]

50. Cf. Ps 147.4, and see *Hymns on the Church* 47.10.
51. Cf. Isa 48.13.
52. For Christ as architect, see *Hymns on the Nativity* 3.15; *Hymns against Julian* 4.22; and *Hymns on Nisibis* 48.10.
53. This is a conjectured translation; the Syriac word is otherwise unattested. See Brock, "Ephrem's Letter to Publius," 299.
54. Cf. Isa 40.12. The same "exegesis" of this verse from Isaiah can be found, almost verbatim, in P. Bedjan, *Homiliae Sancti Isaaci Syri Antiochae* (Paris, 1903) 1:49. This poem is perhaps the only known work that shows acquaintance with this *Letter*.
55. Cf. Gen 1.10.
56. Cf. Isa 40.15.
57. See *Homily on Our Lord* 8.
58. For Christ as "the second," i.e., of the Trinity, as a common designation for the Son in Ephrem, see *Hymns on Faith* 23.13, 40.1, and *Hymns on the Nativity* 26.5. For light, see John 1.4–5.

the treasure house of all riches that have been or will
  be made,[59]
the judge of the tribes,[60]
the measure of justice,
the *scale* without deceit,[61]
the even measuring rod,
the measuring bowl that is not false,
wisdom that does not err,
intelligence that cannot pass away,
the renewer of creatures,
the restorer of natures,
the resuscitator of mortality,[62]
who rolls away the cloud of darkness,[63]
who brings to an end the reign of iniquity,
who destroys the power of Sheol,
who shatters the *sting* of evil,[64]
who brings captives to the light,[65]
who raises up from *Abaddon*[66] those who were cast down,
who removes the darkness,
who makes worthy of rest,
who opens mouths that had been shut[67] and
who breathes in life just as of old.[68]

8. Look then upon that divine child whose names surpass the reckoning of mortals and whose titles are more numerous than the computations of the earth:[69]

59. See *Hymns on Virginity* 31.7; *Hymns on Faith* 24.2; and the *Homily on Our Lord* 9.
60. Cf. Matt 19.28 [=Luke 22.30]. See *Commentary on Genesis* XLIII.6, above.
61. Cf. Prov 16.11.
62. For this image see *Hymns on the Nativity* 3.9; *Hymns on Nisibis* 49.8, 65.15.
63. Cf. John 8.12.
64. Cf. 1 Cor 15.56; Hos 13.14; and the refrain to *Hymns on Nisibis* 37.
65. Cf. Isa 42.7.
66. Rev 9.11.
67. See the *Homily on Our Lord* 10; *Hymns on the Resurrection* 4.2; *Hymns on Nisibis* 59.16, 69.24.
68. Cf. Gen 2.7.
69. For the impossibility of enumerating all the titles of Christ, see *Hymns on Virginity* 4.5; *Hymns on Faith* 44.1ff., 53.13, 62–63, 82.6; *Hymns against Heresies* 53.13; and *Hymns on Unleavened Bread* 5.14.

> *King of kings,*[70]
> the Messiah affirmed by the prophets,[71]
> who spoke through the Prophets,[72]
> who sends the Spirit,[73]
> who sanctifies every soul in the Spirit, for His aid is manifest.[74]

Consider this *Only-Begotten,*[75] the multitude of His names, this one who *does the will of Him who sent Him,* this one whose will fulfills the will of Him who begot Him.[76] Look at Him, on that day, *sitting at the right hand* of Him who begot Him,[77] in that hour, *placing the sheep at His right hand and the goats at His left hand,* at that moment, *calling* out *to His blessed ones,* while giving them thanks, "Come, inherit that kingdom,"[78] which from of old had been made ready for them in His knowledge and *which from the beginning had been prepared for them.*[79]

> When He *was hungry they fed* Him in the poor. He *was thirsty and they gave* Him *to drink* in the disabled.
> He *was naked* and they *clothed* Him in the naked.
> He *was imprisoned* and they *visited* Him in the imprisoned.
> He *was a stranger* and they *took* Him *in* with the aliens.
> He *was sick* and they *visited* Him in the infirm.[80]

And when they did not make their good works known before Him, those same beautiful works, which were depicted on their limbs, sounded the trumpet and gave witness on

---

70. Cf. 1 Tim 6.15; Rev 17.14, 19.16.   71. Cf. Acts 10.43.
72. Heb 1.1.
73. Cf. John 14.26; and *Sermons on Faith* 4.179–80.
74. For Christ's manifest aid, see *Hymns on the Nativity* 3.18; *Hymns on Nisibis* 35.13, 42.5; *Homily on Our Lord* 24; and *Hymns on Unleavened Bread* 1.15.
75. Cf. John 1.14, 18; 3.16, 18; 1 John 4.9; and the general introduction, above.
76. Cf. John 4.34, 5.30, 6.38. See also *Sermons on Faith* 2.601.
77. Cf. Mark 16.19 and notes 36 and 37, above. See also *Hymns on Nisibis* 43.22; *Sermons on Faith* 1.79, 4.181.
78. Cf. Matt 25.33–34. See also *Hymns on the Crucifixion* 3.14.
79. See *Hymns against Heresies* 30.12.
80. For "hungry . . . sick," cf. Matt 25.35–40.

their behalf. Like luscious fruits on beautiful trees they hung on them and stood like bunches in order to be witnesses to the truth that these persons had truly wrought them.

9. For just as the deeds of the wicked are their accusers[81] before *the righteous Judge*,[82] making them bend and bow down their heads silently in shame, so also their beautiful deeds plead cause for the good before the Good One.[83] For the deeds of all mankind are both silent and speak—silent by their nature yet they speak when one sees them.

(2) In that place, there is no interrogation, for He is the judge of knowledge; nor is there any response, for when He sees it, He hears. He hears with sight and He sees with hearing. Because in that one thing, which is not a composite, is hearing and sight, swiftness, touch, sensation, smell, taste, discernment, knowledge, and judgment. Also by that which is not a composite, there is given out the reward of good things and the punishment of evil things to the two sides: those on the right hand and those on the left.[84]

(3) It is not that there really are a right and a left in that place, but rather these are names for those who are honored among us and for those in our midst who are unworthy. Rather we reckon that there is a throne for the Judge in that place and we call the place of the good "the right," while we label the place of the wicked "the left." We call the good "sheep" because of their docility, and we call the wicked "goats" because of their impudence. We call His justice "a balance" and His retribution to us "the measure of truth."[85]

---

81. Cf. Isa 59.12; Wis 4.20; 2 (4) Esd 7.35.
82. See note 29, above.
83. This title for God, stemming from Mark 10.17–18, is frequent in Ephrem. See *Hymns on Virginity* 25.1; *Hymns on Faith* 27.7; *Hymns against Heresies* 51.1; the refrain to *Hymns on the Church* 25, and also *Commentary on the Diatessaron* 25.1–11.
84. Cf. Matt 25.33.
85. See *Hymns on Paradise* 11.4–8, where Ephrem also insists that the terminology used of Paradise is metaphorical.

10. Take firm hold, then, of this clear mirror of the divine Gospel in your two hands and look at it with a pure eye that is able to look at that divine mirror. For not everyone is able to see himself[86] in it, but only the one whose heart is discerning, whose mind is sympathetic, and whose eye desires to see its helper. Look at it, then, and see all the images of Creation, the depiction of the children of Adam, both the good and the wicked. Within it can be observed the beautiful images of the works of the good and the unsightly images of the deeds of the wicked. They are conceived within it so that at their time they might be given birth either to praise those who did [the good works] or to rebuke[87] those who performed [the evil deeds]. See that just as here [the mirror] rebukes the ugly, so also there will it manifest within itself their ugly deeds. Just as here it sets out the good for praise, so there will it also mark out in itself their beautiful deeds.

11. At times even we when we were in error, mired in the pride of our mind as if with our feet[88] in the mud, did not perceive our error because our soul was unable to see itself. Although we would look [into the mirror] each day, we would *grope around* in the dark *like blind men*[89] because our inner mind did not possess that which is necessary for discernment. Then, as if from a deep sleep, the mercy of the Most High, poured out like pure rain, was sprinkled on our drowsiness and from our sleep we were roused and boldly took up this mirror to see our self[90] in it. At that very moment we were convicted by our faults and we discovered that we were barren of any good virtue and that we had become a dwelling place for every corrupting thought and a lodge and an abode for every lust.

---

86. Or, "his soul."

87. This is a conjectured translation as the manuscript is difficult to read here. See the various possible readings in Brock, "Ephrem's Letter to Publius," 302.

88. Dr. S. P. Brock kindly offered us this suggested reading after his edition was already published.

89. Cf. Deut 28.29; Isa 59.10.

90. Or "soul."

LETTER TO PUBLIUS 349

12. I saw there virtuous people and I longed for their beauties, [I saw] the places whereon the good were standing and I earnestly desired their dwellings.

I saw their bridal chamber[91] on the opposite side into which no one who did not have a lamp was allowed to enter.[92]

I saw their joy and I sat mourning the fact that I possessed none of the deeds[93] that were worthy of that bridal chamber.

I saw that they were arrayed in a garment of light,[94] and I was distressed that no noble garments had been prepared for me.[95]

I saw their crowns, which were adorned with victory, and I was grieved that I had no victorious deeds with which I might be crowned.

I saw there virgins knocking [at the gate], and there was no one who would open it for them,[96] and I wailed because I lacked the deeds of that blessed ointment.

13. I saw there many crowds shouting at the gate[97] and no one would respond to them, and I was alarmed that I had none of those virtues that had the power to open the gate of the kingdom.

I heard the clamor of many voices saying, *"Lord, Lord, open [the gate] for us."*[98] And a voice from there fell upon my ears, swearing to itself, *"I do not know you"*[99] to be worthy of salvation.[100]

I saw there those who were pleading, *"We ate and drank in your presence,"*[101] but [the voice] answered and said to them, *"It is not I whom you sought but only that you ate bread and were satisfied."*[102]

---

91. For the image of the bridal chamber in Ephrem, see *Hymns on Virginity* 5.10; *Hymns on Faith* 11.18.

92. Cf. Matt 25.1ff.

93. See *Commentary on the Diatessaron* 18.19, where the "oil of the lamps" also equals "good works."

94. See *Hymns on Paradise* 7.5, 24. See also Brock, *The Luminous Eye*, 65–76; and idem, "Some Aspects of Greek Words in Syriac," in *Synkretismus im syrisch-persischen Kulturgebiet*, ed. A. Dietrich, Abhandlungen der Akademie der Wissenschaften in Göttingen, no. 96 (Göttingen, 1975) 98–104, for the Jewish origin of this image.

95. Cf. Matt 22.12.

96. Cf. Matt 25.11–12.

97. Cf. Matt 25.10 [=Luke 13.25].

98. Matt 25.11 [=Luke 13.25].

99. Matt 25.12 [=Luke 13.25].

100. Or "life."

101. Luke 13.26.

102. John 6.26.

14. I also, like them, had always taken refuge in His name and had been honored in His honors and had always wrapped His name like a cloak over my hidden faults, but fear then seized me, terror shook me, and a great alarm counseled me to turn back so that perhaps those provisions required for *that narrow way that leads to* the land of *the living*[103] might come to me.[104] For I saw no one there who was able to give any relief to his companion or to *moisten* his *tongue* in that burning fire. For that deep *chasm*, which keeps the good separate from the wicked, did not allow them to give any relief to those others.[105]

15. I saw there pure virgins[106] whose virginity, because it was not adorned with the precious ointment of desirable deeds, was rejected.[107] They implored their fellow virgins to give them some assistance, but they received no mercy[108] and [they asked] that they might be given the opportunity to go and purchase for themselves some deeds, but this was not permitted them because the end, their departure from this life, was coming quickly. I drew near to the gate of the kingdom of heaven and I saw there those who did not bear the title "virgin" who were crowned with victorious deeds, for their virtues filled the place of virginity. For just as those who had been espoused[109] to Him only in their bodies had been rejected because they were naked of any garment of good deeds, so too those who had espoused their bodies in a chaste marriage while their spirit was bound to the love of their Lord were chosen, and they wore their love for Him like a robe with [their] desire for Him stretched over all their limbs.

16. And when I saw those there, I said to myself, "No one from henceforth should rely solely on the chaste name of virginity when it is lacking those deeds that are the oil for the lamps." And while I was being reproved by this dreadful vision of others being tortured, I heard another voice from the mouth of the mirror crying out, "Keep watch, O feeble

---

103. Or, "land of salvation."
104. Cf. Matt 7.14.
105. Cf. Luke 16.24–25. See also *Hymns on Paradise* 1.17.
106. Cf. Matt 25.1ff.
107. See *Sermons* I.2.1227–28.
108. Cf. Matt 25.8–9.
109. See *Hymns on Virginity* 5.10.

one, over your wretched soul. *It is a fearful thing to fall into the hands of the living God.*"¹¹⁰ Have you not heard children shouting to you, *"If a man gain the whole world yet lose his soul what will he gain?"* or, *"What shall he give in return for his soul?"*¹¹¹ Do you not see what happened to that man whose land yielded abundant crops because he said to his soul, *"My soul, eat and drink, be at ease, and enjoy yourself for abundant crops have been gathered in for you for many years?"*¹¹² Have you not heard that while this word was yet sweet in his mouth a bitter word was poured into the womb of his ear.¹¹³ Although it had no understanding, it cried out saying, *"On this very night your beloved soul is required of you. This thing which you have prepared, whose will it be?"*¹¹⁴

17. Be alarmed by this your seal, and consider where all the children of Adam are, who *like locust*¹¹⁵ have swarmed over the earth since the first day. Rouse yourself from this deep sleep that is enfeebling you and that is spreading over all your limbs like a shadow of death. Rise, then, and bring yourself back to those former generations about which you have heard. Where is Adam? Where are your fathers who like fatted sheep lived luxuriously in the midst¹¹⁶ of the Paradise of Eden, who like friends spoke fearlessly with God, whose arms made all creatures obedient to their authority, whose power held the authority over sea and dry land, whose feet *tread upon* the dreadful *serpents*¹¹⁷ and before whom those beasts, which are rebellious nowadays, bent their necks, whose minds used to reach up to heaven and to seek out the deepest part of the deep as if it were dry land?

18. Where are those ten generations from Adam to Noah?¹¹⁸ Were they not washed away in that flood of waters?¹¹⁹

110. Heb 10.31.
111. Matt 16.26.
112. Luke 12.19.
113. For the image of the ear's womb, see *Hymns on the Church* 49.7 and *Sermons on Faith* 1.197.
114. Luke 12.20.
115. Cf. Isa 40.22.
116. Literally, "in the womb." See *Hymns on Paradise* 10.1, 15.9.
117. Cf. Ps 91.13.
118. See Gen 5.
119. Cf. Gen 7.1–24.

Where are those generations of the Sodomites? Were they not also swept away in a flood of fire?[120]
Where are those generations from then until today?
Where are those who in that time used to live for almost a thousand years?

Have they not diminished and passed away? If the ink written on goatskins had not preserved for us the memory of their names, we would not even have known that they had ever existed.[121]

19. Come, I will lead you out to the gloomy sepulchres.
Come down, in your mind, with me even to lowest Sheol and I will show you there kings cast down upon their faces, their crowns buried in the dust with them.
Come, see the princes, those who once luxuriated in silks, how the worm has now become their bed and the grub their covering.[122]
Come, look at those military chiefs who used to command thousands of armies, how they have become useless vessels of dust and things of no understanding.

Look carefully at the dust of the earth and consider that it is your kin.[123] How long will you delude yourself and think that you are any better than *the grass on the housetops*?[124] For the heat of one day dries out the grass. The burning fever of a single day also causes a desirable body to become parched.

(2) Where are the kings,[125] their raiment, their crowns, or their purple?[126] Where are their dominions, their battles, their armies, their companies, their treasuries, or their wealth? See how their spears are shattered, their bows destroyed, their swords rusted, their arms eaten by worms. Their generations have departed and passed on, the threads

---

120. Cf. Gen 19.28. The expression "flood of fire" occurs also in *Commentary on Genesis* XVI.8. For similar expressions, see Brock, "Ephrem's Letter to Publius," 303–4.
121. Cf. Wis 2.2.
122. Cf. Isa 66.24; Mark 9.48; James 5.1.
123. Cf. Gen 3.19.
124. Cf. Ps 128.6; Isa 40.7–8.
125. Cf. Bar 3.16.
126. See *Hymns on Nisibis* 74.10, 76.21.

of their lives are severed like a tent full of worms at their death, and like *a web about to be cut*;[127] their military expeditions are cut down and they are brought to ruin.

20. Notice how their songs have turned to mourning, their harps to the sound of weeping, how their laughter is overcome by mourning, their sweet melodies by songs of lamentation. The garment of a spider has been woven for them there and a bed of worms lies beneath them and a covering of moths is spread over them like a tunic.[128] Tables lie upended before them. Their splendid state of luxury is completely reversed. Their administration is destroyed and is rendered useless. Their glory is laid out in the dust and all their luxury is also buried there in ashes. Bridegrooms are plundered and brides are forsaken who have been thrown out of their bridal chambers, and the crowns have withered on their heads and together with them they are sprinkled with the dust from the earth. Over them is spread a garment of darkness which Sheol has woven for them on a dingy loom. From every mouth there you hear the sound of wailing because there is no one there who can console his companion.[129]

21. Everything that their eyes see causes them suffering, for when they reach out to the boundary of the chasm, they quickly pass over it and fly to the garden of Eden and hover over the Paradise of God[130] and see the blessed place of rest and are filled with desire for the banquet tables of the kingdom.[131] And they hear the sound of pure melodies combined with holy songs and intermingled with the praises of God. And as they stretch out they soar to heaven and the gates of the kingdom are opened. Before their Lord they hover with joy, sending only the sound of their mouths back and forth to each other. There the vision of their eyes is allowed to come and go, and on the two sides[132] it either

---

127. Cf. Isa 38.12.
128. Cf. Isa 59.5–6; and also *Sermones* I.4.54.
129. Cf. Luke 16.26; 2 (4) Esd 7.104–5.
130. See *Hymns on Paradise* 1.12, 7.29.
131. Cf. Luke 22.30. See also *Hymns on Paradise* 2.5, 7.24.
132. See *Hymns on Paradise* 7.29.

grieves or gives joy so that when the good look out upon the wicked their lot increases and they rejoice therein. But, as for the wicked, their souls are condemned and their distress is multiplied.[133]

22. Perhaps, for the wicked, that which they see is Gehenna, and their separation is what burns them with their mind as the flame. That hidden judge who dwells in the discerning mind has spoken and there has become for them the judge of righteousness and he scourges them without mercy with torments for the compunction of their soul. Perhaps, it is this that separates them and sends each of them to the place suitable for him. Perhaps, it is this that lays hold of the good with its extended right hand and sends them to the Exalted Right Hand. It also takes hold of the wicked in its left hand, equal in power, and casts them into the place which is called "the left."[134] And perhaps, it is this that silently accuses them and quietly pronounces judgment upon them.

23. In this matter, I believe the inner mind has been made judge and law, for it is the embodiment of the figure of the law and itself is the figure of the Lord of the law. And for this reason there is given to it complete authority

> to be portioned out in every generation although it is one,
> to be imprinted on every body although it is indivisible,
> to be painted on every heart although it is inseparable,
> to fly over all without tiring,
> to rebuke all without shame,
> to teach and guide all without compulsion,[135]
> to counsel them with no constraint on them,
> to remind them of the judgment to come while cautioning them,
> to recall to them the kingdom of heaven so that they might yearn for it,
> to point out to them the beneficent rewards so that they might desire them,
> to show them the severity of the judgment so they might restrain themselves,

---

133. See *Hymns on Paradise* 1.17.
134. Cf. Matt 25.33.
135. See *Hymns on Nisibis* 16.6.

to make known to them the sweetness of the Only-Begotten so that they might be comforted.

With them [the mind] runs after all good things, strengthening them. Over them it flies when they incline to hated things and reproves them. For its mercy is similar to that of its Lord in that it does not turn away from them when they are defiled with impurities and is not ashamed of them when they are wallowing in the mud. As for those who obey it, it will remember them and as for those who do not heed it, it will recall to them. Here it is mingled with them in every form whereas there it stands before them on this day [of judgment].

24. And when I saw these things in that bright mirror of the holy Gospel of my Lord, my soul became weak and my spirit was at an end and my body was bent down to the dust; my heart was filled with bitter groans that perhaps my stains might be made white by the washing of my tears. And I remembered that good Lord and kindly God *who cancels through tears the bond* of those in debt[136] and accepts lamentation in the place of burnt sacrifices.[137] When I came to this point, I took refuge in repentance and I hid myself beneath the wings of compunction. I sought refuge in the shade of humility and I said, "What more than these am I required to offer to Him who has no need of sacrifices and burnt offerings?" Rather, *a humble spirit*, which is the perfect sacrifice that is able to make propitiation for defects, *a broken heart* in the place of burnt offerings, and tears of propitiation in the place of a libation of wine are things which God will not reject.[138]

25. That, then, which I saw in that living mirror that speaks, on which the images of all the deeds of men move—from Adam until the end of the world and from the resurrection until the day of the judgment of righteousness—and that which I heard from that blessed voice that could be heard from inside it, I have written for you in this letter, my beloved brother.

---

136. Cf. Col 2.14.
138. Cf. Ps 51.17.

137. See *Hymns on Virginity* 13.9.

INDICES

GENERAL INDEX

Aaron, 222, 230, 236, 240–41, 254, 256, 262–63, 265; sons of, 260
Ab, 237
Abaddon, 345
Abba Bishoi, *see* Bishoi, Abba
Abel, 59, 69, 124–28, 133; blood of, 127, 130, 143; cheeks of, 131
Aberbach, M., 79
Abercius, bishop of Hierapolis, 7
Abgar V Ukhama, King of Edessa, 8–10, 34
Abgar VIII the Great, 9
Abimelech, 71, 154, 165–67, 172
Abraham, 33, 70–73, 148–60, 165–71, 176, 179, 198–99, 212, 223–24, 226, 230–31, 233, 235, 248–49, 252, 340; *see also* Just One; descendants of, 67, 149, 151–54, 167, 169; *see also* just ones; house of, 71, 152, 158, 168, 196, 258; tent of, 70, 146, 158–59, 168; tribe of, 170; Abram, 148–51, 154, 167; herdsmen of, 150
Absimius, 26
Abu 'Afr, 7
abyss, 77–78, 80, 89, 92, 98, 121, 141; creation of, 77; face of, 77–78; of waters, 77
Achaemenid empire, 26
Acts of the Persian Martyrs, 44
Acts of Thomas, 11, 38, 44
Adah, 131
Adam, 43, 47, 53–54, 60, 64, 69, 90, 92–95, 97, 99–110, 113–24, 127, 130, 133–34, 162, 165, 209, 211–12, 270–71, 284, 286, 314, 351, 355; descendants of, 90, 92, 95, 133, 286, 348, 351; *see also* Abel, Cain, Seth; house of, 69, 107, 115, 290
Addai, 9–10; *see also Doctrine of Addai*
Adiabene, 9–10, 28, 147
adulterer, adulteress, 164, 282–83

adultery, fornication, 163, 166, 183, 185, 282–83
air, 84, 92, 109, 243, 297
Akkad, Akkadia, 26, 147
Alexander, P., 136
Alexandre, M., 94, 100, 123
Alexandria, School of, 68
alien, *see* foreigner
All-knowing One, *see* God, titles of
All-Wise, *see* Christ, titles of
allegory, 62, 68, 74, 338; *see also* exegesis; literary techniques
altar, 71, 142, 168–69, 181, 256, 259–60, 263, 265
Amar, J. P., ix, xvii, 15, 17, 21–22, 25, 27–28, 33, 35–38, 43, 60, 330
ambassador of peace, 72
Amelech, 222, 251, 255–56
Amelechites, 256
Amid, 31–33
Ammianus Marcellinus, 32–33
Amorites, 154, 167, 252; land of, 224
Amphilochius of Iconium, 16, 22
Ananišoˆ, 15
anaphora, 274, 341
Anderson, G. A., 101
Aner, 150
angel, watcher, 14, 43, 70, 72, 76, 105, 109, 112, 116, 123, 135, 145, 155–56, 158, 160–62, 164, 167–69, 173–74, 180–81, 222, 231, 235, 247, 250, 260, 277, 283, 301–3, 314, 326
anger, fury, rage, wrath, 72, 119, 126–28, 136, 143, 159, 176, 194, 201, 207, 209, 234–35, 298–99, 302–4, 306; *see also* God, attributes of
animal, beast, 90–91, 93, 95–96, 99, 103–7, 109–10, 112, 118–19, 121, 124, 132, 137–40, 142–43, 154, 191, 208, 232, 241–43, 245, 351

359

Annas, 331
anti-Jewish character of texts, 30; *see also* Jews, Jewish nation
Antioch, 11, 19
Antioch by the Callirhoe, *see* Edessa
Antiochus IV Epiphanes, 33
antithesis, *see* literary techniques
Apamea, 206
Aphrahat, *Demonstrations*, 3, 10, 20, 30, 38, 41, 44, 63, 235, 247, 275, 297, 328
Apophthegmata Patrum, 3, 60
Apostles, 55, 118, 211, 270–71, 274, 290; *see also* the names of individual apostles; the Twelve, 210
Aptowitzer, V., 124
Aqedah, 167
Arabia, 7
Arabs, 73, 182, 196
Aramaic language, 5, 74
Ararat, *see* Mount Ararat
architect, *see* Christ, titles of; of Creation, *see* Christ, titles of; of the flesh, *see* Christ, titles of; of the mountains, *see* Christ, titles of
Arianism, 50, 277
Arians, 50
Arius, 35
Ark of Noah, 69, 83, 137–45, 141–42; of the Covenant, 59, 206; arm of His glory, *see* Christ, titles of
Armenia, 6
arms, 175, 199, 207, 211, 227, 256, 305, 325–27, 342, 351–52
army, 232–33, 249–50, 252–53
Arpachshad, 148
arrogance, 106, 128, 294, 315; *see also* pride, humility
arrow, 211, 299
asceticism, 11–12, 15, 17–20, 24, 35, 39, 273, 335; *see also* encratism, eremetical life, monastic practices; in Jewish sectarian ideology, 11
Asher, 177, 206, 210
ashes, 242, 353
ass, 139, 155, 204, 254
Assemani, J., xv, xvii, 63, 226
Assemani, S. E., 63, 219
assembly, 309

Assyrian Church, *see* Church of the East (or Assyrian, or Nestorian Church)
astrology, 218–19
astrology, astrologers, 224; *see also* magic, magicians
Atargatis, cult of, 34
Atonement, Day of, 330
Audiens, 50
authority, 30, 104, 143, 186, 207–8, 224, 228, 329, 332, 351, 354; *see also* dominion, rule
avarice, 108
Azema, Y., 3, 39
Azizos, cult of, 34

b'nay q'yama, 20; *see also* Daughters of the Covenant
Babel, Tower of, 67, 70, 147–48
Babu, 28–29
Bailey, L. R., 141
Balai, 3, 38, 42
banquet, *see* feast
baptism, 12, 50, 54, 276–77, 302, 325, 330–31; *see also* Christ, clothing of; John the baptist
Bar Hebraeus, 74
Bar-ammi/Ben-ammi, 164
Barak, 206
Bardaisan, 7, 13, 34–37, 49–50, 61–62, 64, 75–77, 79, 86–87, 218, 243; son of, *see* Harmonius; disciples of, 61; *On Fate*, 37; teachings of, 60–61
Bardaisanites, teachings of, 75
Bardy, G., xvii
Barhadbešabba, 22, 29, 36, 218
Barnard, L. W., 6
Barr, J., 94
barrenness, 71, 149, 152, 155, 157–59, 163, 171, 176; *see also* birth, pregnancy, womb
Barsamya, *see* martyrs of Edessa
Basil of Caesarea, 13, 15–16, 79
Bauer, W., 6, 8, 79
Baumstark, A., 17, 23
beast, *see* animal, beast
Beck, E., xv–xviii, 19–20, 24, 30, 32, 37, 39–42, 45–46, 50, 53, 55, 61–62, 74–75, 79, 120, 137, 211,

INDEX 361

272–74, 277, 280, 306, 310, 336–38, 342
Becker, H., 41
Bedjan, P., 15, 22–23, 28, 344
Behemoth, *see* Leviathan and Behemoth
Being, *see* God, titles of
being, earthly, 181; heavenly, 112, 302; human, 104, 149, 210, 306; living, 99, 123; physical, 275; self-existent, 67–68, 87; self-subsistent, 75, 86; spiritual, 76, 275
Bel, cult of, 34
Bellarmine, R., 3
belly, 118; *see also* stomach
Ben-ammi, *see* Bar-ammi
Benedict XV, Pope, 18
Benjamin, 190–94, 196–97, 200, 208, 211
Bestul, T. H., xviii
Beth Garbāyê, 33
Bethel, 174, 181
Bethuel, 170
Bethune-Baker, J. F., 74, 274
betrayer, *see* Satan
Bevan, E. A., xvi, 43, 47
Bezabdê, 31–32
Bickell, G., xvi
Bidez, J., 13, 25
Bilhah, 72, 176, 201
bird, 80, 91–95, 99, 103–4, 124, 137–40, 142, 152–54
birth, 55, 71, 81, 119, 124, 131, 156, 163–64, 166, 171, 176, 247–48, 254, 275–77, 286, 296, 325; *see also* pregnancy, womb, barrenness; natural, 275; of Christ, 275–77; pangs of, 118–19, 121–22, 166, 171; physical, 274–75, 296; spiritual, 275–76
birthright, 71, 171–72, 200, 206; *see also* Esau, blessings of
Bishoi, Abba, 15–16
bishop, 7, 9, 17, 20, 24, 27–30, 37, 218, 264, 281, 290
bitterness, 254, 280, 300
Blackmann, E. C., 62
Blanchard, M., 16
blasphemy, *see* slander
blessing, 69, 72–73, 82, 95–96, 103, 119, 145–46, 158, 172–73, 180, 183, 191, 199, 207–9, 226, 248, 275, 282, 284; dew of, 84; of Jacob's sons, 73
blind, blind man, 287, 291–92, 308–9, 311, 316–17, 322, 348
blood, 143, 182, 202, 204, 222, 225, 229, 233, 235, 239–40, 246, 252, 260–62, 281, 285, 306, 325
Bloomfield, B. C., 6
blossoms, 275, 344; *see also* flowers
boat, 101, 327
body, 8, 19, 32, 94, 114, 122, 136, 232, 242, 259, 274, 276, 278–79, 281–90, 293, 297, 299, 309, 314, 317, 322, 324, 326, 330–32, 339, 341, 350, 352, 354–55; physical, 276
Body of Christ, *see* Christ, body of
Bojkovsky, G., xvi
bondage, *see* captivity; *see also* captive; slavery, servitude
bonds, *see* chains
Book of Steps, 38
Book of the Laws of the Countries, 37–38; *see also* Harmonius
Borborians, 50
Botha, P. J., xviii
Bou Mansour, T., xviii–xix, 45–46, 48, 53, 68, 218, 227, 240, 243, 284, 306, 337
Bouvy, E., 16
bow, 199, 207, 211; *see also*, rainbow, weapon
Bowder, D., 31
Bowersock, G., 31
Bravo, C., xix, 47
bread, 120, 150, 158, 167, 174, 195, 206, 229, 247, 317, 349; eucharistic, 287; from heaven, 254; *see also* manna; leavened, 260; unleavened, 247
breast, 166, 208
breath, 99
briar, *see* thorn
bribe, 309–10, 319
bride, 163–64, 353
Bridegroom, *see* Christ, titles of,
bridge, *see* cross as bridge
bridle, 280–81, 315; *see also* yoke

Brinkman, J., 7
Brock, S. P., xvi, xix, xxx, 4–7, 25, 33, 41–42, 44–46, 49, 52–54, 59, 63, 66–67, 101, 106, 149, 167, 269, 273–74, 277, 280, 284, 296, 302, 324–25, 330, 335–37, 339, 341–42, 344, 348–49, 352
Brooks, P., 12
brother, 72
Brown, P. R., 19, 47
Browning, R., 31
Bruns, P., xix
Budge, E. A. Wallis, 15
bull, 124, 139, 143, 198, 241, 254, 260
Bundy, D. D., xx, 30, 35, 62, 64–65
buried, *see* dead
Burkitt, F. C., xvi, xx, 4, 34, 43, 47, 77, 335–36
burning bush, 217, 222, 231–32
burnt sacrifices, *see* sacrifices, burnt
Byzantine liturgy, 6; Kontakion *see* Kontakion, Byzantine

Caiaphas, 331
Cain, 59, 69, 124–33, 143; daughters of, 135–36; descendants of, 129, 132–33, 136; house of, 133–34, 136; shame of, 129; son(s) of, 69; sons of, 135; tribe of, 69, 136–37
Calah, 147
calf, 124, 154; fatted, 158; golden, 223, 251–52, 262–65, 282–83, 292–93, 319
Cameron, R., 11
camp, 205, 209; of Egyptians, 250; of Hebrews, 250; of the Hebrews, 264–65
Canaan, 69, 70, 145–46, 149, 153, 189, 224, 253
Canaanites, 151, 167, 169, 173, 182, 240; land of, 232, 253
Canivet, P., 19, 27, 335
Cappadocia, 19
Cappadocian Fathers, 269
Cappadocians (inhabitants of Cappadocia), 146
captive, imprisoned, 345–46; *see also* prison
captivity, 146, 154, 296

captor, *see* Satan
Caquot, A., xx, 123, 149
carpenter, 280, 327; *see also* Christ, titles of
Casetti, P., 168
Caspian Sea, 29
Catastini, A., 229
Cathars, 50
cattle, 93–94, 96, 99, 104, 129, 131, 154, 198, 242–43, 246
cave, 71, 169
celibacy, 11–12, 20, 142
censer, 285
Cersoy, P., 336
Chabot, J. B., 17, 26
chains, bonds, fetters, irons, 123, 182, 187–88, 196, 300–301, 313, 340, 355
Chalcedonians, 47
Chaldeans, 92, 142, 152
chamber, 185, 193; bridal, 349, 353; inner, 339
chaos, 61
chariot, 198, 251–53; of Pharaoh, 187–88
charity, 51
Charlesworth, J. H., 38
Charon, C., 6
chasm, 280, 306, 340–41, 350, 353
chastity, 142, 170
Chaumont, M.-L., 6–7
Chedorlaomer, 150
cherub, cherubim, 54, 109, 123–24, 262
chiasm, *see* literary techniques
children, 106, 119, 134, 155, 163, 165–66, 170, 176–77, 191, 206, 221, 223–26, 231, 235, 237, 241, 244–45, 248–52, 258
Chionites, 28
Christ, 53–54, 133, 169, 174, 213, 260, 269–271, 274, 279, 286–87, 301, 307–14, 325, 329, 337, 342; as teacher, 298; attributes of; *see also* God, attributes of; all-knowing, 318; compassion, 301, 321, 324, 326; equal in essence with the Father, 342; exaltedness, 311; feebleness, weakness, 310, 312–13, 327; fountain of healing,

316; fullness, 287; gentleness, 272; glory, 276, 314–15, 317, 327; goodness, 273, 275, 282, 297–98, 312, 314, 324, 329; humility, 272, 298, 300, 310–11, 313–15; justice, 312, 321, 347; knowledge, 293, 297, 344, 346; majesty, 275, 310–11, 318, 321, 327, 329; meekness, 298; mercy, 355; might, 313; power, 271, 327, 344; silence, 320; splendor, 314–15; sublime, 310; sweetness, 321, 355; tenderness, 289; truth, 295–96; will, 225; body of, 51, 204, 276, 278–79, 281, 284–89, 297, 314, 324, 326, 331; *see also* church (Mystical Body), eucharist; as fountain of life, 284; as treasurer of His wealth, 285; ears of, 331; feet of, 274, 289, 293–94, 320, 324–25, 327; fingers of, 286–87; hand(s) of, 281, 292, 298, 305, 313–14, 329, 344, 346; head of, 324–25; limbs of, 286, 288, 331; lips of, 289, 325; mouth of, 350; saliva of, 287; touch of, 326; voice of, 349, 350, 355; clothing of, 52, 204, 323; baptism as, 330; body, 284–85, 288, 314, 324; clothes, 288–89, 325; garment of flesh, 324; His mother's robe, 276; in priesthood, 329–30; in prophecy, 329–30; swaddling clothes, 329; divine nature, 270, 275–78, 285–86, 290, 296–97, 310, 312, 327–28, 342, 345; human nature, 270, 276, 278, 285, 290, 296, 310, 312, 327–28, 342; teaching of, 290, 324; teachings on, 269, 310; titles of, 52, 271, 285, 345; *see also* God, titles of; All-Wise, 311; architect, 344; Architect of Creation, 327; Architect of the flesh, 286; architect of the mountains, 344; arm of His glory, 342; Carpenter, 271, 280; Christ, 308; compassion, 326; Crafter of the body, 286; divinity, 276, 278, 323, 331–32; ember, blessed, 324; Establisher of all, 52; Exalted One, 52; Exalted Right Hand, 354; Firstborn, 275, 327–29; firstborn of Being, 274; Fisherman, 271, 290; forgiver of sins, 296; gate of life, 343; God, 280–81, 284, 295–97, 316, 319–20, 322; God from God, 344; Godhead, 276; God's Son, 312; good Lord, 355; Good One, 290, 296, 321, 347; grape, 278; He who clothes all, 52; He who gives drink to all, 52; helper, 285; Hidden One, 323; infant, 329, 331; intelligence that cannot pass away, 345; Judge, 347; of knowledge, 347; of righteousness, 342; of the tribes, 345; Just One, 294; King of heaven, 300; King of kings, 346; lamb, 52; Life, 278; Living One, 284; Lord, 52, 204, 209–11, 246– 47, 259, 272–74, 277–78, 281, 284–301, 307–24, 326–32, 338, 349, 350, 353, 355; of all, 283; of David, 203; of stewardship, 330; of the angel, 314; of the Kingdom, 203; of the law, 354; of the light, 313–14; of the Prophets, 291, 316, 319; of the signs, 288, 291; of the Symbols, 53; manifestation of His rest, 342; Master, 312–13; Builder, 271; Craftsman of the Creator, 288; of the debt, 319; measure of justice, 345; measuring bowl that is not false, 345; measuring rod, even, 345; Mediator, 69; Medicine of Life, 45, 210, 271, 279, 283, 289–90; Merciful One, 324; mercy seat, 330; Messiah, 294, 324–25, 346; Mighty One, 52, 281; Most High, 285; near and far from Him, 342; One, 285–86, 288–89, 300–301, 310, 313, 315, 320, 325–26, 329, 331; Only-Begotten, 20, 273–74, 346, 355; Physician, 271, 289, 293, 299, 316–17, 319, 324; priest who remits debts, 343; propitiatory lamb, 343; Provisioner of all, 52; pure sacrifice, 343; ray of His light, 342; receiver of offerings, 326; renewer of creatures, 345; restorer of na-

Christ *(continued)*
tures, 345; resuscitator of mortality, 345; right hand of His mercy, 342; righteous Judge, 347; Rock, 174; Savior, 206, 288; scale without deceit, 345; second, 344; second light of Being 344; servant, 52, 285; Shepherd, 52, 271; Silent One, 320; Son, 51, 54, 68, 94, 115, 133, 147, 175, 203, 209, 211–12, 275–76, 278, 284, 286, 296, 325–28, 330, 331, 344; of David, 203, 307; of God, 204, 209, 270; of Man, 296; of the Most High, 276; of the skillful carpenter, 280; Splendrous One, 52; sprinkling that purifies, 343; steward, 329; sweet root, 331; treasure house of all riches, 345; Treasurer, 271, 285, 329; Treasury of Healing, 289; tree, natural, 331; unreachable power, 285; way of truth, 343; wisdom of His nature, 342; wisdom that does not err, 345; Word, 52, 53; Word of His Father, 342; word of, 280, 289, 300, 303, 308, 312–16; Christensen, A., 26
Chronicle of Arbela, 7
Chronicle of Edessa, 8, 36
Chronicle of Seert, 15, 31
Chrysostom, John, 6, 39; *Homilies on Genesis*, 94
Church, 5, 139, 174, 210, 217, 247, 258, 261, 272, 300–301, 325, 328; as Mystical Body, 312; as rock, 174; of the Gentiles, 204, 209
Church of the East (or Assyrian, or Nestorian Church), 5, 15, 31
circumcision, 71, 228, 230, 235–36, 283
city, 72, 130, 147–48, 162, 188, 201, 204, 209
civilization, 309; *see also* wilderness
clothing, 55, 106, 174–75; *see also* naked, nakedness; fringes on Jews' clothing, 309; incarnation as, *see* Christ, clothing of; Jewish, 319; Joseph's cloak, 182; of Dives, 340; of Egyptians, 189, 249; of false gods, 284; of Joseph, 185, 187; of majesty, 251, 253; white clothes of the synagogue, 283
cloud, 69, 78, 80, 85–86, 88, 144, 207–8, 223, 243, 248, 252, 255, 258, 261–63, 345; of heaven, 77
Colless, B. C., 6
Cologne Mani Codex, 11; *see also* Mani, Manichean
column, *see* pillar
Commander, *see* God, titles of
command, order, 223, 225–26, 233, 245, 252, 265
commandment, 67, 69, 93, 95, 100–104, 106, 108–11, 114–16, 118, 120–21, 126, 162, 170, 209; of circumcision, 236
commandments, 102, 223, 245–46, 258–59, 261, 264; *see also* Law
Commensurate with the nature, *see* Christ, titles of
commerce, 205
compassion, 326; *see also,* Christ, attributes of, titles of; God, attributes of; Moses
compulsion, 86, 226–27, 354; *see also* free will; will
conception, 55, 81, 119, 277
Constantine, 27, 31
Constantinople, 15
Constantius, 28, 31
conversion, 119
Coptic, 16
coriander, 255
corn, 73, 90
corpse, 224, 228, 239, 252, 271, 288
cosmology, 61–62, 76
Council of Ephesus, second, 337
Council of Nicaea, 15, 27, 35
counsel, 72, 108, 110–14, 116, 120, 186, 202, 290
covenant, 69, 71, 132, 143–44, 147, 153–54, 156, 167, 169–70, 172, 179–80, 231, 248, 261; *see* also Daughters of the Covenant; ark of the, 330; blood of the, 260; book of the, 260, 283; of circumcision, 70, 157, 169, 198; of peace, 69–70, 72

INDEX

cows, 186
Crafter of the body, *see* Christ, titles of
craftsmen, 138, 262–63, 280, 305, 311
crafty one, *see* Satan
Cramer, W., xx, 76
creation, 14, 43, 48–49, 51, 59–60, 62, 67, 73–74, 76–80, 84, 86–88, 90–94, 96–98, 104, 114, 116, 121, 142, 162, 169, 212, 277, 284, 287, 305, 327, 339, 344, 348
creatio ex nihilo, 49, 67–68, 75–76, 81, 85; of earth, 74, 77; of heaven, 74, 77
Creator, *see* God, titles of
creditor, 321
cross, 46, 54, 116, 150, 199, 210, 240, 247, 249, 254–56, 276–80, 283, 285, 300; as bridge, 280
crown, 116, 203–4, 208, 229, 331–32, 349, 352–53; of martyrdom, 225; of the Law, 59
crucifiers, killers, 225, 278, 284–85, 288, 299–301, 308–9
crucifixion, 312
Crusades, 6
cure, *see* medicine
Cureton, W., 34
curse, 95, 100, 115, 119–20, 122–23, 128, 130, 136, 145, 172–73, 202, 209
cymbals, 264, 293; *see also* tambourines
Cyril of Alexandria, 65
Cyrillona, 3, 26, 38

Dahood, M., 340
Dalmais, I. H., xx, 46
Damascus, 311, 315
Dan, 176, 205, 210; sons of, 206
Daniel, 301–3
Daniélou, J., 47
Dante, 5, 337
Danube, 100–101
darkness, 61, 75–78, 80–81, 86–89, 98, 161, 227, 245, 250, 340–42, 345, 353; *see also* shadow
Darling, R. A., xx
daughters of Eve, 121
daughters of men, 134–36

Daughters of the Covenant, 24, 36; *see also* b'nay q'yama
David, 61, 92, 202–4, 307; house of, 328, 331; Son of, *see* Christ, titles of; sons of, 203–4
dawn, 80–81, 89–91, 152, 179, 180
day, 70, 80–81, 87–88, 90–92, 102, 115, 124, 129, 136–37, 139–43, 152–53, 157–59, 161, 163, 166, 168–69, 173, 175–76, 180, 182, 190–91, 198, 200–201, 206, 208, 225–27, 234–35, 239, 245, 250, 254, 259–61, 264, 293, 351–52; latter, 211; of creation, 69, 74–78, 80–93, 96–100, 103, 105, 121; of judgment, 346, 355; of Noah, 98; of one's life, 119–20, 135, 146, 153; sabbath, *see* sabbath
de Halleux, A., xx, 39–41, 45, 51, 56, 218
deacon, 14, 21–22
dead, the buried, 278–80, 316
deaf, deaf-mute, 271, 286–88, 341
death, 53, 71–73, 102, 112, 116, 119, 121–23, 128–29, 132, 134, 143, 169, 171, 183, 200–202, 209, 212, 221–22, 224–25, 229, 235, 238–39, 247, 249, 252, 259–60, 270, 276–81, 285, 288, 317–18, 324, 350–51, 353
debt, 210, 291, 294, 319, 322–23, 325, 330, 343, 355
debtor, 291, 321–22
deeds, 116, 135–36, 138, 140, 148, 153, 163, 182, 209, 275, 312–13, 320–21, 325, 332, 340, 342, 347–50, 355
Delehaye, H., 28
deliverance, 70–71, 149, 154, 221, 224, 228, 237–38
deniers, *see* Jews
depths, 78, 285, 297, 305, 344
descendants, 202
desert, *see* wilderness
desire, 72, 350, 353
destruction, 243, 278, 303
dew, 78, 207, 208; of blessing, 84; of heaven, 84
Dewey, A. J., 11
Diatessaron, 279, 297

366 INDEX

Didymus of Alexandria, 133
Dietrich, A., 349
dignity, 73; *see also* honor
Dinah, 177, 181; rape of, 72, 181, 202
Diocletian, 26, 34
Diodore of Tarsus, 79
Dionysius of Alexandria, 7
disabled, 346
disciples, 247, 257, 271, 288, 300–301, 309, 311–13; *see also* Ephrem as disciple; of Addai, 9; of Bardaisan, 37; of Ephrem, 13, 16–17, 22, 39; of Jesus, 9, 54; of Mani, 10; of Thomas, 9
disease, sickness illness, 8, 73, 122, 270, 296, 341
disgrace, 163–64, 187, 192, 201
Dives, 337, 340
divinity, 112–14, 116, 151, 204, 276, 301; title of, 284; *see also* Christ, titles of; God, titles of
divinization, 276
Doctrine of Addai, 8
dogs, 309; image of Moses' house, 309; image of Paul, 309
dominion, rule, 81, 94–95, 103, 117, 187, 305, 352; *see also* authority
donkey, 278
door, 70, 126, 141, 158–59, 161, 195–96, 299, 307, 316, 318–19
doorposts, lintels, 246
doubt, 68, 152–53, 157, 172, 195, 288, 291, 293–94
Draguet, R., 15, 18, 21
dream, 38, 72–73, 105, 165, 173–74, 178, 182, 185–87, 189–90, 193, 196–97
Drijvers, H. J. W., 10, 33–34, 37–38, 47, 61–62, 75–77, 79
dualism, 276
Dummer, J., 3
dust, 32, 99, 118, 120, 205, 241, 265, 324, 341, 343–44, 352–53, 355
Duval, R., 16, 33–35
dwelling, 95, 146, 158, 177, 275, 332, 343, 348–49; *see also* haven, tabernacle; of Christ, 210

earrings, 262–63, 265
ears, 53, 108, 112, 119, 181, 193, 263, 270, 284, 286–88, 303, 307–8, 313–14, 323, 341, 349; *see also* Christ, body of; Eve; Mary, mother of Christ; as womb, 351; of grain, 186
earth, 74–78, 80–85, 87, 89–101, 103, 105, 109, 114–15, 120, 123–24, 126–28, 130–31, 134, 136–37, 139, 141–44, 147–48, 162, 169, 171, 173, 188–89, 196, 205, 241, 243, 272, 288, 298, 301, 312, 343–45, 351–53; face of, 81, 87, 97–98, 127–28, 147; surface of, 272, 298
earth-dwellers, 285
east, 61, 89, 91, 99, 123, 130, 139, 151
Eaton, J. H., 5
Eber, 148
Edar, 129–30
Eden, 46, 99–101, 123, 130, 326, 351, 353
Edessa, 6–10, 12, 15, 22, 29, 32–37, 59–60, 62, 147, 281, 336; Antioch by the Callirhoe, 33; archives of, 9; as Athens of the East, 34; cults of, 33–34; famine of, A.D. 373 12–13, 36; flood in, 8; Mount Edessa, *see* mount, Edessa; School of, 36, 43; Urfa, 33; Urhai, 33
Edom, 253; kings of, 72
Edomites, 157, 171
education, 227
Egeria, *see* Etheria
Egypt, 15–16, 63, 67–68, 73, 78, 149, 154, 180, 182, 186, 188, 191, 195–98, 207, 212, 218–19, 221–25, 227, 232, 234, 236, 238–40, 242, 244–52, 257, 261–62, 282, 292, 315, 318; Ephrem's travels to, 16; gods of, *see* gods; kingdom of, 149; land of, 73, 187, 189, 198, 224, 240–41, 252, 263; monasticism in, 15; Egyptian, 68, 142, 149, 155, 186, 188–89, 193–95, 198, 208, 219, 222, 224, 228–29, 231, 233, 239–42, 247–53, 258, 263, 319; language 189, 192
Ehlers, B., 61
El-Khoury, N., xx, 74–77

INDEX 367

elders, 222, 232, 236, 255, 261–62
elements, 75–77, 79, 87, 212, 240
elephants, 28, 139
Eliezar (son of Moses), 231
Eliezer (servant of Abraham), 71, 183, 198
Elijah, 42, 78
Elim, 254
Elisha, 318
Elkasites, 11
El Shaddai, *see* God, titles of
ember, blessed, *see* Christ, titles of
embryo, 87
Emerton, J. A., 97
Emmanuel bar Shaharre, 59
Encomium on Ephrem, attributed to Gregory of Nyssa, 35, 39, 218
encratism, 8, 11; *see also* asceticism, eremetical life, monastic practices
enemy, 151, 202, 207, 211, 252, 256, 264, 296, 299; Satan as, *see* Satan
Enoch, 129–30, 133–34
Enoki, K., 5
Enosh, 130, 133, 136
Ephraim, 73, 157, 199
Ephratha, 72
Ephrem, 3, 13, 35–36, 38–39, 42–43, 45–56, 352; as deacon, 12, 29; as disciple of Christ, 24; as doctor of the universal Church, 4, 18; as Harp of the Holy Spirit, 3, 39; ascetical image of, 14–15, 17–21, 39, 42, 271; attitudes towards women, 271; baptism of, 25; disciples of, *see* disciples of Ephrem; feast of, 37; iconography of, 18, 37; life of, 12, 18, 25, 28, 32–33, 37; liturgy left in Nisibis, 31; ministry of, 24; relics of, 16; study of, ix; translations of works, 39–40; *Vita* tradition, 14–22, 25, 27–28, 33, 35–38, 43, 60, 271; works of, 3, 20, 30, 38, 40, 271, 274, 342; *Against Heresies*, 41; *Against Julian*, 41; *Armenian Hymns*, 104, 142, 151, 158; *Commentary on Exodus*, 42–44, 64, 200; *Commentary on Genesis*, x, 26, 33, 40, 42–43, 49, 59–66, 345, 352; *Commentary on Job*, 40; *Commentary on the Diatessaron*, 21, 40, 42, 46–48, 53–54, 94, 142, 289, 328, 347, 349; *Homily on Our Lord*, 44–45, 225, 340, 344–46; *Hymns against Heresies*, 25, 29, 35, 45, 49–50, 52, 60–62, 75, 116, 276, 338–39, 345–47; *Hymns against Julian*, 32–33, 41, 344; *Hymns on Abraham Kidunaya and Julian Saba*, 41; *Hymns on Epiphany*, 79; *Hymns on Faith*, 41, 45, 48, 50–55, 75, 77, 94, 99–101, 104, 114, 135, 137, 139, 145, 274, 276, 278, 280, 282–83, 286–87, 292, 310, 338–39, 341, 343–45, 347, 349; *Hymns on Fasting*, 41, 54, 338–39; *Hymns on Holy Week*, 41; *Hymns on Nicomedia*, 32, 40, 114, 140–41; *Hymns on Nisibis*, 17, 24, 27, 30, 32, 41, 53, 55, 82, 94, 108, 113, 116–17, 128, 135, 142, 144, 264, 278, 289, 297, 338, 340, 342, 344–46, 352, 354; *Hymns on Paradise*, 41, 45, 48–49, 51, 59, 63, 66–67, 80, 82, 93, 100–102, 104, 106, 108–9, 111–12, 114, 116, 118, 123, 130, 134–35, 141, 269, 274–75, 306, 339–40, 343, 347, 349–51, 353–54; *Hymns on the Church*, 41, 53, 94, 104, 106–7, 112, 114, 116–17, 119, 134, 280, 301, 306, 330, 342, 344, 347, 351; *Hymns on the Crucifixion*, 142, 231, 346; *Hymns on the Nativity*, 41, 52, 74, 76–77, 87, 94, 106, 114, 117, 133, 135, 142, 145, 165, 167, 176, 184, 203, 296, 301, 343–46; *Hymns on the Paschal Feast*, 41; *Hymns on the Pearl*, 41, 54; *Hymns on the Resurrection*, 237, 328, 345; *Hymns on Unleavened Bread*, 53, 217, 247, 279, 288, 297, 345–46; *Hymns on Virginity*, 25, 41, 49–51, 53, 55, 81, 100, 106, 137, 144, 149, 162, 165, 184, 199, 209, 276, 280, 282, 285, 294, 325, 330, 338, 342, 343, 345, 347, 349–50, 355; *Letter to Hypatius*, 281, 336; *Letter to Publius*, 44, 55, 269, 273, 280, 335–36, 341–42, 344, 348; *Prose Refutations*, 3, 42–43, 47,

Ephrem *(continued)*
  50–51, 61–62, 77, 86, 108, 287;
  Sermones, 146, 336–37, 340–42,
  350, 353; *Sermons on Faith*, 75, 94,
  341–43, 346, 351
Epiphanius, 3; *Panarion*, 151
Equal in essence, *see* Christ, titles of
Er, 182
Erech, Erekh, 33, 147; *see also* Edessa,
  Urfa, Urhai
eremetical life, 14, 17, 20; *see also* asceticism, encratism, monastic practices
error, 68, 226, 277, 291, 293, 348
Esau, 71–72, 151, 171–73, 180–82;
  blessings of, 72; descendants of,
  72; sons of, 156
essence, 74, 120; *see also* God, essence of
Essenes, 11
Establisher of All, *see* Christ, titles of
Eternal, *see* God, titles of
eternal principles, *see* principles, eternal
Etheria, 34
Eucharist, 45, 210, 247, 261, 274,
  279, 281, 287, 290, 324, 326; *see
  also* mysteries; living Body, 247
Euphratensis, 335
Euphrates, 7, 101, 154, 203
Eusebius of Caesarea, 7–9, 37
Eusebius of Emesa, 79, 133
Evagrian terminology, 21
Evagrius, 21
Eve, 43, 53–54, 60, 64, 94, 104–22,
  124, 127, 162; as fountain of
  death, 278; as mother of all the living, 278; as old vine, 278; ear of,
  53
evening, 78, 87–88, 90–91, 152–53,
  179–80, 208, 211, 235
evil, evildoer, 100, 102, 111–12, 116,
  122, 131, 137–38, 155, 178,
  187–88, 191, 212, 243, 282, 297,
  316, 318, 321, 340–41, 345
evil one, *see* Satan
Exalted One, *see* Christ, titles of
Exalted Right Hand, *see* Christ, titles of
exegesis, 54, 82, 101, 344; Alexandrian method of, 47–48, 68; allegorical, 47–48; Antiochene
  method of, 47, 94; Ephrem's
  method of, 47, 60, 62–64, 220,
  223; Hellenistic, 63; Jewish, 63,
  88, 90, 93–94, 99, 102, 104–6,
  110–11, 118, 124, 129, 132, 136,
  140–42, 145, 148–49, 151, 175,
  218, 224–26, 232, 235, 237, 242–
  44, 246, 248, 253–54, 277, 349;
  literal, 48, 50, 74, 220, 270; Nestorian, 74, 76, 87
exegete, 218
exile, 153, 257; from Eden, 69, 96,
  123–24
eye, 24, 55, 70, 107–14, 125–26, 135,
  155, 158, 165–67, 172, 185–87,
  190, 194, 196, 198, 204, 229, 231,
  241, 261–62, 264, 270, 284, 301–
  2, 304–8, 310, 313, 322, 326, 339,
  341, 348, 353; blink of an 98, 105,
  250; twinkling of an 80, 89, 105
Ezekiel, 77

face, 68, 125–26, 128, 145, 157, 160,
  174, 184, 189, 192; *see also* Moses
faith, 50, 52, 55–56, 70, 117,
  152–53, 157, 177, 183–84, 208,
  222, 230, 235, 259, 270, 285,
  291–92, 294, 308–9, 322
faithful, 79
Fall, 59–60, 64, 104, 139
famine, hunger, 73, 102, 110, 149,
  153, 171–72, 186, 188–89, 191,
  196, 202, 205, 211, 224, 279; *see
  also* Edessa, famine of A.D. 373
father, 71–73, 105, 129–32, 144–45,
  149, 151, 154, 157, 162–65, 172,
  176, 178–79, 181–85, 189–93,
  196–201, 207–8, 212, 274, 330;
  see also God, titles of
fathers, 224, 232, 258, 264
feast, banquet, 236, 260, 263, 290,
  320, 324–25; tables at, 353
feet, 73, 115, 159, 174, 182, 187,
  206, 235, 247, 250, 261, 327, 348,
  351; *see also* Christ, body of
Féghali, P., xxi, 63–66, 86, 218,
  224–26, 228–39, 241–42, 244,
  247–48, 254–55, 257, 262–63

INDEX

fence, 102, 123, 136, 278
Festugière, A., 19
fetters, *see* chains
field, 93, 97, 103–4, 107, 120, 126, 177
Fiey, J.-M., xxi, 6–7, 24, 26–30, 37
fig tree, *see* tree
fingers, 116, 127; *see also* Christ, body of; God
fire, flames, 61, 72, 75–76, 78, 81, 85, 87, 89, 116, 121, 125, 152, 154, 162–63, 174, 205, 222, 231–32, 243, 247, 260, 282, 298, 302–3, 319, 340, 350, 352, 354; pillar of, 248, 250
firmament, 76–78, 81, 84, 86–90, 92
firstborn, 171, 211; death of the, 219, 222, 234, 238–39, 246–48, 252–53; *see also* Christ, titles of; plagues; Jews as, 199, 234; laws of the, 166; of Being, *see* Christ, titles of; of the cattle, 246; of the Egyptians, 222, 246–48, 252–53; of flock, 124; of the Hebrews, 247–48; of Jacob, 200, 209, 211; of Joseph, 199; of Judah, 182; of the "briar of sin," Marcion, 62
Fischer, R. H., 44, 63
fish, 92, 94–95, 225, 239, 241
Fisherman, *see* Christ, titles of
Fitzmyer, J. A., 5
flesh, 52, 105, 121, 129, 131–32, 134–35, 138–39, 141–44, 157, 182, 204, 209, 225, 277–78, 283, 286, 303, 305–6, 324, 343
flood, 60, 83, 129, 137–39, 141–42, 144, 147, 162, 304–5; of fire, 162, 352; of waters, 351; floodgates, 84; of heaven, 141; of wrath, 84
flowers, 237, 275, 340, 344; *see also* blossoms
folly, foolishness, 95, 115, 117–20, 127, 147, 159, 197
food, 83, 90, 100, 136, 198, 254, 279, 290, 320; solid, 317
foreigner, alien, 148, 165, 176, 259, 343, 346
foreknowledge, 95
forgiver of sins, *see* Christ, titles of
fornication, *see* adultery

Forshall, J., 335
Foundation of the Schools, *see* Barhadbešabba
fountain, 54, 303, 316; of death, *see* Eve; of healing, *see* Christ, attributes of; of life, *see* Christ, body of
Fraade, S. D., 133
fragrance, 100, 275, 319, 325; *see also* oil, ointment, perfume
Fransen, P., xxi
fraud, 72, 318
freeman, 112
free will, freedom, 195, 218, 226–27, 239, 243, 245–46, 254, 280, 306, 337, *see also* compulsion; God, attributes of; will
Frerichs, E. S., 31
friend, 299–300, 302, 351
Froidevaux, L., xxi
fruit, 38, 82, 90, 108, 111–13, 116, 118, 120, 122–25, 136, 144, 159, 177, 191, 200, 209, 278–79, 300, 323, 325, 332, 344, 347; mortal, 278–79; of womb, 156
Frye, R. N., 26, 29, 31
fury, *see* anger

Gabriel, 277
Gad, 177, 206, 210
Gadar, 165
garden, 43, 96, 101, 104, 109, 120, 123–24; of Eden, 54, 353
garment, raiment, 54, 194, 196, 204, 350, 352; *see also* Christ, body of; naked, nakedness; heavenly, 106; love for Christ as, 350; noble, 349; of a spider, 353; of darkness, 353; of flesh, *see* Christ, clothing of; of glory, 54, 106; of good deeds, 350; of Joseph, 185, 186–87; of leaves, 106, 121; of light, 349; of moths, 353; of skin, 121; of the Egyptians, 222, 249
Garsoian, N. G., 6
gate, 343, 349; of ear, 341; of heaven, 174; of kingdom of heaven, 350, 353; of life, *see* Christ, titles of; of Paradise, 104; of Sheol, *see* Sheol; of Sodom, 160; of the kingdom, 349

Geerard, M., xxi, 17, 39
Gehenna, 336–37, 340, 354
Gelineau, J., xxi
Gemser, B., 74
genealogy, 171
generation, 67–70, 97, 129–41, 148, 154, 162, 212, 221, 223, 241, 244, 255–56, 258, 325, 332, 351–52, 354
Genesis Rabbah, 76, 82, 87, 90, 93, 96, 99, 102, 104, 124, 136, 141, 145, 147, 149, 151, 162, 173, 184
genres; poetry; dialogue poem, 45; hymn, 41, 45, 52, 59, 64; prose; exposition, 42–43, 221; homily, 17, 41–42, 59, 67, 149, 269; paraphrase, 43, 217, 221; *see also* targums, targumic traditions; rhetorical prose, 44
Gentiles, 204, 341; *see* also church of the Gentiles
George Syncellus, 39
Gero, S., 8
Gershom, 230
Gerson, D., xxi, 63
Gideon, 204
Giet, S., 79
gifts, 122, 157, 165, 170–71, 197, 227, 254, 261, 285, 306, 325, 328, 330–32
Gihon, 100–101; *see also* river (Nile)
Gilead, mountain of, 72, 178
Ginzberg, L., x, 63, 88, 90, 92–93, 99, 102, 104, 106, 108, 118, 123–24, 129, 132, 135–36, 140–42, 145, 148, 151, 166, 169, 175, 201, 207, 225–26, 232, 235, 243, 248, 254, 262
Giver, *see* God, titles of
glory, 107, 114, 213, 275–76, 302, 304–6, 314–15, 317, 327, 353; *see also* Christ, attributes of; God, attributes of; clothing with, 96, 99, 104, 106, 108, 122
gnashing of teeth, *see* teeth, gnashing of
gnosticism, 61–62
goat, 152, 154, 336, 346–47
God, 35, 48–52, 55–56, 60, 62, 68–72, 74–79, 81–85, 87, 89–99, 101–5, 107–9, 111, 113, 115–28, 130–35, 137–44, 146–48, 150, 152–54, 156–60, 165–71, 173–75, 177–81, 183–84, 188, 190, 192, 195–97, 199, 201–2, 205–9, 212, 219, 222–23, 225–26, 230–37, 239, 241–42, 245–46, 248–50, 252–57, 259–64, 273, 281, 283, 293–95, 297, 300–301, 304–6, 308–9, 315, 317–18, 325–26, 328, 330, 344, 351, 353, 355; attributes of; *see also* Christ, attributes of; compassion, 119, 326; glory, 223, 261, 304–5, 342; goodness, 252, 296, 305–6; grace, 123; justice, 127; kindness, long-suffering, 128; light, 342; love, 304; majesty, 251, 253, 304; mercy, 136, 342, 348; patience, 244, 258; power 251, 271, 277; praiseworthy, 251–52; rest, 342; splendor, 304; terrifying, 252; transcendence, 306; weakness, 317; will, 234, 259, 306; wrath, 252, 304; bosom of, 274; command of, 265; commandments of, 261; essence of, 304–5, 311; finger of, 241, 261; house of, 174; lips of, 252; mouth of, 252; name of, 260; nature of, 77, 305, 342; titles of; *see also* Christ, titles of; All-knowing One, 281; Being, 75, 274, 344; Divine Being, 306; Commander, 113; Creator, 48–51, 55, 60–61, 67, 75, 89, 103, 212, 271, 288, 306; Divinity, 276, 284–85, 311, 325; El Shaddai, 199; Eternal, 50; Father, 51, 133, 274–77, 284–85, 314–15, 325, 329, 342; Giver, 157; God on high, 297; Godhead, 273–74, 276, 332; Good One, 347; Healer, 51; judge, 115, 282; Just One, 100, 162, 175, 282, 306; kindly God, 355; living God, 232, 351; Living One, 156; Lord, 71, 93, 97–99, 101, 103–5, 107, 109, 115, 121, 124, 130, 133–35, 137, 139, 140–42, 146–47, 150–52, 155–58, 162, 168–74, 177–79, 182–83, 193, 206, 210, 219, 232–34, 236–41, 244–46,

INDEX

248–53, 255–58, 260–61, 263–65, 303, 325, 328; Lord God, 102; Lord of all, 61; Lord of the angel, 304; Maker, 69; Mighty One, 211; Most High, 150, 277, 283, 348; Musician, Divine, 53; One, 68, 229, 264, 273, 282, 305–6; res-cuer, 251; Self-Existent One, 304; Spirit, 50; voice of, 237, 258, 262; warrior, 252; Yahweh, 248, 251, 256, 274; God from God, see Christ, titles of; Godhead, see Christ, titles of; God, titles of; God on high, see God, titles of
gods, idols, images, 32, 60, 68, 75, 116, 149, 178–79, 181, 230, 232–33, 240, 251–52, 257, 259, 262–64, 280–82, 284, 293, 318; of Edessa, 34; of Egypt, 227, 241
God's Son, see Christ, titles of
Gog, house of, 208
gold, 222, 246, 249, 259, 263
Gollancz, H., 31
Gomorrah, 160
Good Lord, see Christ, titles of
Good One, see Christ, titles of; God, titles of
goodness, 326, 328; see also Christ, attributes of; God, attributes of
good will, 180
Goshen, 198; land of, 241
Gospels, 55, 62, 101, 209, 247, 260, 335–36, 338–39, 348, 355
grace, 55, 95–96, 227; personified, 110, 119, 136, 138; see also God, attributes of
Graffin, F. xxi,, 54
Graham, W. C., 74
grain, 124–26, 186, 188–89, 191–92, 198
granaries, 115–16, 224
grape, 231, 278; Christ as, see Christ, titles of
grape stones, 144
grass, herbs, 89–90, 98, 136, 208, 245, 282, 344, 352
Greece, 13
Greek language, 269
Gregory of Nyssa, 14, 35–36, 39, 218;

see also *Encomium on Ephrem* (attributed to him)
Gribomont, J., xxi, 19
Griffith, S. H., xxii
Grossfeld, B., 79
guard, guardian, 102, 204
Guillaumont, A. xxii,, 21, 60, 63, 235
Guillaumont, C., 21
Guria, see martyrs of Edessa
Guy, J.-C., 24
Gwynn, J., 272

Habib, see martyrs of Edessa
Hagar, 70–71, 155–56, 166–67, 176; as the "slave woman," 166–67; descendants of, 155
haggadah, 45, 63, 218
hair, 274
Hallier, L., 8, 36
Ham, 134, 144–46; sons of, 146, 151
Hamor, 181
hands, 68, 99, 103, 115, 118, 121–22, 134, 137, 143, 151, 155–56, 161, 165, 167, 169, 172, 179–80, 182, 184–87, 194–95, 198–99, 202, 207, 211–12, 221, 228–29, 233, 236, 240, 243–44, 247, 249, 251–53, 255–57, 259, 261–62, 264, 278, 282, 298, 310, 313, 325–27, 329, 338, 342–43, 346–48, 351, 354; see also Christ, body of; Moses
Hansen, G. C., 13
Hanson, A. G. P., xxii, 66
Haran, 70, 148, 165, 173
Harmonius, 13; see also Bardaisan; *Book of the Laws of Countries*
Harnack, A. v., 10, 62
harp, harp strings, 53, 108, 273, 323, 353
Hartranft, C. D., 13, 38
Harvey, S. A., 35
Hatra, 7, 33, 147
Hausherr, I., xxii, 52
Hausman, B. A., 18
haven, 273, 332; see also dwelling
Hayman, A. P., 30
Hayyot, 123
head, 113, 119, 151, 169, 182,

head *(continued)*
198–99, 205–8, 211, 347, 353; *see also* Christ, body of
healer, 224; *see also* Christ, titles of; God, titles of
heart, 55, 137, 142, 157–59, 165, 178, 192, 219, 227, 233, 237–41, 243–45, 249, 282–83, 291–93, 296–97, 303, 308, 320–21, 341, 348, 354–55
heaven, 14, 38, 71, 74–78, 80, 85–86, 88–91, 94, 96–97, 147, 152, 154, 162, 167, 173–74, 207–8, 254, 259, 300, 312, 339, 343–44, 350–51, 353–54
Hebrew language, 74, 195
Hebrews, 171, 183, 195, 212, 219, 224–25, 229, 231, 235, 242, 245, 249–52; *see also* Israel; Israelites; Jews; synagogue
Hebron, 169, 181–82, 184
Hedrick, C. W., 8
heel, 119, 139, 205–6
heights, 323, 331; *see also* depths
Hellenistic Christianity, 11, 63
Hem, 71; sons of, 71
Hemmerdinger-Iliadou, D., xxii, 39
herbs, bitter, 247; *see also* grass, herbs
hermit, 17, 37, 43, 60, 273
Herod, 331
Hess, R. S., 97
Heth, sons of (Hittites), 71, 169
Hexaemeron, 16, 59
Hidal, S., xxii, 43, 76–77, 93, 137, 151
hidden judge, *see* judge, hidden
Hidden One, *see* Christ, titles of
Hieronymus, 15
hip, hip joint, 72, 265
Hittites, *see* Heth, sons of
Hodgson, R., Jr., 8
Hoffman, J. H. G., 31
Hoffman, R. J., 62
Holy Spirit, 16, 51, 54, 68, 79, 147, 210, 213, 302, 310, 325; *see also* spirit
holy dwelling, *see* tabernacle
honey, 205, 255
honor, 72, 97, 99, 125, 170, 186, 188, 192, 196–97, 201, 208, 213, 350; *see also* dignity, shame
Hopkins, S., 149
Horeb, 222, 231, 235, 255
horsemen, 251, 253
house, household, 164, 182–85, 187, 191–94, 200–201, 221, 227, 229–30, 240, 246–47, 253, 258, 270, 293–94, 317, 320; *see also* Abraham; Adam; Cain; God; Gog; Isaac; Israel; Jacob; Judah; Laban; Lot; Noah; Pharaoh; Seth; Terah; of forgiveness, 330
Howard, G., 8
Höll, K., 3
humanity, 82, 99, 113–14, 141, 276, 278, 280, 285, 306, 310, 330; *see also* mankind
humility, 298, 300, 310–15, 355; *see also* Christ, attributes of; arrogance, pride
hunger, *see* famine
Hur, 256, 262–63
hymns, 13, 15, 36, 40–41, 45, 60–61, 63–64, 67, 75–76, 79, 99, 101, 106–8, 111, 114, 134–35, 138–39, 209, 217, 269, 271, 274, 337

Ibas, 337
idols, *see* gods
ignorance, 138, 160, 316, 318, 321
'iḥidāyâ, 20
image, 232, 338, 348
of God, 94, 133, 143
images, *see* gods
immortal, *see* life, immortal
imprisoned, *see* captives
Incarnation, 52–53, 55, 74, 269, 276, 278, 284, 310, 323, 331; as clothing, *see* Christ, clothing of
incense, 261, 285
India, 9, 28, 34
Indians, 208
infallible, *see* knowledge, infallible
infant, 221, 224–25, 239, 246, 257, 317; *see also* Christ, titles of
infirm, 346
inheritance, 73, 146, 149, 154, 156, 167, 202–3, 205–6, 208
injury, 298–99, 302

INDEX

inner chambers, *see* chambers, inner
inns, milestones, 211
insect, 104
intelligence, 107, 345; *see also* Christ, titles of
intercession, 71, 264
interpretation, 313, 318; *see also* genres, prose
investigation, 275, 296
Iraq, 141
Irenaeus, Against Heresies, 281, 285
irony, *see* literary techniques
Išōyab of Adiabene, 31
Isaac, 33, 70–73, 151, 165–73, 176, 179, 181–82, 199, 208, 235, 248; house of, 72, 178, 258
Isaac the Teacher, 17
Isaiah, wife of, 253
Iscah, 148; *see also* Sarah
Ishmael, 70–71, 155–57, 166
isocola, *see* literary techniques
Israel, 107, 199, 202, 205–7, 211, 236, 239, 246, 253, 256, 262, 273, 281, 292, 294, 319, 331–32; *see also* Hebrews; Israel; Israelites;Jews; synagogue; as idolatrous, 281; children of, 221, 223–24, 231, 237, 241, 248–52; foolish teachers of, 322; fraudulence of, 318; house of, 72, 261; son of, 281, 291–92, 317–18, 321; unbelief of, 273, 291–92
Israelites, 146, 250, 254, 260; *see also* Hebrews; Israel; Jews; synagogue
Issachar, 177, 204–5, 210
Iyor, 141, 144

Jabal, 129, 131–32
Jackson, B., 25
Jacob, 71–73, 82, 145, 151, 157, 171–82, 188–91, 197–202, 205–7, 209–12, 221, 223, 230–31, 248; as Israel, 199; blessings of, 73, 200, 209; daughter of, 181; descendants of, 181, 202, 209; house of, 188; sons of, 181, 188–89
Jacob of Edessa, 59, 219
Jacob of Nisibis, 15, 21, 24–25, 27–30, 35, 218

Jacob of Sarug, 3, 42, 59
Jaeger, W., 14
Jansma, T., xxii–xxiii, 60, 64, 66, 68, 70, 74–76, 79, 81, 84, 87, 93, 97, 117, 147–48, 171, 203, 218–19, 221–22, 225–27, 230–33, 237, 238, 240–42, 246, 249, 263
Japhet, 134, 146
Jared, 133
Jerome, 3, 39
Jerusalem, 204, 208, 253, 278
Jesus, 53–54, 203, 206, 273–74, 276, 281, 287, 292, 297, 301, 324–25, 328; *see also* Christ; flying, 297
Jethro, 221–22, 229, 234, 257
Jewish Christianity, 62, 106
Jewish community, 10, 31, 45; literary influence of, xi, 45, 62–64, 218; in Nisibis, 30
Jews, Jewish nation, 106, 291, 293, 300–301, 304–5, 308, 318, 330–31, 341; *see also* Hebrews; Israel; Israelites; synagogue; deniers, 301; God's children, 283; holy nation, 258; infidels, 308; liars, 308; most stubborn, 315; stiff-necked, 315; bitter will of the, 300; contentiousness of, 307; hardness of heart of, 233; infantile state of, 69; perversity of, 315; unbelief of, 293
Job, 92
Jochabed, 228, 254
John Chrysostom, *see* Chrysostom, John
John the Baptist, 115, 247, 328, 330–31; as treasurer of baptism, 330
John the Evangelist, 94
Johnston, A. E., 272
Joined with Him and separated from Him, *see* Christ, titles of
Jordan, 150, 331
Joseph, 72–73, 177, 182, 185–200, 202–3, 206–7, 211–12, 223–24; bones of, 73, 248; brothers of, 73, 188–89, 191–200, 206–8, 212; dreams of, 197; head of, 208; sons of, 198
Josephus, 9–10

374 INDEX

Jewish Antiquities, 87, 141
Joshua son of Nun, 96, 146, 255–56, 261–62, 264
Joshua the Stylite, 37
Jovian, 32
Jubal, 131–32
Judah, 72, 176, 182–84, 191, 195, 197, 202–4, 210; house of, 157, 203, 208
judge, 109, 136, 160, 291, 303, 337, 342, 345, 347, 354; *see also* Christ, titles of; God, titles of; hidden, 354; of righteousness, 342, 354
Judge, E. A., 274
judgment, 72, 115, 118–21, 131, 154, 160, 195–97, 209, 341, 347, 354–55; last, 72, 336–37
Julian, Emperor, 28, 31–32
Just One (of Abraham), 340–41; *see also* Christ, titles of; God, titles of
just ones, 68
Abraham as father, 340
justice, 95, 108–9, 137, 195, 201, 209, 258, 265, 282, 312, 321, 340, 345, 347; *see also* Christ, attributes of; God, attributes of; letter of, 340–41; personified, 110, 119, 127–28, 136, 150

Kaczynski, R., 41
Kanjiramukalil, S., xxiii
Kawerau, P., 7
Kechichian, P., xxiii
Kenan, 133
Keturah, 156, 171; sons of, 156
keys, 307, 329–30
Khuzistan, 31
killers, *see* crucifiers
kindness, *see* God, attributes of, titles of
king, 100, 149–51, 153–55, 157, 167, 170, 172, 187–88, 203, 206, 210, 221, 223, 228, 244, 258, 331, 346, 352; *see also* Christ, titles of; of Edom, 72; of Egypt, 239; of Elam, 150; of Gadar, 165; of Israel, 72; of Nabatea, 34; of Salem, 150; of Sodom, 150; of the Philistines, 72;
kingdom, 203–4, 206, 210, 217, 247, 274, 346, 349, 353; gate of, *see* gate of kingdom; of David, 202–3; of Egyptians, 186, 227, 249; of heaven, 339, 350, 354; of priests, 258
King of kings, *see* Christ, titles of
kingship, 328–29, 331
Kirchmeyer, J., xxii, 39–40
Kirsten, E., 9
Klijn, A. F. J., 11, 38
knife, 168
knowledge, 62, 68, 78, 127, 160, 171, 183, 211, 293, 297, 300, 323, 347; *see also* Christ, attributes of; human, 277, 280–81; infallible, 114; natural, 12
Kontakion, Byzantine, 4
Kowalski, A., xxiii
Kronholm, T., xxiii, 61, 63, 67, 74, 79, 82, 94, 99, 101, 103–5, 107–8, 111–12, 114, 118–19, 128, 133–35, 137–41, 218
Kruse, H., 61
Kutscher, E. Y., 5

Laban, 72, 170, 175, 177–81, 185; daughters of, 176, 230; house of, 72, 170, 173, 175, 178; sons of, 178
labor, *see* work
Labourt, J., 6
ladder, 72, 173–74, 231
lamb, 124, 139, 169, 178, 343; *see also* Christ, titles of; propitiatory, 343; *see also* Christ, titles of; Passover lamb
Lamech, 69, 129–34
lamps, 349; oil of the, 349–50
Lamy, T. J., xvi, xxiii, 15, 42, 272
lance, sword, 54, 123–24, 128, 154, 199, 265, 282, 293–94, 352; *see also* weapon
land, 70, 73, 84, 93, 100, 123–24, 130, 132, 135–36, 139, 149–50, 152–55, 167, 171–74, 189, 191, 198, 200, 205–6, 210, 212, 232, 244, 257, 263, 351; *see also* promised land; dry, 79, 83–84, 89, 92–93, 143, 233, 328, 351; of Egypt, 152, 154, 226, 241–42,

244, 258; of Paradise, 99–101; of salvation, 350; of the living, 350; strange, 230
Langerbeck, H., 14
language, 62, 147–48, 195, 269, 286, 288; *see also* tongue; Aramaic, 5, 74; Egyptian, 189, 192; Greek, 269; Hebrew, 74, 195; Syriac, 13, 269, 271
Lattke, M., xxiii
Lausiac History, 21
Lavenant, R., xxiii
law, 101–3, 106, 109, 161, 170, 198, 217, 221–23, 229, 246, 254, 259, 264, 283, 354; tablets of, 223, 261, 264, 283
Lazarus (raised from the dead), 317
Lazarus (the poor man), 337, 340–41
Le Déaut, R., 224, 228–30, 235, 244, 249–50, 254
Leah, 72, 175–78, 200
Lebon, J., 16
Lehrman, S. M., 224, 232, 235, 237, 246, 254
Leloir, L., xvi, xxiii, 20, 40, 47, 56, 203, 328
lepers, 316
leprosy, 226, 270; *see also* Moses, leprous hand of
Leroy-Molinghen, A., 335
letter, 204, 340–41, 355
Letter to the Men of Homs, 336
Letter to the Mountaineers, 336
Levene, A., xxiv, 141, 200
Levi, 176, 201–2, 209; sons of, 205, 265, 282; tribe of, 202; *see also* Levites
Leviathan and Behemoth, 92–93, 109
Levites 293; *see also* Levi, tribe of
Levy, B., 169
liars, 295
libation, *see* sacrifice
Lietzmann, H., 11
Lieu, J., 32
Lieu, S. N. C., 31–32, 41, 62
life, 53, 99, 110, 123, 128, 134, 141, 143, 149, 151, 163, 207, 210, 212, 224–25, 234, 262, 271, 278–81,

283–85, 287–88, 290, 316–17, 326, 343, 345, 349–50, 353; *see also* Christ, titles of; divine, 55; eternal, 114, 117, 120, 123, 173; immortal, 109, 114, 123; mortal, 109; natural, 278; supernatural, 278
Life of Ephrem, 27, 34, 37, 43, 60; *see also* Ephrem, Vita tradition
light, sun, 56, 61, 75–78, 80–92, 96, 174, 182, 227, 244–46, 250, 254, 298, 301–2, 304–7, 309–11, 313–14, 319, 342–45; *see also* God, attributes of; ray; garment of light
lightning, 307; *see also* thunder
limbs, 49, 91, 154, 163, 169, 296, 339, 346, 350–51; *see also* Christ, body of
lintels, *see* doorposts
lion, 139–40, 203, 309
lips, 115–16, 127, 173, 192, 204, 252, 289, 310, 320, 323–24, 329; *see also* Christ, body of; God
literary techniques, 269, 271; *see also* allegory; exegesis; antithesis, 271, 276; chiasm, 44, 276; direct address, 295; irony, 271; isocola, 41, 273; metaphor, 273, 284, 302, 337, 342, 347; parallelism, 44, 47–48, 271, 276; rhythm, 44, 271, 273
liturgical practices, 302, 325, 330; Byzantine, 6; Syriac, 6
Living God, *see* God, titles of
Living One, *see* Christ, titles of; God, titles of
lord, 103, 184, 196; *see also* Christ, titles of; God, titles of; God, *see* God, titles of; of all, *see* Christ, titles of; God, titles of; of David, *see* Christ, titles of; of stewardship, *see* Christ, titles of; of the angel, *see* Christ, titles of; God, titles of; of the Kingdom, *see* Christ, titles of; of the law, *see* Christ, titles of; of the light, *see* Christ, titles of; of the Prophets, *see* Christ, titles of; of the signs, *see* Christ, titles of; of the Symbols, *see* Christ, titles of
Lossky, V., 46

376 INDEX

Lot, 70–71, 148–50, 160–65; daughters of, 71, 161–64; descen-dants of, 149; herdsmen of, 150; house of, 71, 161; servants of, 150; sons of, 161, 164; wife of, 161–64
love, 67, 102, 113, 119, 125, 138–39, 149, 157–58, 168, 180, 183, 185, 207–8; see also God, attributes of
lower regions, 61
Luz, 199
lyre, 131–32

Macedonia, 33
Macomber, W., 274
Madey, J., 6
magic, magician, sorcery, 197, 219, 230, 238–42, 244; see also astrology, astrologer
Mahalalel, 133
Mahr, A., xxiv
majesty, 99, 158, 193, 275, 303–4, 307, 310–11, 318, 321, 327, 329; see also Christ, attributes of; God, attributes of; weakness
Maker, see God, titles of
man, mankind, 82, 91, 93–94, 96, 105, 107, 124, 131–32, 135, 137–38, 142–45, 153, 155, 157, 159–60, 162–63, 165, 170, 175, 179, 182–84, 186, 194, 208, 347; see also humanity
Manasseh, 73, 199
Mandeans, 11
Mani, 10–11, 35, 49–50, 61–62, 64, 86–87, 218, 243, 306; see also Cologne Mani Codex
Manichaean, 10, 49–50, 306; see also Cologne Mani Codex
Manichaeism, 62, 87, 279; see also Cologne Mani Codex; teachings of, 75
manifest aid, 346; see also medicine, cure
Manifestation of His rest, see Christ, titles of
manna, 222, 254–55, 262–63, 319 see also bread from heaven
Marah, 253–54; water at, 217, 222, 254

Marcion 35, 47, 49–50, 61–62, 64, 218, 243
Marcionites, 49, 62, 137, 343; teachings of, 75
Maries, L., xvi, 40, 151
Maronite Church, 5
Marquart, J., 9
marriage, 350
Martha, 324
Martikainen, J., xxiv
Martin, J. R., 18
martyr acts, 28
martyrdom, crown of, see crown, of martyrdom
martyrs of Edessa (Barsamya, Guria, Habib, Shamona, and Sharbil), 34; Barsamya, 35; Sharbil, 35
Marutha of Maipherkat, 28
Mary Magdalene, 324; identified with the sinful woman, 324–25
Mary, Mother of God, 49, 53, 176, 247, 276–77, 324, 329, 331; see also virgin; mother of Christ, 52; as new shoot, 278; as second Eve, 53, 278; as vine, 278; ear of, 53
master, 259, 264, 305, 312, 340, 342; see also Christ, titles of; Builder, see Christ, titles of; Craftsman of the Creator, see Christ, titles of; of the debt, see Christ, titles of
Mathews, E. G., Jr., ix, xxiv, 14, 17, 21–22, 40–41, 54
Mathews, T. F., 6
matter, 49, 62
McCullough, W. S., 8
McVey, K., xi, xxiv, 33, 41, 53, 330
measure of justice, see Christ, titles of
Measuring bowl that is not false, see Christ, titles of
measuring rod, even, see Christ, titles of
meat, 158, 230, 254
Media, 7
Mediator, see Christ, titles of
medicine, cure, remedy, 55, 279, 283, 289–90, 294, 296, 299, 316, 319, 325; see also manifest aid
Medicine of Life, see Christ, titles of
Mehujael, 129–30

Melchizedek, 70, 150–51, 171, 328; *see also* Shem
sons of, 151
Melki, J., xxiv, 40
Melkite (or Greek Catholic) Church, 6
memory, memorial, 256, 264, 325, 352
Mercier, C., xvi, 40
Merciful One, *see* Christ, titles of
mercy, 115, 118, 133, 182, 265, 350, 354–55; *see also* Christ, attributes of; God, attributes of
mercy seat, propitiatory, 262, 330; *see also* Christ, titles of; lamb, propitiatory
Mesopotamia, 7–8, 28, 31, 45, 71, 218, 279
Messalians, 50
Messiah, *see* Christ, titles of
metaphor, *see* literary techniques
Methuselah, 134, 140
Methushael, 129–31
metrical homilies, *see* genres, prose
Meyer, R. T., 13
Midian, 221, 229, 231, 234–35
Midianites, 204
midrash, 63, 218, 235, 237, 246; *see also* genres, poetry
midwives, 224–25
Mighty One, *see* Christ, titles of; God, titles of
Milcah, 148, 165
milk, 27, 55, 166, 204–5, 208, 227, 260, 317
mind, 55, 67, 94, 107–8, 111, 125, 163, 170, 186, 192, 200, 202, 212, 264–65, 275, 290–91, 293–94, 299–300, 318–20, 322, 324, 332, 341, 343, 348, 351–52, 354; human, 50; inner, 245, 348, 354
Mingana, A., 3, 7
mingling, *see* mixing, mingling
miracle, 68, 243
Miriam, 226–28, 230, 253–54; song of, 222
mirror, 55, 79, 280, 297, 336–41, 347, 348, 350, 355; as womb, 339
Mitchell, C. W., xvi, 62
mixing, mingling, 61, 290, 310, 330, 355

Moab, 164, 253
Mobarek, P., 63, 65
Molenberg, C., xxiv
Monastery of Our Lady of the Syrians (Egypt), 63, 219
monastic life, 19; *see also* asceticism; Egypt, monasticism in; encratism; eremetic life; Syria, monasticism in; cell, 12, 24; philosophy, 13; practices, 13, 20, 23; terminology, 20
monasticism, 274
money, 73, 178, 191–94, 198
Monimos, cult of, 34
monk, 15, 18–19, 21, 24, 27, 37, 273–74
Monophysites, 47
moon, 82, 89–92, 182
Moore, G. F., 242
morning, 90–91, 208
mortal, 123, 274, 277, 284, 287, 290, 302, 328, 345
mortality, 345
mortar and pestle, 290
Moses, 43, 48, 60, 63, 67–68, 75, 77–78, 80, 82, 85, 91–92, 94, 96–97, 99–100, 103–4, 106–7, 121, 124, 135, 137, 144, 147, 201, 206, 209, 212, 219, 221–23, 225–45, 248–49, 251, 253–57, 260–65, 282, 292–93, 301, 304–6, 308–9, 315, 318–19, 328–29; beauty of, 226, 228, 230; Canticle of, 44, 217, 251, 253; compassion of, 229; face of, 107, 231, 308; radiance of, 68, 308–9; family of, 226; gaze of, 304; hand of, 292; leprous, 222, 233; house of, 237, 241, 248, 261, 309; humility of, 315; integrity of, 230; justice of, 229; staff of, 69, 96, 217, 222, 233–34, 236, 238, 240–41, 249, 255–56; teaching of, 60; titles of; deliverer, 224; intercessor, 264; servant of the Lord, 251; shepherd, 293; the one who breached their gaps, 264; voice of, 232–33; stammering of, 228, 234, 315
Moshe bar Kepha, 59
Moss, C., xxx

Mosshammer, A., 39
Most High, *see* Christ, titles of; God, titles of
mother, 52, 72, 105, 260, 276, 278, 287, 329, 331; of Moses, 225–28, 253; of all the living, *see* Eve; of Christ, *see* Mary, Mother of God
mount Ararat, 141; Edessa, 43; Qardu, 141; Sinai, 222–23, 257–58, 261–65, 283
mountain, 93, 98, 109, 126, 135, 139, 141, 162–63, 167–69, 208, 255–56, 308, 344; of inheritance, 253; *see also* Jerusalem; Paradise as, 101
mouth, 179, 183, 196, 206, 225, 234, 252, 273, 275, 281, 286, 288–89, 293, 295, 303, 305–6, 314, 323, 325, 340–41, 345, 351, 353; *see also* Christ, body of; God
murder, 69, 126–27, 132–33, 202–3, 228, 262
Murray, R., xxiv, xxv, 4–6, 9–12, 20, 25, 30, 44, 46–47, 52–54, 105, 123, 174, 203–4, 261, 269, 271, 274–75, 277–78, 280, 284–85, 290, 292, 310, 312, 324, 342
Musician, Divine, *see* God, titles of
Mygdonius River, 28
mysteries, 68; *see also* eucharist
mystery, 46, 48, 52, 54–55, 96, 149–50, 174, 199, 232, 269
Mystical Body, *see* church

Naamah, 131
Nabatean kings, *see* kings, Nabatea
Nag Hammadi, 11
Nahor, 148, 170, 179
naked, nakedness, 54, 105–6, 113–15, 117, 121, 144–45, 182, 196, 346, 350; *see also* clothing; garment
names, 74–75, 79, 83, 103–7, 110, 131, 147, 155, 172, 186, 193, 199, 207–8, 211; of the Lord, 133
Naphtali, 176, 206, 210–11
narrow road of the persecuted, *see* way
Narsai, 3, 59
Narses, King of Persia, 26

Nasrallah, J., 6
nation, 232–33, 252, 258, 280–81, 284, 294, 308, 315, 330, 332, 341; *see also* Jewish nation
nations, 71, 146, 148–49, 151, 153–54, 156–57, 164, 167, 169–71, 174, 199, 201, 203–6, 209–10, 253–54, 256, 258, 260, 330, 341; *see also* tribe
nature, 19, 46, 48, 51, 53, 74–75, 82–83, 85, 137, 164, 201, 212, 237–38, 240, 254, 275, 280, 302, 305, 307, 342, 345, 347; deficiency of, 286; divine, 50–51, 69, 275–76, 290, 296–97, 301–3, 310; fullness of, 286; human, 67, 275–76, 290, 296, 307, 310
natures, 75; *see also* Christ, divine/human nature
Nau, F., 7, 26
Near and far from Him, *see* Christ, titles of
Nebo, cult of, 34
needy persons, 188
neighbor, 246, 258–59
Nestorian Church *see* Church of the East (or Assyrian, or Nestorian) Church
Nestorians, 47
Nestorius, 74, 274
nets, 290
Neusner, J., 10, 31
New Testament, 20, 47, 53, 121, 210, 271, 273, 290
night, 78, 80–82, 87–91, 137, 139, 141, 143, 152, 160–61, 163, 173, 177–80, 222, 234–35, 245–48, 250, 314, 319, 351
Nimrod, 33, 146–48
Nisan, 80, 237, 248
Nisibis, 7, 10, 12, 17, 24–33, 35–37, 62, 147, 218; baptistery in, 29; church of, 27, 29–30; School of, 22, 29, 36, 218; siege of, 27–29
Noah, 60, 69–70, 83, 98, 134, 138–46, 148, 151, 162, 351; house of, 83, 141; sons of, 138, 143
Nod, 130
north, 61, 101, 139, 146

INDEX 379

nostrils, 99
Noth, M., 250
Noujaim, G., xxv, 51
Numbers Rabbah, 104
nurse, 227

oath, 71, 170, 172
oblation, *see* sacrifice
ocean, 39
Odes of Solomon, 10, 37–38
offering, *see* sacrifice
Ogren, I., xxv
oil, 174, 206, 289, 294, 319, 324–25, 349; *see also* fragrance, ointment, perfume, Christ, titles of Messiah; for the lamps, 350; holy, 261
ointment, 275, 324, 349–50; *see also* fragrance, oil, perfume
Old Testament, 43, 47, 53, 74–75, 121, 218, 270, 289
olive, 83, 231
On Fate, *see* Bardaisan
Onan, 182–83
One, *see* Christ, titles of; God, titles of
Only-Begotten, *see* Christ, titles of
oppression, 225, 232, 238
order, *see* command
Origen, *Homilies on Exodus*, 254
orphans, 188
Ortiz de Urbina, I., xxv, xxvi, xxx, 17, 24, 29, 42
Outtier, B., xvi, xxvi, 13, 15, 20–22, 271
Overbeck, J. J., xvi, 281

paganism, 10, 15, 25, 31–32, 35
pagans, heathens, infidels; paganism, 106, 229, 232, 281, 283, 292–94, 296, 318–19; of Egypt, 292
Palestine, 8
Palladius, 3, 12–15, 17, 21, 24, 29, 35–36
Palmyra, 33
Palut, 9, 35
Papa, Catholicos, 336
parable, 272, 291, 298–99, 321, 323, 337, 340
Paradise, 15, 53–54, 59, 69, 80, 90, 93, 95–96, 99–103, 104, 107–9, 111, 113, 115–16, 120, 123–24,
126, 133, 136, 141, 209, 212, 336, 339–40, 347, 351; land of, 99–100; of God, 353; trees of, *see* trees of Paradise
parallelism, *see* literary techniques
Parmentier, L., 24
Parthia, 7
Parthian Empire, 34
Parthians, 26
Passover, 217, 277; lamb, 217, 222, 246, 260; ritual, 246
path, pathway(s), *see* way
patience, 115, 176; *see also* God, attributes of; long-suffering, 140
patriarchs,, narratives of, 43–44
Paul, 7, 10, 77, 94, 118, 211, 270, 295, 300–302, 305–9, 311–15; *see also* Saul
Paulinians, 50
Payne Smith, R., 330
pearl, 54
Peeters, P., 17, 27, 37
Peleg, 148
Pelliot, P., 5
Pena, I., 19
Pentateuch, 67, 97
Pentecost, 7
people, 73, 96, 146, 153, 156, 165, 175, 198–99, 205, 210, 212–13, 226, 228, 231–34, 236–39, 242, 244–46, 248–54, 256–58, 260, 262–65; ancient, 212; eternal, 96; innocent, 165; Jewish, 211–12; *see also* Hebrews; Israelites; Jews; of God, 133, 135; temporal, 96
Peral Torres, A., xxvi
perfume, 275; *see also* fragrance, oil, ointment
persecution, 7, 26, 28, 307–8, 311–13; Decian, 35
persecutor, 32, 301, 308, 310, 312–15; wide road of the, *see* way
Persia, 26–28, 31–32, 34
Persian Empire, 5, 27–28
Peshitta, x, 63, 74, 76, 79, 96, 106, 123, 136, 141, 144, 149, 165, 169–70, 178, 190, 193, 198, 200–201, 203–8, 210–11, 218, 229, 261, 274, 303, 317–18, 330, 341
Peter the Apostle, *see* Simon

INDEX

Petersen, W. L., xxvi, 279
Petre, H., 34
Petrus Benedictus, 219
Pharaoh, 70, 73, 149–50, 155, 165, 186–88, 196, 198, 218–19, 221–22, 224–29, 231–34, 236–46, 248–50, 252–53; dreams of, 186–87; eyes of, 229; hand of, 232; hands of, 229; house of, 70, 149, 242; servants of, 73, 186, 244, 246, 248–49; wise men of, 186
Pharaoh's daughter, 221, 226, 229
Pharisee(s), 298, 316, 324; *see also* Simon the Pharisee
Phicol, 167, 172
Philistia, 252
Philistines, 146, 165, 205–6
Phillip, disciple of Bardaisan, 37
Phillips, G., 8
Philo, *On the Sacrifices of Abel and Cain*, 124
philosophy, 34
Philoxenos, 7
Phineas, 202
Photinians, 50
physician, 289–90, 316–17; *see also* Christ, titles of
Piganiol, A., 28
Pigulevskaja, N., 26
pillar, 174, 179, 211; of cloud, 250, 292, 319; of fire, 81, 248, 250, 252, 255, 262, 319; of salt, 162–63
Pishon, 100–101
pit, 73, 182, 185, 188, 190, 196
plagues, 70, 218–19, 233–34, 237–44, 246, 249, 253, 258; boils, 222, 242; darkness, 222; firstborn, 222, 234, 238–39, 246–48, 252–53; frogs, 222, 240–41; gnats, 222, 241; hail, 222, 242–45; insects, 222, 241–42; locusts, 222, 244–45; pestilence, 222, 242; river to blood, 222, 233, 239, 241, 252; ulcers, 239
plants, 98, 120, 134, 208
plunder, *see* treasures
poison, 53
Polotsky, H. J., xxvi, 16
poor, 346

Potiphar, 185, 187–88; wife of, 73, 185, 187
Pouchet, J., 79
power, *see* Christ, attributes of; God, attributes of
praise, 56, 273, 286, 300, 323, 348, 353
praiseworthy, *see* God, attributes of
prayer, 71, 125, 154–55, 170, 184, 226, 249, 255, 263–64, 285, 315, 320
pregnancy, 163; *see also* birth, womb, barrenness
Price, R. M., 24
pride, 233, 298, 300, 313, 315, 348; *see also* arrogance, humility
priest, priesthood, 30, 150–51, 154, 229–30, 258, 260, 262–63, 270–71, 322, 326, 328–32, 343; *see also* Christ, titles of; Aaronic priesthood, 328; lands of, 73, 198
principles (itye), eternal, 61, 76–77
prison, 73, 185, 187–88, 190; *see also* captive, captivity
proclamation, 281, 284, 288, 311
prologue, 59–61, 66
promise, 96, 114, 116, 142, 149, 159, 166–68, 198, 209, 223, 233, 242, 325, 332, 340
promised land, 155, 255
prophecy, 105, 168, 253–54, 261, 270, 324, 328–32
prophet, prophetess, 79, 203, 234, 253–54, 262, 270, 291–92, 295, 299, 316–20, 326; *see also* Christ, titles of
Prophets, 55, 92, 154, 209, 211, 259, 270, 287, 291, 316–20, 346
propitiatory, *see* mercy seat
prose homily, *see* genres, prose
prostitute, harlot, 184, 290
prototype, 261; *see also* shadow; type; typology
providence, 218
provider, *see* Christ, titles of
Provisioner of All, *see* Christ, titles of
public, open, 282, 287, 289, 292–93, 296–97, 300, 319, 323, 325, 342; *see also* secret, hidden
publican, 290, 324

Publius, 335–36; *see also* Ephrem, works of, *Letter to Publius*
punishment, 69, 71, 110, 115, 118–21, 127, 130, 132–33, 147, 153–54, 160, 265, 301
pupils (of eyes), 287, 302, 308, 314
purifications, 329
pure sacrifice, *see* Christ, titles of

Qardu, *see* mount, Qardu
quail, 222, 255, 262
Quasten, J., 7
Qumran, 10–11

race, 225
Rachel, 72, 174–79, 182, 191, 200; children of, 191
rage, *see* anger
Rahmani, I. E., xvi
rain, 84, 97–98, 139, 143, 208, 243, 272, 298, 312, 348
rainbow, 144; *see also* bow
ram, 71, 152, 154, 169
Rameses, 248
ranks, 339
rape of Dinah, 163–64
rationalism, 275
ray, 298, 301–2, 304, 313, 342; *see also* light
ray of His light, *see* Christ, titles of
reason, 99, 107, 114, 119, 149
Rebekah, 71–72, 151, 170–74, 176
receiver of offerings, *see* Christ, titles of
Red Sea, 222, 226, 240, 249–53, 258, 261, 263, 292
redemption, 269
Refson, K., 66
region, 95, 139, 146; above, 61, 95; below, *see* lower region
Rehoboth, 147
remedy, *see* medicine
renewer of creatures, *see* Christ, titles of
rennet, 331; *see also* bread, leavened; yeast
Renoux, C., xvi, xxvi, 40
repentance, 118, 120, 128, 136–38, 237–38, 244–45, 250, 289, 319, 330, 355

Rephidim, 255
reptile, 80, 93, 96, 103, 117, 137–38
rescuer, *see* God, titles of
Resen, 147
Reshaina, 147
rest, 96–97; *see also* Christ, titles of; God, attributes of; temporal, 96
restorer of natures, *see* Christ, titles of
resurrection, 54, 134, 143, 168, 209, 271, 274, 277, 288, 309, 355
resuscitator of mortality, *see* Christ, titles of
Reu, 148
Reuben/Reubel, 176–77, 190, 194, 199–201, 209, 211
revelation, 51–52, 151, 158, 329
rhythm, *see* literary techniques
rib, 94, 104–5, 113, 116, 235
Ricciotti, G., xxvi
Richardson, E. C., 3
right hand of His mercy, *see* Christ, titles of
righteous Judge, *see* Christ, titles of
righteous ones, 154, 275, 331, 336
righteousness, 138–39, 142, 152–53, 194, 342, 354–55
river, 83–84, 92, 100–101, 208, 225; *see also* water
river (Nile), 100, 154, 222, 224–27, 229, 233, 239, 241, 246–47, 252; *see also* Gihon
road, *see* way
Robbins, G. A., 101
Robinson, T. A., 8
Robson, P., xxvi
rock, 173–75, 179, 199, 207, 211, 222, 252, 317, 319; *see also* Christ, titles of
Rolfe, J. C., 32–33
Roman Catholic Church, 18
Roman Empire, 26, 31, 33, 62
Romanos the Melodist, 4, 279
Rome, 7, 26–27, 34
Roncaglia, M. P., xxx
Rosen, V., 335
Rousseau, D. O., xxvi, 16
Rouwhorst, G. A. M., xxvi, xxvii, 237
rule, *see* dominion, rule
ruler, 96, 99, 103, 107, 117, 121, 146, 148, 196, 207, 228

sabbath, 97, 169, 254
Sabellians, 50
Saber, G., xxvii
sacraments, 276, 279–80, 310, 325
sacrifice, holocaust, fat, libation, oblation, offering, 69–72, 124–26, 134, 142, 152–53, 167–69, 174, 180, 189, 192, 232, 239, 245, 257, 260–61, 263, 325–26, 343, 355; *see also* Christ, titles of
Saeki, Y., 5
salt, saltiness, 83–84, 208; pillar of, *see* pillar of salt
salvation, 47, 206, 210, 343, 349–50
salvation history, 123
Samaritans, 151
Samir, K., xxvii, xxx, 65
Samson, 205
sanctuary, *see* tabernacle
sand, 228
Sarah, 70–71, 148–49, 151, 153, 155–59, 165–71, 176; *see also* Iscah; as the "free woman" (cf. Gal 4.21–31), 71, 166; descendants of, 149
Sassanian Empire, 6, 26, 29, 31, 34
Sassanians, 26
Satan, 50, 104, 108–10, 121, 209–10, 224, 235; fall of, 114; titles of; betrayer, 117; captor, 288; crafty one, 117; enemy, 113–14; Evil One, 108, 290; mighty one, 332; tempter, 108–11, 115, 121
Saul (king), 79, 307
Saul (Paul), 300–301, 307–9, 311–13, 315; *see also* Paul
Savior, *see* Christ, titles of
scale without deceit, *see* Christ, titles of
scepter, 203–4
Scetis, 15
Schechter, S., 242
Scheidweiler, F., 24
Scher, A., xxvii, 15, 22, 29, 31, 33, 36, 218
Schiwietz, S., 16
Schmidt, M., xxvii, 52
scribe, 42, 237, 296, 323
Scripture, 14, 47–49, 51, 53, 55, 67, 80, 85–86, 88, 98, 113, 129, 135, 145, 151, 171, 213, 270

sea, 68, 78, 82–84, 89, 92–96, 98, 101, 109, 143, 203, 205, 327–28, 344, 351; *see also* ocean, Red Sea, water
sea coast, seashore, 205, 209, 228, 232, 251
season, 90, 92, 143, 237
Sebeok, T. A., 5
second, *see* Christ, titles of
second light of Being, *see* Christ, titles of
Second Sophistic, panegyrical tradition of, 14
secret, hidden, 280, 282, 285, 287, 289, 292–93, 296–97, 299–300, 317–18, 320–21, 323, 342; *see also* public, open
Sed, N., xxvii, 45, 63, 339
seed, 70, 119, 121, 136, 153, 155, 162–64, 166, 169, 175, 198, 226, 228, 243, 312, 344
Segal, J. B., xxvii, 4, 6, 9–10, 33–34
Seleucia-Ctesiphon, 27, 31, 147
Seleucus I Nicator, 33
Self-Existent One, *see* God, titles of
self-existent being(s), *see* being, self-existent; elements
self-subsistent being(s), *see* being, self-subsistent
Sennacherib, 208
Sephora, 221, 230, 234–36
seraph, seraphim, 109
Serapion, bishop of Antioch, 9
Serjuni, A. H., xxvii
serpent, 53, 69, 85, 92–93, 106–19, 121, 205, 210, 233, 351; *see also* snake
Serug, 148
servant, 71, 73, 96, 112, 150–51, 153, 155, 158, 168–70, 173, 176–77, 185–87, 191, 195–97, 208, 251, 285, 325–26, 328; *see also* Christ, titles of
female, 71, 96, 167, 176–77; *see also* serving girl
service, 78, 80–82, 88, 93, 97, 175
serving girl, 227, 259; *see also* servant, female
servitude, *see* slavery
Seth, 130, 133, 136; daughters of,

INDEX 383

131; descendants of, 136; house of, 133; sons of, 130, 132, 134–37; tribe of, 69, 133, 135–36
Sethites, 132–33, 136
Severus of Antioch, 16
Severus of Edessa, 219
Severus of Gabala, On the Creation of the World, 94
shadow, 78, 80, 86, 88, 351; *see also* darkness; prototype; type; typology
shame, disgrace, 106, 111, 127, 129, 132, 165, 185, 196, 202; *see also* honor
Shamona, *see* martyrs of Edessa
Shapur II, 26–29, 31–32
Sharbil, *see* martyrs of Edessa
Shechem, 72, 181, 201, 209
inhabitants of, 201, 209
sons of, 181, 209
Shechemites, 201
sheep, 104, 198–99, 230–31, 241, 336, 346–47, 351; flock of, 229–30, 245, 309
Shelah, 148, 182–84
Shem, 67, 70, 134, 146, 148, 151; *see also* Melchizedek; descendants of, 146; sons of, 156; tent of, 146
Sheol, 229, 270, 274, 277–80, 340, 345, 352–53; gate of, 128
shepherd (not Christ), 103, 124, 174–75, 207, 232, 293, 309; *see also* Christ, titles of; Moses, titles of
Shunammite woman, 318
sickness, *see* disease
Sidon, 205, 210
siege, 30
signs, 90, 110, 130, 140, 144, 159, 169–70, 183–84, 219, 222, 232–34, 236–38, 240, 244, 249, 255–57, 273, 282–83, 286–88, 291–94, 296–97, 308–11, 315–17, 319; *see also* wonders
Silent One, *see* Christ, titles of
silk, 352
silk route, 34
silver, 222, 246, 249
Simeon bar Sabbae, 27–28
Simeon Metaphrastes, 14
Simeon of Samosata, 16

Simeon the priest, 270, 325–31; as treasurer, 329; as steward, 329
Simeon, son of Jacob, 176, 190–91, 193, 199, 201–2, 209; son of, 202; tribe of, 202
Simon the Apostle, 270–71, 327, 329–30
Simon the Pharisee, 270, 272–74, 281, 289–96, 298–99, 315–23, 327
Sims-Williams, P., xxvii
Sin, cult of, 34
Sinai desert, 205, 254; *see also* Mount Sinai
Singara, 31–32
Sisera, 206
skill, 240–41, 269, 311; divine, 69; human, 240
Skudlarek, W., 20
slander, blasphemy, 61, 229, 273, 295, 299, 306, 316, 319, 323, 342
slave, 31, 145–46, 152, 154, 166, 168, 192–93, 195–97, 205, 221
slavery, servitude, 96, 155, 195, 197, 205, 221, 231, 261
Smith, R. Payne, 4
snake, 222, 233–35, 238, 240; *see also* serpent
Sodom, 71, 150, 159–63
Sodomites, 70–71, 150–51, 160–61, 163–64, 352
soldiers, 309
Solomon, 78
Son, *see* Christ, titles of; of David, *see* Christ, titles of; of God, *see* Christ, titles of; of Man, *see* Christ, titles of; of the Most High, *see* Christ, titles of; of the skillful carpenter, *see* Christ, titles of
songs, 285, 353
sons of God, 135–36
sorcery, *see* magic, magicians
soul, 73, 94, 107, 211, 221, 223, 280, 288, 290, 317, 322, 324, 330, 332, 341, 346, 348, 351, 354–55
south, 61, 101, 139
Sozomen, 3, 13–14, 16, 21, 24–25, 28, 32, 35–36, 38–39
spear, *see* weapon; *see also* lance, sword
speech, 108, 270, 273, 286–88, 299, 307, 315

Sperber, A., 79
Spira, A., 14
spirit, 79, 94, 163, 197, 241, 272, 276, 290, 302, 329–30, 341, 346, 350, 355; *see also* God, titles of; Holy Spirit; evil spirit of God, 79; of God, 135; robe of the, 330
spiritual being, *see* being, spiritual
splendor, 105, 107, 110; *see also* Christ, attributes of; glory; God, attributes of
Splendrous One, *see* Christ, titles of
spoils, *see* treasures
Sprengling, M., 74
spring (of water), 92, 97–98, 100–101, 141, 174, 206, 208, 211
sprinkling that purifies, *see* Christ, titles of
stain(s), 170, 277, 319, 322, 330, 338, 355
star, luminary, 82, 89–90, 96, 152, 182, 189–90
statues, *see* gods
Stephen, 7, 77
steward, 191–94; *see also* Christ, titles of; Simeon the priest
stomach, 163, 279, 289, 324, 339; *see also* belly
stranger, 70, 118, 158, 160, 230, 245, 247, 346
straw, 116, 222, 237, 245, 257
street(s), 144–45, 160, 188, 225, 317; *see also* way
stretcher, 296
struggle, Jacob's with angel, 72
Sturm, J., 26
stylite, 37
substance(s), 49, 67–68, 74–75, 77–78, 81, 86–88, 91
Succoth, 248
Sumer, 45
summer, 90, 143, 237
sun, *see* light; *see also* ray
supplication, 115–16, 118–19, 184
sweetness, 280, 300, 321; *see also* Christ, attributes of
sweet root, *see* Christ, titles of
sword, *see* lance
symbolic theology, 48

symbols, symbolism, 48–49, 51–53, 55–56, 63, 68, 204, 206, 275, 324, 329, 338; *see also* literary techniques, metaphor; mystery
synagogue, 204, 282–83, 300; *see also* Hebrews; Israel; Israelites; Jews
Syrén, R., 200
Syria, 3, 6–8, 10–12, 15, 19, 21, 24, 26–27, 38–39, 65, 269; culture of, 5; language of, 5, 13, 269, 271; literature of, 38, 42, 59, 79, 148, 167, 174, 285, 336; monasticism in, 19, 24, 274
Syriac-speaking Christianity, 3–6, 8, 10–11, 218, 269–71, 274, 280–81, 284, 290, 310, 328, 330
Syrian Catholic Church, 5
Syrian Orthodox (Jacobite) Church, 5
Syro-Malabar Church, 6
Syro-Malankar Church, 6

tabernacle, sanctuary, holy dwelling, dwelling in Jerusalem, 204, 223, 252–53, 261; *see also* cherubim; incense; mercy seat; oil; priest; tent of meeting; vessels; heavenly, 261; temporal, 261
Tabet, J., 65
Tamar, 72, 182–84, 203
tambourines, timbrel, 254, 293; *see also* cymbals
Tammûz, 237
targum, targumic traditions, 43, 63–64, 74, 79, 93, 141, 169, 200, 218, 228–29, 235, 249–50, 254; *see also* genres, prose; *Onkelos*, 79, 169, 207; *Neofiti*, 93, 97, 102, 123, 136, 169, 248; *Pseudo-Jonathan*, 93, 102, 123, 141, 144, 169, 193, 230, 244, 248
Tarsus, 31
taskmaster, 228–29, 237
Tatian, 11
tax, 27
teacher, 298, 322; foolish, 318, 320, 322; *see also* Israel, foolish teachers of
teaching, 86, 204
tears, 118, 126, 176, 182, 226,

289–91, 293–94, 316, 319–20, 324, 341, 355
teeth, 204; gnashing of, 340; *see also* wailing and weeping
Teixidor, J., xxvii, 61
temple, 204, 327–28, 331; *see also* tabernacle; presentation in, 328, 330
tempter, *see* Satan
Ten Napel, E., 59
tent, 129, 131, 144, 173, 353; of meeting, 261
Ter Petrossian, L., xvi, xxvii
Terah, 148, 165; house of, 149
testament, 38
Testament of Ephrem, 17, 35, 37
testimony, 112, 295–96, 316, 319
testing, waters of, 282–83
Theodore of Mopsuestia, 218
Theodoret of Cyr, 19, 21, 24, 27–28, 39; *History of the Monks of Syria*, 24–25, 335; *Questions on Genesis*, 94
thief, robber, 101, 206, 210
Thomas, Apostle, 9, 34; Church of, 34; tomb of, 34
Thomson, R. W., 6
thorn, briar, weed, thistle, 62, 101, 120–21, 232
throne, 347; of Egypt, 187, 227; of judgment, 256; of Yahweh, 256
twelve thrones of judgment, 341
thunder, 52, 243, 307; *see also* lightning
Tigris, 101
title, 232, 251, 253, 271, 279, 284, 289, 324–25, 330, 342, 345, 350; divine, 284; *see also* Christ, titles of; God, titles of; Moses, titles of; Satan, titles of
Tobia bar Tobia, 9
tohu and bohu (void and desolation), 76–77
tomb, sepulchre, 34, 248, 310, 352
tongue, 38–39, 68, 70, 146–47, 159, 193, 195, 234, 271, 282, 286, 291, 300, 306, 315, 340, 350; *see also* language
Tonneau, R. M., xvi, xxvii, 63–65, 68, 101, 171, 220, 226, 244, 246, 263, 282
Torah, 67, 213, 221, 254
Torres, A. P., 65
Trajan, 35
transcendence, *see* God, attributes of
transgression, 95, 100–102, 106, 114–16, 212
treasurer, *see* Christ, titles of; John the Baptist; Simeon the priest
treasures, plunder, spoils, 30, 183–84, 233, 248–49, 252, 278, 284–85, 298, 332
treasury, treasure house, 59, 186, 285, 298, 321, 329, 345, 352; *see also* Christ, titles of; of Sheol, 277–78; of God, 284; of humility, 298; of mercy, 99
tree(s), 71, 89–91, 97–100, 102, 107–12, 115–17, 124, 158, 169, 243, 280, 331, 344, 347; broom, 340; fig, 54, 332; fruit-bearing, 90; natural, *see* Christ, titles of; of knowledge, 69; of life, 100, 109–10, 113–14, 119–20, 122–23, 278, 280; of Paradise, 90, 96, 100, 102, 107, 111, 115; of the knowledge of good and evil, 100, 102, 108–9, 111, 114, 117–18, 120, 122–23; olive, 55; spiritual trees of Paradise, 100
Treppner, M., xxvii
trial, 115, 117, 140, 160, 162
tribe(s), 69, 129, 132, 137, 151, 154, 156–57, 165, 199, 201–3, 205, 207, 210–11, 341, 345; *see also* nation(s); of Israel, 205; of the descendants of Cain, 133; twelve, 157
Trinity, 25, 30, 122, 310, 342, 344; *see also* God; Christ; Holy Spirit; spirit
teachings on, 269
trophies, 300
truth, 25, 48, 157, 164, 179, 187, 190, 192, 197, 204, 210, 273, 288, 291, 295–96, 310, 343, 347; *see also* Christ, attributes of
Tubal-Cain, 131
Tugwell, S., 4

INDEX

type(s), 48, 68, 139, 209, 217, 246–47, 254–55, 260–61, 325; *see also* prototype; shadow
typology, 46–49, 51–53, 55, 60, 101, 145, 217, 220, 247, 287; *see also* prototype; shadow
Tyre, 210

unreachable power, *see* Christ, titles of
Ur of the Chaldees 70, 148, 152
Urfa, *see* Edessa
Urhai, *see* Edessa
uterus, *see* womb

Vaillant, A., xxviii
vainglory, 147
Valens, 335
van den Broek, R., 11
van der Horst, P., 146
Van Rompay, L., xxii, 66, 79
Van Vossel, V., xxviii
vaults, *see* treasuries
vegetation, 82, 90–91, 97–98, 243
veil, 107, 161, 305
Vellian, J., 6
Vermaseren, M.J., 11
vessel, 108, 232, 261, 328–29, 352
village, 144, 159, 174, 182
vine, 38, 60, 204; *see also* Eve as old vine; Mary, mother of Christ as new vine; true, 204
vineyard, 69, 144, 243, 278, 323
virgin, 274, 278, 349–50; *see also* Mary, mother of Christ
virginity, 129, 134, 170, 200, 350
vision, 38, 70, 72, 105, 109–10, 152, 156–58, 160, 163, 231–32, 235, 248, 261, 309, 336–37, 350, 353
Vologeses, 29
Vööbus, A., xiv, xxviii, 12, 17–19, 22, 29, 37, 42, 336

wailing and weeping, 340, 349, 353; *see also* teeth, gnashing of
Walsh, J., xxviii
war, 148, 150, 167
warrior, 204, 210; *see also* God, titles of
watcher, *see* angel/watcher

water, 61, 75–80, 82–85, 87–90, 92, 98, 100, 103, 141, 144, 162, 167, 200–201, 208–9, 222, 225, 229, 233, 239–40, 252–55, 263–64, 293–94, 298, 317, 319, 327, 330, 351; face of, 78; of wrath, 134
wax, 302–3, 307
way, path, road, pathway, 55, 84, 116, 123, 129, 131, 134–35, 138, 204–5, 210–11, 236, 274, 277, 298, 311, 315, 322, 343; narrow, 350; narrow road of the persecuted, 315; wide road of the persecutor, *see* way, 315
Way of truth, *see* Christ, titles of
weakness, 303–4, 307, 310, 313, 317–18, 327; *see also* Christ, attributes of; God, attributes of; majesty
wealth, 181, 352
weaning, 71
weapon, bow, spear, 201, 209, 278, 300, 352; *see also* lance, sword
weed, *see* thorn
Weinstock, S., 7
well, 71, 156, 167, 170, 174–75, 221, 229
west, 61, 89, 91, 101, 139, 146
Westermann, C., 193
wheat, 116, 158, 243; grain of, 285
whispers, 315, 342
White, H. G. Evelyn, 16
wickedness, 69, 137, 321, 336, 340
wide road of the persecutor, *see* way
Widengren, G., 87, 279
widows, 188
Wiessner, G., 28
wilderness, desert, desert waste, 19–20, 68, 81, 155, 167, 174, 182, 185, 188, 205, 207, 211–12, 236, 244, 254, 257, 282, 292–94, 309, 315, 328; *see also* civilization
will, 82, 84, 98, 125, 146, 156, 170, 173, 176–77, 189, 194, 201, 225, 259, 278, 300, 303, 306, 346; *see also* free will; compulsion; divine, 346; *see also* Christ, attributes of; God, attributes of
Wimbush, V., 17

INDEX

wind, 61, 76, 78–80, 85, 87–88, 250, 298, 327
wine, 71, 144–45, 150, 162–63, 204, 206, 286, 355
wineskins, 252
Winkler, G., 20
winter, 90, 143
Wischmeyer, W., 7
wisdom, 103, 106–7, 197, 208, 225, 342–43, 345; divine, 104; *see also* Christ, titles of
Wisdom of His nature, *see* Christ, titles of
witness, 49, 179, 184–85, 347
woes, ten, 270, 301
wolf, 139, 208, 211, 309
woman, 119, 166, 201–2, 324; foreign, 165, 176; free, 71, 166; of Eve, 104–5, 107–8, 111, 113, 116–18, 121; of Mary, 276; of Rachel, 72; of Rebekah, 170; of Sarah, 152, 159, 165–66; of Tamar, 184; pregnant, 259; Shunammite, *see* Shunammite woman; sinful, 270, 272–74, 289–95, 316–24; slave, 166–67; sterile, 227, 247; with a flow of blood, 289, 325
womb, 52, 71, 85, 87, 98, 124, 151, 153, 156, 158, 171, 176, 208, 246, 277, 287, 310, 331, 339, 351; *see also* birth; ear, womb of; mirror as; pregnancy; barrenness
women, 24, 118, 163, 221, 225, 253, 271, 283; adulterous, 261; Egyptian, 248; free, 176, 205; Hebrew, 227, 248
wonders, 233, 236, 245, 249, 252, 255–57, 263, 286, 289, 292, 294, 314–17, 319, 322; *see also* signs
wood, 138, 142, 168–69, 222, 232, 254, 282

word, 96
word (of God), 83, 89, 92, 96–97, 103, 172, 180
Word, *see* Christ, titles of
Word of His Father, *see* Christ, titles of
work, labor, toil, 96, 120, 122–23, 134, 179, 205, 211, 224, 232, 236, 245, 254, 325
workers, 323; hired, 254
works, 68, 74, 81, 90, 96–97, 121, 137, 311, 348; beautiful, 346; good, 346, 349; mighty, 68, 255
world, 48–49, 53, 61, 67–68, 95, 97, 121, 123, 130, 137, 153, 159, 162, 169, 188, 209, 211, 269, 275, 289, 325–26, 351, 355; eternal, 96
worship, 55, 223, 284
wrath, *see* anger; *see also* God, attributes of
Wright, W. C., 23, 28, 37, 335

Yahweh, *see* God, titles of
Yarshater, E., 26
yeast, 287; *see also* bread, leavened; rennet
yogurt, 55
yoke, 245, 298; *see also* bridle
Yousif, P., xxviii, xxix, 46, 279

Zacchaeus, 324
Zarpanalean, G., 65
Zebulun, 177, 205, 209, 211
Zechariah, 247, 328
Zeugma, 335
Zillah, 131
Zilpah, 72, 177
Zimri, 202
Zingerle, P., xvii
Zoar, 161–62

INDEX OF HOLY SCRIPTURE

Old Testament

Genesis
1–11: 67
1–3: 44, 49
1–2: 59–60
1.1: 62, 74–75, 85
1.1–2, 4: 66
1.2: 76–79
1.4: 81
1.7–8: 87
1.9: 83, 89
1.10: 83, 344
1.11–13: 90
1.14: 90, 92
1.14, 16: 90, 91
1.16–17: 343
1.17: 82
1.20–21: 92
1.20, 24: 103
1.21: 93
1.24: 93
1.26: 93–94
1.27: 94, 105
1.28: 95
1.31: 81, 89
2.1–2: 96
2.4: 69, 97
2.5–6: 97–98
2.7: 99, 343, 345
2.8: 99
2.9: 100
2.10: 100–101
2.15: 101
2.16–17: 102
2.19–20: 104
2.19: 103
2.21–24: 235
2.21–22: 105
2.23: 105
2.24–25: 106
3.1: 107
3.2–3: 111
3.3: 280

3.4–5: 111
3.5: 122
3.6: 108
3.7: 113
3.8: 115
3.10: 115
3.11: 117
3.12: 118, 130
3.13: 118, 121
3.14: 118–19
3.15: 119
3.16: 119–20
3.17: 130
3.17–18: 120
3.19: 120, 352
3.20: 121, 278
3.22: 122
3.23: 123
3.24: 55, 123
4.1–4: 124
4.5: 125
4.6–8: 126
4.9–11: 127
4.12: 128, 130
4.13–14: 128
4.15: 128–30
4.16–17: 130
4.17–22: 131
4.17–20: 129
4.18–24: 131
4.20: 129
4.23: 131
4.26: 133
5: 351
5.3–18: 133
5.3: 133
5.24: 133
5.29: 134
5.32: 134
6.1: 131, 134
6.2: 134
6.3: 135

6.4: 136
6.5, 7: 137
6.12: 129, 131, 134–35
6.13–16: 138
7.1–24: 351
7.2: 139
7.4: 139–40
7.11: 84, 141
7.12, 16: 141
7.23: 141
7.24: 141
8.3–5: 141
8:13–14: 141
8.16–17: 142
8.20: 142
8.21: 142
8.22: 143
9.1–2: 143
9.4–7: 143
9.11–15: 142
9.13: 144
9.21–22: 144
9.24: 145
9.25: 145
9.27: 146
10.9: 146
10.10–12: 147
11.1–9: 67
11.1, 4–7: 147
11.10–29: 148
11.31: 148
12.1–2: 149
12.2: 223
12.5: 149
12.10–13: 149
13.7: 150
13.11,
13–14: 150
13.16: 152
14.1–2: 150
14.10–16: 150

388

INDEX OF HOLY SCRIPTURE 389

14.18–20: 151
15: 248
15.1–9: 152
15.3: 154
15.11: 152
15.12: 154
15.13: 152, 154,
   224, 228, 248
15.14–16: 154
15.15: 153
15.16: 154
15.17: 153
15.18–20: 153–54
16.2–5: 155
16.7–15: 156
17.1–2: 157
17.6: 157, 170
17.10: 157
17.16–20: 157
17.23: 157
18.1–2: 158
18.3: 158
18.6–8: 158
18.9–13: 159
18.15–18: 159
18.19: 159, 170
18.20–21: 160
19.1–2: 160
19.3–5: 161
19.7–13: 161
19.16–22: 162
19.16: 161
19.24: 162
19.26: 162
19.28: 352
19.31–32: 162
19.37–38: 164
20.1–6: 165
20.8–9, 12: 165
21.10: 166
21.11–13: 167
20.16: 165
20.17–18: 166
21.4–9: 166
21.12: 169
21.14, 17–18: 167
21.22–24: 167
22.1–18: 34
22.1–2: 167–68
22.7–12: 168

22.13: 169
22.15–18: 169
23.1–2, 19–20: 169
24.2–3: 169, 198
24.9–32: 170
24.12–14: 183
24.34–51: 170
24.57–67: 170
25.1–7, 10: 171
25.11: 171
25.21–26: 171
25.22–23: 151
25.29–34: 171
26.1, 12, 26–31: 172
27.1–14: 172
27.18–33: 172
27.29: 173
27.33–34: 173
27.39: 84
27.41–45: 173
28.1–13: 173
28.10: 231
28.15–19: 174
28.15: 180
28.20–22: 174, 181
29.10–11: 175
29.26–27: 175
30.1: 176
30.3–9: 176
30.9: 176
30.10–14: 177
30.17–28: 177
31.1–8: 178
31.14–16: 178
31.19–30: 179
31.24: 178
31.34–35: 179
31.42–46: 179
31.53: 179
32.1–26: 180
32.26–29: 181
33.18: 181
33.19: 199
34.1–29: 181
35.1–5: 182
35.16–21: 200
35.27–29: 182
37.1–11: 182
37.13–14: 182
37.24: 182

37.28: 182
37.32–33: 182
37.36: 182
38.1–11: 183
38.14: 183
38.16–19: 184
38.16: 183
38.24–25: 184
38.26: 184–85
38.27–30: 185
39.1: 185
39.7: 185
39.11–23: 185
40.1–23: 186
41.1–36: 186
41.37–45: 186–87
41.48–49: 188
41.53–57: 188
42.2: 189
42.6–7: 189
42.9: 189
42.13: 189
42.15–17: 190
42.21: 190
42.24: 190
42.29–38: 191
43.9: 191
43.14–16: 191
43.18: 192
43.20–23: 192
43.26–29: 192
43.30–34: 193
44.1–5: 193
44.9: 193
44.11–13: 194
44.15: 194
44.16–34: 195
45.1: 195
45.3–4: 195
45.5–6: 196
45.13–16: 196
45.21–24: 196
45.27–28: 197
46.3: 197
46.4: 180, 198
46.5–27: 198
46.33–34: 198
47.7, 10: 198
47.13–26: 198
47.29–31: 198

INDEX OF HOLY SCRIPTURE

Genesis *(continued)*
48.1–6: 199
48.7: 200
48.9: 199
48.14: 199
48.16–20: 199
48.22: 199
49: 200, 205
49.1: 200
49.3–4: 209
49.3: 200
49.4: 200–201
49.5: 201, 209
49.6: 201
49.7: 201–2
49.8: 202
49.9: 203
49.10: 203–4
49.11–12: 204
49.13: 205, 209–10
49.14: 204, 210
49.15–16: 205, 210
49.17: 205
49.18–21: 206, 210
49.21: 211
49.22: 206–7, 211
49.23: 207
49.24: 207, 211
49.25: 207–8
49.26: 208
49.27: 208–9, 211–12
49.33–50: 212
50.15–26: 212

Exodus
1.1, 5: 223
1.15–16: 224
1.17: 225
1.19: 225
2.2–3: 225
2.2: 227
2.7–10: 228
2.7: 227
2.13–14: 228
2.15–16: 229
2.18–20: 229
2.22: 230
2.23: 231
3.1–2: 231

3.5: 231
3.7–8: 232
3.11: 232
3.14: 75, 274
3.16: 232
3.18: 232
3.19–22: 233
4.1: 233
4.2: 69
4.6–9: 233
4.10: 228, 234
4.11: 315
4.12: 234
4.18–19: 234
4.22–24: 234
4.24–26: 235
4.26: 236
5.1, 4: 236
5.6: 237
5.8: 237
5.23: 237
7.9: 69, 238
7.11: 238
7.14–15: 239
7.22: 239–240
7.23: 240
8.2–3: 240
8.5: 69
8.11: 241
8.13: 241
8.15: 241
8.21: 241
8.24: 242
9.7: 242
9.10–11: 242
9.11: 239
9.16: 242
9.19: 242–243
9.25: 243
9.27: 243
9.33: 243
9.34–35: 244
10.1–2, 4–5: 244
10.7: 244
10.13: 69
10.16–17: 245
10.21: 250
10.22–23: 245
10.22: 78
10.24–25: 245

10.27: 245
11.2, 4, 6 : 246
11.8: 246, 248
12.2–7: 246
12.11: 247
12.19: 260
12.31–32: 248
12.37–40: 248
12.37: 315
13.19: 248
13.21: 81, 248, 293
14.5: 249
14.10: 249
14.14–16: 249
14.16: 69
14.17: 249–50
14.19: 250
14.21: 250–51
14.24–25: 251
14.26–28: 149
14.27, 31: 251
15: 45, 217
15.1: 251
15.2: 252
15.3: 251–252
15.4–11: 252
15.13: 252
15.14: 252
15.15–17: 253
15.18, 20: 253–54
15.25: 254
16.27: 255
17.4: 255, 309
17.5–9: 69
17.6, 7: 255
17.6: 207
17.8–16: 251
17.8: 255
17.11: 256
17.14–16: 256
18.3: 230
18.4: 231
18.5–7: 257
18.9–12, 27: 257
19.4, 6: 258
20.5–6: 258
20.13: 258
20.25–26: 259
21.7–8: 259

INDEX OF HOLY SCRIPTURE 391

21.12: 259
21.22–23: 260
21.28: 143
22: 45
22.7: 136
22.28: 260
23.18–21: 260
24.4–8: 260
24.9–11: 261
24.13–16: 261
25.9: 261
25.17–19: 330
25.22: 262
32.1: 262, 292, 293, 318
32.3–8: 263
32.10: 264
32.14: 265
32.17: 264
32.19: 264
32.20: 264, 282
32.21: 265
32.25–27: 265
32.26–28: 282
33.13, 18: 223
33.17–23: 304
33.22: 305
34.33–35: 107
34.33: 305

Leviticus
14.7, 17: 343

Numbers
5.16–28: 283
5.19: 282
8.7: 343
14.10: 309
20.11: 207
21.4–9: 210
25.6–9: 202
25.12: 69

Deuteronomy
8.4: 319
28.29: 348
29.4: 319
33: 200
33.6: 201
33.14: 82

33.24: 206
33.28: 84

Joshua
2.9–10: 253
4.12–13: 206
9.9: 253
17.13: 146
24.32: 199

Judges
4.4–22: 206
6.33–7.25: 205
15.1–8: 206

1 Samuel
4.11: 206
16.14: 79

1 Kings
18.44: 78

Nehemiah
8.15: 275

Job
38.30: 87
40.15: 92

Psalms
8.5: 96
8.6: 106
9.8: 342
15.1: 101
24.2: 98
24.3: 101
32.9: 281
50.10: 93
51.17: 355
74.13–14: 92
78.20: 317
80.8, 14: 204
85.12–13: 325
91.13: 351
96.10–13: 342
98.9: 342
104.2: 343
104.26: 92
115.5, 6: 284
120.4: 340

128.6: 352
139.1: 297
147.4: 344

Proverbs
3.20: 78
15.1: 298
16.11: 345
26.3: 281

Ecclesiastes
1.7: 83

Wisdom
2.2: 352
4.20: 347

Isaiah
2.2: 101
6.6: 324
9.1–2: 211
27.1: 92
29.18–19: 316
30.28: 281
35.5–6: 316
38.12: 353
40.7–8: 352
40.12, 15: 344
40.22: 343, 351
42.5: 343
42.7: 345
44.24: 343
48.13: 344
53.8.: 277
54.10: 69
59.5–6: 353
59.10: 348
59.12: 347
61.1: 316
66.24: 352

Baruch
3.16: 352

Ezekiel
1.1, 22: 77
28.13–14: 101
34.25: 69
37.26: 69

392 INDEX OF HOLY SCRIPTURE

Daniel
7.10: 68
10.6: 303
10.8: 302–3
10.11, 20: 303

Hosea
13.14: 345

Joel
2.6: 341
3.4: 210

Najhum
2.10: 341

Zechariah
12.1: 343

Pseudepigrapha

4 Esdras
7.35: 347
7.104–5: 353

Jubilees
41.6: 183
41.19: 184

New Testament

Matthew
2.19: 332
3.11–12: 116
4.1–11: 109
4.13–16: 211
5.29: 339
6.3: 298
7.14: 350
8.12: 340
9.2: 295
9.4: 297
9.12: 316
9.20: 289, 325
10.16–23: 309
10.26: 342
11.5: 316
12.38: 291
14.28–33: 327
15.22, 27: 283
16.19: 329
16.26: 351
18.7: 301
19.28: 341, 345
21.1–11: 278
21.40: 323
22.12: 349
22.13: 340
22.40: 259
23.37–25.46: 278
23.5: 309
23.13–29: 301
25.10–12: 349

25.12: 349
25.1: 349–350
25.8–9: 350
25.30: 340
25.33: 346–347, 354
25.34–40: 346
26.7: 324
26.12: 324
26.13: 325
26.24: 301
26.64: 343
27.50–52: 278
27.52–53: 279
28.12: 309
28.13: 288

Mark
1.15: 231
1.17: 290
2.17: 316
4.22: 342
4.39: 327
5.27–29: 325
7.32–37: 271
7.32–33: 286
7.33: 287
9.48: 352
10.17–18: 347
11.1: 278
12.9: 323
14.3, 8: 324

16.17: 147
16.19: 346

Luke
1.26–38: 54
1.35: 277
1.36: 247
1.41: 331
2.12: 329
2.28: 325
2.29–30: 326
2.34: 329
4.28–30: 297
5.20–21: 295
5.24: 296
5.31–32: 316
7.22: 316
7.36–50: 273–74
7.37: 290
7.38: 289
7.39: 291–92, 295, 299, 316–17
7.40: 299
7.41: 291
7.41: 321
7.44–47: 290
7.44: 293–94
7.45: 289, 294
7.46: 294
7.47: 289, 293
8.17: 342
8.44: 289, 325

INDEX OF HOLY SCRIPTURE

10.42: 324
12.2: 342
12.19–20: 351
13.25–26: 349
15.10: 283
16.19–31: 340
16.24–25: 350
16.25: 341
16.26: 280, 340–41, 353
17: 270
19.2–10: 324
19.29: 278
19.31: 204
20.15: 323
22.30: 341, 345, 353
22.43: 314
23.34: 299

John
1.1: 342–43
1.3: 94, 212, 277, 343
1.4–5: 344
1.11: 283
1.14: 346
1.18: 274, 346
1.29, 36: 343
2.1: 286
3.16, 18: 346
3.34: 329
4.34: 346
5.30: 346
5.46: 308
6.26: 349
6.27: 133, 290
6.38: 346
7.37: 316
8.12: 345
9.1–3: 287
9.6: 287
9.19–20: 287
9.24, 30: 322
9.39–41: 322
10.9: 343
11.50: 331
12.3: 324
12.12: 278

13: 312
14.2: 275
14.2–3: 340
14.6: 343
14.23: 273, 332
14.26: 346
16.11: 121
18.13–14: 331
19.2: 331
19.7: 281
19.17: 278
19.30: 312

Acts
2.4: 147, 288
2.33: 343
7.55–56: 77, 343
9.3: 77
9.4: 300–301, 308–9, 311–13, 315
9.8: 301
9.13: 302
9.36–43: 288
10.43: 346
20.9–12: 288
22.6: 77, 301–2
22.11: 301
26.13: 77, 301–2

Romans
2.29: 283
4.3, 22 : 152
8.29: 274
12.2: 343

1 Corinthians
1.24, 30: 342
3.1–2: 317
5.6: 287
8.6: 277
10.4: 207, 211
13.1: 288
15.27–28: 284
15.36: 285

2 Corinthians
3.18: 280

10.4–5: 310
11.25: 309

Ephesians
1.18: 308
2.14: 283
5.2: 343

Philippians
2.6, 7: 285

Colossians
1.16: 94, 277, 343
2.9: 328
2.14: 291, 294, 355

1 Timothy
2.14: 118
6.15: 346

2 Timothy
4.8: 342

Hebrews
1.1: 346
1.2: 277, 343
2.17: 343
5.6: 328
5.12: 317
7.3: 151
10.31: 298, 351

James
5.1: 352

1 Peter
2.24: 277

1 John
4.9: 346

Apocalypse
5.10: 258
9.11: 345
17.14: 346
19.16: 346